To Be Born A Nation

Department of Information and Publicity, SWAPO of Namibia

To Be Born A Nation

The Liberation Struggle for Namibia

Department of Information and Publicity, SWAPO of Namibia

**SOLIDARITY FREEDOM
JUSTICE**

Department of Information and Publicity, SWAPO of
Namibia, CP 953, Luanda, People's Republic of Angola.

Zed Press, 57 Caledonian Road, London N1 9DN.

To Be Born a Nation was prepared and issued by the Department of Information and Publicity, South West Africa People's Organisation (SWAPO) of Namibia, CP 953, Luanda, People's Republic of Angola.

Published by Zed Press, 57 Caledonian Road, London N1 9DN in June 1981.

Cover design, maps and diagrams by Jan Brown
Typeset by Margaret Cole
Proofread by Penelope Fryxell
Printed by Biddles of Guildford

British Library Cataloguing in Publication Data

To be born a nation: the liberation struggle for Namibia.
1. Namibia—Politics and government
I. SWAPO. *Department of Information and Publicity*
968.8'03   DT714

ISBN 0-905762-73-8 Pbk

Zed Press would like to thank the following for the use of photographs:

International Defence and Aid Fund: cover, 5, 19, 27, 37, 41, 53, 73, 81, 88, 90, 115, 134, 142, 149, 157, 173, 181, 182, 195, 220, 227, 228, 243, 252, 260, 261, 284, 296.
SWAPO: 7, 14, 19, 27, 61, 75, 77, 88, 90, 113, 129, 149, 161, 163, 204, 211, 212, 249, 260, 261, 275, 277, 288, 294, 299.

Second Impression, May 1983

U.S. Distributor:
Biblio Distribution Center, 81 Adams Drive, Totowa, New Jersey 07512.

Acknowledgements

SWAPO wishes to acknowledge the kind assistance it has received from the Southern Africa Committee, Amsterdam and the International University Exchange Fund in the process of preparing this book.

Contents

List of Maps and Figures

Maps

Figures

Foreword

The year 1980 marks the 20th anniversary of the formation of SWAPO — the South West Africa People's Organisation of Namibia — the national liberation movement dedicated to the complete overthrow of South African rule in our country.

Formed on April 19 1960, SWAPO drew together various anti-colonial forces in Namibia. Then, it was the realisation of the Namibian people's need for a nation-wide movement to confront effectively the South African regime. Now, it has become the embodiment of their aspirations for freedom, locked in combat with South Africa in a war of liberation, and recognised by the international community and the United Nations as the 'sole authentic representative of the Namibian people'.

The South African regime which now occupies our country succeeded the German colonial regime in Namibia under a League of Nations Mandate of 1919. South Africa was instructed to ensure the well-being and development of Namibians as a 'sacred trust'. Instead, however, it drove the people into subjection under a battery of repressive apartheid legislation and organised brutality. It divided the people into segregated 'native reserves' and bound the men as contract labourers to work in the mines, in the factories and on the farms.

Systematically, South Africa has exploited Namibia's people and resources. Its Mandate to administer the country has been revoked by the United Nations (1966); its presence has been declared illegal by the International Court of Justice at The Hague (1971) and it has been hated and reviled by the Namibian people who have never accepted this foreign domination. Yet South Africa has persistently defied the people of Namibia and the international community, and has refused to withdraw from Namibia.

The past 20 years of direct opposition to the South African occupation regime have taken us through a variety of stages, the experience of which has in turn further shaped and transformed our movement. Of particular importance was the decision to launch the armed struggle (26 August 1966) which has become the main form of our resistance. The initial clashes between our combatants and the South African troops led to increased repression and organised violence from the South African regime against the

Namibian people. It was necessary to put equal effort into our work of
political mobilisation throughout the country as a prerequisite for the
successful development of the armed struggle and the liberation struggle as
a whole. The heightened level of activity on the political and military fronts
brought about increasing support for SWAPO, and established it firmly as
the vanguard party of the liberation movement in Namibia.

Today SWAPO encompasses people from all sectors of Namibian society.
We have thus been able to weather the storms of South African repression
and, indeed, more than that, to undermine South African rule in Namibia
so successfully that the occupation regime has been pressed to fraudulent
forms of administrative devolution aimed at trying to retain control. The
bantustan governments, the Consultative Council of the early 1970s, the
Turnhalle Constitutional Conference of 1975—76 and the Constituent
Assembly which grew out of it, the so-called National Assembly now in
Windhoek, are all symptoms of South Africa's desperation — the last kicks
of a dying horse.

Thanks to the political consciousness of the people of Namibia and the
determination of our liberation movement, SWAPO, to forestall the
machinations of our enemies, these moves by the South African regime have
been unmasked and have failed. Armed with the will and determination of
the people of Namibia, and the tools and skills forged through the bitter
experience of the liberation war, SWAPO will continue our struggle until
our goals of freedom and national independence are achieved.

In the words of our leader Herman ya Toivo, currently imprisoned on
Robben Island, when he addressed the court at his trial in Pretoria in 1968:

> We do not now, and will not in the future, recognise your right to
> govern us; to make laws for us in which we have no say; to treat our
> country as if it were your property and as if you were our masters.
> We have always regarded South Africa as an intruder in our country.
> This is how we have always felt and this is how we feel now . . . Only
> when South Africans realise this and act on it, will it be possible for us
> to stop our struggle for freedom and justice in the land of our birth.

We have deemed it important and necessary to communicate with as many
people as possible about the situation in Namibia and our liberation struggle.
We believe that this struggle should not be fought in a vacuum; it is part of
the world-wide struggle against imperialism and for independence and social
liberation. We have therefore made the effort to widen international understanding and seek international solidarity for our cause.

It is in this spirit that we have produced this book, *To Be Born a Nation*.
The title is taken from a saying of the Mozambiquan liberation struggle —
'to die a tribe and be born a nation.' It encapsulates the drive for unity and
the bonds forged through common endeavour and sacrifice that are such
vital elements of the national liberation struggle. Our intention is to provide
the widest possible documentation on Namibia and on the role of

SWAPO in the liberation struggle against the South African occupation
regime. Moreover, at this crucial stage in the history of our people's
resistance, we felt it imperative that SWAPO itself should provide a comprehensive analysis and authentic version of our history.

There is much that remains to be done — not least to close the last chapter
of the liberation struggle itself. That moment, however, will only herald the
beginning of a new task of national reconstruction, a new era of control over
our own lives, a time when, free of imperialist domination, we can begin not
only to write, but to make our own history.

Peter H. Katjavivi
SWAPO Secretary for Information and Publicity
August 1979

Map 1 – Namibia.

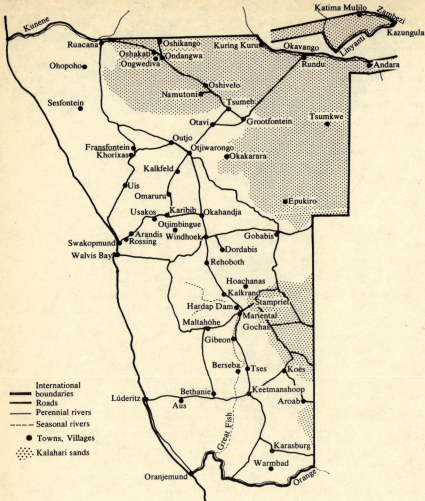

Kunene

Katima Mulilo
Zambezi
Kazungula
Ruacana
Oshikango
Kuring Kurus
Okavango
Linyanti
Andara
Oshakati
Ondangwa
Ohopoho
Ongwediva
Rundu
Oshivelo
Sesfontein
Namutoni
Tsumeb
Otavi
Grootfontein
Tsumkwe
Outjo
Fransfontein
Otjiwarongo
Khorixas
Okakarara
Kalkfeld
Uis
Omaruru
Usakos
Karibib
Okahandja
Otjimbingue
Epukiro
Arandis
Windhoek
Gobabis
Swakopmund
Rossing
Dordabis
Walvis Bay
Rehoboth
Hoachanas
Kalkrand
Stampriet
Hardap Dam
Mariental
Maltahöhe
Gochas
Gibeon
Berseba
Tses
Koës
Lüderitz
Bethanie
Keetmanshoop
Aus
Aroab
Great Fish
Karasburg
Warmbad
Oranjemund
Orange

International
boundaries
Roads
Perennial rivers
Seasonal rivers
● Towns, Villages
Kalahari sands

iv

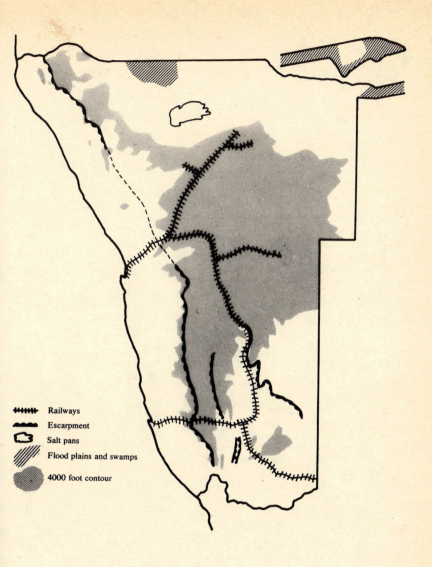

+++++	Railways
⌒⌒⌒	Escarpment
⌒⌒	Salt pans
⫽⫽⫽	Flood plains and swamps
▓	4000 foot contour

1. Introduction

Namibia forms a vast, wedge-shaped block of territory in the south-western corner of Southern Africa. Today it is the setting for a grim struggle to overthrow one of the last vestiges of the old colonial order, the South African apartheid regime, which occupies it illegally in defiance of United Nations sovereignty and of the will of its people represented by their national liberation movement, the South West Africa People's Organisation (SWAPO) of Namibia. With the collapse of Portuguese colonialism in Angola and Mozambique, and the defeat of settler rule in Zimbabwe, Namibia is now in the frontline in the liberation struggle in Southern Africa to end all forms of colonial and imperialist domination.

The name which the colonisers gave to the territory — first 'German South West Africa', then, after the South African conquest in 1915, 'South West Africa' or simply 'South West' — expresses perfectly their conception of it as a zone of economic exploitation, in which the interests of the people they ruled had no place. But the character of colonial oppression has inevitably called into being a national liberation movement dedicated to its overthrow. To symbolise their commitment, the people have chosen the name 'Namibia' for their country. It is derived from the Nama-Damara word *Namib* (meaning 'shield' or 'enclosure'), which designates the barren coastal desert of the country. Stretching unbroken from the Orange to the Kunene rivers, for centuries it protected the people of the interior from colonialist marauders. Today it is also the source of great natural wealth — under its sands lie vast deposits of diamonds and uranium, while off its bleak coastline lies one of the world's richest fishing grounds. In the name of their country and in the emblem of their liberation movement SWAPO, the people of Namibia have signalled their commitment to the creation of a new and liberated social order, both in their own country and in the whole of Africa.

The present boundaries of Namibia were laid down in the late 19th Century, when the major European imperial nations, then at the height of their power, carved up the world and divided it amongst themselves as colonies. To the imperialist negotiators in their conference halls, such boundaries were mere lines on a map. They knew little of the lands and societies they were subjecting to their rule and cared not whether their arbitrary borders disrupted the lives of the local people. Thus, between 1884 and 1890, the territory of Namibia was enclosed between the Orange River to the south, the Kunene and Okavango rivers to the north and the 20th and 21st parallels to the east. Because the Germans, the first colonisers, believed that the Zambezi River might be navigable eastwards to the Indian Ocean, they also demanded, and got, a finger of land reaching to its banks, the Caprivi Strip, so named after their Chancellor of the day.

Overnight the local people found themselves rigidly divided by sharp frontiers imposed on them by alien rulers. People living in the Orange and Okavango river valleys saw their kinfolk on the other side of the river suddenly become subjects of a different colonial regime; the San nomads of the Kalahari Desert (the European misnomer for the Kgalagadi), who hunted over great distances for their livelihood, saw an invisible barrier to the east bisect their hunting grounds. In the north integrated kingdoms were torn between the Germans and the Portuguese. Worse still, for decades the rival colonial regimes could not agree where the boundary was to be located, and when, in 1926, it was finally moved south, thousands of people were uprooted once more.

Within the new boundaries a number of distinct African societies, loosely bound by ties of trade and diplomacy but politically independent, were broken up and thrown together, common prisoners of an alien colonial state. In recent years, the South African apartheid regime has involved these historic identities and pre-colonial boundaries in the name of its infamous bantustan policy, in a desperate attempt to divert the national unity of the liberation movement into ethnic chauvinism. A few years ago, it even considered grabbing part of Southern Angola to make a 'greater Ovamboland' out of its show-piece northern bantustan. But the ideology of apartheid is a caricature of historical reality, and the bantustan areas conveniently leave the people's ancestral lands in the hands of settlers. Above all, 90 years of brutal subjection to a system of colonial exploitation has irrevocably welded a new social order amongst the oppressed people of Namibia, has given them a common experience of national oppression. It is on the rock of this new social and political reality that SWAPO has forged a united and nationally representative movement for national liberation, a movement which has weathered each succeeding storm of colonial oppression and withstood each new imperialist intrigue to the point where its goal of genuine national independence is now clearly within sight.

Geographically, Namibia is a country nearly four times the size of the U.K., nine-tenths that of Nigeria and two-thirds as big as its colonial master, South Africa. Its coastline stretches for 1,300 km and its northern border for 1,450 km. It lies astride the western rim of the vast sub-continental Kalahari Basin, to which it rises in a sharp coastal escarpment 80—130 km inland and from which it then slopes gradually to the east and north into the sandy fastnesses of the Kalahari Desert. Nearly all the interior lies at an altitude of over 1,000 m and the central plateau often reaches 1,500 m, with mountain ranges of more than 2,000 m around Windhoek and Grootfontein. This height gives cool summer nights and bitterly cold spells in winter — even

the far north has the occasional frost — for all that the Tropic of Capricorn
lies south of Windhoek and Walvis Bay.

Despite its size, Namibia is sparsely populated because of the lack of rain.
Only in the far north-east and around Grootfontein does the average yearly
rainfall exceed 500 mm, the lowest limit for reliable grain crops, and south
of Windhoek it drops well below 300 mm. The Namib Desert, sandwiched
between the escarpment and the cold offshore Benguela Current, is bone
dry and completely barren. Inland, all the rains come in summer showers,
highly unpredictable as to when and where they fall. In this precarious
environment, finding permanent water supplies has from time immemorial
been the key to survival for people and animals alike. Between the Orange
and Kunene, both of which run through inhospitable rocky valleys, not a
single river flows all year round. Natural springs are few, and water has to
be extracted from seasonal pans, sandy river beds, wells, and in recent times,
boreholes and small dams. Counting the Namib Desert (15%) and the Kalahari
Plains (30%), whose deep salty sands leave no fresh ground-water for winter
consumption, just under half the land is uninhabitable. Nonetheless, as the
pre-colonial inhabitants proved, with careful pasture management, the vegetation of the central plateau makes excellent grazing for cattle in the north,
and sheep and goats in the south. And in the Eastern Caprivi Strip, the
Okavango Valley and the flood plain of Ovamboland, where year-round water
supplies are sufficiently reliable, grain cultivation has enabled peasants to
settle densely on the land.

Figure 1 — Home languages spoken by Namibians.

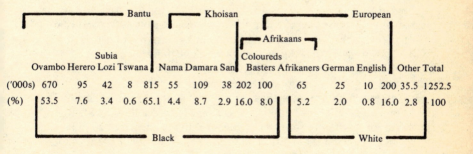

	Bantu				Khoisan			Afrikaans		European			
		Subia						Coloureds					
	Ovambo	Herero	Lozi	Tswana	Nama	Damara	San	Basters	Afrikaners	German	English	Other	Total
('000s)	670	95	42	8	815	55	109	38	202	100	65	25	10	200	35.5	1252.5
(%)	53.5	7.6	3.4	0.6	65.1	4.4	8.7	2.9	16.0	8.0	5.2	2.0	0.8	16.0	2.8	100

Black — White

Source: 1970 census, UNIN 1977.

This natural environment has led to an extreme imbalance in the distribution of Namibia's population, an imbalance which the South African
apartheid regime has deliberately worsened in order to force tens of
thousands of black Namibians to work as migrant labourers. Nationally and

in the inhabited central plateau region, the population density is about 1.6 per sq km, which compares with 21.4 for South Africa and 71 for Nigeria. In Ovamboland, on the other hand, there are 40 people per sq km, a figure which approaches 130 in the crowded central Ovamboland Plain. In other words, whereas half the Namibian people live on 50% of the national territory in the centre and south of the country, the other half are crammed on to 5% of the land along the northern border between the Kunene River and the eastern tip of the Caprivi Strip. In reality, the contrast between north and south is even greater, since 60% of the latter's population lives in towns and mines and another 20% has been dumped in the small reserves which the apartheid regime has dotted around the desert fringes of the white-owned central plateau. Here the population density is a mere 0.4 per sq km; each white ranch has an average of 7,250 hectares of land, the average African household in Ovamboland a mere 15 hectares and in central Ovamboland and less than 5 hectares.

Few other colonies in the modern era of capitalist imperialism have as extreme a record of economic exploitation as Namibia under German and South African rule. The nation is well endowed with natural resources – substantial mineral reserves (diamonds, uranium, copper, lead, tin), extensive pastures (cattle, sheep) and rich offshore and deep-sea fishing grounds – which for decades the colonial state, South African settlers and foreign companies have been busy stripping bare for their own profit. Much of the wealth produced by Namibian workers – a massive 30–35% of the Gross National Product by current estimates – disappears into the foreign bank accounts of the settlers and transnational corporations who monopolise the economy. Even after this crippling imperialist levy has been paid, Namibia remains a moderately wealthy country by any standards, its 1977 Gross National Income of about R7000 per person putting it amongst the top ten African nations and well above such countries as Nigeria (R350) and Kenya (R225) and Zimbabwe (R415). Yet, such a large proportion is taken by settlers, foreigners and the colonial government that the income of black Namibian workers and peasants, at about R112 per person in 1977, is amongst the lowest in the world – below those of even the poorer African countries.

It is to regain control over their own political and economic destiny that the Namibian people, led by SWAPO, are fighting a deadly war. Their struggle is for freedom, not only from the oppressive rule of the hated colonial regime but also from the political and economic stranglehold of its imperialist allies, and for the end of class exploitation and all forms of social injustice. The 1950s was the decade of the first stirrings of nationalist resistance, when the early leaders began to organise in opposition to colonial oppression. The 1960s was the decade of apartheid and the launching of the liberation struggle, when the South Africans began to impose their apartheid master-plan and SWAPO, left with no peaceful alternative, commenced the armed struggle for the complete overthrow of colonial oppression. The 1970s was the decade of generalised popular resistance, when the combined force of mass action and the growing power of the People's Liberation Army of

Namibia (PLAN) destroyed the credibility of first South Africa's bantustan programme and then the neo-colonial manoeuvres of South Africa and its imperialist allies as they desperately sought an alternative to the liberation movement. In this 20th anniversary year (1980) of the foundation of SWAPO, as South African colonialism stands naked of any means of maintaining its hold other than by brutal repression, the long and bitter struggle for liberation, for which many Namibians have laid down their lives and thousands of others have suffered imprisonment and torture, is entering surely its final phase.

This book presents the history and present context of that struggle. Its chapters are grouped in two sections. The first analyses the way in which colonialism and imperialism have exploited the Namibian people — the German colonisation, the Mandate and its revocation by the U.N., and current imperialist strategy; the political economy of South African colonial rule; and the Namibian people's experience under the apartheid regime. These are the factors which have shaped the economic, social and political reality with which the national liberation movement has had to contend and the legacy it will face after final victory. The second section depicts the liberation struggle from its earliest moments, through the heroic resistance to the German military conquest at the turn of the century and the dark inter-war years of forced labour and land robbery, to the formation of the national liberation movement, the launching of the armed struggle in 1966 and the mass campaigns and military and political successes of the 1970s. At the end of the book, appendices bring together useful information on several topics: a documents' section presents a selection of statements from key phases in the history of the Namibian people's struggle against foreign domination; and a statistical section gives basic facts and figures which the South African occupation regime has obscured in order to camouflage the degree of its exploitation.

SECTION 1
Namibia Under Colonial Rule

2. The Colonial Conquest

Colonialism has always sought to legitimise its authority by confronting its subjects at every turn with a caricature of their historical identity. The South African occupation regime, true to form, propagates a fearsome set of myths about pre-colonial society in Namibia — of endless intertribal warfare and disunity. In this nightmare, only with the colonial conquest does Namibia enter historical time; only under colonial hegemony is 'progress' conceivable.

The colonial myth is, of course, an inverted image of reality. The societies described by the first explorers from Europe possessed varied and constantly evolving forms of self-government. Later, they successfully turned the technology and culture of intruding traders and missionaries to their own use and self-defence. It was the German military conquest which robbed Namibians of control of their own history. The colonisation of Namibia irrevocably subjected a number of distinct societies to a single system of exploitation, and thereby, in due course, called into being the means for its eventual overthrow — the people's movement for national liberation. It is a measure of the desperation of the occupation regime that it now seeks, in its bantustan policy, to resurrect a deformed tribalism and to divide a people whom its oppression has welded into a single united nation.

Before colonisation, the people of Namibia had evolved a variety of forms of subsistence. In the barren coastal Namib Desert, isolated Khoisan communities lived on the produce of the sea and the game and plant-life that existed in the valleys of the few seasonal rivers. In the southern interior, where the country was often too dry for cattle, the Nama herded sheep and goats. On the better-watered central plateau, the Herero raised cattle in vast numbers. In the Kaokoveld, the Tjimba, a section of the Herero, were limited by the rugged terrain to raising small livestock and hunting. Scattered across the highland plateau, the Damara cultivated small plots, kept goats and hunted game, while the San hunted across the waterless plains of the Kalahari Desert. The people had complete freedom to move from one area to another within their economic zones, seeking out pasture for their herds, following the seasonal migration of game, collecting wild herbs or searching out precious supplies of water.

Only in the far north was there sufficient ground-water for the people to

Map 2 — Namibia before the Holocaust.

a) Southwestern Africa, c1800

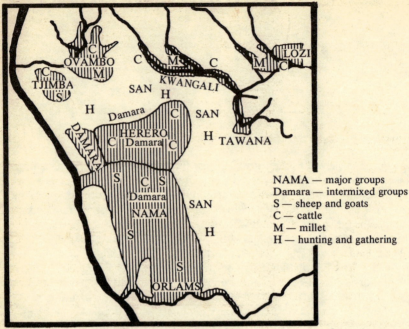

NAMA — major groups
Damara — intermixed groups
S — sheep and goats
C — cattle
M — millet
H — hunting and gathering

b) Central and Southern Namibia, c1890

The people

	Original name	Colonial name
1, 3	Ounin	Topnaar
2	‖Khou-ǀgõan	Swartbooi
4, 15	‖Ai-Xa-‖Ain	Afrikaner
5	‖O-Gein	Groot Doden
6	Gei-ǀkhauan	Amraal
7	‖ Khouben	Rooi Nasie
8	!Kowesin	Witbooi
9	!Kara-gei-khoin	Franzmann
10	ǀHei-ǀkhauan	Berseba
	or !Konan	
11	!Karo-!õan	Tseib
12	⧸⧸Hawoben	Veldschoendragers
13	!Aman	Bethanie
14	!Gam- nun	Bondelswarts
16	Basters	Rehoboth Basters
17	Basters	Rietfontein Basters
18	Damara	Berg-Dama
19	Herero	Herero
20	Mbanderu	Herero
21	Tjimba	Tjimba
22	San	Bushman

c) The Police Zone under German rule, 1903

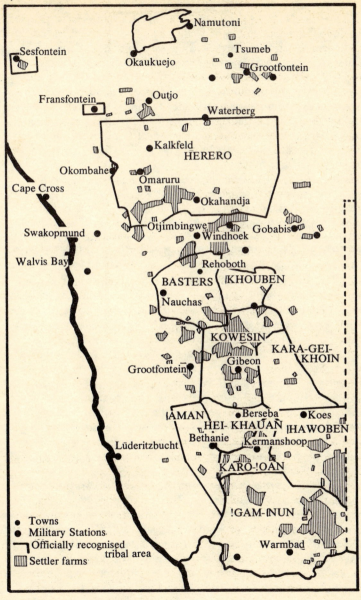

Sesfontein
Namutoni
Tsumeb
Okaukuejo
Grootfontein
Fransfontein
Outjo
Waterberg
Kalkfeld
HERERO
Okombahe
Omaruru
Cape Cross
Okahandja
Otjimbingwe
Gobabis
Swakopmund
Windhoek
Walvis Bay
Rehoboth
BASTERS
|KHOUBEN
Nauchas
KOWESIN
KARA-GEI-
KHOIN
Grootfontein
Gibeon
|AMAN
Berseba
Koes
HEI- KHAUAÑ
|HAWOBEN
Lüderitzbucht
Bethanie
Kermanshoop
KARO-!OAN
!GAM-|NUN
Warmbad

- Towns
● Military Stations
⌐ Officially recognised tribal area
▥ Settler farms

cultivate the land on a regular basis. Densely settled on their huge but isolated flood plain, the Ovambo grew millet, vegetables and fruit, caught fish in the seasonal floods and raised cattle and goats. Along the Okavango River people related to the Ovambo cultivated the rich valley soils and sent their cattle into the neighbouring grasslands. Farther to the east, in today's Caprivi Strip, the Mafue and Masubia were settled in the southern reaches of the Zambezi flood plain.

The people were bound together by ties of reciprocity and a network of long-distance trade. Long before the appearance of capitalist mining companies, Ovambo and San smiths mined copper at Otavi, iron ore at Kassinga and salt from the Etosha Pan. Ovambo and Damara artisans traded salt and copper and iron artefacts for livestock far into Namaland, the Kalahari and Central Angola.

But this pattern of peaceful co-existence was soon shattered by the intrusion of external forces. Before the end of the 18th Century, an aggressively expanding colonialism at the Cape had begun to push waves of migration out from the lands it was usurping. Small groups of Nama were followed, after 1810, by parties of Dutch-speaking Orlams, equipped with guns, horses and ox-wagons. Most settled in the south, although a couple pushed up into the Kaokoveld. Later in the century, small parties of Griqua and Boer trekkers came to rest temporarily on the Kalahari fringes. Long before the arrival in 1870 of the final group, the Rehobothers, the interior highlands had become overcrowded and the people pitted against each other in desperate competition for scarce resources.

At the same time, Christian missionaries from Europe began to penetrate the Namibia interior. By the 1840s, the Rhenish Missionary Society (R.M.S.) had established a virtual monopoly with a string of stations throughout Nama and Herero territory. The missionaries disrupted the way of life of the people, who needed to be constantly on the move in order to seek out the best pastures for their stock, by inducing them to settle permanently around their stations. Their indoctrination of the people in European culture and religion also introduced a new dependence on imported goods and a foreign ideology. Ultimately, their diplomatic pressure on Namibian leaders was to prepare the ground for German colonialism.

Hard on the heels of the missionaries came the traders. Drawn from most of the nations of Europe and North America by the lure of quick profits, they had penetrated the far interior of Southern Africa from their supply bases at Walvis Bay, Mossamedes (in Southern Angola) and Kimberley by the mid-19th Century. Greedy for ivory, cattle and slaves, they plied the people with guns and ammunition, liquor and clothing. Increasingly, Namibian rulers, already competing for pasture and water, became dependent on them for arms and fell into debt. For the most part, the Herero could meet the cost of their imports from the sale of their own herds. But the Nama and Orlams had to resort to plundering the herds of their neighbours in order to meet their trading debts. Under similar pressures, the Ovambo kings raided far to the north for cattle and slaves, and taxed their people heavily in cattle. In this way the rapacious demands of commercial capitalism played the people off against each other and destroyed the stability of Namibian independence long before Germany began dreaming of empire-building in Africa.

The late 1870s and early 1880s witnessed half-hearted attempts by the Cape Colony and Britain to secure the right to colonise Namibia. But who would be the colonial power ultimately, and the boundaries of the territory, were determined not in Africa but at the Conference of Berlin in 1884-85, at which the major imperialist powers divided the continent of Africa between themselves. Even so, it was not until the early 1890s that the Germans made a serious attempt to subjugate the people of Namibia by force. Delayed by the forceful diplomatic and military resistance of Herero and Nama leaders, the colonial regime under Governor Leutwein (1894–1905) employed cynical divide-and-rule tactics, dispossessing some groups while attempting to bribe and coerce others into collaboration. Unscrupulous traders fell upon the Herero cattle herds, bartering goods on credit at outrageous prices, and then used the colonial courts and police to enforce their barefaced robbery. By 1903, more than half the Herero cattle had passed into the hands of the settlers, whose farms were encroaching alarmingly on Herero pasture land.

Early in 1904, the Herero took up arms against their colonial oppressors. Later that year, they were joined by almost every section of the Nama in the south. The uprising had become a national war to resist colonisation. The German regime took a terrible retribution. Given command of the colonial forces, the racial extremist General von Trotha, having inflicted final military defeat on the Herero in the Waterberg, issued his notorious 'Extermination Order':

> The Herero nation must leave the country. If it will not do so, I shall compel it by force. Inside German territory every Herero tribesman, armed or unarmed, with or without cattle, will be shot. No women and children will be allowed in the territory; they will be driven back to their people or fired on. These are the last words to the Herero nation from me, the great general of the mighty German emperor.

To his military superiors, who backed him to the hilt, von Trotha declared: 'I believe that the Herero must be destroyed as a nation.'

The Herero retreated fighting into the waterless Kalahari, where they died in their tens of thousands of starvation and thirst. The Nama, resorting once more to the guerrilla warfare tactics of which they were masters, held out tenaciously for several more years, but one by one they eventually succumbed. By 1907, fewer than 20,000 of the original 80,000 Hereros survived, and more than half of the Nama and Damara were also dead. Altogether, the German war machine had exterminated some 60% of the population of Central and Southern Namibia. Many more were to suffer the same fate in the German concentration camps and labour gangs as the colonial government imposed a savage forced labour system on the survivors. Dispossessed of land and cattle, Namibians were compelled, by a thicket of pass, vagrancy and contract laws, to work for the colonists in conditions of appalling degradation and violence, in the aptly-named Police Zone. This Zone covered that part of Namibia which the colonial administration brought under direct rule, it being so named to distinguish it from the border zone north of the so-called 'Red Line', which the Germans never attempted to administer in any way. (Today, the apartheid regime uses this internal border to divide its northern bantustans — especially Ovamboland, Okavango and the Caprivi Strip, where the liberation war is fiercest — from the rest of Namibia.)

Victims of the German genocide

Out of the country's pre-colonial population, only the Ovambo escaped the full rigour of German rule. The Portuguese had mounted intermittent and largely ineffectual military expeditions to colonise the region, and gradually the more distant parts fell uneasily under Portuguese authority. But Ukwanyama, by far the largest and most powerful Ovambo kingdom, retained its independence to the last. The Berlin Conference of 1884—85 had driven the international boundary between Angola and Namibia quite arbitrarily through the middle of Ovamboland. But the Germans, preoccupied with their subjugation of the Herero and Nama and deterred by Ovambo numbers and military power, left them alone. Even when, after the genocidal suppression of the 1904—07 national uprising, the colonial economy became heavily dependent on Ovambo migrant labour for its mines and railways, the colonial

> This bold enterprise shows up in the most brilliant light the ruthless energy of the German command in pursuing their beaten enemy. No pains, no sacrifices were spared in eliminating the last remnants of enemy resistance. Like a wounded beast the enemy was tracked down from one water-hole to the next, until finally he became the victim of his own environment. The arid *Omaheke* was to complete what the German army had begun: the extermination of the Herero nation.
>
> *Official German war account*

regime limited its contacts with the Ovambo kings strictly to 'protection' treaties and diplomatic 'persuasion'.

The outbreak of war in Europe in 1914 between the major imperialist powers brought Namibia under new colonial domination. Acting as allies of the British, South African forces seized the territory from the Germans, and then collaborated with Portuguese forces to bring the independence of Ovamboland to a bloody end in 1915. But imperialist rivalry prevented South Africa from gaining complete sovereignty over its conquest. The United States, which did not have much of a colonial empire, objected to those who did adding to their territories from the German ex-colonies. Thus, at the Versailles Peace Conference in 1919, the spoils of war were allotted to their conquerors as Mandates in three classes, subject to the supervision of the newly-constituted League of Nations. Namibia was duly awarded to South Africa as a 'C' Class Mandate, to be administered as an integral part of the metropolitan area, subject only to the obligation 'to promote to the utmost the material and moral well-being and the social progress of the inhabitants of the territory'.

However, the real motive behind the new rhetoric was very soon exposed when General Smuts, then Prime Minister of the Union of South Africa and one of the architects of the Mandate system, told a German deputation in 1921 that 'the Mandate over South West Africa was nothing else but annexation'. And in 1925 he announced in Parliament: 'It gives the Union such complete sovereignty, not only administrative but legislative, that we need not ask for anything more.' And indeed, the record of South African rule in Namibia has followed that interpretation to the letter up to the present day.

3. The Economics of Exploitation

Colonisation and Expropriation

The occupation of Namibia at the end of the 19th Century took place at the threshold of a new epoch in the history of modern imperialism. The great age of economic liberalism, during which British manufacturers had colonised world markets under the banner of 'free trade', had come to an abrupt end as other capitalist countries industrialised in their turn. For 30 years (1870–1900) the major powers vied with each other to carve up the world. Like a pack of wolves they fought bitterly over the spoils, but took for granted their general right to conquer. And all began to establish capitalist relations of production and exchange in their colonies.

The German Conquest: Land Robbery and Forced Labour

Imperial Germany was a late-comer in the scramble for colonies. Its hunger was fuelled more by political than by economic considerations. Colonial possessions enhanced national prestige against other imperialist powers and deflected the formidable challenge of the socialist opposition at home. For a long time after Germany had formally declared a Protectorate over Namibia in 1884, German capitalists showed little interest in the new territory which their government had secured for them to exploit. At first, the imperial authorities left Namibia entirely in the hands of a monopoly company, the Deutsche Kolonialgesellschaft fur Sudwestafrika (D.K.G.). But this concern, in which leading German banks held a major interest, remained virtually inactive, as did the multitude of speculative concession companies which mushroomed in the 1890s when the government lost patience and broke the D.K.G.'s monopoly.

The inactivity of the concession companies forced the colonial administration itself to take the leading role in creating a colonial economy. In a series of military campaigns (1890–96) it established a network of army and police posts throughout the south and centre of the country up to the borders of Ovamboland. It seized every possible pretext to expropriate land for settler farms. Its forces of repression were on hand to enforce every fraudulent land or trading deal as a motley collection of immigrants – subsidised settlers, ex-soldiers, traders and Boers – drained the economic lifeblood from the

Herero and Nama people. To service its military and economic objectives, it
built a network of roads, railways, harbours and communications.

The overall strategy of the German colonial regime was to reproduce
German society in Africa by creating a colony of European settlement. It
was left to Paul Rohrbach, head of the Settlement Commission, to spell
out with brutal frankness its implications for the people:

> The decision to colonise in Southern Africa means nothing else than
> that the native tribes must withdraw from the lands on which they
> have pasfured *their* cattle and so let the *white man* pasture *his* cattle
> on these self-same lands. If the moral rights of this standpoint are
> questioned, the answer is that for people of the cultural standard of
> the South African natives, the loss of their free natural barbarism and
> the development of a class of workers in the service of and dependent
> on whites is above all a law of survival of the highest order.

In 1904, as we saw in the last chapter, the Herero and Nama people
rose against the inexorable destruction of their independent economic base
by 'indirect rule'. In retaliation, the German imperial army set out systematically to eliminate the Namibian people and their economic resources from the
face of the land. 'At a cost of several hundred millions of Marks and several
thousand German soldiers,' remarked Governor Leutwein in 1906, 'of the
three economic assets of the colony — mining, farming and native labour —
we have destroyed the second entirely and two-thirds of the third.' Central
and Southern Namibia was a wasteland from which most of the population
and nearly all the cattle and small livestock had been driven or killed. The
colonial regime expropriated nearly all the land within the Police Zone not
already in its hands and proceeded forthwith to parcel it out to white settlers.
Only Rehoboth and Berseba, whose inhabitants did not join the uprising,
escaped to a limited extent the full force of repression during and after the
war. By April 1913, a total of 1,331 farms, comprising 13.4 million hectares
— nearly a third of the central plateau — had been sold or leased to settlers,
while further large tracts had been taken methodically, particularly by Boer
immigrants in the south.

By now, mining capital had also found minerals it could exploit very
profitably. In 1906, the copper mine at Tsumeb, still the country's richest
base mineral site, started production. And when, in 1908, diamonds were
discovered in the sands of the southern Namib Desert, German companies
and adventurers scrambled to lay their hands on this lucrative resource.
Almost overnight, the administration found itself bloated with tax revenues
to channel into its settlement programme. Railways snaked between the main
towns and ports; transport and construction contractors grew fat on the
pickings; and a new commercial petty bourgeoisie mushroomed in the towns
and villages.

German capital found its long-awaited paradise in the diamond fields. The
mining companies exported 5.5 million carats between 1908 and 1915. In

> Our people . . . were being robbed and deceived right and
> left by German traders, and their cattle were taken by
> force. They were flogged and ill-treated and got no redress.
> In fact, the German police assisted the traders instead of
> protecting us. Traders would come along and offer goods.
> When we said that we had no cattle to spare as the rinder-
> pest had killed so many, they said they would give us
> credit. Often when we refused to buy goods, even on credit,
> the trader would simply offload goods and leave them, say-
> ing we could pay when we liked, but in a few weeks he
> could come back and demand his money or cattle in lieu
> thereof. He would then go and pick out the very best cows.
> Very often one man's cattle were taken to pay other
> people's debts. If we objected and tried to resist, the police
> would be sent for and, what with floggings and threats of
> shootings, it was useless for our poor people to resist . . .
> They fixed their own prices for the goods but would never
> let us put down our own valuation on our cattle.
> *Daniel Kariko, Herero leader, quoted in Troup, 1950 p.38.*

1913 alone, they exported one and a half million carats, earning R5.4 million.
One company sold its diamonds at 15 times what it cost to recover them
from the Namib sands, and paid its gloating investors a dividend of 175%.
Another paid a staggering 2,500%. The colonial regime in its turn raked in
R6 million in taxes between 1908 and 1913 on services and finance to its
settlers. And what of those who produced this vast wealth? In 1913, the
3–4,000 Ovambo contract workers, earning a mere R2.50 per month, cost
the companies an annual wage-bill of about R100–120,000 — a mere 2% of
the value of diamond sales in that year.

The sudden eagerness of imperialist capital to plunder Namibia's resources
created a massive demand for labour. Even before the 1904–07 uprising, the
government had experienced shortages on its major construction projects,
despite the steady supply of prison labourers from its frequent war expeditions against the local people. Many Namibians would only work for farmers
or contractors if protected and supervised by representatives of their own
tribal governments. In the north, the Ovambo kings kept a frosty distance.
But genocide transformed the situation dramatically. No sooner had German
military barbarism reduced the black population of the Police Zone by some
60% than mining began to boom and settlers flooded on to the land.
Motivated by fear and a desperate need for wage-labourers, the regime imposed
a ferocious forced labour code upon the survivors. No black person was
allowed to own land or stock — all were compelled by law to labour at whatever job their colonial masters allotted to them. Overnight, the Police Zone,
that desolate graveyard of the people's rebellion, became a vast prison camp.

Prisoners of the German colonial regime

Victim of a German flogging

But repression came nowhere near to meeting the demands of the farms, mines and railways. Poverty and the routine violence of the colonisers killed thousands of workers and drove many others to flee for safety into the bush or across the border to Botswana. The regime urgently sounded out foreign sources of indentured labour, but to no avail. Its reputation was notorious — even fellow German colonies refused to oblige. Only the South Africans, long experienced in exploiting migrant workers, came to their assistance, sending thousands of indentured labourers from the Cape and the Transkei.

Even this was not enough. One last resort was open to the Germans: the Ovambo peasantry in the far north. Impoverished by their kings' cattle taxation to meet trading debts, Ovambo men had already begun to take short-term contracts on the construction sites in the south. When the Germans crushed the national uprising, the Ovambo kings, intimidated by the brutality of the German war machine and perceiving a new source of taxation, finally co-operated with the colonial regime in promoting labour migration. By 1910, some 10,000 Ovambo workers were streaming south each year to the mines and railways on contracts lasting six months or more.

It was in this way that the last years of German rule laid the foundations of modern colonialism — cheap forced labour and the contract labour system.

South Africa's Colony: A Paradise for Foreign Capital

In 1915, Namibia changed colonial masters, an incidental consequence of the war then being fought in Europe. But the incoming South African administration soon made it abundantly plain that the mode of exploitation would not change in the slightest, and its form only in minor aspects. Black leaders, deliberately misled into believing that the South African invaders were but agents for 'the British', expected the Germans to be dispossessed and the land returned to the people. The brutal simplicity of the South African reaction has been typical of their rule ever since. 'Almost without exception, wrote the South West Africa Administrator (South Africa's top official in the territory) in 1922, 'each section asked for the allotment of the old tribal areas, in which vested rights had accrued, and the utmost difficulty was experienced in making them realise the utter impossibility of complying with such a request.' These 'vested rights' of which the Administrator spoke so glibly were the very birthright of the Namibian people, expropriated under German colonialism, first by the deception and intimidation of 'indirect rule', and then by the terrorism of armed conquest and genocide. South Africa had inherited the German colonial heritage and, for all the fine-sounding words of the Mandate, proceeded to exploit the natural and human resources of the territory in its own interests.

By the time the South African army marched into Namibia in 1915, the capitalist economy of South Africa had completed the first stage of its industrial revolution and was hesitating on the threshold of the second. The discovery of diamonds in the late 1860s had not been enough to finance the Cape Colony's efforts to annex Namibia a decade later, and by the time the gold rush started on the Rand in 1886, imperial Germany had already pounced on the territory. Now, 30 years on, the all-powerful diamond- and gold-mining corporations, backed by Western imperialism, had created a united South African state and a powerhouse economy which dominated the whole of Southern and Central Africa. Their recruiting organisation, the Witwatersrand Native Labour Association ('Wenela'), was sucking in over 300,000 black migrant workers a year from as far north as Angola and Tanzania, and impoverishing the entire sub-continent. The mines' need for cheap food for their workers was transforming settler agriculture from subsistence into commercial production. In the mushrooming ports and mining towns, manufacturing and service industries were struggling into existence against a flood of imports from the factories of the industrial West.

Both the South African Government and South African-based capitalists thus had quite specific interests of their own to serve, as well as their role as agents of imperialism. In the first place, the crisis in their country's settler agriculture was in full swing and thousands of destitute Afrikaners were pouring into urban slums from the platteland — the bastion of the white minority government — as capitalist farmers enclosed the land. It was, therefore, with unrestrained greed that the South Africans fell upon the vast unoccupied areas of prime stock-farming land which the Germans had expropriated from the Namibian people, and cancelled the rights of the concession companies. These new lands provided an outlet for their surplus white population, as well as promising future supplies of cattle and hides to South African markets. They also established a backbone of colonists who would remain loyal to the regime through thick and thin.

White farmers from South Africa were not slow to grasp so rich a prize and poured on to the central plateau of Namibia in their thousands. By the end of the 1950s, all commercially viable ranch land was fully occupied. The great majority of ranchers today are Afrikaners of South African origin, though a sprinkling of Germans survive from before 1915, whose numbers have more recently been supplemented by West German immigrants.

Of the other sectors of South African capital, however, at first only the large mining houses were strong enough to stake their claim, and even then only in partnership with their Western financiers. Given the dominance of European- and American-financed capital in South Africa, the regime could do little more than preside over the transfer of ownership from the vanquished Germans to the monopoly capitalists of the imperialist victors of 1914–18. U.S. monopoly capital snapped up the diamond fields: in 1919, the Anglo-American Corporation ('Anglo' for short), backed by a loan from top U.S. banker J.P. Morgan, bought out the captive German interests for a paltry R7 million and brought them under a single subsidiary, Consolidated Diamond Mines (C.D.M.) — a monopoly it has retained ever since. A decade later, Anglo bought its way into the South African mining industry by taking over the de Beers diamond empire, and has since become the leading South African-based transnational corporation. For the rest, German capital retained some hold. The Tsumeb copper mine was allowed to continue under its former German ownership, in which British/South African mining capital already had a strong interest through the South West Africa Company (SWACO), which also ran most of the smaller mines. And in commerce and services, South African businessmen could make few inroads as the German traders and shopkeepers, who were to give the regime a torrid time in the 1930s when Nazi Germany demanded the return of its former colony, maintained their dominant position.

After the stagnation and crises of the 1920s and 1930s, the Second World War marked a watershed in the foreign exploitation of Namibia's resources. Although the basic balance of power between South Africa and its imperialist partners changed little, the pace of exploitation increased sharply. On the one hand, new industrial technologies, together with imperialist wars in the Middle East and South East Asia, created a voracious appetite in the industrial West for base and strategic minerals. Transnational mining corporations ransacked the world for profitable deposits. They found a rich treasure trove under the soil of Namibia, and the long post-war mining boom saw an influx of foreign companies anxious only to strip the country's assets bare before the people could take power into their own hands. Though some of this foreign capital was routed through South African subsidiaries or mining houses, most of it came directly from abroad. First on the scene, in 1946, were two North American giants, the Newmont Corporation and American Metal Climax (AMAX), which, like Anglo before them, picked up a rich prize by jointly buying the lucrative Tsumeb mine, which had been seized from its German owners during the war for a mere R2 million. Many others were to follow in their footsteps over the next three decades.

On the other hand, South African capitalists substantially strengthened their own economic stake. By the 1940s, South Africa was industrialising rapidly and, by the 1960s, had become a strong industrial country, although still heavily dependent on Western investment and technology. Furthermore, the National Party Government which came to power in 1948 was deeply committed to securing a share of the economic prosperity for local South African (and especially Afrikaner) capitalists, while taking care not to damage the economic interests of its imperialist allies. In the late 1940s and early 1950s, a cartel of Afrikaner-owned companies established a modern fish-processing industry at Walvis Bay and, protected by government licences and quotas, have since plundered Namibia's rich fishing grounds almost to extinction.

At the same time settler agriculture was also rising to commercial prosperity. South African manufacturers and construction firms, often the subsidiaries of Western corporations, moved into the limited but expanding market for their products, carefully protected from cheaper foreign imports by high tariff walls. In the 1960s and 1970s, Afrikaner- and state-owned enterprises were even beginning to make small inroads into the foreign-dominated mining sector, chiefly to supply their processing plants in South Africa itself. By far the biggest is General Mining's half-completed uranium mine at Langer Heinrich. Always politically sensitive, the mining transnationals have increasingly combined with Afrikaner companies and South African public corporations in joint ventures. The most notorious is the huge Rossing uranium mine, in which British and French transnationals have joined in partnership with General Mining and the parastatal Industrial Development Corporation (I.D.C.). And it is the royalties, taxation, customs dues and foreign exchange handed over to the South African state by the mining corporations that have made the whole colonial enterprise so hugely profitable for the occupation regime. Such harmony between Western-based transnational corporations and the national capitalists of the colonial state has made Namibia one of the most deeply exploited countries in the history of modern imperialism.

The Structure of the Economy

Colonised Namibia's economy is characterised by two prominent

features:
> (a) the capitalist component of the economy, based on the extensive extraction of the country's varied natural resources, fishing and ranching activities; and
> (b) a subsistence agriculture enveloping the majority of the African population who are forced to live in the Bantustans.
> This economic state of affairs has been consciously designed in accordance with the social interest of the white settler group and international monopoly capitalism.

With these words SWAPO's Political Programme of August 1976 captures the central dynamics of economic exploitation in Namibia under the South African occupation. As the colonial power, the South African regime has structured the economy of Namibia according to those foreign interests which it serves: in the first instance, South African-based capital, and, where this cannot compete, Western-based monopoly capital. It is also concerned to rake in as great a surplus from its colonial venture for itself as its alliance with foreign capital allows. To these interests the local settlers are subordinate but useful junior partners in exploitation. Finding the peasant economy* of the Namibian people already partially destroyed by their German predecessors, the South Africans have systematically subordinated its surviving pockets to their central design: the building of a system of exploitation based on cheap wage-labour. On the one hand, the peasants have been impoverished to force them to work for wages; on the other, the resulting rural reserve army of labour has been used, together with totalitarian labour controls, to keep the wages of all black workers at starvation levels. For the foreign settlers and capitalists, this system of labour repression has guaranteed stability and exorbitant profits; for the colonial regime, it results in a useful source of revenue and a valuable corrective to South Africa's chronic trade deficit.

The Growth of Colonial Capitalism

The growth of capitalist production in the 60 years of South African occupation falls into three broad stages. During the inter-war period, between 1915

---

* Few economic statistics cover the production and consumption of the black peasantry. Their standard of living has troubled South African researchers and statisticians so little that not even rough estimates are available. Yet, according to the latest census in 1970, some 64% of the black population was living in the reserves. South African census figures are thought by the U.N. to be underestimates by as much as 50% and, in addition, the 'hidden' population will be largely rural. In this way, nearly two-thirds of the Namibian people are made to 'disappear' by means of a statistical sleight-of-hand; they produce very little for the capitalist market, and are therefore deemed insignificant. By comparison, the colonial capitalist economy is well covered. Even so, basic information which is published for virtually every other country in the world is withheld by the regime or merged with South African statistics in order to disguise the scale of its plunder of Namibian resources.

and 1945, there was only limited investment and output as all sectors stagnated and suffered periodic catastrophic collapses. After the Second World War, both investment and output expanded at a high rate, with only short-lived minor interruptions. But, in the mid-1970s, the advances of the liberation struggle throughout Southern Africa, and above all in Namibia itself, combined with the effects of the world recession in the industrial West, halted growth and dried up most new investment.

Taking a broad overview, the Gross Domestic Product (G.D.P.), all but a tiny fraction of which is within the capitalist sector, increased, according to South African figures, from R13 million in 1920 to R22 million by 1946, R142 million by 1956, R300 million by 1966 and R830 million by 1977 (see Figure 2). These figures are, however, measured in current prices. If we allow for inflation, the growth is by no means so spectacular: static between the wars, with a near total collapse in the early 1930s when the Great Depression closed the mines and a severe drought brought farming to a halt; rapid after 1946, increasing fourfold within a decade and doubling again between 1960 and 1970; but tailing off into stagnation in the 1970s. A report prepared by the United Nations Institute for Namibia (UNIN) gives a revised estimate for the Namibian G.D.P. of R1,135 million in 1977, a mere 2.2% of which was generated within the peasantry outside capitalist production.

The capitalist economy of Namibia has developed almost exclusively within three distinctive export-oriented sectors: stock farming, inshore fishing and mining (see Figure 3). Very few links exist between the three, and each has expanded according to its own particular circumstances. Nevertheless, the most rapid phases of growth in each have tended to coincide, producing the rapid post-war spurts in the national economy as well as the recessions of the late 1950s and the 1970s.

Commercial farming has developed in two main branches, cattle ranching on the central grasslands north of Windhoek and karakul sheep rearing in the south. Despite a massive state-aided influx of settlers, white farming between the wars was hardly more advanced than that of the subsistence peasantry which the colonial regime was forcibly dispersing to barren reserves in order to make prime land available. It was after the severe drought of the early 1930s that commercial karakul sheep farming took off; and cattle ranching, hitherto halting and slow, followed suit. In mining, the two large-scale operations, the Namib diamond fields and the Tsumeb copper mine, were virtually the only producers before 1950, and even then they periodically closed down because of war or world price fluctuations. But during the 1960s and 1970s, a large number of medium- and small-scale mines were prospected and opened up, and in the mid-1970s, as other mining investment dried up, a third large-scale concern, Rio Tinto Zinc's open-cast uranium mine at Rossing, began production. Before the Second World War, fishing comprised little more than a rock lobster industry at Luderitz, hand-line fishing and sealing. After 1945, groups of South African fishing companies established a modern pilchard industry based on inshore trawlers and processing factories at Walvis Bay. During the 1970s, mining rose to overwhelming dominance in primary

Figure 2 – Namibia's stop-go colonial economy: rates of growth of the GDP at constant (1938) and current prices, 1920–78.

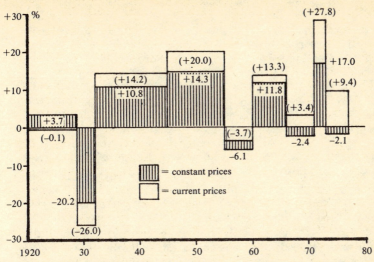

Note: Current prices include inflation; constant prices exclude inflation and are reduced to the base year 1938.

Source: as for Table 4.1a, SWAPO.

Figure 3 – The dominance of export-orientated primary production: share of the main sectors of the economy in GDP, 1920–77.

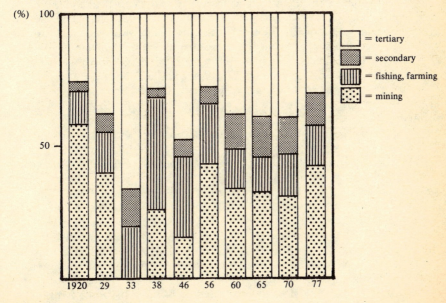

Sources: UNIN 1977, as revised. See Table 4.1b.

25

production and processing for export, from just over half of the sector's output in 1974 to about three-quarters in 1978. Its rise has been matched by the collapse of the fishing industry from 20% to a mere 5%; while cattle and karakul sheep ranching have together maintained a share of over 20%.

Because the three main branches of primary production are so self-contained, it is useful to separate them out for more detailed analysis, as we will also do for the manufacturing and service sectors of the economy. In each case, we outline the raw materials used, how far they have been exploited, who owns the means of production, the methods and scale of the production processes, the profitability generated for their owners and the volume and value of output.

Settler Ranching

Commercial farming in Namibia has been from the start an artificial plant, the creation of the colonial state. By 1915 the Germans had, with isolated exceptions, expropriated from its Namibian inhabitants, the plateau hard-veld of Central and Southern Namibia, which is the only viable farming country outside the far north. Far from returning this area to its rightful owners, the incoming South African administration encouraged the remaining German farmers to stay, and divided up huge tracts of prime grazing land into individual farms, distributing them to settlers from South Africa. In the 1920s, the regime allocated 10.4 million hectares — some 25% of the viable agricultural land in the Police Zone — to about 1,500 new settlers. The number of white farms increased from about 2,000 in 1920 to just over 3,300 in 1938, encompassing 25 million hectares. Drought, depression and the Second World War drastically slowed the influx of new settlers, but the post-war boom and additional subsidised settlement rapidly swallowed up nearly all of the remaining 'white-zoned' land, so that by 1960 39 million hectares — nearly half the total area of the country and 95% of viable pasture on the central plateau — was occupied by some 5,000 white farms. By the mid-1970s, white commercial farming comprised 8,500 land units occupying 37 million hectares and divided between some 5,100 farms containing 6,500 farming households.

It has always been the object of official policy to establish a stable stratum of commercial farmers on the land. To that end, the regime granted easy credit to new settlers to purchase land and equipment, provided expert advice, back-up research, technical services and drought relief, and gave access to the subsidised South African agricultural marketing system. During the first flood of land settlement between 1920 and 1932, it lavished an average R1,200 in cash advances and borehole subsidies on farms whose state-regulated purchase prices averaged no more than R1,340 each. In the late 1920s, the South African Government granted an additional R1 million to settle 301 Boer families from Angola — at a time when the entire G.D.P. was a mere R13 million. Official South African reports in recent years boast of the value of its subsidies, services and protected markets for the white farmers. By contrast, virtually nothing was spent on peasant agriculture in the reserves.

The Karakul industry

Worker catching a lamb for slaughter . . .

. . . and the end product

swakara IS FASHION
IS MODE
IST MODE

By these means, thousands of white settlers were planted on the best agricultural land and raised from impoverished subsistence in the 1920s and 1930s to the mechanised commercial prosperity of the post-war years. Most settlers still own and live on a single farm and large-scale company farming has not made great inroads. However, in the last 20 years, their increasing wealth has enabled some farmers to buy up other farms and form partnerships or syndicates, often linking their businesses with farming or trading concerns in South Africa. Their widely dispersed interests, luxurious lifestyle and, recently, the spread of the armed struggle have induced some of them to move to the towns or to South Africa itself, leaving their farms in the hands of managers. In recent years, also, non-farmers, particularly from South Africa and West Germany, have bought up farms as profit-yielding investments. The stereotype of the settler family with its roots in the soil for generations past is gradually giving way to the dominance of the absentee landlord and the agricultural businessman.

The rise of commercial settler farming has been built almost exclusively on stock farming. In a small zone around Grootfontein, the rains are just sufficient for dryland maize cropping, and elsewhere, small quantities of cereals, vegetables and fruit are cultivated under irrigation; but they amount, all told,

27

to little more than 1% of agricultural production. With careful pasture conservation, the plateau hardveld is ideal for low-density stock raising — cattle
in the centre and north and sheep and goats in the south. The replacement of
communal ownership of grazing land by the individual tenure of capitalist
farming destroyed the seasonal flexibility of pasture control which is so vital
in a fickle rainfall climate, and often spelled disaster in drought. Fencing
and boreholes have only partly compensated for this under normal rainfall
conditions by making possible improved range management, protection
against wild animals and reliable water supplies.

The farmers' main motive for fencing in recent years, however, has
probably been to reduce the number of black workers, partly out of fear of
the latter's hostility towards them. As a result, the total agricultural labour
force has been gradually dropping since 1970. Most farms not only have a
small work force but are also very isolated: both karakul and cattle ranches
have on average only about ten black workers each, and are often 10—15 km
from their nearest neighbour and 50—100 km from the nearest small town.
The average size is about 7,850 and 8,100 hectares respectively for cattle and
karakul ranches, and for most of the working day the workers are spread
across these huge ranges, sometimes — particularly in the south — completely
alone. Stock densities are of necessity very low, about 5—10 hectares per
head of cattle in the north and the same for sheep in the south. But, despite
the distances, extensive stock raising of this kind requires relatively little
capital expenditure — mainly fencing, boreholes, sheds and transport. The
average ranch is valued today at about R265,000 for cattle and R160,000
for karakul sheep, of which land accounts for about half in each case. There
are, in addition, a few very large ranches as well as some fairly small maize
growers or market gardeners, but the great majority of farms are between
4,000 and 20,000 hectares in size and, as a result, the settler farmers are a
fairly cohesive class. They rely on taking 30—40% of their sales as net profit,
on average a comfortable R10,000—12,500 a year (1977), which although
nowhere near the profits of the big companies, puts them on a par with
middle-ranking civil servants and managers.

Cattle (45—50%) and karakul pelts (35—40%) make up four-fifths of the
farm sector's output, with dairy produce, mutton and wool as by-products
(see Figures 4 and 5). About a third of the farms (1,700) are cattle ranches,
two-fifths (2,000) raise karakul sheep for the pelts of their lambs (the 'black
diamonds' of the south so popular in the fashion markets of the West) and
maybe a quarter (1,400) combine both. The number of white-owned cattle
has shown a gradual rise since the last major drought in the early 1960s to
some two million in the early 1970s. The average farm herd has remained
at about 600, with an average commercial off-take of 20—25%. This high rate,
taken with the static farm herd size over the last 15—20 years, indicates that
capitalist ranching in its present form has long since reached its saturation
point. The national karakul herd (around 4—5 million sheep) and the volume
of pelts sold (3—4 million a year) have both risen by roughly half since the
1950s, particularly in recent years, with a slow increase in average farm herd

Figure 4 – The rise of settler ranching: numbers of beef cattle and karakul pelts marketed, 1930–78.

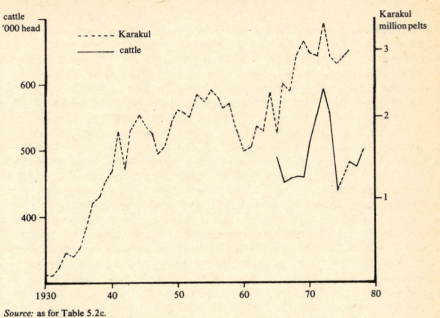

Source: as for Table 5.2c.

Figure 5 – The rise of settler ranching: sales of farm produce, 1977.

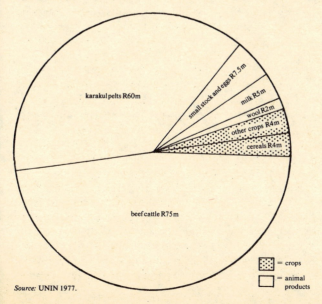

Source: UNIN 1977.

size to about 2,000. But since pelt sales had already shot up from 97,000 in 1931 to 2.6 million by 1950, capitalist sheep farming has also reached its limits in the last 25 years.

Fish Processing

Fishing, the second major sector, presents a complete contrast. Before 1945, it consisted mainly of a small rock lobster industry at Luderitz and seal culling — this extending far back into the 19th Century — from the coast around Luderitz and at Cape Cross, north of Walvis Bay. Both these resources have long been exploited to near their full potential. Some 50,000 seals were caught each year and processed for pelts, oil and bonemeal, worth about R1 million. The long-established rock lobster factories in Luderitz, five in all since the early 1960s, produced an estimated R14 million in 1976, mainly of frozen tails, with canned tails and meal as by-products. The main activity is, however, pelagic fishing — mainly pilchards and anchovy. The cold Benguela Current which sweeps north from the Cape produces the climate which renders the Namib a desert wasteland, but it also makes for one of the world's richest fishing grounds, and after the Second World War, South African-based fishing companies were quick to stake their claim. Exclusively based in Walvis Bay, at least five modern canneries were built between 1948 and 1954, and by 1956 the present nine were in production.

The two sides of the industry — trawling and processing — operate quite differently. The canneries are owned by a tightly knit network of companies, which over the years have combined even further. By the mid-1970s, the entire production and much of the marketing, as well as all the Luderitz lobster factories, were controlled by just four groups, two of which also jointly own the one deep-sea factory ship to join the large-scale international fleet which harvests the vast quantities of white fish further offshore (see Figure 6).

Figure 6 — The Afrikaner fishing cartel.

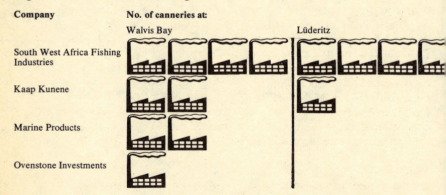

The canneries are mostly large and highly mechanised units employing an average of 400 workers each. A visitor in the mid 1970s described the production process at one of the most modern:

> [From the boats], vacuum pumps sucked the fish straight into the
> factory . . . [Inside], workers were engaged in laying pilchards on the
> conveyor belt and picking out the other types of fish which were
> accidentally caught in the net. Everything else is done by machine:
> cutting off heads and tails, mechanical extraction of the gut, placing
> in line, adding tomato sauce, closing and cooking, and finally the
> mechanically labelled tins are packed in cartons ready for despatch.

Fishing, on the other hand, is mostly done by small trawlers with an
average crew of nine. The fishing grounds are inshore, and the factories are
served by a fleet of about 80 which returns daily with its catch. Many are
owned by their captains, although often financed by the companies, and landing prices are settled seasonally by contract.

Figure 7 – The principle fish products, 1962–78.

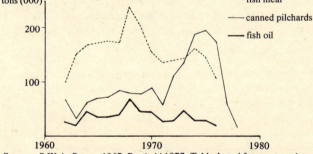

Sources: S.W.A. Survey 1967, Barthold 1977, Table 4, and fragmentary data.

Fishing quotas are set by licences which are issued by the South African
regime to the companies – a lucrative source of patronage. The quantity of
fish landed and processed has fluctuated markedly as over-fishing has
depleted fish stocks. The record total in 1974 of 830,000 tons, valued at
R102 million, was triple the mid-1960s average; but by 1979, the total had
been more than halved to little over 300,000 tons. The fish are processed into
meal, canned pilchards and, to a lesser extent, fish oil, the proportions varying according to market prices and the quality of the catch (see Figure 7).
Fishing in Namibia is a classic 'enclave' industry – all production being
concentrated at the country's two ports in a small number of large, highly
mechanised factories owned by an interlocking clique of companies.

Mining
Mining, the last and most important of the three sectors, is also an 'enclave'
industry, differing only in that its centres of production are necessarily
located on the sites of its raw materials. Namibia is rich in mineral resources
in demand throughout the industrial economies of the capitalist world. The

31

coastal sands of the Southern Namib cover extensive fields of diamonds. On the central plateau and escarpment a large variety of base mineral ore bodies are located, notably copper, lead, zinc and coal, as well as rare metals and semi-precious stones. The ore bodies are widely scattered, mainly in the Groot-fontein area, the centre and the far south of the country. There are several large concentrations, but also numerous small deposits. Along the coast, between Swakopmund and Cape Cross, conditions are good for the large-scale production of salt. Inland, the Namib holds yet another valuable resource: vast reserves of low-grade uranium. Intensive prospecting has shown that the Walvis Ridge, off Walvis Bay, is potentially rich in supplies of oil and natural gas, although the regime has refused to admit this publicly. In both variety and quantity Namibia is well endowed with mineral resources, some of which have not yet been properly prospected, much less put into production. Of those which have, the diamond fields are estimated to contain roughly 5% and the uranium deposits 10% of the world's reserves.

As with stock ranching, it did not take the intrusion of foreign exploiters to teach Namibians the value of their natural resources. For hundreds of years before the coming of the colonialists, the San inhabitants of the Etosha Pan area had been mining copper extensively at Otavi, near Tsumeb. They sold the ore to Ovambo metal-smiths, who smelted it and turned it into a wide variety of artefacts which they bartered in Ovamboland and beyond, ranging as far south as the Orange and as far east as the Zambezi. The Ovambo also mined and processed iron ore from Kassinga and salt from the Etosha Pan, which they exported far north into Angola. Today Tsumeb, near Otavi and still the largest and most profitable base mineral mine in Namibia, is owned by transnational corporations, the colonial regime's partners in exploitation. Together with Consolidated Diamond Mines (C.D.M.), it has until recently accounted for some 90% of the value of mining output, C.D.M. monopolising diamonds and the Tsumeb Corporation (T.C.L.) producing 80% of base minerals from its principal mine at Tsumeb and three smaller mines. Since 1976, these two have been joined by a third major producer, Rio Tinto Zinc's (R.T.Z.) uranium mine at Rossing (R.U.L.).

The pattern of mining in Namibia has thus been dominated by a very few large isolated operations (see Figure 8). Between them T.U.L., C.D.M. and T.C.L. today control about 95% of mineral production and exports. Smaller mines have, however, proliferated since 1950, in particular in the decade since the mid-1960s, during which a number of medium-sized mines were opened up. Official figures in 1969 claimed 9 'large', 13 'medium' and 34 'small' mines and quarries (many of which are insignificant and intermittent operations); since then, another 7 medium-scale ('large') mines in addition to Rossing have started production. These are nearly all widely scattered — there is no 'Band' or 'Copperbelt' in Namibia — but fall mainly within the centre-west and Grootfontein regions. Despite its diversity, virtually none of the industry is locally-owned, even partially, with the exception of a handful of small mines and the salt works north of Swakopmund, which is owned by a local syndicate. In fact, all major assets, and many of the smaller

Figure 8
The Major Mines, Their Mineral Reserves and Ownership, 1977–78

Year Opened	Location of Mine	Capital Invested[1] (Rm)	Minerals	Reserves (000 tons)	Local Holding Co.	Management	Ownership (%)[4] 1st tier	2nd tier
1976	Rossing	260	Ur	500,000 (ore) 100 (conc.)	RUL	RTZ	M (10), IDC (13.2), GM (6.8), RTZ (46.5), RA[3] (10)	CFP, PUK (100), SA (100), FVB, FVB, RTZ (51.3)
	Trekkopje		Ur		development stage	GFSA	GM (100)	CGF (49)
	Langer Heinrich		Ur	500,000	development stage	FM	GM (100)	FVB
1908	Oranjemund	210	D		CDM	DBCM	DBCM (100)	AAC (100)
1906	Tsumeb	55	Cu, Pb, Zn, Cu	5,000	TCL	NMC	NMC (29.6), AMAX (29.6), OCC (9.5), ST (14.2), UC (9.4), KP SWACO (9.4), others (5.3)	NMC (57.5), AMAX (18), CC (27), AMAX (12), GM (48), GFSA (53), AAC (30), MG
1975	Otjihase	62	Cu, Zn, Ag	16,000	Otjihase Mining Co.	JCI	JCI (67), TCL/RUL (33)	AAC (48), as above
	Asis Ost/West		Cu		TCL	NMC	as above	as above
	Matchless	8	Cu	1,280	TCL	NMC	as above	as above
	Kombat	25	Cu, Pb, Zn	2,750	TCL	NMC	as above	as above
	Otjosundu		Mn		SAMC	JCI	JCI (100)	AAC (48)
	Brandberg West		W, Ag	7	SWACO	GFSA	KP (100)	GFSA (53), AAC (30), MG

Year	Mine	Life (yrs)	Minerals	Output	SWACO	GFSA	KP	
1966	Berg Aukas	20	Van, Pb, Zn	1,600			KP (100)	as above
	Klein Aub	9	Cu	6,000	Klein Aub Copper Co.	GM	GM (90) MP (10)	FVB
1971	Rosh Pinah	10	Zn, Pb	12,000		ISCOR	IMCZ (51) MCMEC (49) ISCOR (100) ID (48)	ISCOR (100) ID (48) SA (100) SA (100)
1971	Uis		W, Zn, Sn		Uis Mining Co.			
1971	Oamites	12	Cu, Ag	4,300	Oamites Mining Co.	FNM	FNM (75) FNM (?100)	FNM (75) FNM (?100)
	Elbe	12	Cu, Zn, Ag		development stage	FNM		
1972	Krantzberg	9	W, Sn			NRC	NME (40) EMC (60) GMC (100)	NRC BS
1967	Onganja		Cu	320		ZNL	GMC (100)	ZNL (93)
1960	Lorelei		Cu		Lorelei Copper Mines		ID (33.3) MCMEC (33.3) ID (48) DMUC (33.3) MCMEC (12.5)	
	near Karibib[2]		Li		SWA Lithium Mines	NRC	DM (majority) MG (100)	
	Witvlei		Cu	7,000	development stage		AV, GM	
	Orange River		Ta		Tantalite Valley Minerals		(owned in Namibia)	
	Swakoppmund coast		S				(owned in Namibia)	

Notes

1. Rough estimates from a wide range of references.
2. A group of small mines south of Karibib.
3. RTZ's Canadian subsidiary. In fact RTZ controls fewer voting rights (26.5%) in RUL and IDC more under a weighted share structure — in

this way RTZ concentrates on making profits while the South African government keeps the real power.

4. The first tier indicates the percentage stake held in the local holding company by parent companies. However, some of these companies are themselves owned by larger parent companies. The second tier therefore indicates the latter's stake where this is the case. The inter-locking ownership of British/South African mining corporations is shown separately (see Figure 9).

Key – minerals

CU = copper   Ag = silver
Pb = lead   W = wolfram/tungsten
Zn = zinc   Sn = tin
Ur = uranium   Li = lithium ores
D = diamonds   Ta = tantalite
Van = vanadium   S = salt

Key - companies

European and North American
RTZ   Rio Tinto Zinc (UK)
RA   Rio Algom (UK/Canada)
CFP   Companies Francaise des Petroles (France)
MG   Metallgesellschaft AG (W. Germany)
DM   Duisburg Mannheim Gesellschaft (W. Germany)
NMC   Newmont Mining Corporation (U.S.)
AMAX   American Metal Climax (U.S.)
ZNL   Zapata Norress Ltd. (U.S.)
NRC   Nord Resources corporation (U.S.)
FNM   Falconbridge Nickel Mines (Canada)
OCC   O'Kiep Copper Company (SA/US)
EMC   Ebco Mining Corporation (U.S.)
BS   Bethlehem Steel (US)
M   Minatome SA (France)
PUK   Pechiney-Ugine-Kuhlmann (France)

British/South African
DBCM   De Beers Consolidated Mines
AAC   Anglo-American Corporation

ST   Selection Trust
AV   Anglo-Transvaal Consolidated Investments
CC   Charter Consolidated
SWACO   South West Africa Company
JCI   Johannesburg Consolidated Investments
GFSA   Gold Fields of South Africa
CGF   Consolidated Gold Fields
KP   Kiln Products

South African national and parastatal
GM   General Mining/Federale Mynbou (Afrikaner)
FVB   Federale Volksbeleggings (Afrikaner)
UC   Union Corporation (Afrikaner)
ISCOR   Iron & Steel Corporation (State)
IDC   Industrial Development Corporation (State)
MCMEC   Moly Copper Mining & Exploration Company
DMUC   Diamond Mining Utility Company
ID   Industrial Diamonds of SA
MP   Marine Products (Afrikaner)
SA   South African government

Local holding companies
CDM   Consolidated Diamond Mines
TCL   Tsumeb Corporation Ltd.
SAMC   South African Minerals Corporation
NME   Nord Mining and Exploration
RUL   Rossing Uranium Ltd.
IMCZ   Industrial Mining Corporation Zinc (SWA)

Sources: Mining 1974, 1979, NGG 1979 ...

35

ones too, are controlled by transnational corporations and, to a lesser extent, South African parastatals.

Black workers collecting diamonds at Oranjemund

The industry has on the whole a clear two-tier capital structure. At the upper level, some 17 companies, all foreign-based, hold major and usually complete ownership in the 18-odd significant mines on Namibian soil. Of the former, ten are European- and American-based mining transnationals (predominantly AMAX, Newmont and R.T.Z.), three are Rand-based mining houses founded on British and South African capital (mostly Anglo-American Corporation and Federale Volksbeleggings), and two are South African parastatals (ISCOR — the Iron and Steel Corporation, and I.D.C. — the Industrial Development Corporation). At the lower level, each mine is usually run by a single locally registered company, the one major exception being T.C.L., which owns one large and three medium-sized mines. Most of these companies are directly bound to their parent corporations as majority- or wholly-owned subsidiaries.

There are two exceptions to this pattern. First, most of the South African-based corporations are interwoven with each other and with their subsidiaries through a network of intermediate companies and minority or reciprocal shareholdings — in this way they can exercise a powerful influence while appearing to own very little. Second, in a few cases several transnationals have clubbed together in a consortium of exploiters, and these include two of the three large-scale mines in the territory. While C.D.M. is a part of the A.A.C. empire as a wholly-owned subsidiary of de Beers, T.C.L. is jointly controlled by two U.S. transnationals, with South African mining houses holding minority interests, and Rossing Uranium is predominantly controlled by R.T.Z. with powerful and politically useful minority holdings by the parastatal I.D.C. and the Afrikaner giant F.V.B. In such cases, the leading shareholder usually provides the management. In short, mining in Namibia is completely dominated by a tightly knit group of transnationals, which operate in close collaboration with the colonial state.

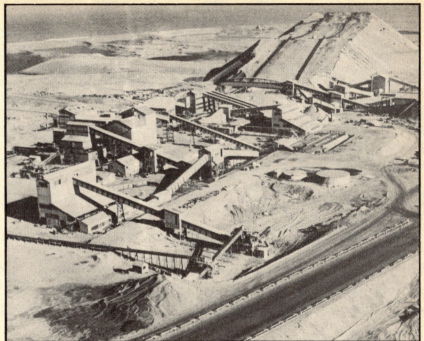

Consolidated Diamond Mines (CDM)

Namibian mines vary greatly in size and methods of extraction. In terms of employment, the three largest, Tsumeb, C.D.M. and Rossing, which employ 4,000, 5,000 and 2,000 black workers respectively, account for three-fifths of the 17,500 black miners and most of the estimated 3,500 whites in the industry. If the 2,000 black workers in the Otjihase copper mine, shut down since 1976, were added, the share of the big mines would be even greater. Most of the medium-scale mines employ only a few hundred each and the scattered small outfits a few score. The workers are fairly evenly divided between underground and open-cast mining, for, although nearly all the base mineral mines are underground operations, two of the others (C.D.M. and Rossing) undertake surface excavations. Nor does the type of mining greatly affect the size of the capital invested. All are highly mechanised, and the surface plant of C.D.M. and Rossing accounts for as much as two-thirds of all mining investment. It was not always so: in the early years of the diamond rush, lines of black workers searched the dunes for stones on their hands and knees or carted loads to their bosses for sifting or primitive processing. Nowadays, the deep top layer of sand, like the ore-bearing earth at Rossing, is removed by massive vehicles and conveyor lines. Most black workers, right down to those at the rock-face or diamond-bearing gravels, are therefore not unskilled labourers but machine operators, some gaining considerable skill on the job, although they are rarely given formal training or qualifications. Furthermore, since most of the mines are integrated operations with their plant and living quarters concentrated together in isolated company towns, the workers are crowded together in a highly authoritarian environment both in and outside working hours.

Mechanised mining, particularly with several large operations, has required capital on a considerable scale — in fact, only the mining trans-nationals have had the resources for such investments (see Figure 9). Four mines absorbed over 80% of the R740 million invested in the sector by 1978 — C.D.M. (R210 million), Rossing (R260 million), Tsumeb (R55 million) and Otjihase (R61 million). The lure for the companies has been the prospect of vast profits, most of which a benevolent colonial regime has allowed them to remit abroad to their gloating shareholders. Of the two old-established concerns, in the decade up to 1972, T.C.L.'s net profit averaged R13 million and C.D.M.'s about R32.5 million. Since 1974, the slump in the world price of copper has wiped out T.C.L.'s profits and forced the expensive new Otjihase mine to cease production in 1976, within a few years of starting up. But Rossing, despite its huge capital outlay and teething troubles, is assured of high profitability by the West's hunger for nuclear energy (and weapons). By 1978, after only two years of limited production, it was returning a profit of R7.5 million, and C.D.M., riding a sustained surge in diamond prices, has seen its net profit soar to R80.6 million in 1974 and R148 million in 1978. Even this figure may understate C.D.M.'s real return to its owners: its shares and reserves were valued at a massive R373 million in 1974, the last year before separate accounting was stopped, and they are likely to be higher now.

Figure 9 — The big three in mining: Rossing, CDM and Tsumeb.

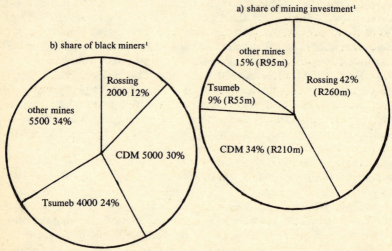

a) share of mining investment[1]

other mines
15% (R95m)

Rossing 42%
(R260m)

Tsumeb
9% (R55m)

CDM 34% (R210m)

b) share of black miners[1]

Rossing
2000 12%

other mines
5500 34%

CDM 5000 30%

Tsumeb 4000 24%

[1] excludes mines which have been closed down or not yet opened

In other words, in the early 1970s, it was taking T.C.L. a mere three years
to recover its total investment to date, while C.D.M. had proved even more
lucrative — despite recent heavy investment — since the early 1970s, consistently returning more than three-quarters of its entire capital *each year*.
Small wonder then that not only have existing companies stepped up production (C.D.M. increased its output by 25% in 1976–77), but also that
many other mining corporations have recently invested in prospecting or new
mines in defiance of the U.N. Decree of 1974 which declares such actions
illegal. In 1962, Marcus D. Banghart, then Vice-President of Newmont Mining
Corporation, described the profits of American companies in South Africa
as 'tantalising', and declared: 'We know the people and the government and
we back our conviction with our reputation and our dollars.' Since then,
foreign mining companies have continued to do precisely that.

Despite the huge profitability of individual mines, the mining sector has
had mixed fortunes in recent years. Taken as a whole, the value of production
hardly increased between 1964 and 1971, and fell markedly in real terms,
despite the buoyancy of base mineral prices. Since then, as diamond prices
have soared and uranium output has mounted, output has increased sixfold
to 1978 and more than doubled in real terms, easily compensating for the
depressed base mineral markets which closed at least six mines between 1973
and 1977. Such fluctuations expose a central feature of the Namibian mining
industry: because its entire product is exported, it depends totally on the
political and economic priorities of the industrial West. On the one hand, the
victory of the Vietnamese people over the U.S. aggressors reduced the
demand of imperialist arms manufacturers for such metals as copper. On the
other, the industrial capitalist nations' increasingly desperate resort to nuclear
power to appease their voracious energy needs is pushing up the price of
uranium, and the deep crisis of the world capitalist economy in the 1970s
has sent the speculative price of gem diamonds soaring upwards.

Industry, Commerce and Services
Three export sectors — farming, fishing and mining — account for nearly all
commercial primary production in Namibia. The balance, no more than 3%,
is made up of small, isolated concerns — government-controlled forestry in
the northern bantustans, irrigated market gardening near the large towns,
sales of milk and eggs from ranches and the Herero reserves. By comparison,
secondary industry is only weakly established. Even today, manufacturing
barely exists in its own right. The processing of mineral ore cannot properly
be distinguished, so integrated is it with the extraction process. The three
largest mines (Tsumeb, Rossing, C.D.M.) have all built concentrators or
reduction plants and process their products to near the quality of second-
stage industrial inputs — uncut gem diamonds from C.D.M., uranium oxide
(commonly known as 'yellow cake') from Rossing, and refined copper and
lead from Tsumeb. T.C.L's smelter/refinery takes concentrates on commission
from several other mines, including Otjihase when in production — another
link in the chain of interlocking interests which, like the growth of joint

prospecting in recent years, bind the companies together.

Much the same is true of food processing for export, which is best regarded as the final stage of the primary sector of which it is an extension. It accounts on average for more than two-thirds of sectoral output, which excluding ore processing, amounted to about R85 million in 1977. Most of this derives from fish processing, above all canned pilchards, as well as fish oil and meal, which produces some three-quarters of the value added in the fishing industry — the rest mainly comes from trawling. As described earlier, the production process is highly integrated in large factories, all of them owned by the cartel of Afrikaner fishing companies, as in the factory ship. The processing of animal exports is much more limited: karakul pelts are shipped in their raw state, while 80% of the cattle off-take is exported live by rail to South Africa. Three-quarters of the remaining cattle are slaughtered at Namibia's three abattoirs and either frozen or canned for export to South Africa and Europe. This processing was worth perhaps R10 million in 1977, and a comparison with neighbouring Botswana, with a national herd about the same size as that of white farmers in Namibia, whose offtake is a mere third of Namibia's but whose frozen beef production is worth three or four times as much, exposes graphically the severe underdevelopment which the colonial regime has forced on the Namibian cattle industry. Even these limited processing facilities are owned not by Namibians but by two Afrikaner-owned South African companies.

Apart from fish and cattle processing, there is little else but small-scale food and drink preparation, repair workshops and local assembly plants, mostly located in the larger towns with a few, under government patronage, in the bantustans. Most are tied to the consumption of the white elite or to the supply or servicing of foreign equipment in the primary export industries. Many, too, are no more than the local branches of South African or foreign firms. This includes nearly all of the handful of sizeable import-substituting plants, such as the British-owned Metal Box Company's can-making factory at Walvis Bay, which supplies the fish factories.

The construction sector has been dominated over the past 12 years by higher levels of government spending, to a very limited extent on 'developmental projects', but increasingly on strategic roads and military installations. The bloated spending power of the white minority has been reflected in new commercial building and a rash of affluent housing, which, however, dried up rapidly in the 1970s, as the liberation struggle gained ground. Again, although small local contractors have profited, it is the big subsidiaries of foreign firms, mainly British or South African, which have taken the lion's share. Two-thirds of the sector's output of R60 million (1977), as well as large-scale unrecorded military spending, derives from public expenditure, and most of it is farmed out to a few large contractors.

Public utilities (electricity, water, sanitation) play but little part in the lives of most Namibians. Only urban industry and white residential areas have a full range of services, while the mines and settler farmers mostly use plant of their own. Provision for black workers in the locations and compounds and on the farms is extremely primitive and as good as non-existent for the peasants on the reserves and bantustans. Namibia is not hooked into the South African national grid, and generates most of its electricity from thermal power stations. The liberation of Angola and frequent military operations by the People's Liberation Army of Namibia (PLAN) have effectively crippled supplies from the large-scale hydro-electric scheme on the Kunene river at Ruacana — the 'place of hurrying waters'. The R100 million South Africa has sunk in the Kunene Scheme is in effect a hostage for the future, and in desperation in 1979 the authorities laid emergency plans for a cross-border power-line from South Africa.

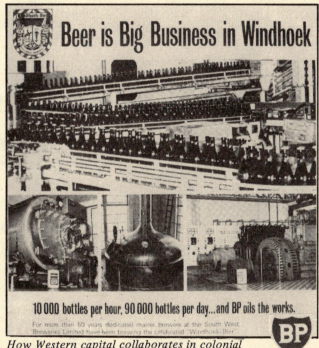

How Western capital collaborates in colonial exploitation

The distributive and service sector is retarded for lack of a mass market and moulded to the consumption patterns of the affluent white elite. Commerce caters primarily for the wealthy town-dwellers, and the urban poor have to buy their basic necessities in town-centre shops or black-owned location stores. A number of farmers run their own stores, at which they force their workers to buy on credit, often at inflated prices, thus keeping them in permanent debt. In the bantustans, on the other hand, a sizeable class of black traders and transport contractors has sprung up in the last decade, particularly in Ovamboland, where there were over 5,000 full- or part-time traders by the mid-1970s. Such apparent success in breaking the

colonial stranglehold is deceptive, however, for the state-run Bantu Investment Corporation (renamed the First National Development Corporation
— ENOK — in 1978) and its bantustan subsidiaries have a complete monopoly
of wholesale supply and credit. Even in the urban locations, black shopkeepers have hitherto only been allowed to rent their premises. Apart from a
few supermarkets and chain stores, most retail outlets are small and locally
owned, many by long-resident Germans. Nevertheless, both the wholesale
and retail sectors are dominated, as are hotels and finance, by large South
African companies which treat Namibia as a mere extension of their South
African operations. In recent years, South African supermarket chains and
banks have in fact been extending and tightening their grip, despite the fact
that, since 1977, a number have begun to register their local branches as
separate Namibian subsidiaries.

Of those people working in the service sector, selling their skills rather
than goods, independent professionals (such as lawyers and doctors) and
artisans are with few exceptions town-based, operating as individuals or in
partnerships and small firms serving the needs of the white settlers. Most are
relatively recent expatriates from South Africa. The services provided by the
regime itself are fairly limited in size and scope. The central and local admin-
istrations provide a range of transport, utility and research services adequate
for the present level of capitalist production in Namibia. These are very often
simply an extension of their South African operations. But social services are
very limited, even for whites, and are virtually non-existent for blacks. It is
typical of this classically colonial society that the great majority of settlers,
whether businessmen or employees, also employ blacks as servants in their
own households to do their child-care, domestic work and gardening. Taken
together, the tertiary sector is estimated to have generated a meagre 30.5%
(R400 million) of G.D.P. in 1977 (with social services a miserable 1.3% —
R35 million). By contrast, even in South Africa itself, in the midst of mass
poverty and scanty welfare services, the proportion was 48%.

The productive forces of the Namibian economy have thus been given a
characteristic shape by the capitalist interests which control their expansion.
The direct production of material goods within the capitalist sector is devoted
overwhelmingly to the large-scale extraction of a few natural resources,
primarily for export. Our 1977 estimates put mining at 42% of the G.D.P.,
settler agriculture at 13% and fishing at 3%, with food processing adding
another 1% to the second and 2% to the third — altogether 61% of the total.
Other direct production (manufacturing, construction, utilities) accounts for
a mere 9.5%, and distribution and services 30.5%, most of it geared to
capitalist producers or the settlers and very little to the needs of the masses.
Likewise, nearly all large-scale, capital-intensive production is concentrated
within the exporting primary and processing sector. Large companies, transnational corporations or financial institutions dominate mining, fishing,
banking, manufacturing, much of construction, commerce and accommodation, and have considerable indirect influence with the small local businesses
in the last four categories, as well as farming, whose main protector is the

state. This domination, the core of imperialist and colonialist exploitation
in Namibia, has given the structure of the economy an extreme distortion
at the expense of the Namibian people.

The Ravages of Imperialism and Capitalism

Economic exploitation in Namibia appears in two principal forms: imperialism and capitalism. Imperialism in turn has two main aspects. First, it denotes
the economic domination of weaker capitalist economies by stronger ones,
achieved both through the systematic draining of surplus from the weaker to
the stronger and through the structuring of the former's national economy to
serve the interests of the metropolitan centre. Second, it may also take the
form of colonialism, through which the colonising state serves both its own
interests and those of the capitalists it represents by means of direct
conquest. Both these components have been powerfully present in Namibia
since the early years of colonial rule.

   Capitalism, on the other hand, specifies the method by which the product
of the labouring masses is appropriated by non-labourers who own the
machines and resources by means of which the workers transform their
labour into material goods and services. The two forms of exploitation are,
of course, mutually compatible. Over the last hundred years, capitalism has
been the vehicle through which imperialism and colonialism have translated
their domination over weaker peripheral economies into flows of surplus
back to the metropolitan centres. Imperialism ensures that the re-investment
of part of the profits extorted in the periphery takes place elsewhere, retard-
ing the local development of the productive forces. In a country like Namibia,
where imperialism's grip is very strong, most of the profits generated by
capitalist production are taken abroad.

The Dominance of Foreign Monopoly Capital

The most striking measure of the impact of imperialism on Namibia's
economy is the net outflow of funds repatriated abroad year after year, part
to the South African capitalists and occupation regime, and part to their
allies in exploitation, the transnational corporations. A United Nations
Institute for Namibia (UNIN) study estimated in 1977 that a staggering 36%
(R425 million) of Namibia's G.D.P. is remitted abroad in the form of profits,
salaries, taxes and state enterprise surpluses, leaving the Gross National
Income (G.N.I.) available for use inside the territory at less than two-thirds
of actual output.* The proportion of foreign remittances increased dramatic-

* The UNIN estimate for 1977 is probably fairly accurate. Our own calculations suggest
the slightly lower range of 30–35% for 1977 and 1978, partly because of heavy investment and limited initial output at Rossing. On the other hand, settlers and capitalists
have been running down their assets and savings more rapidly as the tide of liberation
has advanced.

ally as foreign capital extended its grip on the natural resources of the country. From 5.1% between 1920 and 1930, it rose to 13.3% in the period up to 1945 (see Figure 10). The post-war surge of foreign investment, mainly in mining but also in fishing and commercial agriculture, held it down to 90% for the succeeding four years; but it has steadily grown since then, from 17.2% for 1950—56, the last years for which reliable official figures are available, to some 30—35% during the 1970s.

Figure 10 — The imperialist levy on Namibian workers: the foreign appropriation of GDP, 1920—77.

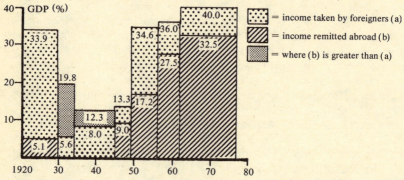

Sources: Krogh 1960, table 2; Odendaal 1964; Thomas 1978, table 6; Rijneveld 1977; UNIN 1977.

Even these figures do not tell the whole story, for they omit that portion of profits which foreign-owned companies re-invested in Namibia to expand their regime of exploitation. During the 1920s, when mining was virtually the only commercial producer, the proportion of G.D.P. accruing to foreigners averaged a very high 33.9%, but most of it (28.8%) was re-invested in mechanised plants rather than remitted. During and after the Great Depression, as output ground to a virtual standstill, foreigners actually managed to remit more than their ostensible net income (7.7% for 1931—45 leaving a negative difference of 5.6%). After 1945, new and ploughed-back investment rapidly expanded the foreign share, reaching 34.6% for 1950—56 and a remarkable 41.8% in 1956 — well ahead of remittances. Since then, the gap has closed gradually, but foreign income is still some 5—10% above remittances, giving foreigners as much as 40—45% of G.D.P. in the 1970s. Taking UNIN's 1977 estimates of population and G.D.P. R370 out of the value produced by the sweat of each black Namibian's labour every year is drained abroad — three times the average *per capita* income (R126) for black Namibians in a whole year.

The transnational mining corporations are responsible for the bulk of the outflow. In 1956, foreign investors in mining took 84.9% of foreign income (R60.4 million) and 86.4% of remittances (R28 million) (see Figure 11). The fact that the repatriated salaries of the foreign personnel (R3.63 million) accounted for most of the remainder indicates that the surpluses of foreign capital in fishing and farming were still either small or spent locally. Even

Thus economic reconstruction in a free, democratic and united Namibia will have, as its motive
force, the establishment of a classless society.
Social justice and progress for all is the governing
idea behind every SWAPO policy decision. The
government of a truly liberated Namibia will,
therefore, be called upon to take the following
measures:

1. Wage the struggle towards the abolition of all
   forms of exploitation of man by man and the
   destructive spirit of individualism and aggrand-
   isement of wealth and power by individuals,
   groups or classes.
2. Ensure that all the major means of production
   and exchange of the country are in the ownership of the people.
3. Strive for the creation of an integrated national
   economy in which there is a proper balance
   between agricultural and industrial development along the following lines:
   — the establishment of processing industry;
   — a comprehensive agrarian transformation
   aimed at giving land to the tiller;
   — the establishment of peasants' cooperatives
   or collectives;
   — the establishment of state-owned ranching
   and crop farms, aimed at making Namibia an
   agriculturally self-sufficient nation;
   — the cultivation of a spirit of self-reliance
   among our people.

   SWAPO Political Programme, 1976

in the more broadly based 1977 estimate, which reflects the rapid growth of
profits in foreign-dominated fishing, farming, commerce and finance, 'large
enterprises' registered 70% of remittances (R300 million out of R425 million).
More than 60% of this came from mining, the remainder from processing
and assembly plants, commercial chains and financial institutions. Nevertheless, even when this remittance figure for 'large enterprises' is added to the
remaining 30% — 'small businesses' 8% (R32.5 million), probably some two-
thirds of it from farming, the state 9% (R40 million), and white salaries 13%
(R52.5 million) — nearly 45% of the total, a massive R200 million of remittances a year, is attributable to mining alone. The two mining giants, C.D.M.
and the Tsumeb Corporation, are responsible for nearly all of this outflow,

although they will shortly be joined by Rossing, with predicted annual profits at full production of R100 million or more. Indeed, with the slump in the copper market and the steep rise in diamond prices over the last three years, C.D.M. alone probably accounted for over 80% of remittances by mining companies in 1977 – over a third of the total outflow in that year. This is the very core of imperialism, when corporate capital, hitting upon a lucrative resource (diamonds, uranium, oil) chooses not to spend or re-invest its vast profits locally but to export them to the industrial centres where its political power is assured.

Figure 11 – Who profits from imperialism: breakdown of foreign remittances, 1977.

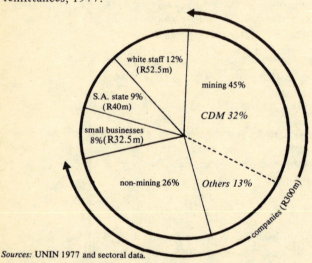

Sources: UNIN 1977 and sectoral data.

Such a high rate of imperialist exploitation is a necessary consequence of the complete control which foreign capital and the South African regime hold over all sectors of Namibia's economy. According to a conservative official estimate* in 1966, out of R92.2 million invested in mining, manufacturing and fish processing, 53% (R49 million) was European and North American and most of the rest South African. Since then, the three main export sectors have received a flood of new investment, nearly all of it foreign. Most has gone into mining, up from R75 million to some R740 million by 1978. Fish processing plant is worth about R40 million, all of it owned by the South African canning companies, which also put up most of the R20 million invested in the trawler fleet. The most recently available

* This and the following estimates (except for agriculture) are for historic investment, that is, they compensate neither for inflation nor for depreciation but simply add up the costs of each investment at the time it was made. The two factors (inflation and depreciation) roughly balance each other out.

figure (1978) for assets in stock farming is much larger, probably around R1,000 million, half of which, requiring little fixed capital, is derived from land, much of it bought with 'soft' loans from the colonial regime. Even here, foreign interests hold a virtual monopoly — over two-thirds of the settler farmers are of South African origin and most of the rest are German, with growing recent investment from West Germany.

Overall, of the 1978 total of about R1,800 million invested in means of production in the three export sectors and related processing and suppliers, not more than R40 million was owned by specifically local interests, and little even of this by black Namibians. The South African share was 75% (R1,350 million), while European and North American companies controlled 29% (R250 million). This inflates the South African position substantially: if agriculture, which is 90% South African or local German, is excluded and the foreign shareholdings in South African companies are exposed, the South African share drops to 59% and in mining alone to 40%. Corporate capital from the metropoles of the industrial West has taken care to invest in the most profitable enterprises in primary production, the large mines, and, as a result, it holds a dominant stake in Namibia's strategic assets and in the export of natural resources and profits (see Figure 12).

The Destructive Impact of Resource Imperialism

But the impact of imperialism is not to be measured solely in terms of the profits it extorts from the toil of Namibian workers. The very structure of the economy has been tailored from its inception to the needs and demands of foreign capital. There is a grotesque inbalance in the productive forces between the different stages of production: capitalists have invested heavily in the extraction and basic processing of raw materials, hardly at all in manufacturing and in a limited and lopsided manner in commerce and services. As a result, Namibia can process for its own use only a fraction of what it produces — meat and canned fish are the chief examples. Furthermore, it can manufacture hardly any of its own consumer needs, whether from local or imported raw materials. Thus, instead of a metal and engineering industry using base metals, diversified fish and meat processing and dairying to meet local food and fertiliser needs, or a leather and textiles industry using local hides and wool, foreign capital goes no further than smelting metals, basic fish canning and processing and limited dairy output. Worse still, its export priorities block the development of useful resources. Dams and windmills, for instance, are used to water cattle for export rather than for the more widespread irrigation of cereals, vegetables and fruit for the consumption of those on the land and in the towns.

The eyes of the foreign companies have always been turned towards the lucrative mass markets of the industrial metropoles, and those of the occupation regime to its own particular requirements. Virtually the entire output of the three primary sectors is exported — all minerals, all processed fish, all karakul pelts and over 90% of marketed cattle — leaving only a few ranch by-products, such as the carcases of karakul sheep, and locally-grown maize as rations for black farmworkers. Indeed, according to the 1977 UNIN estimate, exports from farming, fishing and mining even exceeded the value of their production — the difference being made up mainly by the cost of inputs (fuel and materials used in production) which are, of course, included in the selling price.

Figure 12 — The foreign stranglehold on Namibia's productive resources: nationality of ownership of means of production in the three main extractive industries, 1978.

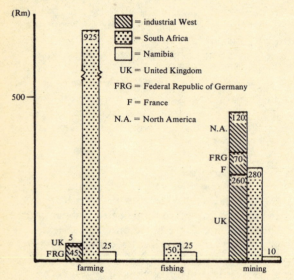

Exports are calculated at 62% of G.D.P., a startlingly high proportion, and probably amount to over 90% by value of the direct production of material goods. In the words of the UNIN study, 'Namibia is therefore almost a classic case of an economy which, in respect of goods, produces what it does not consume and consumes what it does not produce ' This distortion reaches the depths of absurdity when the country's entire supply of canned meat has to be imported because its own production is all exported and when it has to re-import from South Africa the very same tinned pilchards and fish-meal which its own factories have produced for export. Of the small pro-portion of food production marketed locally, most is bought by white settlers, for the wages of black workers are so low that such products become luxuries. While black shepherds shiver from hunger and cold in the highveld winter, farmers export their cattle to the tables of the affluent in South Africa and Europe and breed karakul sheep to feed the whims of high fashion in the Republic and the West. While malnutrition haunts workers and peasants throughout the land, vast quantities of protein-rich pilchards and anchovies are processed into fertilisers or animal feeds and canned for Western super-

markets or as pet foods. For the Namibian people the cruel logic of imperialism reaches extreme depths of degradation.

The Namibian economy is also vulnerable to sudden fluctuations in the
price of its main exports. Karakul pelts depend entirely on a fashion market,
which although hitherto stable could vanish almost overnight, as did ostrich
feathers after the First World War. Even diamonds, despite the iron grip
of de Beers on the world market, have been subject to speculative pressure
during 1977 and 1978, to the extent that in April 1978 de Beers was forced
to slap on a premium which brought prices crashing down. Fish products
may be able to rely on a more stable long-term demand, but base minerals,
so dependent on the requirements of manufacturing industry and high technology armies, have suffered depressed prices since 1974, as the world
capitalist depression began to bite. Between 1975 and 1977, several big
copper mines, including two with heavy recent investment, were either
not opened (Elbe) or put on a 'care and maintenance' basis (Otjihase, Asis
East, Kombat). Even Tsumeb was running at an annual loss of R2 million
through 1975–76.

The systematic plundering of natural resources by foreign companies is
a form of asset-stripping which will have serious consequences for the future
well-being of the Namibian people. This applies particularly to resources
which cannot be renewed, above all to the reserves of minerals. As the
prospect of independence draws nearer, the transnationals have been stepping
up production from their mines so as to strip the country bare before a
government of the people can bring its natural resources under its control.
C.D.M., for instance, has in the late 1970s maintained production at 25%
above average levels earlier in the decade. In 1979, it was an open secret that
C.D.M. was going all out with a round-the-clock three-shift system to raise
output to the highest possible level – and such is de Beers' tight control
over diamond marketing that not even the South Africans can check whether
it has secretly stockpiled undeclared gems from Oranjemund. To cover its
tracks the company is currently claiming that it is extending its prospecting
programme in order to increase proven reserves, which at the present rate of
extraction are not expected – by the company and the South Africans themselves – to last more than 15 years. Ore grades at the big Tsumeb mine are
already declining and management has admitted that reserves are expected
to run out by the early 1990s. These and other exports by foreign companies,
illegal in terms of the International Court of Justice verdict of 1971 and the
U.N. Decree on Natural Resources of 1974, are systematically stealing the
birthright of the Namibian nation.

There is a further cost of imperialism which may leave a permanent
and damaging legacy: destructive development. Minerals are wasting assets;
other resources are not, yet without adequate conservation they may become
so through the competitive greed of their exploiters. Already the desert has
encroached inland along the Namib and Kalahari fringes as settler farmers
overburden the fragile grazing. The process may still be in its early stages,
for settler farming is barely 80 years old, but the danger is real and imminent.

When regression sets in, it is not easily reversed. Once the best grazing is denuded and coarser vegetation takes over, it may take more than a century for the pasture to be restored, even if left fallow, as has already been shown in other parts of Southern Africa. In the overcrowded reserves and bantustans the deterioration is, of course, far more advanced. This is especially serious where, as in Ovamboland, large numbers depend at least in part on stock raising and cultivation. The Ovamboland flood plain, where the soil is so fragile that even regular ploughing destroys its fertility, is being increasingly intensively cultivated and its natural resources, in particular woodland and fruit trees, severely depleted.

It is the fishing industry which provides the classic instance of how short-sighted capitalist greed can destroy Namibia's natural resources. The owners of the canning companies are well connected with the ruling circles in South Africa and during the 1960s and early 1970s, as one report had it, their 'balance sheets proved that a fishing quota was a licence to print money.' Under lax and benevolent colonial supervision, the companies have hunted the prized pilchard to the verge of extinction. A timely warning at the end of the 1960s, when stocks ran dangerously low, was ignored and by 1974 the companies were once more hauling in record catches. Two years later, the pilchard catch suddenly began to drop. Grudgingly, and ignoring the pleas of scientists to declare the area a temporary sanctuary, the colonial authorities began to bring the permitted maximum catch down, from 568,000 tons in 1975 to 200,000 tons in 1977 and a mere 29,000 tons in 1979. The pilchard has practically vanished from one of its richest feeding grounds, and most of the canneries will remain silent for some years to come.

South African officials desperately attempt to cover their criminal failure to control overfishing by pointing an accusing finger at the large international fishing fleet further offshore. But these trawlers are equipped to catch deep-sea white fish and have little interest in inshore varieties. Compounding their irresponsibility is the bribery which has frequently allowed the companies to exceed their quotas, the dumping overboard by boats which reached their ceiling for pilchards but not for other species, and the failure to take the pilchards spawning period out of the fishing season. The Namibian people will not forget this sordid plundering of one of their most valuable resources by the capitalists and government of the colonial power.

Within the orbit of imperialism the weakness of South African capital in competing with the Western monopolies has forced the colonial regime to allow foreign corporations not only the choicest opportunities for exploitation but also to keep the bulk of their profits. The immediate spin-off for the colonial state is customs revenue and the taxes paid by the mines which, given the limited South African capital available, would otherwise not exist. More generally, such corporations are powerful political allies in keeping Western governments friendly towards South Africa. In return, foreign capital has had its interests well protected by the regime. The rate of tax on profits at 32.5% is lower even than its South African equivalent (40%), and so wide-ranging are the allowances for capital spending that companies can plough back profits into local investment virtually tax free — in fact new investors get a three-year tax holiday until the full cost of their initial capital outlay is recovered.

In practice, foreign companies have reinvested only to expand their own operations, and very little of their profits is put into more general local circulation. In 1977, C.D.M. announced a R25 million fund to promote mineral prospecting and both it and Rossing have put small sums into technical education facilities for black workers — but that is as far as it goes. There are no exchange controls between Namibia and South Africa, and all South African firms and South African-based foreign subsidiaries send their funds there rather than hold or invest them inside Namibia. All foreign companies may freely repatriate their dividend income, the chief method whereby foreign capital drains its bloated profits out of Namibia. How lightly the companies escape is well illustrated by the record of two of the largest mining enterprises. In its most profitable years, 1963–72, the Tsumeb Corporation paid out no more than an average 36% of its gross profits in taxes, and distributed 95% of the remainder in dividends to its shareholders abroad. In the four years 1971–74, C.D.M. paid only 35% in taxes, and deposited huge sums in cash and investments — as much as R370 million in 1974 — with subsidiaries and its parent de Beers outside Namibia. Some idea of the scale of profiteering which South Africa allows can be seen by comparison with Botswana, whose government is taking a substantial stake in the three diamond mines which de Beers is developing, and is taxing de Beers' profits on the scale 66–70%.

The South African Stake
Nonetheless, despite the low tax rates which they have extorted as the price of their participation, the transnational mining corporations have been an indispensable ally in enabling the South Africans to make their colonial regime a profitable venture. In recent years, mining taxation has provided 40–45% of the South West Africa account's revenue* and together with customs and excise 50–60%; other companies contribute an additional 12%. Once again it is diamonds which, with few interruptions, have principally fuelled the colonial machine over the last 70 years. During the 1960s and early 1970s C.D.M. generated an average 75% of mining sector taxation. This proportion has increased to well over 90% since 1974, following the slump in base mineral prices and profits, which had accounted for most of the balance. In 1978–79, the mining sector's contribution was estimated to be a massive R163 million — fully 45% of the total state revenue. This is the solid sinew which binds the apartheid regime to the corporations and

* Since 1969 most taxes have been paid directly to the South African Treasury but kept in a separate account. The S.W.A. Administration itself collects only about 30% of all revenue derived from Namibia.

to its colonial enterprise. Although the South African Government disguises its budgetary accounts, the UNIN study estimates that in 1977 the South African regime and public services made a net surplus on current account spending of about R40 million, and this is now probably a considerable underestimate.

But the economic benefits to South Africa are much wider than a mere budgetary surplus. South Africa's 'national' capitalists may be small compared with the international giants, but the political control which their government exercises over Namibia on behalf of imperialism in general enables them to secure some special advantages, both direct and indirect, which they would not have a chance of obtaining in open competition with the more powerful capitalists of the industrial powers. Companies and parastatals possessing strong links with the Afrikaner political establishment (this excludes C.D.M.'s parent, de Beers/A.A.C., which is a transnational corporate group in its own right) have invested some R160 million* in the mining, fishing and processing sectors, about 20% of all foreign investment in these sectors. This includes a virtual monopoly of fish canning (R40 million) and some R100 million in mining, R70 million of it in the strategically vital Rossing uranium mine. Several have exploited Namibian ore reserves for their own industrial use in South Africa. For instance, the state steel monopoly, ISCOR, has developed its Rosh Pinah mine to supply zinc to a South African refinery in which it has a 33% interest and which supplies its steelworks. In addition, of course, settler farming is totally dependent, financially and politically, on the colonial state.

The particular character of South African interests in Namibia has further distorted the pattern of exploitation. Some South African companies have been inefficient, if nonetheless destructive, exploiters. In fishing, which the colonial regime handed over to its capitalists on a plate, the companies allowed short-term greed, as we saw, to take priority over long-term productivity, and as a result have all but destroyed the basis of their prosperity. This does not worry them as greatly as it might, because they used their profitable years neither to update the fishing fleet, with its primitive, and consequently wasteful equipment,** nor to diversify into deep-sea fishing, but instead re-invested outside fishing altogether, mainly in property in South Africa. Behind them they leave a ruined industry which, studies have shown, if tightly regulated and with an internationally recognised 200-mile limit, could sustain catches of 1.5 million tons of inshore fish and 1 million tons of deep-sea fish a year, worth about R300 million at current prices.

---

* These totals exclude the large sums invested by General Mining in developing its uranium reserves at Lager Heinrich; this partly built mine has apparently not yet been put into production.
** When in recent years some R4 million was spent on installing chilled conveyance tanks in 23 boats — a quarter of the fleet — wastage was reduced from an astonishing 80% to a more moderate 45%.

The South African Government has also forced food producers in the territory to serve its own interests before either their own or those of the Namibian people. Before exporting fishmeal, for example, producers must supply the whole of the South African home market at government-controlled prices well below world levels — so that recently little Namibian fishmeal at all has been exported to other countries. Likewise, South Africa now has a shortfall in domestic meat production and consequently imports Namibian beef — but only in sufficient quantity to meet that shortfall and no more. When it comes to a conflict, the politically dominant South African farmers will always win out over their Namibian counterparts, who have been complaining with increasing bitterness over the last few years that the all-powerful South African Meat Board has restricted their quotas, held prices well below the rate of inflation and refused them the facilities to export anywhere else.

Since 1978, perhaps sensing that with the liberation war now in their midst the morale of the northern cattle ranchers was cracking, the South Africans have let through some cattle for export and now plan improved abattoir facilities in Namibia itself so that beef can be shipped direct to Europe. But there is another motive for this apparent change of heart which is probably quite as strong. South African Railways (SAR), with its monopoly of long-distance transport, has always forced Namibian ranchers to send their cattle live in rail trucks, a costly method which results in lower market prices as the exhausted cattle lose condition on the long journey. This, of course, has made perfectly good business sense to SAR — which would otherwise have to return the trucks which bring Namibia's imports empty. Only recently has the situation begun to change as SAR is being forced by world shipping trends to switch to containerisation. Consequently it will have fewer trucks but more refrigerated containers, thus making the movement of frozen beef rather than live cattle more suitable. Here is but one example of the ruthlessness with which the colonial regime is prepared to subordinate the interests of even its own settlers if the wellbeing of its own agencies or capitalists demand it.

South Africa uses Namibia not only as a protected field for investment and a supplier of those primary products of which it is short, but also as a captive market for its exports. Namibia is imprisoned behind the same tariff walls which give South African manufacturers such heavy protection. As a result, South African goods make up a high proportion of Namibian imports and the prices of all foreign and most South African imports — and nearly everything (95%) consumed or invested in Namibia is imported — are forced up. About two-thirds of imports originate in South Africa. Even worse, fully two-fifths of imports from third countries are transported via South Africa, considerably raising their transport costs.

One consequence of this, especially damaging to the development of Namibian industry, is that there is a good deal of scope for competition between South African exporters and local producers, whatever their nationality. Where such conflict arises the colonial state usually sees to it that the South African exporters have priority. A good example is the planned cement factory, long justified even in terms of capitalist standards of profitability by the scale of the Namibian construction industry, but still not yet built. Similarly, the Namibian dairy industry, which used to supply all local needs and even export butter to Europe, was severely restricted in the 1960s when the regime imposed hygiene regulations suitable to South African intensive production on the *extensive* production of Namibian ranches. Today, 20% of fresh milk and most other dairy products must be imported, mostly from South Africa. And again, in the case of karakul wool, a product which in its raw state contains 40% fat (by weight) and whose transport costs to South Africa are paid by the farmer, when a wool-scouring plant opened for direct export, the regime simply closed it down.

Figure 13 — South Africa's cheap imports from Namibia: proportions of the value of exports taken by South Africa, 1977.

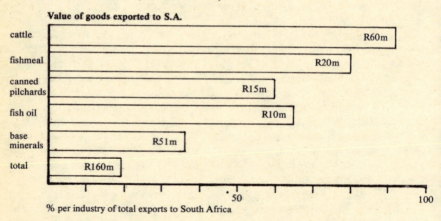

Sources: Thomas 1977 and sectoral data.

Whether devious or heavy-handed, South Africa has structured the Namibian economy to serve the needs of its own capitalists and state corporations, sometimes at the expense of local Namibian businesses and always at that of black Namibian workers and peasants. The cost of integration with the South African economy, with its periodic trade deficit, its recessions, its high-cost manufacturing, its heavy tariffs on imports, its inequitable taxation, its expensive subsidies to farmers and its massive spending on its machinery of repression, is a crippling burden on the Namibian people.

Namibia's pattern of trade, deliberately imposed by the occupation regime, is also a major benefit to the South African economy, and here the collaboration with foreign corporations in maximising production for export has paid handsome dividends. The impoverished living standards of Namibian workers and peasants have kept internal consumption very low; thus imports today are way below exports in value — the bulk of imports are consumed anyway either by the affluent white settlers or as industrial inputs and plant. As a result, the visible trade surplus of R40 million in 1965 (25% of imports) rose by 1977 to about R390 million (85%). But the positive balance of trade is even greater when expressed in terms of foreign currency, for only a third of all imports are bought outside the Rand currency zone, costing R160 million in 1977, while over three-quarters of exports are sold to third countries fetching over R680 million. After net remittances (R140 million) have been deducted and South Africa's imports from Namibia (R160 million), plus their subsidy element (R20 million) added, this leaves a net overall gain in foreign currency to South Africa amounting in 1977 to R630 million. This huge surplus is used to help finance South Africa's own imports and heavy arms purchases from the West and the interest it bears, because Namibia has no monetary authority of its own, goes entirely into the coffers of the South African treasury. This feature is a major gain both for the South African state and for all South African capitalists, and in itself gives them a strong vested interest in perpetuating colonial rule in Namibia.

The Poverty Imposed by Capitalist Exploitation

Such are the costs of imperialism and colonialism in the economic life of the Namibian people. Even so, they do not account for the full weight of economic exploitation, for capitalism imposes its own additional costs on the workers and peasants who produce its wealth. So complete is the stranglehold that very little of the profits of foreign-owned concerns is put into local circulation for further investment and almost no local manufacturing for the internal consumer market is possible. Those small-scale capitalists who do survive (food processors, traders, service and catering proprietors, independent professionals and artisans) are little more than appendages of the extravagant consumption of the white colonial elite. Nevertheless, both

Figure 14 — The division of the spoils: distribution of the GDP between workers, peasants, capitalists and the state, 1977.

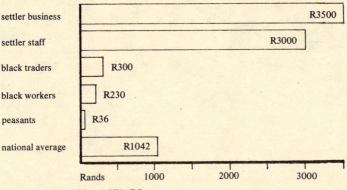

Sources: UNIN 1977 and SWAPO

they and the rest of the settler class, most of whom are the technicians and administrators of the system of oppression and already employers in their own homes of domestic servants, are a further burden on the working masses, either directly, as exploiters of Namibian labour, or indirectly, through their inflated salaries, as consumers of the surplus which the companies or the colonial state rake off from that labour.

Just how extreme are the consequences for the Namibian people is revealed by the 1977 UNIN estimate of income distribution, which puts black wages at no more than 9.3% (R105 million) of G.D.P., black businesses at 1.3% (R15 million) and peasant output at 2.2% (R25 million) — a total of 12.8% for over nine-tenths of the population (see Figure 14). By contrast, large-scale capital took 44%, small colonial businesses 9% and state taxes on profits 15% — a total of 68% in gross profits. Even white salary-earners, who with their dependants make up less than a twelfth of the population, received half as much again (18.5%) as all black Namibian workers, peasants and traders put together. This is the true measure of the depth of exploitation which the engine of colonial oppression is grinding from the labour of the workers and peasants of Namibia.

A miner at the American-owned Tsumeb copper mine

4. Life Under South African Rule

With the help of the imperialist interests to which it is allied, the South African occupation regime has created a system of extreme economic exploitation in Namibia which is backed up by a repressive state machinery and legal system. It is a society where a white settler elite lives in great wealth and enjoys privileges entrenched in law, while the black majority has little chance to escape the poverty, degradation and misery into which it is institutionally bound.

Colonial Oppression and Cheap Labour

The impoverishment of the black population of Namibia is no historical accident. It has from the start been a deliberate and comprehensive strategy through which the people have at all times been subordinated to the labour needs of the colonisers. It is part of deliberate South African policy that the peasants in the reserves and bantustans are starved into migrating as wage-labourers, and that only a handful of Namibians can earn cash other than by wage-labour. Most peasants must depend for part of their subsistence on wage remittances from relatives working in the so-called white areas. But so systematically does the South African regime exploit Namibian labour that the wage-rates of the majority are well below family subsistence levels, usually providing for not much more than the immediate needs of the workers themselves. By these means, the standard of living of black Namibians is kept at the barest minimum. So ruthless and pervasive is the system of cheap labour that many urban families can only survive if several of their members are employed at any one time, while few migrant workers earn enough to bring their families to live with them, even if the apartheid laws allowed it.

Both employers and contract workers perceive the central economic rationale of the migrant labour system with unambiguous clarity. When farmers, the employers paying the lowest wages, voice their perennial complaints against the 'labour shortage', it is taken for granted that the 'shortage' is of labourers prepared to work on their terms, usually because other sectors offer better wages or because peasant impoverishment is lagging behind the

the pace of expansion in commercial farming. When, in 1960, the South West Africa Administrator, making a public appeal for more efficient use of black labour, declared that 'we must create a surplus of labour', his understanding of the wage-cutting potential of a permanent pool of unemployed workers desperate for jobs at any price was accurate enough. Tsumeb's General Manager, also, was quite clear that it was not pay or conditions of service but the cutting edge of poverty which drove Ovambo workers to his mine. In 1971, shortly before the general strike of contract workers, he commented: 'If it is a good year and they don't have to work, they stay at home.' And during the strike itself one building contractor stated baldly: 'there are many thousands of Ovambo to choose from, and when they are hungry they will return to work.'

But workers, too, understand the vicious trap which binds them. Nearly four-fifths of a 1968 sample of contract workers at Tsumeb gave 'poverty' or assistance to their families as their reason for migrating, and only 1% were seeking 'adventure'. Many men and women in Voipio's survey of Ovambo migrant labour two years later expressed deep awareness and frustration at the structural poverty which was tearing their families apart. A few months later, it was Commissioner-General De Wet's assertion that contract labour was not slavery, since workers did not have to volunteer, that fired the campaign for a general strike, for all were bitterly conscious that the very survival of themselves and their families hung upon their jobs. For most it was and remains a 'choice' between work and slow starvation.

This totalitarian system of social engineering has drastically changed the composition of the Namibian population within the space of three generations. Before colonisation, Namibian society was certainly not without its divisions. There were Nama and Orlam war-lords, wealthy Herero cattle-owners, and powerful Ovambo kings and their courts; equally, there were travelling metal-smiths, many Damara and San clients, and refugees of all kinds. But nowhere was systematic class exploitation deeply entrenched, and all were entitled to fields or pasture for producing their own means of subsistence. The colonial conquest robbed all Namibians of this birthright and subjected them, directly or indirectly, to ruthless class exploitation. Overnight, most of the peasants in Central and Southern Namibia were dispossessed and turned by force into wage-labourers. The remainder, together with their more numerous compatriots in the north, were propelled into ever deeper poverty and thus into sending out their men as migrant labourers. Today, the dominant form of colonial oppression is the class exploitation of wage-labour by capitalists and the colonial state, and few Namibians, wherever they live, can escape its clutches for long.

Seventy-five years of full-blooded colonial oppression have irreversibly transformed Namibia from a society of peasants into a society of capitalists, workers and residual peasants — that is, families who live on the land but depend on cash income from wage-labour for part of their basic subsistence. Of all able-bodied black Namibians, some 44% are wage-labourers at any one time, 5% the non-employed wives of workers and 49% peasants in the reserves — less than 2% are store-keepers, traders and small farmers (see Figure 15). In reality, half of all peasant households have at least one of their number away working for wages, and the great majority of male 'peasants' spend the best part of their adult lives as migrant labourers. Perhaps a quarter of their number at any point in time are either between jobs or un-employed — kept penned up in the reserves, like their families, by the laws of apartheid. So most black Namibians are closely bound to wage-labour, whether they live in the towns, ranches and mines or in the labour pools which the apartheid regime has created out of the reserves.

Figure 15 — Exploiters and exploited: the class composition of the working population, 1977.

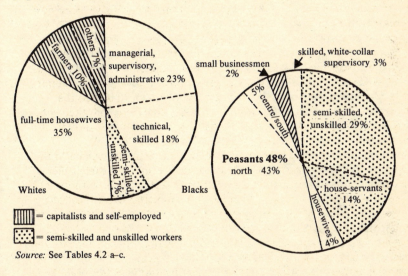

Source: See Tables 4.2 a–c.

The system of oppression which enforces this exploitation controls every aspect of the daily lives of Namibian workers and peasants. Where to live, in what type of accommodation, what kind of job, promotion prospects, per-mission to travel, permission to move outside one's township, farm or reserve, the right to walk the streets, to live with one's family, to marry the person of one's choice, even to die in decency — all depend on the say-so of colonial officials and police and are governed by a host of restrictive laws and regula-tions. In recent years, reforms have modified and refined the legislative frame-work, but in most of its basic features the system remains unchanged and as harshly repressive as ever. A white colonial class of about 100,000 (9% of the Namibian population) and an occupation army of over 60,000, with a few thousand black Namibian collaborators to help them, are the enforcers of the system. A quarter of the working white population are capitalists, mostly farmers and small businessmen; an eighth are the senior managers and administrators who mastermind the economic exploitation and the repressive machinery which enforces it; and nearly half are the bureaucrats, supervisors and police who impose it on the Namibian people. In other words, fully 80% of white employers and employees are themselves exploiters or agents of repression.

The apparatus of repression run by the employers and the South African state is truly formidable. In the towns, mines and factories, there are municipal police, location police, 'Bantu Affairs' inspectors, compound guards, company security guards, foremen and supervisors. In the reserves and bantustans, there are dictatorial 'Bantu Affairs' officials, white South African Police (SAP) and their black minions, the tribal headmen and their armed thugs, and the ethnic 'armies' which South Africa is building in each bantustan. There are the 'unofficial' associations and terror groups, the all-white gun clubs, light aircraft clubs and commandos, the heavily armed private army of the pro-South African Democratic Turnhalle Alliance (D.T.A.), the mushrooming white terror organisations, given free rein by the police. Behind all this is the huge army of occupation, the regular and 'dirty tricks' units of the South African Defence Force (S.A.D.F.), including their mercenaries such as ex-soldiers of UNITA, the paramilitary SAP infantry, the Security Police and the spies and *agents provocateurs* from BOSS (recently renamed) and Military Intelligence. This powerful and ruthless security apparatus indicates a deep South African commitment to its colonial enterprise. No matter which way they turn, it confronts all Namibians in every aspect of their daily lives and in every attempt they may make to improve their social, economic or political conditions.

Bantustans and Peasant Impoverishment

When the League of Nations Mandate came into force in 1920, the South African Administrator for Namibia declared that 'the Native question is synonymous with the labour question.' He appointed a commission to work out an appropriate solution: it was to be based on land ownership and labour control. The South African regime lost no time in continuing the German strategy of expropriation of land, and ensured that nearly all viable farming land in the centre and south of Namibia was reserved for, and taken by whites. As mineral deposits were found, that land too has been taken into white hands.

Apart from a handful of treaty areas* the regime appropriated the entire plateau hardveld — the only good stock-farming land in the country — and allocated land to the dispossessed Namibian people only in ethnic reserves

* Principally Rehoboth (1,312,000 hectares), Okombahe (175,000 hectares), Berseba (388,000 hectares) and Bondelswarts (175,000 hectares). Of these, the second straddles the border of the Namib Desert, and the third and fourth embrace rugged country with little water.

on the semi-desert fringes. Areas where blacks had succeeded in regrouping after the Germans had been ousted were condemned as 'black spots' or 'temporary reserves' and the people were gradually driven out of them by official intimidation and harassment.

South African troops at Grootfontein, the S.A.D.F.'s military H.Q.

From the very start, there was never any question that Namibians should be allowed sufficient land for their own subsistence, let alone for a viable peasant agriculture. In 1922, the Native Reserves Commission recommended a mere 9% (5 million hectares) of the Police Zone for African occupation, of which only a tiny fraction outside the Rehoboth Gebiet (300,000 hectares or 0.5%) had good ground-water.

But even this was too extravagant for the regime, for in the following year it actually proclaimed less than 2 million hectares. By 1947, it had allowed the total to creep up to 5.4 million hectares (10%) and by 1962 to 6.1 million (11%). Under the regime's apartheid masterplan, proclaimed in the Odendaal Commission's report in 1964, the total was to reach a maximum of 13 million hectares, but these additions were almost all desert or mountainous terrain and actually entailed the loss of most of the surviving patches of good pasture which the existing reserves still possessed. The bantustan programme is a bitter mockery of the historical rationale on which it supposedly rests, for the so-called 'homelands' have been sited in precisely those areas which were shunned before colonisation by the very people for whom they are now designated. The Herero have been dealt the crowning insult — a reserve in the very *omaheke* in which over three-quarters of their people perished of hunger and thirst in the German genocide.

The reserves and projected bantustans are sited on land which is almost useless. For the Herero there is the Kalahari sandveld with hardly any ground-water — surface supplies exist permanently only at isolated spots or for short spells after rain. On top of this, mineral deficiencies in the pasture cause endemic stock diseases. The Nama bantustan will comprise rugged terrain in the arid south — precisely that area where, with good white farming country on either side, usable ground-water becomes scarce. The Damara have been allocated a block two-thirds of which is barren Namib Desert, and the remainder, being dry, rugged and remote, is of limited use for pasturing. Only the Rehoboth Gebiet, which has survived largely intact since its foundation over a century ago, possesses good pastoral land

Figure 16 — 'Homelands' in the desert: the proportion of viable farmland in the designated bantustans.

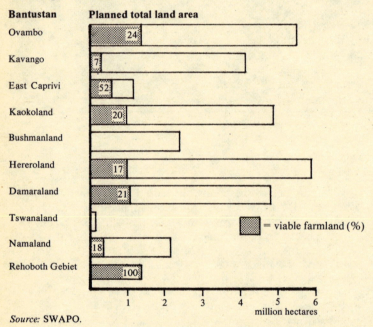

Source: SWAPO.

In the northern region, by contrast, the South African regime confirmed the pre-colonial boundaries of settlement and added large tracts of land from the uninhabited territory which surrounded them. Ovamboland itself has always been presented in South African propaganda as a model of benevolent colonial administration — the ideal 'homeland' where the people live in primitive luxury and venture out as wage-labourers in order to savour the material and cultural delights of Western civilisation.

But the hard economic reality has been the impoverishment of the peasantry of the north as well. Out of the 5.6 million hectares promised to Ovamboland under the Odendaal plan, only 1.35 million can support a settled peasant population. This area, a flat inland delta which traps the summer rains and the seasonal streams from Angola, has one vital resource that the vast tracts of the Kalahari sandveld lack — a year-round supply of water. Even though, in 1915, over half of the flood plain was uninhabited, the Ovambo peasantry exploited the resources of the land fully and efficiently, growing millet, raising cattle on the stubble and summer grass of the surrounding sandveld, fishing in the seasonal streams, and scouring the woodlands for vegetables, herbs, fuel, building materials and game. Today, the whole flood plain is intensively cultivated, but the population is at least four times larger, most of the summer grazing for cattle is cut off by the bantustan boundaries and game, food, plants, fuel and building materials are scarce. The position of the people living further east in the Okavango Valley and the Eastern Caprivi is equally isolated and desperate, and they are subject to the same poverty trap. Land shortages and underemployment, severe in Central Ovamboland, also affect most people in the north.

In this way the chief function of the reserves in apartheid's grand design, to convert the peasant areas into pools of cheap labour, has been fully achieved. Two supporting clamps complete the regime's iron grip on the Namibian peasantry. It had to ensure that no-one could escape, by becoming independent commercial farmers themselves, but also that no-one became completely landless and destitute — otherwise, either wages for migrant workers would have to be raised or their families would simply starve to death.

The South Africans have blocked any chance of Namibian peasants buying their way to self-sufficiency in two ways. First, they made sure that blacks had very little opportunity to gain access to their ancestral lands, which the regime converted to private ownership and distributed to its subsidised white settlers. Although there is no absolute ban on black ownership of private farmland, the state has the legal power to stop the transfer of such land from whites to blacks. In practice, only a handful of blacks (mostly D.T.A. adherents, returned exiles and other puppets of the regime) have been permitted to buy farms in the 'white' area. In any case, with no access to the lavish credit which the state gives to white ranchers, blacks have been virtually denied any chance of accumulating sufficient funds to buy commercial ranches, which today cost on average R200,000 each (see Figure 17).

Second, the regime saw to it that no sizeable group of peasants could ever rise to commercial self-sufficiency by selling cash-crops. Land in the reserves is not owned by the peasants, either individually or communally, but by a state institution, the South African Native Trust, which distributes and controls it through the South African appointed hierarchy of chiefs and headmen. Official regulations ensure that there is no security of tenure — peasants are given their plots for life but can be thrown off on a number of pretexts — and impose a ceiling on the number of stock or area of land any individual may hold. In the north, even when peasants have produced a surplus despite these handicaps, they have found it almost impossible to sell. Cattle exports are banned, ostensibly because of disease — in other words to guarantee that there is no risk of competition to the settlers' cattle. The recently constructed meat canning factory in Ovamboland is too small to make much impact. Grain crops are too expensive to export to the towns because the regime has deliberately never completed the railway to Ovamboland which the Germans began in 1914. And whenever black traders have tried to run vegetables and other food supplies through to urban markets by road, their lorries have been harassed, pillaged and driven off the highways by the police.

Figure 17 — The colonial land robbery: land and livestock ownership under the apartheid regime.

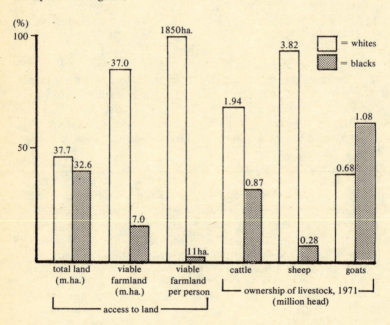

Whether in the northern bantustans or the southern reserves, few blacks have any alternative for earning cash to escape their poverty other than to become migrant workers in some form. Rising taxation and fees for health and education services make a cash income essential for *all* households. For most blacks, getting a job, however badly paid, is a matter of life or death.

The System of Labour Repression

Forced Labour
The colonial economy is therefore founded upon forced labour in the funda-

mental sense that black Namibians are systematically denied any means of providing adequately for themselves other than by wage-labour. The message of the apartheid regime is grim and stark: *work for us on terms we dictate, or starve*. It is forced labour in a second sense too, that for most blacks to be unemployed and not registered at a government Labour Bureau as a 'work-seeker' — whether you want to or not — is a crime. This applies even in the reserves, where officially any man without adequate means of self-support may be deemed a 'work-seeker'. When the call goes out for more (cheap) labour, black Namibians do not even have the right to starve. There is also a third dimension to forced labour, the sheer severity of labour repression, which in the case of the most deeply oppressed section, the contract labourers, is so extreme as to put their 'rights' on a par with those of convicts. Forced labour has been an efficient mechanism of exploitation in Namibia since the German genocide and the first years of South African rule.

Just as the regime denies peasants any opportunity to become commercial farmers, so with few exceptions it blocks the way for workers to become self-employed or capitalists in their own right. Blacks are prohibited from obtaining licences to prospect for minerals in the Police Zone, where most of the large mineral deposits are located, and even in the reserves the Bantu Mining Corporation, a state monopoly, has in recent years simply parcelled out prospecting rights to the big mining corporations.

In the commercial sector, residential segregation in urban areas, imposed through the Native (Urban Areas) Act of 1923 and the Native Administration Act of 1927, prevents blacks from running shops or businesses outside the isolated locations or townships to which they are restricted. Nowhere in the towns are blacks allowed to own land. As the older locations, in which some blacks had previously owned houses and shops were demolished, shopkeepers have come to depend on the patronage of state officials for their rented premises and licences.

In the reserves, the state-owned First National Development Corporation (ENOK) has a complete stranglehold on black business. It and its associates have a monopoly of credit, wholesale supplies, industrial sites and marketing outlets. Since no black can own land and then build up fixed assets, without which capitalist banks will not give credit, ENOK holds would-be black businessmen in the palm of its hands. Not surprisingly, there are very few black capitalists in Namibia. Nearly all of the 10,000 or so black business-men are small shopkeepers, traders, transporters or builders, with a handful of independent professionals such as lawyers and doctors. Two-thirds are storekeepers in the reserves (mainly in Ovamboland), often owning no more than a ramshackle shop on their peasant plots, the achievement of years of hard saving from contract labour. For the overwhelming majority wage-labour remains the only option.

The structure of labour exploitation is classically colonial. Because most capitalists in Namibia are producing for export, they do not need a home market, and it does not matter if Namibians cannot afford to buy their products. Thus the lower their labour costs, so much the better for their profits. The starvation-level wages imposed by the forced labour regime on Namibian workers more than compensate for the premium they pay to recruit their skilled manpower from abroad. Since the early years of South African rule, all managerial, supervisory, technical and skilled staff have been imported from the industrial centres of world capitalism, thereby taking advantage of the latters' advanced educational and training facilities and at the same time conveniently avoiding any need to establish such facilities in Namibia. This makes high salaries and extravagant fringe benefits, which attract white immigrants from South Africa and elsewhere, well worthwhile, especially for large employers like the big mines.

Racial Discrimination and the Migrant Labour System
Racial discrimination is the first and primary method of labour exploitation. The occupational structure of most employment in Namibia is sharply divided between a majority of unskilled, mainly manual, black workers and a white clerical, technical, supervisory and managerial superstructure. There is little statutory job reservation, except on the mines, but an impenetrable wall exists in the hiring practice of most employers. Not only are there virtually no vocational or trade training facilities for blacks — the first technical training institute was recently opened in Ovamboland not by the state but by C.D.M. — but also very few firms will take on blacks as apprentices. There are only a dozen or so black managers and administrators, and few in white-collar jobs generally, except for teachers and nurses, many of whom have been able to get only the most basic of training and are not sufficiently qualified for their posts.

Even here appearances are deceptive. For the South African Government, realising that there are not enough whites to go around, has divided off a section of black workers and given them a more privileged, although still subordinate, place in the apartheid hierarchy, labelling them 'Coloureds'. This category includes persons of mixed racial descent, with or without white ancestors, the Rehobothers and in, recent years, the Nama — though in practice the latter are treated much the same as other indigenous blacks. 'Coloureds' are exempted from the pass laws and can thus move freely and seek employment. Many work in construction and skilled manual occupations, and have been used as foremen and low-grade office staff — in fact, they form the majority of black workers in skilled and white-collar jobs outside teaching and nursing. Because of the lack of training facilities a good many are actually relatively recent immigrants from South Africa.

But in reality their 'privileges' are small and do not breach the major black-white divide — whites are always on top of the pile. In any case, 80% of 'Coloured' workers are only semi-skilled or unskilled. To this day the pattern remains unbroken: whites command, organise and hold most of the skilled posts; blacks do the productive labour and the lowest-grade administrative, white-collar and skilled manual work. Whites hold nearly all senior, middle management and civil service posts and form over 90% of senior supervisory, professional, technical and scientific staff. Over 70%

of artisans and 40% of clerical staff are also white. In fact, only 12.5% of white employees are semi-skilled or unskilled workers — and most of these are simply there to direct the labour of black workers. Blacks are simply being realistic when they refuse to recognise white employees as fellow workers with a common interest, for their privileged position is founded upon the super-exploitation of black labour.

Thus, for all but a tiny proportion of black workers, the only alternative under the forced labour regime is manual work requiring little or no training. But racial discrimination is by no means the only weapon in the regime's armoury of repressive devices. There are two major subsidiary forms of discrimination which it uses to divide the black working class: by job sector, and by supposed place of residence. From its earliest days, the South African colonial regime realised that some of the capitalists it served were much weaker than others and would lose out in a free-for-all competition for labour. Accordingly, the regime allocated each sector its own reservoir of cheap black labour and erected walls of legislation between them so that black workers, trapped by the pass laws, could move from one to the other only with great difficulty. It also created three legal categories of black worker, each with fewer rights than its predecessor. Workers who qualified under the stringent 'influx control' laws to live permanently in the towns or on farms were given automatic preference for any jobs going. Migrants from the Police Zone reserves usually had to take whatever they were given, but could, with difficulty, get permits to look for work themselves or to change jobs, and with extreme difficulty they could gain the right to settle permanently at their place of work. But contract workers (a misnomer for the indenture signed depriving workers of all rights) from the northern reserves had no choice of job or employer at all, could not resign or change their job, and had to return to the reserve as soon as it ended.

Employers have used this system of double discrimination to render all black workers powerless and to dictate wages and conditions of their own choosing. The towns and ranches each have their resident labour forces, augmented by migrants from the Police Zone reserves which are carefully positioned around the fringes of the white heartland. Only the mines and the state utilities have had the resources to organise a supply of migrant labour on a large scale. From the very start they tapped the northern reserves, principally Ovamboland, for thousands of 'contract' labourers. As the capitalist economy expanded and the impoverishment of the peasantry gathered pace, other sectors were allowed to take on those recruits the mines did not need. By the 1960s, there were few menial jobs that contract workers did not do, from house servant to rock-face miner. The regime and the employers have used them as an industrial reserve army of labour, available to fill any gaps and paid so little that they undercut every other section of the Namibian working class.

This of course is the main purpose of migrant labour, to remove any bargaining power which workers might gain by reason of the scarcity of their labour, and thus force down wages to the minimum necessary to support life

— and less if the employer can get away with it. 'Permanent' workers have only their wages to support their families, but 'migrant' workers, even if they live and work for many years in a town, farm or mine, can be forced to leave their families in a reserve to produce part of their subsistence from the land. The declared ultimate aim of apartheid is to make all remaining 'permanent' workers in the so-called 'white' area into 'migrants', stripping them of what few rights they have hitherto clung to. Today, just over 50% of all black workers (excluding about 20,000 migrants from Southern Angola) are migrants — 30% being contract workers from the northern bantustans and 21% coming from the Police Zone reserves. Although the original colonial plan was to tie the latter to the farms, the former to the mines and make the towns self-sufficient, so keen have employers been to use migrants in order to render *all* black workers powerless that nowadays every type of business, from restaurants to the biggest mine, employs migrant labour extensively. Today, migrants comprise over 95% of black workers in mining, 65% in fishing and 50% in farming.

The Legal Apparatus of Apartheid

To impose this harsh regime of forced labour on Namibian workers, the South African Government erected a comprehensive and highly repressive framework of labour legislation in the early years of its rule. This legislation has a fourfold design: to enforce a draconian code of labour discipline, to prevent workers from leaving their jobs against the wishes of their employers, to give the state complete control over the recruitment and distribution of black labour, and to drive all non-workers, except those with the right of permanent residence (including wives and children), out to the reserves. The main instrument of control was the pass laws, that maze of official permits which black workers were forced to obtain in order to do virtually anything, wherever they might live or work. Every single permit had to be in order, otherwise workers could be arrested without warning, anywhere, anytime, and handed out a fine, imprisonment or deportation to a 'homeland' they might never have even seen. In 1963, Ruth First described the situation thus:

> Each reserve, town or farming area is an island surrounded by a sea of restrictions. Once a man is ordained to live and work in one area, there is little or nothing he can do to change his situation. If he steps beyond the limits recorded in his passes, he risks arrest by the police, the detectives in plain clothes, the labour inspectors, who search everywhere for transgressors. The dragnet of the pass laws is inescapable.

The pass laws are made up of proclamations and regulations, many of whose provisions overlap. The general pass law, the Native Administration Proclamation (1922), ordered that 'a native found beyond the confines of a location, reserve, farm or place of residence or employment shall exhibit on demand to the police his pass and on neglect to produce may be arrested.'

Map 3 — The Namibian economy: primary production and communications.

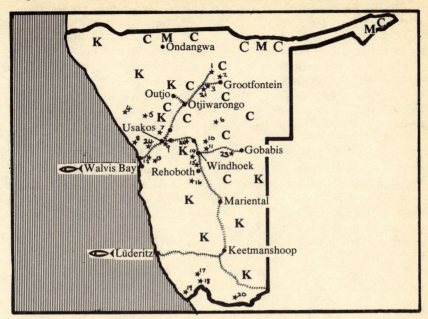

1	Tsumeb
2	Berg Aukas
3	Kombat
4	Brandberg West
5	Uis
6	Otjosundu
7	Krantzberg
8	Coastal salt works
9	Lithium mines
10	Onganja
11	Otjihase
12	Rossing
13	Langer Heinrich
14	Matchless
15	Oamites
16	Klein Aub
17	Rosh Pinah
18	Lorelei
19	Oranjemund
20	Tantalite Valley
21	Asis Ost
22	Elbe
23	Witvlei
24	Trekkopje

K = small stock, mainly karakul sheep
C = large stock, mainly cattle
M = crops, mainly millet and maize
= industrial fishing and fish processing

69

The Natives (Urban Areas) Proclamation (1924) imposed a more comprehensive and detailed set of controls on the towns and mines, and other laws provided additional restrictions in particular industries, notably the Mines and Works Proclamation (1917) in mining and the Masters and Servants Proclamation (1920) in farming. By requiring that all blacks outside the reserves have state-registered jobs, they were designed to enforce the inhuman apartheid doctrine that black Namibians were only allowed in the so-called 'white' area for as long as they served the labour needs of the white employers. All workers had to have a 'service contract' usually valid for 12 or 18 months at a time, and no worker could resign his or her job without the employer's permission. To be found without this basic document or without the employer's endorsement on it when leaving a job rendered urban workers liable to summary deportation, farm or contract workers to heavy fines and imprisonment for 'desertion', and all workers to be forced afterwards to serve out their 'contracts' with their former bosses — an intimidating prospect given the vindictive and violent practices of many Namibian employers. So limited were the rights left to black workers under this legislation that it amounted to forced labour in all but name.

Each body of employers was given controls tailored to its specific needs. In the towns, employers needed a stable, locally settled work-force; consequently, blacks were allowed to live permanently with their families in the towns. But since wage-rates were usually higher than on the surrounding farms, those looking for work were usually more numerous than jobs going, so the authorities imposed stringent conditions on permanent residence and surrounded the towns with a rampart of restrictions on blacks coming in from outside. Under the notorious Section 10(1) of the Natives (Urban Areas) Act, blacks could qualify to stay in the towns only by being born and residing there continuously, by working there continuously for 15 years or for a single employer for 10 years, and without being convicted of any crime more serious than a minor pass offence, or by being the wife, unmarried daughter or minor son of a qualifying worker. A few days' illness, unemployment from redundancy or sacking, changing jobs, a visit to a relative living elsewhere, even in childhood — any of these could bring a worker's precious Section 10 rights to an abrupt end and risk him or her being 'endorsed out' to an unknown 'homeland'. Basic insecurity is a permanent condition of life, even for the most favoured of black workers.

Once outside the urban fortresses, workers could only return through the migrant labour queue, condemned to live for the rest of their working lives in single quarters, with wife or husband and children trapped in the reserves unless they themselves qualified under Section 10. And few migrants from Police Zone reserves ever gained Section 10 rights if they did not have them already, while northern contract workers did not stand a chance because their short-term indentures forced them to return to the reserves before they could extend them or take out new ones. Such discrimination between the two categories of migrant workers also extended to access to jobs.

Migrants from within the Police Zone were allowed limited rights to seek work on their own account. In the reserves, anyone intending to look for employment had first to obtain a 'workseeker' pass, issued only for towns and districts with a local shortage of labour. On arrival in the towns they had to register immediately with the official Labour Bureau and could only stay if they found work within 14 days. All jobs had to be approved and registered at the Bureau, making any attempt to bypass it highly vulnerable to pass checks. The same procedure applied for changing jobs or for moving from one town to another. Such controls made it extremely difficult to get a job and very risky to try and change it. At any time the whim of a Labour Officer, his ear always turned to employers' complaints, or a random pass check in the street could mean sudden deportation to the reserves.

But contract workers from the north were not granted even this limited freedom of choice. The only discretion allowed by the South West Africa Native Labour Association (SWANLA), the semi-official labour recruiting organisation set up in 1926 by the big mines, was whether or not to 'volunteer' for recruitment. Since for many the alternative was slow starvation in apartheid's poverty-stricken labour reservoirs and since the regime permitted no one to set foot outside the reserves except through SWANLA, migrants had no choice but to take whatever they were given. The 'contract' which workers were compelled to sign was in reality a standardised indenture enforced by legal sanctions. It placed them under controls which were even more disabling than those which bound migrants from the central and southern reserves. First, they had to sign for long periods – 12 or 18 months, but sometimes longer – without any right to give notice, 'desertion' being a criminal offence. Second, on completion of their contracts they were compelled to return to the northern bantustans and sell themselves anew to SWANLA, thereby automatically losing any chance of getting Section 10 rights or a regular job.

At the Ondangwa and Grootfontein recruiting centres, a crude and degrading medical examination determined which of three broad categories of work recruits were eligible for, and each worker was then arbitrarily allocated to a job requisition which had been sent in by an employer. There was no choice of job, no bargaining over wages (which were fixed in advance at a standard rate) or hours of work. The transformation of human beings into anonymous labour units could hardly have been more complete.

White farmers, the political favourites of the colonial regime, have always received special protection – and they have needed it, for they have consistently paid the lowest wages, provided the worst conditions and meted out the most violent treatment of all employers in Namibia. Two laws, although applying nationally, were particularly designed to enable them to immobilise their work-force. First, a Vagrancy Law made any black 'found wandering around abroad and having no lawful or sufficient means of support', or simply 'wandering over any farm', liable to arrest and magistrates were required to distribute first offenders to employers at whatever wage the latter deemed fair. In other words, any black in the rural areas without a job, for whatever reason, could be picked up and press-ganged into forced labour on local farms — indeed farmers used to hang about the magistrates courts just to take on such prisoners. Second, a Masters and Servants Law made 'desertion' a criminal offence. The only way a farmworker could escape from his boss was to make a complaint of maltreatment to the police — a sick joke, because even to get to the police station required a farmer's permission, and the police habitually beat up any worker who complained and handed him back to the farmer. In practice, many farmers never bothered with the courts, hunting down any workers who tried to leave and beating them savagely in full confidence that even if a worker died they would not be prosecuted. The farmers' power to hire and fire their work-force was absolute.

In its essentials, as we show later in this chapter, this same forced labour system remains in force today. Most of South Africa's much trumpeted 'reforms' in recent years have done little more than strip away overlapping legislation, leaving the basic provisions intact, and rationalise archaic regulations which employers no longer need. The general pass law has been repealed but the specific enactments, above all the 'influx controls', have not, and workers can still be deported as readily as before. The contract laws also remain and workers are as tightly bound to their employers as ever. For most black workers, choice of job, employer and place of residence and the right to seek employment, to resign from one's job, to legal protection from maltreatment by employers, and to live with one's family are still illusions of the South African propaganda machine.

The Poverty of Apartheid

Peasant Subsistence

The standard of living for most blacks in Namibia is low by any comparison. The poverty is greatest in the peasant areas, where nearly two-thirds of the black population depend on the land for most of their subsistence. Few peasant families can produce enough to keep themselves the year round, and in the central and southern reserves, where crops can rarely be grown, they depend on imported cereals for their staple supplies. The few estimates of *per capita* income are rough, but they still provide a telling indicator of the grinding poverty which is the general condition of 55% of the territory's population. In 1951, peasant output from the north contributed a mere 3.5% of the G.D.P., or R17 per head, according to South African figures. In 1977, peasant output for the whole country was estimated in the UNIN study at about 2.1% of G.D.P. or R39 per head; down to R16 in real terms allowing for inflation. These are the prices their produce would fetch with wholesalers; the same goods purchased at retail stores would cost roughly twice as much. In physical terms, food production amounts to as little as half the average quantity *per capita* in Tanzania. In other words, in 1977 the average peasant household in the northern bantustans produced food to the value of about R100 — less even than the cost price of their annual grain requirement measured in maize, let alone other foodstuffs, clothing, utensils and fuel. A household might expect to receive R80–100 a year in cash remitted by members on contract from their wages, and if cash income from trading were evenly spread (which it is not) would pick up another R60–70, making a yearly cash income of R140–170. Even the average is barely enough to survive on, and certainly not to live decently, and most families get less. Hunger haunts many peasant families in the north in all but the very best harvest years. As for the Police Zone reserves, they are little more than dustbowls — dumping grounds for the elderly, the sick and disabled, wives and children.

A slum near Rehoboth — typical housing conditions for black workers in the towns

Wages

Wage levels for black workers provide a standard of living scarcely better than that of the peasants and, for the majority, well below the level of bare subsistence. Few town dwellers have any other form of income than their wages. Unlike many towns elsewhere in Africa, the Namibian climate is too harsh to give workers much scope for growing some of their own food. In any case, official housing policy denies land or water for growing vegetables and grain. A handful of people in the towns, mainly women, manage to augment their wages by operating illegal beerhouses, selling handicrafts or taking in washing. But their services are mostly paid for out of the meagre earnings of their fellow workers, and always the regime's officials and police are on the watch to stamp out any form of livelihood which reduces people's dependence on wage-labour. On the settler farms, workers may be allowed to keep a few goats, a 'privilege' always vulnerable to the whims of the farmer.

An austere Poverty Datum Line (P.D.L.*) for Windhoek, the biggest and wealthiest town in Namibia, estimated a minimum of R50.82 as necessary in 1967 for a family of five to live on per month. A sample survey revealed that only 13% of the city's black workers earned over R50 a month, only 5% over R60, while 80% earned between R20—49, 63% under R40 and 7% under R20. In the following years the situation has scarcely improved. In October 1973 the Windhoek P.D.L. was set at R81.25, in October 1976 at R151.14 and in 1977 at R161.96.

This threefold increase has made nonsense of the much vaunted percentage rises in basic wages. Only in 1972 did the contract workers' strike force employers to raise wages in real terms, and the rampant inflation caused by the economic crisis in South Africa — into which Namibia was inevitably dragged — has eaten away most of these gains. In 1973, the big mines such as Tsumeb and SWACO were paying average cash wages of R30—40, and the Windhoek municipality, the Railways, the construction industry, hotels and catering and the food industry all paid R25—30, though because the fish canneries operate for only six months a year their effective wage was half that. By 1977, most cash wages had roughly doubled, but then so had the rate of inflation. Today, few black workers are better off in real terms than in the immediate aftermath of the 1972 general strike.

Employers and South African officials have always made much of the non-cash supplement which many employers add to the cash wages they pay. In hard reality this is little more than a humiliating and patronising way of cheapening the cost of labour. The 'wage-in-kind' is usually simply basic accommodation and food, which employers lay on so as not to have to pay their workers enough to provide these things for themselves. The 'accommodation' provided is often no more than a corner of a shed or a corrugated iron shanty for the farm workers and house servants, and grim, overcrowded barracks for contract workers in the towns and mines. The 'food' may be nothing more than sacks of maize and the occasional carcass on the farms, and bleak canteen meals in the compounds. It is no coincidence that the employers paying the lowest cash wages are the ones who provide the most in kind. In 1977, figures released by a farmers' spokesman, despite being

* A crude device for estimating the minimum earnings at which a family can survive in passable health. It omits even minor luxuries as well as many items most workers would regard as essentials. Below this level, workers do not die, but their babies do in large numbers, their children are stunted by malnutrition, and their own health is increasingly badly damaged. The Minimum Effective Level is usually set at 50% higher and claims to provide a frugal but adequate standard of living. Neither bear any relation to the undoubted ability of employers to pay higher wages.

highly inflated, revealed that cattle ranchers have a full 70% of their wages in kind — worth two and a half times more than the cash wage the workers actually received. And in 1975, Tsumeb, notorious for its harsh management and bad conditions, paid its black miners only half their average wage in cash.

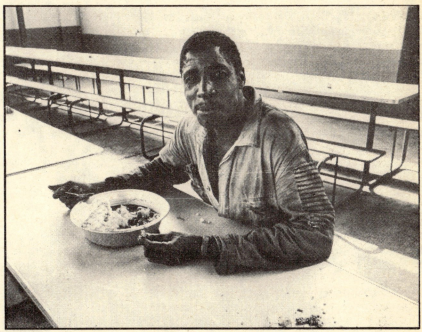

The contract workers' canteen at the Matchless mine

In practice, the supposed 'benefits' of these cheap provisions to the workers are largely illusory. The quality of food and housing is often appallingly bad — so bad that when they can workers have to spend part of their precious cash wage to compensate. A large number of farmworkers are bound more or less permanently by debt to their employers, who advance their workers credit to buy essential provisions from them at prices of their own choosing. In the huge mine and town compounds food is often the workers' biggest problem and their biggest source of resentment. Many have to miss breakfast altogether to get to work on time, because of the queues at the canteen and the pass checks, and sometimes arrive back too late for the evening meal. The food itself is monotonous, barely nutritious and detested by the workers. In 1977, one Walvis Bay worker estimated that 'easily three-quarters of them don't eat that food any more . . . Because of the fact that workers have to go without food, they are forced to use their own money, which is very little, so that they can buy their own food, otherwise they are going to starve.' But all of them have to pay for the compound meals in full, because their employers deduct the compound fee from their wages in advance. The worker, just quoted, exposed another trick the company and municipally-run canteens play — substituting cheap bad food for good, for instance, fish for meat. 'Everybody's salary is reduced, because he's paying for the food he never gets.' Above all, the workers have absolutely no choice whether to accept these 'benefits.' They are required by law to live in the compounds or in whatever 'accommodation' the employer chooses to provide, and to pay whatever deductions the employer makes for 'services' such as housing and food.

Although the 1970s have seen a gradual increase in the proportion of black wages paid in cash, the compulsory deductions discussed above usually leave the workers no better off, and sometimes even overall losers. A comparatively high cash wage is often less impressive when such deductions are taken into account. Rossing, for instance, was paying a minimum of R146 per month early in 1978, but charging R20 for accommodation in compounds rated by the workers as amongst the worst in Namibia and for food many did not even get a chance to eat. Government agencies can be quite as cynical as private capitalists. At a workers' meeting in early 1977, a Windhoek contract worker recalled: 'I know railway workers who . . . were told that they were going to get R40 a month. When they arrive here in Southern Namibia they find that R12 has to be subtracted from the R40 for food and R4 for accommodation.' In other words, a staggering 40% was deducted from a cash wage that was already well below its 1973 value in real terms.

Farmers simply do as they please, as they always have. At the same meeting a farmworker recounted an experience many of his comrades have shared.

> Sometimes workers are told — before they leave Northern Namibia — that they are going to get, for instance, R15 a month. Now if you go down to the farm where you are going to work, that farmer is only going to give you R6 a month. And if you happen to complain about it, he is going to tell, 'Hey, Jonas, when I brought you here, I bought you from the Bureau, therefore I can do what I want.'

Many employers compel their workers to work longer hours than are laid down in their contracts — which is illegal — and then pay them nothing extra or refuse to give overtime rates. Hotels and the catering industry generally are notoriously bad — workers regularly have to put in a 100-hour week for a cash wage that is only a half or a third of the poverty line.

Cash wage-rates vary greatly between jobs. There are sizeable differentials between the main economic sectors. For a 'normal' working week of 40—60 hours, in late 1976 unskilled and semi-skilled workers earned on average over R100 a month at C.D.M. and on the fishing boats, R70—80 at Tsumeb and Rossing, and less at other mines, R40—60 in state employment, factories and urban commerce, R30—40 in catering, and, at rock bottom, R10—20 as house servants and R10—15 in farming. It is impossible to present comprehensive or up-to-date data on black wages, not only because both government and employers have a great deal to hide, but also because many employers have two wage-rates: the one they give out to government inspectors and the press, and the other, a good deal lower, which they put in their workers' pay packets. Certainly wage-rates vary a good deal amongst the smaller urban businesses, even in the same industry. Early in 1977, one Windhoek garage labourer was getting only R15 a month and he knew of many others getting even less. But some factories or workshops were paying over R60 and building contractors in a hurry to finish a good contract would pay even more.

A worker at the American-owned Matchless copper mine

From this survey one conclusion is devastatingly clear: even today not one employer, state or private, pays its general labourers — over 85% of black workers — a cash rate above the poverty line (see Figure 18). A few large mines reach about 80% of this level and one (C.D.M.) may exceed it if free food and accommodation are included. But nearly all urban employers pay only between a half and a quarter of the P.D.L., and farmworkers and house servants get no more than 10% — perhaps 50% with provisions if they are lucky.

The only relatively well-paid black workers are those with skills or trades, such as lorry and bus drivers, sales and clerical staff, many of whom are Coloureds, and teachers. Even here the rates are mostly less than 50% above the P.D.L. In other words, few black households can hope to avoid degrading and crippling poverty on the wage of one worker alone, and many struggle to avoid it even on the wages of two. Most working-class families must send out all their able-bodied members, including the old, those in poor health, youths and even children, in order to scrape together a bare subsistence.

Figure 18 – The poverty of apartheid: wage-rates[1] for semi-skilled and unskilled black workers, late 1976.

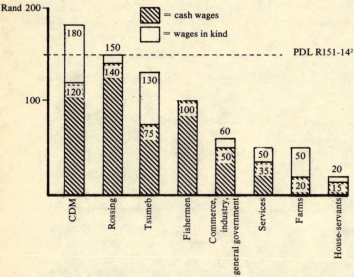

Notes: [1] Because no comprehensive wage data are published by the authorities, these estimates are only approximate. They are, however, based on the testimony of workers themselves, of workers' representatives and the National Union of Namibian Workers.
[2] Poverty Datum Line for Windhoek, October 1976. The PDL, at best a crude measurement of the minimum income needed for an average family to survive from day to day, is taken from ILO 1977, p61.

Labour Repression

Working conditions are uniformly harsh. They range from the regimented discipline of the big mines to the arbitrary violence of many small employers in the towns and on the ranches. Violence and humiliation are the daily experience of most black workers. As one colonial official explained: 'You know the mentality of a certain sort of South African – if he cannot kick or beat his black men he thinks he has lost some of his own basic rights.'

An early flurry of legislation, which was to stand unaltered for over half a century, gave all colonial employers wide-ranging coercive powers over their workers. Three Proclamations, the Mines and Works (1917), the Masters and Servants (1920) and the Natives (Urban Areas) (1924), and regulations issued under them, made a whole series of breaches of 'discipline' into criminal offences whether in the mines, on the farms or in the towns. Absence from work for whatever reason, even sickness, 'disobedience'.

negligence, 'abusive language', drunkenness, even simply being late — for all of these workers risked not merely the sack but also being hauled before a magistrate, and sentenced to heavy fines or imprisonment. Even then the ordeal would usually not be over: if the employer wanted them back afterwards, they still had to serve out their full contract period; if not, they could be distributed to other employers as forced labour or deported to a reserve.

In practice, most white employers have used the law only to reinforce the repressive methods they habitually use anyway. Verbal insult and physical violence are the standard ways in which employers or supervisors communicate with the workers under their command. 'When we go to work in the morning,' recounted one worker, 'the white workers don't greet us, they just order: "Go to work here, go and do that."' The withdrawal of many of the statutory criminal sanctions since 1976 has changed attitudes and customs very little. Small employers, particularly farmers, are the worst. Where previously the farmer could use the Masters and Servants Law to force a stock-herd to account for every one of the animals under his care and to compensate him if he thought any were missing, now the farmer simply docks his wages. 'If one of, for instance, the sheep gets lost,' recounted one shepherd in 1977 two years after the repeal of the Master and Servants Law, 'then that worker is going to be maltreated by that farmer. He's going to beat him up or even shoot him, or he's going to let him work without any wages . . . He has sometimes to work for months and he is not paid.'

Farmers are notorious for their brutality, and the complete isolation of farmworkers (the nearest town may often be 50 kilometres away) makes them easy prey. Any attempt to stand up for their rights or for treatment as human beings brands them as 'trouble-makers', fit only for beating. In practice, no worker can escape. Failure to complete an impossible work assignment or even simply misunderstanding — few employers can speak the home language of their workers — are frequent pretexts for violent punishment. One worker described how the farmer for whom he worked 'hit another Ovambo who died shortly afterwards in hospital. That worker could not lift the iron bar up alone, so Mr. X hit him with it on the head, smashing his skull.' The farmer, of course got off scot-free.

> You see, in Namibia if a white man kills he will have his excuses. For instance, he will say that the man he killed is a 'terrorist' or that 'he's a politician, he used to speak politics.' The police don't get their information from the dead man's fellow workers; no, they only ask the killer 'how did you kill him?' and the reply will be 'he was not very nice, he spoke rudely to me, so I got annoyed and hit him.'

Many workers know of similar cases, and in the few instances where they come to court, the murderer usually gets no more than a suspended sentence or a few months in jail. Blacks who kill, on the other hand, rarely escape with less than hanging or life imprisonment, however desperate their circumstances.

The police are willing and sadistic accomplices to this brutal treatment. Both on the farms and in the towns a farmer or overseer who cannot be bothered to beat up a worker simply calls in the police to do the dirty work for him. Vinnia Ndadi described one such incident in the Walvis Bay cannery where he worked. A brutal foreman attacked a worker, who successfully defended himself. 'He went straight to the phone and called the police, who came and arrested the workers . . . This fellow was taken to the station and badly beaten.' Later the worker told Ndadi why. 'I just refused to clean my machine while it was going . . . It's too dangerous. Lots of guys have lost fingers trying to do it. You start cleaning and zip, your finger is gone.' At the police station, he said, 'they just grabbed me and started beating and kicking — two of them. Then, without a word, they brought me back to work.' Whether it is foremen, employers or police who do the beating makes little difference to the Namibian workers who daily experience it: they are but different agents of the same oppressive system.

The brutality of labour exploitation is intensified by the *baas* or 'master' mentality shared by all whites, whatever their position, and ultimately rooted in their basic dependence on colonial oppression. Even those classed as wage employees usually do little more than supervise the work of the black labourers placed under their command. As one miner explained:

> At every section of the mine there are white and black workers. Especially in manual work the white does nothing except give orders. The black is always working hard to finish all the job, including that of the boss.

Another commented:

> Although we do know that there are also white workers, we do not see them suffer like ourselves, we don't see them working. What we do see are the so-called white workers standing with their hands in their pockets, supervising while we are working.

At Rossing, stated one contract worker,

> All the officers today, they're only boers — mostly foremen. There is great dissatisfaction that they are whites, especially migrants that's coming from abroad . . . But [such a person] knows *nothing* about the job. He has failed his Standard 8 and he's coming here, he's promoted, and they give him a large sum of money. The man who knows how to work with machinery is being mishandled every time by such a boss. In some departments I think you'll find more foremen there than workers.

Employers and supervisors delight in subjecting their workers to petty humiliation in order to flaunt their power. A kitchen worker described with bitter irony how his employer had him cook and wash dishes for his table, yet forced him to eat his rations outside from a tin while giving food to the dogs on a plate inside the house. One farmworker recounted how

> every morning at five o'clock you must come on the farm and say
> 'Goeie more, baas,' [Good morning, master] and then you go back.
> If you don't do it, you are going to be thrashed. So no matter
> whether you are sick or not, you have to go in there.

Physical degradation and authoritatian repression are the order of the day wherever a black worker finds employment in Namibia.

An everyday scene throughout Namibia: settler prosperity is built on the sweat of black labour

Working Conditions

Conditions at work are primitive and often highly dangerous. What little factory legislation has been enacted is more concerned with providing segregated toilets for whites than ensuring the safety of production workers. Where there are regulations they can be flaunted with impunity because the state will always take the employer's side. In the fish cannery where Ndadi was employed, the contract labourers were called to work as soon as the first boats came in, which was usually around 2 a.m.

> We quickly dressed and ran the 50 yards to the factory. Then we
> worked until the fish were finished. If, say, five boats came back full
> we'd work from 2 in the morning until 5 the next evening. Sometimes
> even till 9 p.m. — and without a single break! You couldn't stop or 'the
> fish would get stale'. So the machines were going continuously, belts

full and moving all the time. Many men got swollen legs and feet from standing so long. Eighteen hours! It's too much for a human being. Sometimes a man's feet were so swollen he could no longer pull on his boots . . . There were no medical services; you were taken to hospital in town only if seriously injured. And even then you had to return to work the same day, if possible. If your feet got so swollen you couldn't pull on your water boots, you were simply given a bigger pair.

Conditions underground in the mines are probably the most arduous of all. One white observer, writing about the northern Otjihase copper mine in the mid-1970s, declared:

It is difficult to imagine, let alone describe, these working conditions without actually experiencing them. To gain a small impression, try to imagine 15 pneumatic drills going full blast in a small enclosed room with a temperature of over 90°F and the operators working knee-deep in water and drilling not down, but horizontally.

To the employers and their minions, workers are just so many units of labour power, and if one gets damaged it is just discarded and thrown out on to the rubbish heap of wrecked humanity in the reserves. Protective clothing and guards on machines are regarded as extra expenses and therefore dispensable in the drive for greater profits. Most workers still have to buy from their own wages whatever protective clothing they can get. Overseers are anxious only to force up the pace of production to the maximum, and the comfort and safety of the workers under their control are mere sacrifices on the altar of productivity for their bosses.

Not surprisingly, industrial injury and occupational disease are the common experience of many black workers. One horrific accident at Ndadi's cannery exposes the devastating consequences of the lack of safety procedures and guards on dangerous machinery. One day two men were working at a machine which sucked out the fish and filtered them on to a belt below.

One man stood at the top of the tank on a plank across the middle, raking fish down into the mouth of the filter. Well, this fellow slipped and fell right into the machine. It just kept on turning and ground up his leg until it got clogged and stopped. He was taken off to hospital but lost so much blood that he died on the way.

Lesser injuries such as broken limbs, burns or the loss of fingers are common. And diseases, such as chest conditions from breathing dust in the mines, to which workers are prone because of a poor working and living environment and inadequate food, as well as those which are directly related to unregulated exposure to dangerous substances, are rife. In recent years, workers at Rossing, for instance, have protested against the long-term hazard of prolonged exposure to radioactive ore.

There is very little protective industrial legislation which workers can call on to secure even the most basic rights from the exploiters of their labour. Even where the law does impose restrictions, workers face almost certain reprisals if they try to get them implemented. Hours are long. The best conditions are to be found on the big mines, which have standard eight-hour shifts. Some mines, however, operate a six-day week, and some still use a 'ticket' system under which a 'month' means 30 working days — so that the actual work period is quite a big longer than that laid down in the contract, even though wages stay the same. And most of them, despite their huge profits, give no holiday pay, so that workers have to save from their ordinary wages to cover the unpaid leave which the migrant labour laws compel them to take.

In the canneries of Walvis Bay, where the work-load varies from day to day, the factory operatives can sometimes be kept on the job for 18 hours at a stretch, as we have seen. The workers have been campaigning for years for a proper shift system with overtime rates, but with only limited success so far. They may also be forced to work seven days a week throughout the season, and this pattern is widespread amongst many small urban employers and farmers. During the 1971—72 strike, one hotel worker said that his hours were 6 a.m. — 7 p.m., seven days a week — for a basic R27 a month without overtime. Farm labourers work from dawn to sunset — 12 to 15 hours a day in the summer — with a half-day off each week if they are lucky. Shepherds on the vast karakul farms in the south must spend days out alone in the veld with flocks several hundred strong and no shelter or proper provisions, and all for a monthly wage equivalent to the value of one un-tanned karakul pelt. Full-time house servants must similarly serve the daily routine of their masters and mistresses from start to finish, with maybe an hour or two off in the afternoon and a half-day on Sundays. The laws of apartheid extend the working day even further by forcing most workers in the towns and now in some mines (Rossing is the latest example) to live in ethnic ghettos far from their place of work. Every day these workers face a long and tiring journey to and from their work-places, either in buses or, very commonly, in the backs of their bosses' lorries.

The refusal of many employers, especially the smaller ones, to recognise a regular working day deepens the exploitation even further. Concepts such as the 'eight-hour day' or the 'five-day week', which trade union campaigns have established as the norm in most industrial countries, are rarely conceded in Namibia. Workers in domestic service, the hotels and the retail trade, as well as on the farms, are often expected to work even more hours when the work-load is heavy, not only without overtime but even without any addition to basic pay. The issue of better and regular overtime rates has been the objective of some of the bitterest and most prolonged struggles in the history of the Namibian working class, particularly in the docks, the railways and the fish factories. In the early 1960s, Ndadi relates, 'there was no such thing as a week-end' in the canneries. 'We worked seven days a week throughout the fishing season. We got overtime for anything more than 13 hours a day, but it amounted to only 6d. an hour.' The workers' struggle has won improved rates since then, but the overall situation has not changed greatly. Even when regular working hours and overtime rates are written into labour contracts, employers can simply ignore them without any fear of persecution.

Denial of Bargaining Rights

Central to the entire system of labour repression is the denial to black workers of any right to determine, either collectively or individually, their own wages or conditions of work. No Bantu worker in Namibia may legally seek or take a job on his own — everything must be licensed and endorsed by the government labour bureaux. SWANLA first sorted them out, by means of a crude and degrading medical examination at the Ondangwa reception centre, into three grades of physical fitness, and then dispatched them to its huge compound at Grootfontein, where it indentured them to labour contracts.
'When they came in from Ondangwa,' related Ndadi, who worked as a clerk in SWANLA's Grootfontein headquarters in the 1950's, 'they were put into groups for the fishing industry, diamond mines, smaller mines, farms, hotels and domestic work, and so on. The loudspeaker called them to the office where they got their papers . . . Once I got all the papers I listed their names, then took the lists and papers to the office next door. There, SWANLA officials assigned jobs, matching names with the notices from companies and individuals wanting workers. When that was done the workers were called into the office and lined up. Each man's name was called and he was given a contract to sign . . . Of course, there was no choosing or refusing.' Should workers later try to bargain with an employer, they would run up against the standard rebuttal Ndadi encountered: 'Your wages are set by SWANLA; you have no right to ask for an increase'; and if the worker persisted: 'I'd like to raise your wage, but that would be violating the rules of SWANLA and the law.' Job seekers from the north, prisoners of the contract labour system, have virtually no choice at all. The so-called reforms of recent years have done little more than substitute official Labour Bureaux for the now defunct SWANLA, and the system itself continues in most of its essentials.

Other 'Bantu' workers have slightly greater freedom to seek work and to bargain with their employers over wages and terms. But all are bound by the contract law, which makes it extremely difficult to leave a job without the employer's permission. In the towns they may only take new jobs if they have registered with the Labour Bureau and taken out a work-seeker's permit, and a Bureau official will only issue one if they can produce contracts properly cancelled by their previous employers, who can, of course, refuse to do so before the contracts have expired. Without a legal job or a permit, no worker is entitled to live in the towns, and to this day the colonial police surround and sweep the main urban ghettos three or four times a year and interrogate every single person found inside, fining all 'deserters' and 'illegal residents' and sending them under guard back to the reserves.

In addition, there are the black lists of 'deserters' and 'trouble-makers', so that any worker who stands up for his rights runs the risk of being victimised for the rest of his working life, even of being banned from wage employment altogether. A white personnel officer described the system thus:

> The permanent trump card in the Labour Officer's hand of informal rules is his 'black list', a list which he keeps of all workers who are or might be 'agitators' and 'troublemakers' . . . Such 'listed' people simply find that there is no work available for them . . . Many people are placed on the list by the Labour Officer on the basis of information received from the South African Security Police . . . [or] of complaints he has had from white employers. Apparently, there is no impartial investigation into the alleged misbehaviour, and it certainly is difficult for the black-listed worker to appeal against his listing as the Labour Officer can simply deny the existence of the 'black list' and claim there is no 'suitable' employment.

The system is designed to give management total control over the labour force and to deny workers the slightest power to influence their conditions of employment.

Under these circumstances any direct resistance by black workers, whether as individuals or via concerted action, is a highly risky business. To complain to the colonial authorities about an employer is to invite victimisation and physical maltreatment. To leave the job means automatically breaking the law and certain retribution if caught. To strike as a group is likewise to be branded as 'contract-breakers', and the police are quick to intervene and heavy-handed on the slightest pretext. All strikers risk losing their jobs and their homes and being deported to reserves where they may have no land or relatives. If the police or management can track down any rank-and-file leaders or SWAPO members, they are invariably earmarked for detention in solitary confinement as 'agitators' and are frequently beaten up and tortured as well, and after that black-listed from any but the most menial jobs. The cost of mounting open acts of resistance and of organising trade unions is so high that it is not surprising that black workers use the strike weapon with great care and mostly organise underground rather than expose their resources and leaders to attack by the employers and police.

Social Conditions

The web of controls on where people can live, together with discrimination in housing, welfare, education and recreation, is every bit as ruthless as the labour legislation. Every town has its location, where all blacks, except living-in domestic workers or catering staff, are compelled to reside. Moreover, since most blacks are not allowed to build their own houses, the authorities can deliberately engineer the type of housing in furtherance of their apartheid designs.

Accommodation is segregated not simply between black and white but also amongst black: first, by work status, and second, by ethnic labels in terms of which every black is identified. Contract workers are forced to live in enclosed compounds, the bigger ones, as in Katutura, being little more than fortified concentration camps with controlled entrances. Migrants from outside the town or from one of the reserves must live in separate single quarters. Section 10 residents are allowed to live in houses, albeit tiny primitive constructions. But even here, in townships such as Katutura, they are divided up into 'ethnic zones', their doors daubed with big letters signifying their allotted ethnic group — an 'H' or an 'N', for instance, meaning 'Herero' or 'Nama' — just as the homes of Jews were branded in Nazi Germany.

This remorseless fragmentation further divides 'Bantu' from 'Coloureds', who have to live in segregated townships (for example, Khomasdal in Windhoek), and also applies to schools, which are exclusively 'ethnic' right through primary and secondary levels. Thus, in a multi-racial township such as Katutura, the people are forced to live in their so-called ethnic zones, and send their children to 'ethnic' schools staffed by teachers from their own 'ethnic' group.

Few leisure facilities in the 'white' areas of town are open to blacks, while almost nothing — apart from the profitable municipal beer-halls — is provided in the locations. Petty apartheid restrictions keep blacks off the sidewalks, in inferior and segregated railway carriages and buses, and buying food and drink from the back windows of shops. A curfew keeps blacks off the streets at night.

The occupation regime makes very little provision for the social needs of black workers — peasants, of course, are left to support their every requirement from their own resources, no matter that it is the bantustan policy which drives them into abject poverty. There is no child allowance, indeed nothing for mothers beyond the crudest maternity provisions at clinics and hospitals. The old do receive a state pension, but it is so small that even the most frugal cannot survive on this alone. And together with this total lack of welfare provision is the pressure of the higher costs of urban living and of the pass laws dragnet which together force those condemned by the regime's policy as 'superfluous appendages' — in other words all those not in productive employment — back to the reserves and bantustans.

Housing

In the reserves and bantustans the people must build their own housing with no materials provided. Where there is wood, as in the far north, this may not prove a great problem (although wood is now becoming quite scarce), but in the barren reserves of the south the only usable materials are usually scrap corrugated iron and sacking or, at best, sun-dried bricks. Conditions in the reserves on the southern plateau are indescribably bleak — a stony wilderness with hardly any trees or bushes for shelter and extremes of temperature between a baking hot summer and the bitterly cold, dry winds of winter.

Ramshackle huts and scanty clothing provide the people imprisoned there by the laws of apartheid with no protection at all from this harsh climate, and their suffering is great.

On white-owned farms, accommodation for labourers is totally in the power of the farmer. Until recently, a fair number neither provided any nor allowed their workers enough time to build an adequate structure for themselves. Today many families still live in tiny *pondokkies* (tin shanties), although in recent years a few farmers have built concrete huts for their workers — one worker or family to a room. But many farmers still provide nothing. A recent study by the International Defence and Aid Fund summarised the testimony of a number of Namibian farm workers as follows.

> [Thomas's] sleeping quarters were in the garage, 'but I divided it with a piece of material, and on the other side was the car. I was lucky. Some people used to sleep just under the tree. When it was raining they were given a piece of canvas and sticks' to erect a shelter, and they had to do their own cooking outside. This testimony was born out by Hans, Anne and other Namibians interviewed by the authors. Anne said that in most cases the only accommodation was 'what we can build ourselves from sticks and bits of material,' while Hans (a pastor who travelled widely between farms) said that 'workers on farms have no sleeping room, they sleep outside the owner's house'.

When they do build huts, farmers provide no fuel or electricity, so that the workers have to burn scrap wood for cooking and lighting.

In the towns, the people are herded into municipal-owned housing built on the cheap in bleak uniformity. Contract workers are incacerated in sordid compounds surrounded by walls or barbed wire: 'single' workers are sent to bachelor hostels only slightly less severe. A few domestic servants and hotel workers live in servants' quarters at the back of their employers' premises; while the big employers, mostly the mines, build their own compounds. Those allowed to live with their families are allocated spartan little four-roomed houses in the location, without internal doors and with uninsulated corrugated-iron roofs which turn them into ovens in the summer and ice-boxes in winter and at night. Their only sanitation is an outside toilet containing a cold water shower fixture, with a single tap in the yards. There is no electric lighting or heating. And because the government refuses to allow more houses to be built, many are crammed with relatives or friends, sometimes 15 or 20 to a single house, with no additional rooms permitted. A women from Katutura described this desperate overcrowding:

> Most of the houses don't have less than ten people in the house. There are only four rooms — without ceilings, without doors, and there is no privacy. The walls are so thin that you can hear people in the next room talk. And houses have been built very badly — there are big cracks in the walls and the municipality does nothing about it.

The homes of black Namibians frequently lack basic services such as running water, drains and electricity

A typical shanty for black farm workers

Even the mayor of Windhoek has described Katutura as a ghetto, referring on one occasion to the visible symptoms of the people's poverty: 'Daily, hordes of black children and adults swoop down on the Windhoek refuse dumps, scratching in the dirt, looking for food and useful articles.'

A visiting journalist has described the even worse conditions at the contract workers' compound in Katutura initially built to house 3,000 workers:

> 5,000 Ovambos are being housed in circumstances that would disgrace a 19th century prison. A visitor can only be appalled by the compounds' unrelieved bleakness — the barbed wire fences; the food being prepared with spades and pitch forks; above all, the overpowering stench of urine which hangs over the compound.

Generally, 16 to 20 workers are packed into a single room, and sleep in double concrete bunks on a half-inch thick felt mattress. Each worker literally has only his concrete block which acts as a bed and private living space.

In the Walvis Bay municipal compound, related one worker:

> The people are not sleeping on beds, they are sleeping in a sort of case made out of cement, and one has to climb up there . . . You have got to store all your stuff there, and you just retain a little space for your sleeping . . . If they want to sit and discuss things, if they want to drink, they must drink there; if they want to sing — everything else they must do there.

In the Katutura compound, declared another worker:

> There are no beds. The so-called beds which are there are just walls which are built to the height of a bed — two rectangular walls. Within those four walls there is a hole, like a grave, where somebody has also to keep his property.

So many workers are on the run from the pass laws that compounds are invariably overcrowded. Workers are constantly harassed by pass checks, and when they are at work, police and black officials regularly comb the compounds, breaking and often stealing their meagre possessions.

Few families are not torn apart by the enforced separation of migrant labour, which keeps the man away without visits for periods often exceeding a year. Both husbands and wives suffer the emotional hardship of long separations and only brief intervals between one contract and the next; and children grow up hardly knowing their fathers. The women do indeed gain greater independence and managerial control during the men's absence, but they have to bear alone the cost of child-rearing and to take on all the labour of running the peasant farm, with small and sometimes unreliable

Katutura compound: Ovambo compound dormitory buildings

Living space for a contract worker inside a compound

cash remittances from their menfolk. In the barren southern reserves the old people, women and children, gathered in little clusters of iron shanty huts, can often do little but huddle in the shade of their huts from the fierce summer sun and suffer the biting cold of the highveld nights, denied all opportunity of work or self-sufficient farming.

Education

The only services which the occupation regime makes any attempt to provide on a national scale are health and education, and even here, the extent and quality of what is provided is severely limited. Up to the early 1960s, the South Africans left nearly all education and health care in the hands of the missionaries, particularly in the peasant areas. As international pressures intensified and employers increasingly demanded workers who were at least numerate and literate in the language of their bosses, the regime moved to take over both, but always within the framework of apartheid policy as laid down in the Odendaal Report.

In education, the almost total neglect which persisted into the 1950s was radically reversed in the 1960s. By 1976, 167,000 black students, or about two-fifths of all those of school age (6 to 17 years old), were enrolled in schools (see Figure 19). But the structure is overwhelmingly bottom-heavy: nearly half were in the first two years of primary school, and all but a fraction had dropped out by the end of the primary stage. Secondary school students made up a mere 6.3% (10,573). Under the Department of Bantu Education, which controls 83.5% of enrolments, secondary schools numbered only 34, as against 830 primaries, and a mere 10 provided classes to matriculation level. In the whole of Namibia, only 220 students (74 Africans and 146 Coloureds) were studying for matriculation in 1976. Another 494 were in teacher training, but only 18 of them for secondary school diplomas. And black teachers themselves have rarely been given adequate training for their posts. Over a quarter in 1976 had had no teacher training at all; while only 30% had matric and a mere 2.5% (134 out of a total of 5,272) university degrees. In a nation of over one million people there is no university and few technical training facilities, and Namibians must apply to the tribal colleges in South Africa for almost all types of higher education. In 1974, only 40 were studying at universities in South Africa and another 15 by correspondence courses. By 1977, these figures had risen to 134 and 113 respectively, but even then amount to only an eighth of the number of Namibian whites (1,988) enrolled at South African universities. Very few can afford to go even if they get places. A few of the larger firms and management associations have set up literacy programmes of their own. C.D.M. has financed a small technical training institute in Ovamboland and Rossing hands out a few bursaries each year. But these are designed to go no more than enable workers to understand and implement the instructions of their bosses.

The expansion of state education has in fact been part and parcel of the apartheid masterplan. Since the early 1960s, the regime has pressured most mission schools into closing by withdrawing subsidies, banning private classes, dictating the syllabus and restricting or expelling teachers. At the same time, school provision has expanded under the control of the Departments of Bantu Administration and of Coloured Affairs, in an ideological drive to 're-tribalise' the Namibian people. Instruction has to be exclusively in the mother-tongue in primary school, which has left the vast majority who leave at the primary stage with only a smattering of Afrikaans or English. In secondary schools, the medium of instruction is invariably Afrikaans, which denies Namibians access to an international language such as English. New high schools have been built not in towns but in the reserves, and the single training college open to all Africans and Coloureds, the Augustineum, has been pressured to become a Coloureds-only college. Black parents have to pay for various extras, such as school books and uniforms, and many are too poor to afford this burden. With overcrowded schools, scarce equipment and unqualified teachers, this is truly education for subservience, and the syllabus content is sometimes nothing more than racist indoctrination.

Health and Welfare Services
Health services have remained grossly biased towards whites and town dwellers at the expense of blacks and the rural population, especially peasants. Clinics began to appear in the small towns and reserves, while prestige hospitals rose alongside major administrative centres. But the clinics are often badly-stocked outposts, given cursory visits by doctors from distant centres and without transport and qualified staff of their own. Too much is concentrated in the big hospitals, which are difficult, and often impossible, for blacks to reach from the peasant areas or the farms.

There are only two government hospitals in the whole of the north, servicing a population of 700,000, and they are regularly understaffed — the Oshakati government hospital in Ovamboland should have a complement of 20 doctors, but recently was down to only four. This seriously worsens the already marked gap in quality and availability between white and black hospital facilities: there are still twice as many beds per head of population for whites as for blacks. Mission hospitals now have their running costs subsidised, but not their capital expenditure; and so extreme has government hostility been to some missions that it has forced the closure of their hospitals — for instance, the Anglican St. Mary's Hospital at Odibo — expelling staff and blocking replacements. Many of the hospitals are overcrowded, their services constrained by inadequate finance and apartheid regulations and their staff poorly trained and overworked, with a high proportion of medical students and national servicemen, and a mere handful of qualified Namibians among them. Preventive health programmes barely exist, and many workers and peasants simply cannot afford to travel to the hospitals' outpatients departments or to pay the fees demanded, even though they are low. Doctors in general practice are private, charge fees few blacks can afford and are geared almost exclusively to the needs of white settlers, for whom there is an average of one doctor for every 900 people. There are less than half a dozen black doctors in the whole country (see Figure 20).

Figure 19 — Education for subservience.

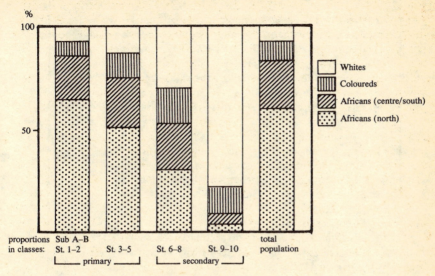

proportions Sub A–B
in classes: St. 1–2   St. 3–5   St. 6–8   St. 9–10   total
                                                             population
             └──── primary ────┘   └──── secondary ────┘

Whites
Coloureds
Africans (centre/south)
Africans (north)

Source: Melber 1979, tables 27, 36, 52, 69, 89.

Figure 20 — Apartheid and health: access to health care and infant mortality rates in Windhoek, 1973–75.

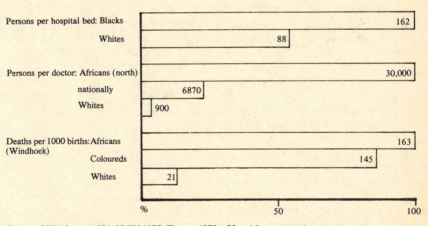

Persons per hospital bed: Blacks — 162
Whites — 88

Persons per doctor: Africans (north) — 30,000
nationally — 6870
Whites — 900

Deaths per 1000 births: Africans (Windhoek) — 163
Coloureds — 145
Whites — 21

Sources: SWA Survey 1974, UNIN 1977; Thomas 1978, p23 and fragmentary data.

A deep-going socio-economic transformation of
Namibian society requires fundamental change in
production relations which will ensure the speedy
development of the Namibian productive forces,
particularly the development of the skills, knowledge and cultural creativeness of the toiling
masses. Hence, our movement is called upon to
embark on:

1. Urgent training of technical and professional
   cadres at institutions of technical and higher
   education in different parts of the world as well
   as the newly established United Nations Institute
   for Namibia;
2. Provision for work-orientated, comprehensive
   education and training for illiterate and semi-
   literate adults (with a literacy component built
   in) at SWAPO schools;
3. Laying the foundation of a free and universal
   education for all Namibians from primary,
   through secondary to university level by
   training many teachers and educationalists
   now;
4. Developing the people's cultural creativeness
   as a weapon in the struggle for liberation;
5. Making the sufferings and aspirations of the
   masses the central themes of all artistic
   expressions, namely, drawings, music, paintings,
   dancing, literature, etc;
6. Striving toward the elimination of all vestiges
   of tribal or feudal mentality, particularly un-
   scientific or superstitious conceptions of
   natural and social phenomena.

SWAPO Political Programme, 1976

Apart from occasional visits to local clinics, few Namibians therefore have
access to health care. At Swakopmund, workers explained recently, there is
only one clinic staffed by a single nursing sister. One session with a private
doctor costs R4, well beyond the means of most blacks. At the government

hospital in Walvis Bay, 'Bantu' or 'Coloureds' pay the same fees but are
segregated into separate sections where the latter get 'white' rations and the
former get 'just a cup of soup and two slices of bread.' South African propaganda claims that treatment is virtually free for the poor, but workers can
still be trapped with heavy debts — one worker was faced with a bill of R70
for a mere seven days' treatment. And the quality of that treatment is often
very poor, especially at the hands of arrogant and poorly qualified Afrikaner
doctors. A Windhoek woman related how 'at the hospital you experience that
most of the doctors, who are white South Africans, feel that you are trying
to be very wise and they chase you out and tell you to use the medicine, and
be content with the results.' Describing the attitude of Afrikaner doctors, a
Walvis Bay nurse described how one of them who would say: "Now, to
which group do you belong? An Ovambo?' 'Yes, I am.' Then he just helps
you roughly and then says, "Go to SWAPO, you belong to SWAPO, go to
your fellow SWAPO doctors . . ."'

In no way is this largely inaccessible state health service compensated for
by company schemes and insurance. A few large-scale mines, notably C.D.M.,
provide free medical treatment of reasonable quality for their black workers.
Most companies do not; indeed, illness or injury can often be a pretext for
victimisation. One Walvis Bay worker described such an instance:

> At one plant you have got a small clinic, and if someone is treated just
> three times . . . I have seen in one case where they tried to get rid of X.
> They wanted to discharge him because the training sister said, 'No,
> you will cost too much money.'

And workers cannot rely on first aid or even emergency cover while on the
job because of the indifference of the white foremen. As a Windhoek contract
labourer explained

> Sometimes it happens that while workers are working and one of them
> becomes ill, he won't be taken to the hospital because the white man is
> going to say: 'I can't take you because the others are working.' . . . It
> means that once one of them has become ill he has become unproduct-
> ive, and the employer is no longer concerned about him.

On the ranches few workers get any medical attention at all, and contract
workers, with no relatives living locally, can be in great danger of simply
vanishing, because many are not told the identity or address of their
employer until they arrive on the farms.

> The family of the worker wouldn't know where he is. Even if he
> happens to die, they won't know that he has died because his employer
> is not going to trouble himself to find out where the family or the
> relatives of the worker are. He's just going to keep quiet and go and
> buy another worker from the Bureau.

> Our health and social services programme in an
> independent Namibia shall strive for preventive
> as well as for curative medicine for all citizens
> along the following lines:
>
> a. There shall be comprehensive, free medical
>   services in an independent and democratic
>   Namibia;
> b. There shall be hospitals and clinics in every
>   district of our country;
> c. There shall be nurseries and clinics in every
>   community for the working people and their
>   families;
> d. There shall be health education centres for
>   preventive medicine and family planning;
> e. There shall be training institutions for the
>   training of medical and para-medical
>   personnel;
> f. There shall be rehabilitation centres for dis-
>   abled and infirmed persons, and
> g. There shall be an International Red Cross
>   Society.
>
> *SWAPO Political Programme, 1976*

Although a state compensation scheme for industrial injury, disease and
death does exist, it excludes nearly all blacks, either by its qualifying condition or by sheer bureaucratic obstruction. Most are simply not eligible. For
the rest, injury compensation and payments to relatives are assessed according
to previous earnings. Thus the personnel officer quoted earlier found that at
his mine, 'as far as I could ascertain, a black would get R400 for the loss of
an eye, while a white would get R6,000 plus other sickness and accident
benefits'. Blacks get small lump-sum payments, leaving them jobless and
destitute for the rest of their lives; whites get life pensions at rates which
guarantee their future comfort indefinitely.

Private insurance is far beyond the means of black workers except for the
few in well-paid white-collar and professional occupations. Over the years,
they have struggled to set up benefit schemes under their own control, but
in such grinding poverty their resources are pitifully few. Yet it is private
insurance which most white employees use to guarantee high quality medical
treatment and adequate compensation, and often it is one of the prize baits
which the big companies offer to attract skilled or managerial staff from
South Africa and the West.

Government welfare is pitifully slight. Sickness and unemployment benefit is as good as non-existent for black workers and few employers bother to try and fill the gap. Except in the few mines which provide free medical treatment, for most black workers injury or illness can mean total social disaster and destitution. There is no law to prevent a worker being sacked for falling ill, without any compensation. Smaller employers usually have the rule, 'no work, no pay'. For women in particular, who have to bear the burden of child-raising and can rarely get jobs other than as low-paid house servants, the hardship this causes can be very severe.

There is also no proper state pension scheme. The rate for blacks is set far below subsistence, is only a fraction of that paid to whites, and even this is denied to the vast majority of black workers. The Turnhalle Conference itself calculated, in 1975, that 88% of the labour force was excluded. Again, few companies run pension schemes, and those that do pay very little and demand impossible qualifications.

All this is completely in line with the remorseless logic of apartheid, which decrees that all 'superfluous appendages' shall be dumped in the reserves to be looked after by the peasants there. But the peasants are themselves destitute, and cannot adequately look after the old and sick. Instances have been reported where groups of old people, torn from their urban communities and dumped in the reserves, have all died within a couple of years. Such an inhuman policy amounts to little less than genocide.

A woman from Windhoek describes with feeling the plight of the elderly:

> There are so-called homelands, to which the old people have been forced to go. These old people have been offered a so-called old-age home, which is in reality only a little corrugated room in this terrible heat of Namibia. While they build beautiful flats and houses, with lawns, trees and shade, and every possible convenience, for the white old-age people, our people have to live in these iron huts where they are being burnt by the sun and where they have no facilities whatsoever. It's very difficult for us because we live in the cities and we don't know what's happened to these old people. We need a permit to visit them in the first place, then we are worried because they don't get their food regularly, although it is only porridge in most cases.

Here we see the full horror of the economic logic of the apartheid system. In order to force down wages and social security expenditure to the minimum needed by the productive workers to survive, it has loaded most of the cost of unemployment, industrial disease and injury, child-rearing and care of the sick and elderly on to a peasantry which it deliberately impoverishes so as to force out cheap migrant labour. By this insane, inhuman logic the weakest naturally go to the wall. As recently as 1975, infant mortality for Africans in Windhoek was a staggering 163 per 1,000 births, for Coloureds 145, but for whites a mere 21.

The most searing indictment of the reality of apartheid is to be found in the city centres where shop-windows display an opulence only the self-indulgent rich can afford while black cripples beg for their life-money; and in the blazing wastelands of the reserves where the old the sick, the human debris of apartheid, huddle together in the cramped shade of their tiny iron huts, following the shadow around the walls from dawn to dusk as they wait to die.

Women Under Colonialism

In colonial society women carry a double burden of disabilities. First, as in most forms of society known in history, they suffer exploitation on grounds of sex. Second, under colonial capitalism they are subject to discrimination by race and by class. The two kinds of oppression interact and reinforce each other. The key factor in the particular form of oppression suffered by women in Namibia, as in South Africa, is the system of migrant labour and influx control.

The fact that systems of migrant labour effectively destroy family life is widely recognised. Mrs. Magdalena Shamena, of the SWAPO Women's Council, describes some aspects of this destruction:

> [In the migrant's family] the wives have to work hard. They have to do jobs that they shouldn't do. They have to look after the children alone. In this way Namibian women have no chance to be with their husbands and enjoy human rights . . . no chance to study . . . no chance for anything else.

The special implications of such a system for women need to be carefully considered. Under migrant labour, women are condemned to raise their children virtually single-handed, with only a little help from elderly or sick relatives. They suffer long, wasting years of loneliness as their husbands appear fleetingly, only to be driven by hardship to depart on contract once more after a few short weeks or months. But on top of their single-parent-hood, women in the reserves, barred from nearly all types of employment, are compelled to provide by their own labour for most of the subsistence needs of themselves, their children and their elderly relatives. Tied to small and increasingly impoverished plots, which the puppet 'tribal authorities' allot not to them but to their husbands, they must wait endlessly and anxiously for money to arrive from their relatives to supplement what meagre living they manage to scrape from the soil.

It is government policy to provide single quarters for male workers from the 'homelands' in the urban areas, but not for women. The colonial regime recognises and exploits the fact that women are 'home-makers' whether or not they are also workers and peasants. By systematically denying them the right to resettle in the towns it both contains women in that role and also forces them to remain producers in order to sustain the system as a whole (see Figure 21).

Figure 21 — The migrant labour trap: composition of the black working population by sex, 1977.

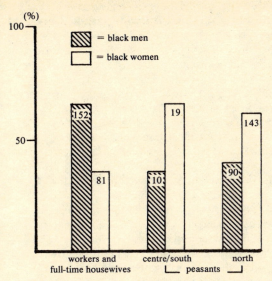

Note: The figures indicate thousands of persons in each category.

The right to work for wages is thus denied to the majority of Namibian women. Of the few who do manage to slip through the influx control net and secure residential rights in towns or on farms, most can only retain those rights through dependence on a male worker who himself qualifies. Even this possibility becomes increasingly problematic as apartheid officials 'endorse out' women and children as 'superfluous appendages,' who once deported never return. Few jobs are open to women outside domestic service and those who do find wage-labour have to tolerate the worst pay and conditions of all. The fact that women have fewer legal rights than men and that their role as home-makers imposes heavy extra demands makes them all the more vulnerable to deportation to the reserves. Even there, the women has few legal rights. She can normally only secure access to land — the only remaining means of survival — by marrying. In terms of the repressive 'tribal' law imposed by the regime, marriage robs her of what limited personal and property rights she possesses. Under South African colonialism in Namibia, there is not one area of her life which the black woman can call her own — discrimination by sex, race and class combine in a system of total oppression.

Namibian women are well aware of these overlapping layers of exploitation. Often girls are the first to leave school to help at home, in the fields or in the houses of white settlers. 'Most of us have no education — or no formal education. We have had no school because we did not have the opportunities. We had to leave school early to go out to work to supplement the income.' Most women in the towns or on the farms end up as cleaners and house servants. 'As a woman I have to work for another woman, a white woman. And I am a woman with six or seven children — we are mostly women with big families.' As house servants, they often average nine- or ten-hour days, seven days a week. Nearly all professional occupations are barred, mostly by custom rather than by law. 'Nurses and teaching and then in offices — that's about all. And shop assistants — "tea-girls" is what they're called, "tea-girls" that make tea in the offices and clean in the offices.'

But this is only half the story. Under their double oppression women find that their involuntary duties as home-makers are in no way diminished by their being wage-earners or peasant farmers as well; and the state makes little provision for supervised child-care facilities which could ease the burden. As women from Windhoek explained:

> We as housewives must leave our children at home during the day because there are no centres to look after our children. We have to get out and go and look for work; and if we get work then we have to start early. We work for the white housewife — we have to look after her children while we have to leave our children at home. We come home after work; we find our houses dirty; we have to clean the children now without care — they have stayed hungry the whole day. When we come home, we don't know whether they have been to school. And we don't know whether they have eaten. Most of the time children go to the dust bins to scratch for food.

Single women often face intense pressures. 'I earn R30 a month. I must care for my parents, I must pay for the house in which I live, I must eat, I must drink, I must clothe myself. And I have a child to care for.' Most black men, whether married or not, do little to ease the burden.

> Most of the men don't help their wives. They still believe that the housework is solely here for the women; and if you want to go some-where, you just have to leave the children at home in their own care and go where you want to be. There is nobody to help there — *very* few men volunteer to help at all.

All this puts a severe extra hardship on women trying to educate themselves, organise their fellow-oppressed or join actively in the liberation movement.

Political and Military Oppression

Denial of the Franchise
At the political level the true character of the occupation regime as a repress-ive colonial regime is sharply exposed. White settlers, citizens of the present and former colonial powers, South Africa and Germany, have had the vote in

local and national elections since 1925 and, since 1948, in South African general elections as well. This latter right was removed for political expediency in the last South African general election, but can be restored at any time, and since the great majority of settlers are South African nationals, they can vote through South African constituencies whenever they wish. Whites alone elect the S.W.A. Legislative Assembly, a body which had considerable power over national administration and policy-making until 1969, when most functions of any importance were hived off to South African government departments. Whites also have the sole right to elect local government councils.

The indigenous inhabitants of Namibia, on the other hand, have been denied the franchise wherever real power is at stake. Instead, the occupation regime has forced on them a cynical caricature of democracy, toothless institutions run by its own clients. In the Police Zone, some reserves and town locations have elected boards, though in the case of the former elections are not always by secret ballot. But none of these have executive powers except by delegation from the colonial officials or town councils to which they are advisory appendages. In recent years, the occupation regime has been trying to bolster the image of its bantustan policy by staging elections in its northern bantustans – Ovamboland, Kavangoland and Eastern Caprivi. At no stage have the inhabitants of these areas been allowed a referendum on the bantustan plan itself, and in the elections for the bantustan legislatures – themselves largely powerless, even at the highest stage of 'self-rule' – rejection of the bantustan policy has not been an option. Under these conditions, merely to vote is to imply acceptance of the regime's divisive strategy, and the people have either boycotted the polls or voted under coercion. To all intents and purposes the colonised Namibian people are completely disenfranchised.

The Apparatus of Repression

Until the tide of popular resistance began to put its rule under serious pressure in the 1960s, the occupation regime was a confused but effective machine of repression. Writing in the early 1960s, one South African militant described it as 'a tangle of divided authority'. At one level, the South Africans bought the loyalty of the settlers by giving them their own all-white Legislative Assembly (which ran most of the territorial budget and many government functions) and municipalities under all-white councils. At another, like any colonial power, they kept control of key areas, such as defence, foreign affairs and police and 'native administration', through reserve powers vested in their top civil servant, the South African Administrator, whose office was similar to that of a British Governor-General. But at a third level, they treated Namibia not as a colonial possession but as an integral part of the metropolitan territory. Most South African legislation was applied to Namibia, and all important policy was determined not in Windhoek but in the apartheid citadel, Pretoria. Many of the Administrator's reserve powers, especially his dictatorial powers over Africans as 'Supreme Chief', were delegated to South African government departments to carry out. Yet there was, with few exceptions, a single bureaucracy: the Administrator was at one and the same time the executive of the Legislative Assembly, the over-lord appointed by the South African Government, and the agent of various South African government departments.

A Bill of Rights

86. It is customary, when drawing up constitutions for modern states, to include Bills of Rights. They take various forms, and their legal effectiveness varies also.

87. SWAPO will do all in its power to ensure that the Namibian Constitution includes a detailed and effective Bill of Rights. We are especially determined about this because the Namibian people, more, perhaps, than any other people who have been under colonialism, have suffered persecution, extermination, repression, wholesale denials of the most basic rights of Man. This must never be allowed to recur here under any government. By the same reasoning we, who have suffered under the most evil form of discrimination, South African apartheid, are determined to eradicate this dehumanising perversion in all its forms. Discrimination is indivisible. A state which permits discrimination in whatever form is in the end wholly corrupted by it.

88. Our Bill of Rights will include a comprehensive anti-discrimination provision, with machinery which will ensure its effectiveness. We will ratify the UN Convention Against Discrimination.

89. The Bill of Rights will reflect the developing international standards of human rights. We shall ratify the two UN Covenants on Human Rights — on Economic, Social and Cultural Rights, and on Civil and Political Rights. The rights protected will be based on these Covenants.

> 90. We shall ensure that these rights are effective
>   on behalf of the citizen. Our Constitutional
>   Court will oversee their implementation in all
>   situations.
> 91. It does not, perhaps, need to be emphasised
>   that human rights standards exist to protect
>   the citizen against the state — normally,
>   against the government itself. Being available
>   to all persons without discrimination, they
>   will provide the single most effective line of
>   defence for any minority; or for that matter,
>   for any majority.
>
> Extract from SWAPO, *Discussion Paper on the
> Constitution of Independent Namibia*, (4th revise,
> 1975).

As international and internal pressure has intensified, the South Africans have increasingly administered Namibia as an integral part of the Republic. Their first major move, in 1955, was to transfer 'Native Administration' from the Administrator to the Department of Bantu Administration and Development. Thenceforth, Pretoria ruled supreme over nearly all aspects of the lives of 85% of the Namibian population. Then, in 1969, they removed all important functions from accountability to the local white settlers and distributed them amongst the different government departments of the South African state, leaving the Legislative Assembly with merely routine tasks and little revenue of its own. Their intention was to reduce Namibia to the status of a region of the metropolitan country — South Africa's fifth province. At the same time, they were fulfilling part of the Odendaal Plan of 1964, by recasting the powers of the Legislative Assembly in the mould of a self-governing homeland for whites. An Act of the South African Parliament in 1968 laid the basis for the imposition of bantustans on Namibia and, in the years following, the powers of the puppet tribal authorities, particularly those along the northern border, were steadily built up towards 'self-governing' status.

The full application of apartheid, fragmenting the nation into a dozen impotent ethnic units amongst which only the white area could be strong, has had the effect of streamlining the administration and concentrating power in the hands of central government departments based in Pretoria. Tribal chiefs have become 'Chief Ministers' with the trappings of democratic institutions behind them; but even where their formal powers are considerable, it is Pretoria which pays their salaries, provides their budgets, suppresses all opposition to their rule and installs the white administrators who dictate their every statement and action. Control over the oppressed people of Namibia has passed almost entirely to the bureaucratic racial empires of the apartheid state — 'indigenous peoples' (over 90% of all blacks) fall under the Department of Bantu Administration, and 'Coloureds' under the Department of Coloured Affairs. Thus, to take one example, there is 'Bantu Education' and 'Coloured Education', white schools coming under the all-white Legislative Assembly. The grotesquely misnamed Department of National Education, which runs higher education in South Africa, where most white matriculants go, is for whites only — there is no national education system.

Each bureaucratic empire has gained virtually exclusive powers over the racial category assigned to its control: education, health services, welfare, the forced labour system, the pass laws, the ethnic bureaucracies, the bantustan trading and credit corporation in the reserves, even the enforcement agencies. The tentacles of these monolithic apartheid machines have entered every corner of the lives of 'their' racial group. Only a couple of urban hospitals (which fall under the Department of Health) and housing and local police (run by the municipalities and the big mines) have escaped their clutches, though of course these also enforce the laws of apartheid. And always, at the back of this whole administrative superstructure have been the powerful forces of the South African Police (SAP) and Defence Force.

Namibia is an imprisoned society, held down by the heavy yoke of a colonial regime which can only survive by means of massive repression (see Figure 22 for a summary of the apparatus of repression). Namibians rarely meet their colonial overlords except in the guise of their agents of repression. In the town locations it is the location superintendent and his staff and the municipal police patrols. In the contract worker compounds, whether municipal or private, it is the compound manager and his 'police boys', periodically supplemented by mass police raids and constant pass checks at the guard posts at the compound entrances. On the streets it is the ubiquitous policeman who at any time can snatch people away for questioning and force them to produce any of a range of permits they need to have outside the reserves. In the factories and mines it is the authoritarian and often brutal white foremen, backed up by the local police should 'trouble' become too much to handle. On the farms it is the white farmers and their overseers, who act as their own policemen and do not scruple to use violence to enforce their authority.

Behind all employers, rural or urban, lies the willing collaboration of the police, always ready to hand out a beating to 'troublesome' workers and baton-charge or shoot up a strike or protest meeting. In the reserves it is the colonial 'welfare' officers and the supporting network of stock and other inspectors who keep the peasants under tight control. In the northern bantustans the regime has established a massive armed presence to combat SWAPO's freedom fighters — tribal police, bantustan armies, SAP and Security Police, in all over 60,000 frontline troops backed by heavy arms, helicopters and jet aircraft. Even the civil administration has been militarised with gun-toting white soldiers acting as doctors, teachers and officials.

As the liberation struggle has advanced, so the forces of repression have multiplied. Four independent forces of political police with their networks

Figure 22 – The apparatus of repression: South Africa's 'Security Forces' in Namibia and their chains of command.

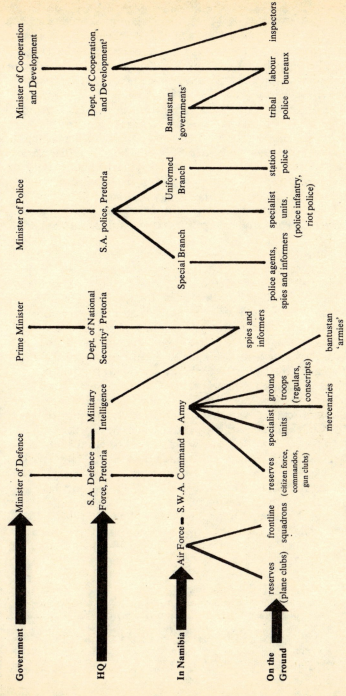

Notes: [1] Note that this does not exhaust the full range of repressive agents of the regime, of whom there are many others such as company guards, compound police, municipal police and commandos, railway police, armed DTA bully-boys and their like.
[2] Formerly the notorious Bureau of State Security (BOSS).
[3] Frequently renamed, but still known to Namibians as the hated Department of Bantu Affairs.

of informers — the Special Branch, BOSS, Military Intelligence and the private security staff of the big mines — spy on all political activity by Namibians detaining and torturing large numbers of activists. Five kinds of regular police — the national SAP, municipal and compound police in the big towns and mines, 'Bantu Affairs' inspectors, and the tribal bully-boys of the bantustan puppets — impose the maze of oppressive apartheid laws and engage in counter-insurgency operations. In the frontline the military are divided into five branches — ruthless paratroopers of the regular army, battle-trained SAP infantry, conscripts who are mostly white, bantustan tribal armies, and UNITA mercenaries.* In all, this army of occupation numbers over 70,000. In the northern border zone, where the liberation struggle is fiercest, South African aircraft bomb the countryside indiscriminately. The troops landmine the footpaths, poison the water supplies and plant poisonous vegetation. They terrorise the local population with indiscriminate attacks and mass interrogations, destroying houses, burning crops, and to torturing and killing anyone they suspect of assisting the freedom fighters.

The whole of the northern part of the country has been under martial law since 1972, and early in 1979 this was extended to central parts as well, covering over 80% of the population. Along the border with Angola a free-fire zone has been declared, and the border itself is peppered with small South African military camps. There are over 20 primary and secondary military bases, some, such as Grootfontein, with underground facilities and air-strips. A sophisticated micro-wave radio-telecommunications system, imported from the British firm Marconi, connects the northern war zone with military nerve-centres in Walvis Bay and South Africa. The two main centres in the north, Ondangwa and Oshakati, are fortified towns. They are surrounded by security fences and have military encampments within. Nobody can enter without first going through an army-controlled gate. Even Oshakati Hospital is heavily patrolled by armed soldiers.

In the rest of the country the whole white population is armed to the teeth and organised into reserve and commando units, police reservists and gun clubs. And black members of the Turnhalle circus (about which more later) are given arms, even machine-guns, for their swollen armies of bodyguards and hired thugs. Increasingly, the burden of repression has shifted from the civilian administration to the armed forces of the police and military: it is only by brute force that the occupation regime maintains its hold.

* UNITA units are not only confined to the north. While one group has been stationed there and is used as South Africa's first line of defence against PLAN fighters, the other section is stationed in Central Namibia and in Windhoek. They are used to create disturbances by beating up SWAPO members and supporters. In Katutura and at Rossing and other mine compounds, UNITA has been responsible for stealing money, clothing and food, and for destroying people's belongings.

The Cost of Resistance

Since the 1971 ruling of the International Court of Justice that South Africa's occupation of Namibia is illegal, it follows that South Africa has no right to try, judge or sentence Namibian men and women. Nevertheless, it has remained intransigent in its defiance of international law, and continues to violate the rights of the people of Namibia and to attempt to crush any resistance to its occupation. Today, many Namibian men and women who have stood firm against the South African regime are in gaols in Namibia and South Africa. There are about 60 long-term Namibian political prisoners incarcerated on the notorious Robben Island, and thousands of others are in prisons and detention camps throughout Namibia, never brought to trial.

South Africa's main legal weapons in the detention and trial of Namibian political prisoners are the Suppression of Communism Act (1950), renamed and reinforced as the Internal Security Act (1976), the so-called Sabotage Act (1962) and, more particularly, the Terrorism Act (1967). They are all worded so as to create an extremely wide range of offences. The Sabotage Act, for example, outlaws any action intended 'to embarrass the administration of the affairs of the State' or to disrupt power supplies, communications, trade or public services of any kind. Thus, not only strikes but even go-slows or pickets could be construed as 'sabotage'. Similarly, the Terrorism Act makes illegal the 'prejudicing of any industry or undertaking or production or distribution of commodities or foods', encouraging 'social or economic change by force of violence', or 'causing financial loss to any person or the State'. If a sheep strayed, the shepherd could conceivably be accused of 'terrorism', and indeed the possibility is not so far-fetched as it seems, for the fear and extremist mentality which has grown amongst white settlers as they have watched their impregnable fortress crumble before the tide of liberation has induced them to attach the most sinister motives to the simplest of events. The Terrorism Act carries a minimum penalty of five years' imprisonment and a maximum of death by hanging.

In fact the 1967 Terrorism Act, so widely used now in South Africa itself, was introduced specifically to cover the new situation created by the launching of the armed struggle in 1966 by SWAPO. It was rushed through the South African Parliament and made retroactive to 1962 to allow for the trial, under its provisions, of 36 Namibian patriots, most of whom had been arrested in 1966. The notorious Pretoria Terrorism Trial followed in 1967–68.

South African security laws provide for indefinite detention without trial of political offenders, during which time suspects may be held incommunicado, without obligation by the South African authorities to inform relatives. South African laws governing the conditions of prisoners in jail have also been made specifically applicable to Namibia. Scores of Namibians, including top Namibian leaders, have simply disappeared without trace behind this wall of silence.

As Namibian resistance to South Africa's illegal occupation has grown in strength and intensity, South Africa has extended further security legislation to Namibia. In 1976, the provisions of the Riotous Assemblies Act of 1956 were applied to Namibia, under which the authorities can, without recourse to the law, ban assemblies which in their opinion could become 'riotous'. Other laws which apply to Namibia are also used to undermine political activity and harass and victimise any person who dares to confront or oppose the occupation regime. Pass laws have been used to prevent people from travelling to political meetings. Indeed, the all-embracing scope of the laws which regulate where people can live, work and travel, makes it easy for them to be used for specifically political purposes by the occupation regime.

The South African regime has, furthermore, issued proclamations which apply only to Namibia, and this tendency has increased since the imposition of direct rule on 1 September 1977. This legislation serves two objectives, both directed solely against the liberation movement: to repress any open political opposition to South African rule, and to provide legal cover for the occupation army's campaign of terror against the armed liberation struggle. On the political front, existing South African legislation already applied to Namibia not only created a wide range of political 'crimes' but also provided for detention without trial. Indeed, Section 6 of the Terrorism Act allows the police to hold anyone in indefinite detention in solitary confinement without recourse to the courts or contact with any person or agency except the police themselves. And it has been frequently used, both to mount political trials and to imprison SWAPO leaders without trial. The declared aim of the Terrorism Act, however, is to produce results in the form of successful prosecutions and state witnesses who have been tortured into obedience to their captors, and its application is therefore somewhat restricted. For this reason, on 18 April 1978 the Administrator-General, using the assassination of Chief Kapuuo as a pretext, proclaimed a new law which gave the police the power of indefinite detention without trial and without access to the courts. The proclamation, which expressly excluded interrogation, was clearly aimed not only at the leadership but also at the ordinary members and supporters of the liberation movement, in fact at all opponents of colonial rule. Since April 1978, the scale of the regular nation-wide sweeps against SWAPO has grown, and by mid-1979 Namibian political detainees were being held no longer in hundreds but in thousands in over a dozen concentration camps scattered across the country.

Legislation to support the army and police has become progressively more severe as the liberation war has expanded and the occupation forces become ever more desperate. Not surprisingly, the north has borne the brunt, for it is here that the fighting has been fiercest. Ovamboland has been under emergency rule since February 1972 (Regulation 17–72), when the regime sent in police and soldiers to crush the peasant revolt which accompanied the 1971–72 contract workers' strike. The regulations outlawed all open political activity, imposed blanket censorship, gave tribal chiefs and headmen dictatorial powers, allowed the police to hold any suspect indefinitely for interrogation, and sealed off the bantustan from the rest of Namibia. In May 1976, shortly after the South African defeat in Angola and the rapid escalation of guerrilla attacks by PLAN, emergency rule was extended to the whole of the border zone from the Zambezi to the Kunene, and its provisions tightened. Henceforth, the army had all the powers previously vested in the police alone. They could search people, vehicles and houses at will and arrest anyone they suspected and hold them indefinitely without access to a lawyer. A night curfew was imposed and, most important of all, a duty was laid on all local people to report the presence of guerrillas or cadres returning from abroad, on pain of a R600 fine or three year's imprisonment. These regulations amounted to virtual martial law, and gave the occupation army a licence – which it used to the full – to terrorise the local population indiscriminately in its war against PLAN. It was from this point that torture, rape and killing, which had previously been only occasional occurrences and mostly on a restricted scale, became the general and widespread experience of blacks in the north.

On 11 October 1977, in one of his early cosmetic gestures, Administrator-General Steyn replaced Regulation 17–72 with slightly less draconian regulations (A.G. 9–77). Meetings were to be allowed provided 24 hours' notice was given, the ban on entering and leaving the northern bantustans was lifted, detentions were restricted to 96 hours and the judicial powers of the hated tribal chiefs and headmen were cancelled. But the occupation forces could still search, seize, arrest and interrogate at will. In June 1978, all vehicles were ordered off the roads at night in Ovamboland.

In May and June 1979, as the U.N. negotiations broke down and the latest PLAN offensive made rapid gains, martial law was tightened again and extended to cover the whole of Central and Northern Namibia. The detention period was extended to 30 days, powers to search, arrest, interrogate and confiscate property were fully applied, the ban on meetings without permission was reimposed, and an all-night curfew was clamped on Ovamboland. For eight long years the people of the north have suffered grievously under the indiscriminate terror of an ill-disciplined and unrestrained army of occupation unable to come to grips with its 'enemy'. Today, many of the farms and towns, including the capital, lie under military occupation. Martial law is used to round up and interrogate thousands of urban blacks at a time, to set up concentration camps, to send army patrols into the black locations and to guard white farmers. In addition, the Democratic Turnhalle Alliance's (D.T.A.) first act, on being given legislative powers in the National Assembly, was to reimpose the nation-wide pass law repealed in 1977 in the form of so-called 'identity cards'. Under the new law, finally enacted on 15 November 1979, every Namibian is required by law to produce this card on demand to any policeman or soldier or face a fine of R500 or six months' imprisonment. Each card has the bearer's thumbprint and photo, and is clearly designed to facilitate the mass round-ups and security checks already so frequent in the towns and on the highways of Central Namibia.

It is the members and supporters of SWAPO who especially suffer such treatment. As the U.N. Ad Hoc Working Group of Experts commented in its report for 1976, 'the SWAPO leadership was particularly singled out for prosecution and arrest.' Repeatedly, large police swoops have rounded up hundreds of SWAPO members. In 1974, 313 men and women, mostly SWAPO members and sympathisers, were arrested in the space of three weeks on charges such as failure to produce travel and identity papers. In August 1975 alone, over 500 SWAPO members were being held in solitary confinement. SWAPO Acting President Nathaniel Maxuilili has been banned and restricted to Walvis Bay since 1972. He is prohibited from entering factories and schools, attending social gatherings and political meetings, and writing or publishing. His banning order was extended in 1977 until 1982.

In recent years, this victimisation has intensified, taking the form of open and violent disruptions of SWAPO public meetings and the arrest of SWAPO leaders, and by withholding the meagre social services, such as medical treatment and pensions, from SWAPO members and supporters. As SWAPO has grown in strength, its supporters have been told by the occupation regime that they must look to SWAPO for such assistance. Many have also lost their homes and jobs as a result of their political activity.

Detention is used by the South African regime not only to intimidate and harass, but also as an opportunity to keep political activists in prison for months on end when no case exists against them, even under South Africa's all-embracing laws. Many have completely disappeared and their fate is not known. In 1970, eight Namibians were being held in Pretoria: no further news has been heard of them to this day. Two further groups, tried on various charges under the Terrorism Act in Ovamboland and Windhoek in 1972, have also not been heard of, and the outcome of the proceedings is not known. There is also the case of Brendon Kongongola Simbwaye, the Vice-President of SWAPO, who was arrested in July 1964 after organising a political meeting, and restricted to his home area for an indefinite period and later moved around the country in secret. In 1972 he disappeared and his whereabouts remain unknown and his survival uncertain.

Military Terrorism and Torture
Torture is commonly and routinely used on Namibian political prisoners and detainees. The testimony of countless individuals bears this out. But as the U.N. Ad Hoc Working Group of Experts on Southern Africa has reported, 'the police use of torture was not a case of cruel treatment by isolated individuals but a system. Before questioning had even begun the victim was hit and kicked.' As the Working Group observed in another report:

> The South African authorities inflict cruel, inhuman and degrading treatment on African political prisoners in order to obtain information from them. Many witnesses stressed that brutal acts of unspeakable sadism were committed on the persons of freedom-fighters captured on the battlefields.

In the north, the full-scale reign of military terror has lasted since early 1976, when the South African army, retreating from Angola, took its revenge on the local population. One white soldier, like most of the rest a conscript, later escaped to Europe and gave a detailed account of the horrific mass torture he witnessed. It is worth listening to him at length:

My name is Bill Anderson. I was born in Cape Town in 1955 and I was called up into the 6th Battalion, South African Infantry (S.A.I.) on 2 July 1975. I did my basic training at Grahamstown. My number was 7153773 BA and I served on operations in a HQ platoon.

On 22 November, we were sent 20 km north of the border with Angola where we guarded Cunene Dam [in Southern Angola] until February 1976. We detained cattle thieves who were suspect MPLA/ SWAPO agents. I saw three of them beaten by my battalion commander with his stick and I saw one of them subjected to water torture. A rag was placed on his face and water poured on continuously until he suffocated. My battalion commander was there and ordered this to be done. The men remained silent under the beatings but after the water torture they admitted to being cattle thieves. One rifleman-driver of 'A' Company in my battalion . . . [was] ordered to take the three suspects down to the river by the battalion commander and shoot them.

We were then moved back to a military camp at Sodoliet in South West Africa, and stayed patrolling the border until mid-April when we were given one week's leave at home. We were then sent up to Groot-fontein, the main South African camp, and then to the north-east base at Ondangwa, the military centre for Ovamboland operations. We drove in convoy to a new base near the small village of Inahna, 12km from the Angola border. For the first four weeks we were on battalion patrols with other battalions patrolling nearby. They were the 4th and 5th S.A.I., Witwatersrand, East Rand and Uitenhage regiments. Our battalion covered about 200 square kilometres up to the border. We had helicopter support based with a paratroop battalion at Ondangwa. This was all known as Operation Cobra. Our patrols, which were on foot, usually lasted about three days.

Torture began almost at once when the suspects were brought back. The first few were interrogated by a section of 10 South African Police inside the tent of battalion H.Q. I saw the troops beating the suspects with rifles and fists and kicks for two hours before they were taken into the tent. All the troops were welcome to join in the beating. Whenever the torture was going on, either in battalion H.Q. or in the open space behind, a crowd would gather to watch. I would not watch but every night I heard the screams. [Anderson explains that there was a drinks tent, for the use of the regular soldiers only, mainly officers and N.C.O.s, where beer and spirits were served. It closed at about 9 p.m.] Torture would begin when the club closed. The screams would go on until well after midnight. Officers boasted in front of me of using field telephones for electric-shock torture to genitals, nipples and ears.

111

It was common knowledge that this was being done.

I saw two suspects given water torture at the camp near Inahna. Their heads were stuffed into an ordinary iron bucket full of water and they were held under until they ceased to struggle. It lasted a good minute. I saw one large suspect who struggled so that five men had to hold him into the bucket. I often saw young boys being roughly man-handled and kicked. They were blindfolded. Some were 13 and some were a little older.

All suspects were blindfolded and beaten when brought in. The conditions they were kept in were appalling. They were handcuffed to trees at night. Some were kept in pits. It was winter and very cold, approaching freezing point at night. Suspects were handcuffed to trees, dressed only in loincloths and drenched in cold water. I was the cook and the only food I know they were given was scraps once a day which were piled into a big bin. On average, they were interrogated by our battalion for two days before being 'coptered back to Ondangwa.

Early in June the five battalions mounted a joint operation, sweeping into the centre. My battalion swept down from near the border, while other battalions moved in from the flanks towards a stop battalion in the south. My battalion swept 100 sq km with one section per kilometre at 1 km a day. Every male over the age of puberty was brought in. The orders were to kill those who ran and arrest those who did not run. All arrested men were beaten, tortured and interrogated without exception. They were then taken to Ondangwa. Our battalion captured between 200 and 300 men, and other battalions captured a similar number, I believe. Of the 1,000 or so detained men, we were later told that 40 were to be charged with terrorism offences. All went to Ondangwa where those not charged were ordered to fill sandbags endlessly, empty them and then fill them again. They filled the bags with their bare hands.

Another tactic was to swoop on homesteads with helicopters and check the bantustan identity cards of all residents. Those who had none or could not find them were automatically presumed to be 'terrorists' and were taken to the detention centre at Oshakati military base for prolonged interrogation and torture.

Since 1976, these conditions and barbarous practices have become general throughout Northern Namibia, and in 1979 they were being rapidly extended to the farms and towns of Central Namibia. Armed raids have been mounted on town locations such as Katutura and contract workers' compounds such as Tsumeb. In the north, prisoners have been taken up in helicopters and told they will be thrown out if they do not talk — indeed a number of witnesses have seen people being thrown out of army helicopters.

One particularly gruesome instance of the repeated torture of war captives is the fate of 130 or so Namibian refugees captured during South Africa's murderous raid on Kassinga refugee camp in Angola on 4 May 1978 and taken back to Namibia. The regime never even acknowledged that it was holding them, but in mid-1979 word leaked out that they were in a concentration camp at Hardap, near Mariental, without access to lawyers or the courts. So severe has their torture been that a number have lost limbs and many have had ears, lips, fingers and genitals cut off, eyes gouged out, and have been subjected to electric-shock torture. They are also forced to do hard labour such as digging, road construction and tree-felling. At the same time, a leading foreign churchman, Rev. Paul Wee of the Lutherans, who visited Northern Namibia, accused the army and tribal police of 'harassing, intimidating, blackmailing and bribing the population' and of stealing anything of value from homes that they raid. He concluded that 'there is no longer any semblance of order and the rule of law in Ovamboland.'

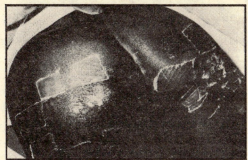

The infected wounds of a victim of the barbaric political floggings in Ovamboland.

Mental as well as physical torture is used to extract information from detainees and can leave as many scars. The most common forms are sleep deprivation and solitary confinement. A SWAPO member, who escaped from Namibia in 1975, described his own and his fellow prisoners' experiences:

> Our legs and arms are tied, we are hung from the roof, and tortured. We are given only a cup of water at 12 p.m. The people in jail are watched over by soldiers so that they do not get a chance to sleep. The soldiers do that in turns. To tell the truth — and I want to tell this as I know from experience, not by theory — if the others were being treated in the same way I was treated for those days I was in jail, then they will die or their mental capacity will be damaged. I cannot really understand what will happen to someone who is forbidden to sleep even half a second, day or night.

The most common forms of torture are:
— being suspended by handcuffs and beaten and, when bleeding starts, left to sit in the hot sun;
— being kept standing for several days, without sleep, and given little or no

food;
— burning with cigarette ends;
— being hung by a chain around the wrist of one arm, with the tips of the toes just reaching the floor, and left for up to 12 hours;
— being punched and beaten on the head and stomach;
this is especially done to pregnant women who are accused of making 'little terrorists';
— being tied to a stick under the knees and over the elbows while in a crouching position, and suffocated by means of a tyre held over the nose and mouth;
— being tied as above, hung by means of the stick, upside down, and given electric shocks;
— being tied as above, lifted to a height of about one metre, and dropped repeatedly to fall on the spine;
— tied to a stick passed between back and elbows and hung up by the stick,
— being bound and blindfolded and pushed off platforms up to six feet high on to concrete blocks or upturned corrugated iron, spikes, etc.;
— electric shocks to all parts of the body, in particular the head and genitals.

The Persecution of Axel Johannes

Sadistic and repeated torture is the common experience of most senior leaders of the liberation movement inside Namibia and of a good many branch officers and ordinary members as well. To take on the historic burden of leadership under such conditions, knowing that intense personal suffering is certain and death a real possibility, requires qualities of courage, tenacity and dedication to the cause of freedom which it is virtually impossible for those living under a democratic government to comprehend fully. The case of Axel Johannes, SWAPO Administrative Secretary inside Namibia, is a classic example of what systematic persecution means in personal terms and of the utter failure of the South African torturers to break the spirit of a leader who has provided inspiration to all Namibians. His 'extensive experience of detention without charge, imprisonment, interrogation and torture' was listed by the International Defence and Aid Fund (I.D.A.F.) in its bulletin *Focus* (No. 21,1979):

1974: spent five months in solitary confinement under the Terrorism Act.

August 1975: arrested in Windhoek following the assassination of Ovamboland Chief Minister Filemon Elifas, along with virtually the entire leadership of SWAPO inside Namibia. Detained incommunicado for more than five months, during which he was tortured. Sentenced in March 1976 to a year's imprisonment for refusing to give evidence in the trial of Aaron Muchimba and five other SWAPO members.

February 1977: rearrested in Ovamboland and detained after failing to respond to a subpoena requiring him to appear as a state witness against Victor Nkandi, charged with complicity in the Elifas assassination.

On 14 April 1978, Axel Johannes was again arrested under Section 6 of the Terrorism Act, and told that he was being held for questioning in connection with the assassination of Chief Clemens Kapuuo.

Axel Johannes

Summarising 'detailed information compiled by SWAPO in Windhoek', *Focus* continues:

[On 28 April] he was brought to a first floor office of the Security Police Headquarters in Windhoek. Captains [Koffee] and Nel, Sergeant Botha and four black security policemen began interrogating him about his participation in the Chief's assassination, an allegation which he denied. His interrogators then hancuffed his arms behind his back, attached a rope to the handcuffs and led the rope through the bars on the overhead window and back to the floor. The four black policemen pulled on the rope until Axel's feet left the floor, putting a great strain on his arms and shoulders. A cloth was tied over his mouth behind his head, and Captain Nel struck him repeatedly on the face with open hands. The other policemen struck him in the buttocks and stomach with a map pin causing bleeding. A blanket was tightened around his neck making breathing impossible. The cloth gag caused bleeding from his mouth. He was hit over the upper arms and shoulders with a wooden plank. Hairs were pulled out of his head and beard. He was then taken by his interrogators to his house to search for a pistol, the murder weapon, allegedly hidden there. Nothing was found.

A little while later, when they were back at the Security Police Headquarters, the police suggested that Axel had hidden the pistol in a river bed north of Windhoek. They drove him along the Okahandja Road to a bridge over the Okapaka River. They walked along the dried-up river bed, and when Axel was unable to show them the pistol, handcuffed his wrists from behind, attached a rope which they threw over a branch and began pulling him off the ground. According to Axel, 'I was crying and screaming.' He finally 'confessed' that he had buried the pistol in the hole in the sand and would show them where. He was let down and began digging a hole in the sand nearby. The policemen then forced him into the hole, and covered his whole body with sand, including his head. Three policemen stood on top. He was unable to breathe and lost consciousness. He was taken out and, when he revived, placed in a nearby pool of water. One police-man held his feet while another held his head under to get another 'confession'. (Another SWAPO member, Festus Thomas, was under-going the same treatment of being buried alive about 100 metres away – Axel could hear him screaming.)

Other forms of torture used during Axel Johannes' detention included being hit on the nose, causing bleeding, and being forced to lick up the blood from the floor; being struck on the ears, causing bleeding; being forced to fight with an ex-SWAPO man, Moses Paulus Iriko, who had also 'confessed' responsibility for Kapuuo's death; sleep deprivation; denial of toilet facilities, during which he was forced to lie face-down on the floor, his wrists handcuffed to two chairs, and repeatedly struck on the buttocks with a rubber petrol hose; having bullets fired so close to his legs that he could feel them pass.

Axel Johannes eventually signed a full 'confession' prepared by the police. On 5 May 1978 he was interrogated by a magistrate who promised to send a doctor (who never arrived). On 7 May he was returned to Seeis Prison and held in solitary confinement until 27 June 1978. On 28 June he was told he was being released from custody under the Terrorism Act but would continue to be detained under the Administrator-General's Proclamation A.G.26. He was then transferred to Gobabis Prison, further to the east, where he joined 15 other SWAPO members also detained under A.G. 26. They were finally released on 16 September 1978 on condition that they did not participate in public meetings or ask people to boycott the South African organised elections planned for December 1978. In December 1978, SWAPO's headquarters in Windhoek pointed out that Axel Johannes, now aged 33, had spent 7½ years of his life in detention and imprisonment.

Johannes was detained again for the duration of South Africa's 'internal election' in December 1978. Free once more, on February 1979 he left Windhoek to drive to his parents' home in Ovamboland. On the evening of the second day of his journey he passed two South African police vans, and was stopped. His account of what followed, reported in *Action on Namibia* illustrates vividly the routine violence to which any SWAPO activist is liable to be exposed at a moment's notice.

> The policemen jumped out and asked me what I thought I was at in having passed them on the main road: I should have realised that it was police vehicles that I was overtaking. They asked my name, but before I could respond one of the policemen recognised me and remarked: 'Ah, it is Axel Johannes! What are you doing here in Ovamboland and what are you looking for?' I told the policemen that I was on my way to visit my parents whom I had not seen for two years, because I have been under continuous arrest and detention and have not had the opportunity to visit my parents. I also remarked that as far as I was aware there is not a law against overtaking police vehicles. The policemen ordered me to get out of my car and surrounded me at my truck pointing their guns at me and starting to kick me mercilessly on my stomach. One policeman hit me with a butt of a pistol on my forehead and the other one hit me with a butt of a gun on my upper lip.

Johannes was blindfolded and driven to a police camp at Uutapi-Ombalantu, where he was interrogated and further kicked and beaten. Then, still blindfolded, he was made to lie down on a concrete bench, where his hands and feet were tied to iron standards at either end, cold water poured over him, and electric shocks given to his body. 'The first time they put two electrodes on either side of my midriff. The second time they put electrodes on the inside upper parts of my thighs adjacent to my scrotum. The third time they put the electrodes on my penis; the fourth time ... in my anus; the fifth time into the nostrils, and the sixth time again on my midriff ... During the interrogation the police put the proposition to me that it was not so easy being a member or leader of SWAPO, was it?'

Seven days later Johannes was found guilty in Ondangwa Magistrate's Court of driving outside the permitted hours (the night curfew imposed under martial law regulations) and sentenced to R200 or 100 days.

In late April 1979, the entire SWAPO national and branch leadership, including Johannes, were swept into indefinite detention under A.G. 26. This time very few were later released, and at the end of 1979 the attack on SWAPO as an open political party was being prosecuted relentlessly. The handful of detainees to have been released since have without exception been tortured by the police. During a brief visit to London in March 1979, Johannes explained that it is the unswerving solidarity of the Namibian people – the vital bond of unity between leaders and the masses – which has sustained him. 'When I am in gaol I think I am going to leave the country as soon as I am released, I can't carry on like this. But as soon as I come out there is the support of the people and I forget everything. I can't believe it myself really.'

Turnhalle: A New Dispensation?

Much rhetoric has been spent by South African politicians and their propa-
gandists in the last few years, as the pressure of the liberation struggle has
grown more urgent, to demonstrate the 'good faith' of the occupation
regime's strategy for so-called self-determination and independence. That
strategy has unfolded on two fronts, the social and the political, for increasingly the credibility of South Africa's neo-colonial political plans for Namibia
have come to depend on the extent to which Namibians can be deceived or
coerced into supporting them. So far, the political promises have remained
mere rhetoric and the social reforms have been belated and severely limited
in their scope.

The repeal of the Masters and Servants Law and the amendment of the
Mines and Works Law in 1975, the first labour reform since the 1972 ration-
alisation of the contract labour system, removed the criminal sanctions
behind the authoritarian labour discipline on the settler farms and in the
mines. But it hardly touched the effective power of farmers over their
workers or of the authoritarian mine managements over their contract
labourers. The pass laws were still in force and the contract workers were still
tied to the employer who had 'bought' them.

It was during the life of the Turnhalle circus that the hypocrisy and fraud
of South African propaganda was most blatantly exposed. Launched in
September 1975, supposedly to work out a constitutional future for Namibia
independent of South Africa, the Conference spent most of its first year
divided into four committees which held desultory discussions on proposals
for social and economic reforms. 'A large number of resolutions and recom-
mendations on equal pay for equal work, uniform taxation, pension schemes,
the establishment of a multi-racial university, improved housing, sporting
facilities, education, and so on have in fact been adopted by the conference,'
reported an IDAF analysis in August 1976, and by June 1976, about 50 of
them were reported to have been referred to the South African Government.
At the same time, the Turnhalle propaganda machine flooded the country
with posters and radio broadcasts promising the 'new deal' which these
proposed reforms were supposed to inaugurate.

In reality, almost nothing was done: the Turnhalle itself possessed no
legislative power whatsoever, and the occupation regime was not prepared
to allow more than a few minor cosmetic changes in 'petty apartheid'
regulations — barely more advanced than the minor relaxations already
allowed in South Africa itself. A hotel that went multi-racial found its social
gatherings smashed up by white thugs tacitly encouraged by the police; the
administration closed a swimming pool rather than let it go multi-racial;
and when, at the end of 1976, the Anglicans and Catholics declared their
intention to implement integration in their schools, the government promptly

withdrew all subsidies. A financial committee set up in March 1976 to cost the Turnhalle proposals came up with a figure of R500 million over 10 years, and dedicated its time to proving Namibia's economic dependence on South Africa. For Namibians suffering under an unchanging and brutal social order, the powerlessness of the Turnhalle puppets was blindingly obvious.

Politically, the Turnhalle strategy collapsed shortly after the constitution for the interim government was finally agreed in March 1977. Under pressure from the Western powers, the South Africans installed a conventional colonial-style administration under an appointee, Judge Steyn, who was given full powers to legislate and administer the territory. He began his term of office on 1 September with a flurry of decrees. In practice, these added up to little more than administrative reorganisation, undoing the 1969 'annexation' by taking over once again most of the local branches of South African government departments. Several apartheid laws were abolished, notably the Immorality Act and Mixed Marriages Act thereby, restoring the freedom to marry or have sexual relations across the colour line. On 20 October, he repealed the Pass Law, allowing freedom of movement for all across the country. On 11 November, he replaced martial law in the north with a slightly less severe decree, Proclamation A.G. 9, which abolished the judicial powers of the tribal puppets and the need for permits to enter or leave the northern bantustans, and allowed political meetings to be held, subject to certain conditions. In December, he announced the establishment of a common syllabus in all schools, although not the ending of racial segregation nor the gross imbalance in educational spending. Finally, on 4 July 1978, the Industrial Conciliation Ordinance was amended to bring 'natives' within its scope for the first time, theoretically granting Africans the right to join registered trade unions and to register their own unions.

These moves appeared to be principally designed to remove some of the more obvious obstacles to a free political process, a pretence at which is essential to the credibility of any national election or independence constitution. But they leave the core of the apartheid system undisturbed. The historical legacy of land theft, the corner-stone of migrant labour, has hardly been touched. Blacks may in theory be allowed to buy farms in the 'white area', but very few can afford to do so, and they remain excluded from the extensive credit and technical aid to which white farmers have access. Since no land redistribution is on the agenda, the peasants face a future of deepening impoverishment. Since no crash programme of building family houses is contemplated in the towns and the mines, labour migration, with all the hardship and social misery it causes, is bound to increase for economic reasons alone. Since no redistribution of ownership of the main wealth-producing assets and no major increase in taxation on profits is envisaged, the wages and standard of living of black workers can at best increase marginally, if at all. The Turnhalle programme, which assumes the permanence of the present distribution of political and economic power, has nothing concrete to offer the Namibian people — sufficient land, premises and credit for a handful of blacks to become small businessmen and cash-cropping small farmers is about the limit of its vision of social reconstruction. Yet it is to further the D.T.A.'s cause — itself a puppet creation of the occupation regime — that South Africa's much-trumpeted 'reforms' have been made.

On closer examination the above legislative changes have little depth. The 'abolition' of the Pass Law in fact only means the removal of general travel restrictions on blacks and the need to produce passes on demand. Passes or permits are still necessary to do almost anything and be almost anywhere: to live in a town or on a mine, to seek work, to be out of doors at night, to enter or leave parts of the combat zone in the north. To avoid persecution, blacks also need to be able to produce on demand D.T.A. membership cards and in the north, bantustan identity cards. To cap it all, in November 1979 new legislation was enacted to force every black to carry a new 'identity card' which any policeman or soldier could demand to see on pain of immediate arrest. To Namibians, the 'abolition' of the Pass Law has become a joke in very bad taste.

In any case, the rigorous 'influx controls' remain in full force. Workers may now travel to a town and walk its streets without being picked up in a random pass checks. But they may neither seek or take employment nor change jobs without a work-seeker's permit from the Labour Bureaux, or at the least their official approval. And a Bureau can refuse a permit or registration whenever it pleases, especially if the applicant is on its unofficial blacklist. Furthermore, any Black person without Section 10 rights of permanent residence may not legally stay in a town without a 'legal' job or a permit. Even though 'desertion' is no longer a criminal offence, there is still no provision for workers to give notice to their employers before their labour contracts expire.

The net result has been that deportation to the reserves has replaced prosecutions under the Pass Law for breach of contract as the main weapon of labour repression in the towns. Any black who remains unemployed for long or who leaves a job against the wishes of the employer is immediately at risk in the frequent military-style police raids on the locations and compounds — anyone found without their papers fully in order is summarily dumped in whichever reserves are deemed their 'homelands'. The authorities can still use the Vagrancy Law to pick up anyone unemployed or homeless. Since municipalities have a legal monopoly on black housing, they have a powerful weapon for enforcing the labour laws, and they have moved ruthlessly against any 'squatters' who have attempted to build homes and havens for themselves. For example, shanties in the Coloured quarter of Windhoek were razed to the ground and over 2,500 Blacks sheltering in the derelict buildings of the old contract labour compound in Katutura were driven out. Once deported, workers can only return through the Labour Bureaux in the reserves, and although more employers than before now use the 'call-in card' system to enable workers to return to their previous jobs, the overall change is very slight. The forced labour system and its migratory component may have been rationalised of its worst excesses, but in all its essentials it remains the same.

The other legislative changes have touched minor issues only, mainly in the field of 'petty apartheid'. Namibians are no longer forbidden to marry and have sexual relations across race lines, but most leisure and social facilities remain segregated, as do schools, health and social services and public transport. In education, segregation even amongst Black Namibians is actually being increased as the few remaining mixed schools and colleges are broken up and new ones, segregated on strict ethnic lines, are built in the reserves or in ethnic residential quarters of the towns. There is little sign yet of the promised national curriculum, and the resources devoted to education are still heavily weighted towards whites. The same is true of the government health service, pensions and official salary scales.

Even the progressive reform of trade union law disguises a reactionary intention. 'Africans' may now be defined as 'employees', but the conditions for trade union registration are so restrictive as to make it very difficult for independent black unions to get themselves officially recognised, and furthermore give the colonial state dangerous powers of supervision over their affairs. Even when registered, the procedures to be exhausted before industrial action may legally be called are so complex as to make lawful strike action virtually impossible — and industrial action under any other circumstances is illegal. 'To strike is a crime,' as a senior South African official succinctly put it in 1978. Not only will black trade unions find it difficult to get legal status, but existing white unions may also set up sub-sections for black workers in their trades. In this way they can both block independent black unions from recruiting these workers and keep control in the hands of their white members by rigging their constitutions. One such union, the S.W.A. Municipal Staff Association, is reported to have done precisely that. An even more sinister move was the amendment of the original Ordinance to make it illegal for any registered trade union to affiliate to any political party or 'to grant financial assistance to or incur expenditure with the object of assisting' any political party, and the reverse applies as well. This is clearly aimed at the National Union of Namibian Workers, which is affiliated to SWAPO and operates within the liberation movement.

In any case, the regime's campaign of political repression continues unabated. Most of the formidable armoury of security laws remain in force, and to reinforce them even further Steyn assumed blanket emergency powers in April 1978 under Proclamation A.G. 29, which gives the authorities even greater powers of indefinite detention without charge, and he reimposed and extended martial law under Proclamation A.G. 9 in the middle of 1979. The system of exploitation and the repression remain intact, challenged only in the partially liberated areas in the north where the freedom fighters are constructing a new social order.

5. South African Colonialism and Imperialist Strategy

The League of Nations, the United Nations, and Namibia

Namibia's status in international law was from the outset determined by imperialist interests. Having decided to possess itself of the territory of Namibia, Germany's right to do so was recognised by the other major imperialist powers at the Berlin Conference in 1884–85. When Germany lost the First World War and the ideological pretensions of the victors made outright annexation inexpedient, her former colonies were granted to their conquerors as wards of an international body, the League of Nations, created to represent imperialist interests collectively and to prevent future wars between its leading members.

Whereas major imperialist powers such as Britain could integrate their acquisitions smoothly into their colonial systems, for South Africa the Mandate, which was finally conferred on 17 December 1920, was never more than disguised annexation, as its leaders Botha and Smuts clearly admitted at the time. South Africa's only concrete obligation was to submit annual reports on her administration to the Permanent Mandates Commission. This body could criticise – and it found ample and repeated cause to do so – but possessing no sanctions for enforcement, its strictures were ineffectual and were treated with contempt by the South African white minority regime.

The League of Nations died with the Second World War, to be replaced in 1945 by the United Nations (U.N.). The South African Government refused to submit its Mandate to the new Trusteeship Council, and demanded instead the right of annexation. The General Assembly's rejection of the South African case was the opening shot in a long campaign to enforce U.N. jurisdiction over Namibia. Legal loopholes and ambiguities, both in the powers of the League over Mandate-holders and in the transfer of those powers to the U.N., took 25 years and a massive volume of legal argument at the International Court of Justice (I.C.J.) to resolve.

In 1950, an I.C.J. Advisory Opinion confirmed that the Mandate was still in force and could not be altered unilaterally by South Africa, and that the U.N. had succeeded to the supervisory powers of the defunct Permanent Mandates Commission. It also ruled, however, that South Africa was not obliged to submit to a trusteeship agreement. Ten fruitless years later, two former members of the League, Ethiopia and Liberia, returned to the I.C.J. in an attempt to settle the issue by having the Mandate revoked on the grounds that South Africa had systematically failed to fulfil its obligations. The litigation dragged on for years, until, on 18 July 1966, the Court declined, on dubious grounds, to rule on the substance of the case. Although this ruling had no bearing on the merits of the applicants' case, it did effectively close one legal avenue, to have the Mandate annulled on the grounds that South Africa had broken its terms.

The League of Nations Mandate

Article 22: 1. To those colonies and territories which as a consequence of the late war have ceased to be under the sovereignty of the States which formerly governed them and which are inhabited by people not yet able to stand by themselves under the strenuous conditions of the modern world, there should be applied the principle that the well-being and development of such peoples form a sacred trust of civilisation and the securities for the performance of this trust should be embodied in this Covenant. 2. The best method of giving practical effect to this principle is that the tutelage of such peoples should be entrusted to advanced nations who by reason of their resources, their experience or their geographical position can best undertake this responsibility, and who are willing to accept it, and that this tutelage should be exercised by them as Mandatories on behalf of the League.

Treaty of Versailles, 28 June 1919

Article 2: The Mandatory shall have full power of administration and legislation over the territory subject to the present Mandate as an integral portion of the Union of South Africa, and may apply the laws of the Union of South Africa to the territory, subject to such local modifications as circumstances may require.

The Mandatory shall promote to the utmost the material and moral well-being and the social progress of the inhabitants of the territory subject to the present Mandate.

> *Article 3:* The Mandatory shall see that the slave trade is prohibited, and that no forced labour is permitted, except for essential public works and services, and then only for adequate remuneration . . .
>
> *Article 4:* The military training of the natives, otherwise than for purposes of internal police and the local defence of territory, shall be prohibited. Furthermore, no military or naval bases shall be established or fortifications erected in the territory.
>
> *Article 5:* Subject to the provisions of any local law for the maintenance of public order and public morals, the Mandatory shall ensure in the territory freedom of conscience and the free exercise of all forms of worship, and shall allow all missionaries, nationals of any State Member of the League of Nations, to enter into, travel and reside in the territory for the purpose of prosecuting their calling.
> *Part of the Mandate for South West Africa, ratified 17 December 1920*

Hitherto, while there was still a chance of resolving the issue before the I.C.J., the U.N. had held back from taking executive action on its own behalf. Now that the proceedings had ended in stalemate, on 27 October 1966 the U.N. General Assembly, assuming its powers as successor to the League of Nations, finally took the initiative, formally revoked the Mandate and assumed direct responsibility for the territory. Since that date Namibia has been U.N. sovereign territory in international law. On 19 May 1967, the General Assembly established a U.N. Council for South West Africa with full legislative and executive powers, to be assisted by a Commissioner, and charged with the responsibility to oversee the territory's transition to independence in accordance with principles laid down by the U.N. After SWAPO had chosen the name 'Namibia' for the territory, the U.N. adopted the name in 1968 and its responsible body came to be called the Council for Namibia. On 20 March 1969, the Security Council at last recognised the General Assembly decision, condemned South Africa's continued occupation as illegal, and demanded that South Africa withdraw its administration forthwith. On 29 July 1970, the Security Council requested an Advisory Opinion from the I.C.J. which would in effect test the legality of the U.N.'s revocation of the Mandate. In a historic ruling on 21 July 1971, the I.C.J. endorsed the revocation of the Mandate and declared that South Africa was under obligation to withdraw its illegal administration immediately and that it was the duty of all U.N. members to recognise the illegality of South African rule and refrain from any act which would support it.

At last the jurisdiction of the U.N. over Namibia had been settled beyond all doubt. But victories in international law alone do not liberate a colonised people from their oppressors. The people of Namibia have never recognised the right of successive colonial regimes to rule them; and their right to self-determination is quite independent of the niceties of international law. Indeed, the legal battles of the past quarter century have often masked the nature of the power struggles which have decided the fate of Namibia. As with the League, the U.N. Charter was drawn up by the imperialist nations in their own interests. But its highest organ, the Security Council, was vested with powers which the League never possessed: to invoke mandatory sanctions binding on all members in the event of a threat to international peace. It is the potential use of this power which deterred South Africa from ratifying in law the annexation it completed in all but name.

So far, the complicity of the imperialist powers in protecting South Africa from Security Council sanctions has prevented the U.N. from becoming an effective instrument for the liberation of Namibia. The rapid dissolution of the colonial empires in the late 1950s and early 1960s, particularly in Africa, turned a minority, comprised mainly of communist states, into an anti-imperialist majority in the General Assembly and established the cardinal principle of self-determination as the inalienable right of all subject peoples. As a result, the veto rights of the three Western permanent members of the Security Council have become a collective defence against attempts by socialist and Third World nations to translate the fine-sounding rhetoric of U.N. resolutions into effective executive action. Anxious not to surrender their self-appointed role as guardians of world order to international control, and concerned to protect their massive economic and political stake in the exploitation of the peoples of Southern Africa, on 18 October 1976, the United States, Britain and France cast their third triple veto to block sanctions against South Africa for failing to meet yet another Security Council ultimatum to withdraw from the territory.

Imperialist Strategy Today

The change in the balance of world forces since the Second World War, against the interests of imperialism and in favour of national liberation, has raised loud the demand for freedom in Southern Africa. On the one hand, the growing power of Third World nationalism has forced the dissolution of the great colonial empires and the adoption of a more subtle, though equally effective, strategy of neo-colonialism. On the other, popular movements of workers and peasants have confronted imperialism with forces that can equal its own, and have shown, in the case of Angola, that they are prepared to unite across the world to do so. The final victory of the liberation move-

Map 4 — The completion of the colonial land robbery

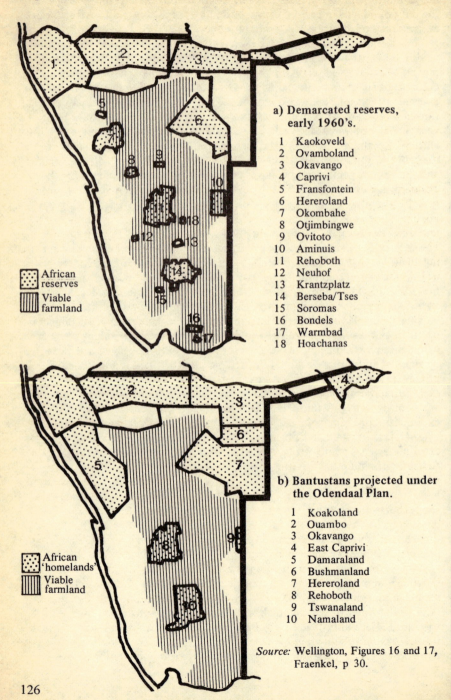

a) Demarcated reserves, early 1960's.

 1 Kaokoveld
 2 Ovamboland
 3 Okavango
 4 Caprivi
 5 Fransfontein
 6 Hereroland
 7 Okombahe
 8 Otjimbingwe
 9 Ovitoto
10 Aminuis
11 Rehoboth
12 Neuhof
13 Krantzplatz
14 Berseba/Tses
15 Soromas
16 Bondels
17 Warmbad
18 Hoachanas

African reserves

Viable farmland

b) Bantustans projected under the Odendaal Plan.

 1 Koakoland
 2 Ouambo
 3 Okavango
 4 East Caprivi
 5 Damaraland
 6 Bushmanland
 7 Hereroland
 8 Rehoboth
 9 Tswanaland
10 Namaland

African 'homelands'

Viable farmland

Source: Wellington, Figures 16 and 17, Fraenkel, p 30.

ments in Vietnam, Laos and Kampuchea in 1975 dealt a crushing blow to the self-confidence of imperialist rulers and forced them into a fundamental reassessment of their strategy for maintaining their world domination. Imperialism has learnt to its cost that a liberation struggle conducted by a united, committed and armed people can defeat even the mightiest military power, and that it cannot afford to become tied down in a protracted colonial war without facing collapse at home.

Heeding this warning the imperialist powers have realised that the preservation of their interests may not be best served either by direct military intervention on their part or by open colonial rule on the part of their subordinate allies. In Southern Africa, the final collapse in 1974—75 of Portuguese colonialism, which the imperialists had complacently supported to the very end, and the coming to power of socialist governments in all Portugal's African ex-colonies drove home the lesson with added urgency. A new approach was needed, and it was not long before it showed its hand. Starting in 1975, the imperialist powers made a series of attempts to negotiate between the white minority regimes and the liberation movements in Namibia and Zimbabwe. The victories of the liberation forces in Angola and Mozambique not only put these two countries in the frontline but also ensured the Namibian and Zimbabwean liberation movements, together with the African National Congress of South Africa, of steadfast and principled support. The imperialists were compelled to recognise that no settlement which excludes those movements would be lasting or stable. Anxious to avoid an intensified and protracted armed struggle and a violent transition to independence which would disrupt the economies of both countries and lead to a further radicalisation of the forces of liberation, they sought 'solutions' which would guarantee and speed up the transfer of formal political power to the black majorities. Their motivation was clear: they aimed to interrupt the political mobilisation of the people because it is this which threatens the establishment of class alliances favourable to imperialism.

That a controlled transition to some form of independence in Namibia and Zimbabwe was essential for Western interests in the whole of Southern Africa and that a more active role by them in managing such a transition was essential was generally accepted by political leaders in the West. There was less agreement on *how* active that role should be or how tightly the screws should be turned on the minority regimes. The appearance of inconsistency and division in the West's collective standpoint has therefore been a reflection of the real policy differences between sections of the political leadership of the imperialist powers as how best to secure their vital interests.

At first the more conservative strategists held sway, particularly in the U.S., the dominant capitalist power. When South Africa used Namibia as a springboard to invade Angola in August 1975 in order to prevent the coming to power of the M.P.L.A., the Ford Administration tried desperately to organise covert political and military support for them. When the U.S. Congress eventually vetoed this secret aid, it dealt a crushing blow to the right-wing camp. The South African army was defeated and driven out early in 1976, and the M.P.L.A. Government consolidated the victory of the Angolan revolution. Nor was a second U.S. intervention, an attempt by Secretary of State Kissinger in late 1976 to force the Smith regime in Zimbabwe to accept a limited degree of black majority rule, much more successful. Because Kissinger ignored the Patriotic Front altogether, the terms to which Smith agreed, which were eventually enshrined in the 'internal settlement' of March 1978, were totally and resoundingly unacceptable to the people of Zimbabwe. The American strategy of attempting to intervene directly and to bypass the liberation movements was clearly failing to establish the conditions for a 'stable' neo-colonial settlement. By this time, too, the Soweto Revolt was shaking the foundations of imperialism's citadel in South Africa itself.

In 1977, the incoming Carter Administration, working closely with the Labour Government in Britain, cleared the way for the more active 'liberal' wing of imperialism. On Zimbabwe this produced the Anglo-American proposals and attempted to negotiate a compromise btween the rebel regime and the Patriotic Front. On Namibia they organised the so-called Contact Group and intervened forcefully in April 1977 to prevent the South Africans from setting up their Turnhalle tribal circus as an 'interim government'. As in Zimbabwe, the principal imperialist concern was to achieve a negotiated and peaceful transfer of power to a government which would be sure of international recognition and with which they could therefore intervene strongly to safeguard their interests. For this reason the liberation movements and the African frontline states played a prominent role in the negotiations for the first time.

During early 1979, however, this offensive by the 'liberal' wing of imperialism began to falter badly, at least in Namibia. One reason for this was the revival in the political fortunes of the conservative wing of imperialism, who were victors in general elections in Britain (and, for a short time, in Canada) and very nearly strong enough in the U.S. Congress to force the lifting of sanctions against Rhodesia. But even before this, a question-mark had arisen over the strategy's implicit assumption that class allies of imperialism could be recruited from the ranks of the oppressed of sufficient political stature to win ahd hold majority support in a democratic transition to independence. In Namibia, where colonial oppression has prevented the emergence of any black elite, the idea has always been a non-starter, and the imperialists seem to be relying on the immense economic power of the transnational corporations to keep any post-independence government docile, whatever its political aspirations.

The second and equally fundamental contradiction in the 'liberal' imperialist strategy was the expectation that South Africa, overlord of the subcontinent, could be persuaded by reasoned argument to risk the coming to power of liberation movement governments on its borders — however limited their freedom of action might be. When the five Foreign Ministers of the Contact Group confronted the Botha Government over Namibia in Pretoria on 16–18 October 1978, they were not prepared to take effective

steps — such as oil sanctions — to coerce the apartheid regime to comply
— just as their predecessors had refused to do so. When the South Africans
once more called their bluff, the Western powers could do little more than
wring their hands and play for time.

NATO weapons captured in battle from the South African army

What is abundantly clear is that, although the Western powers were now
pressing for independence in Namibia and Zimbabwe, they were not pressing
for majority rule in South Africa itself. President Carter, instead, tried to pose
the issue in South Africa solely as one of human rights, and called for the
granting of such rights to South Africa's black population, without disclaim-
ing the political economy which enforces their oppression. Having seen it
survive a massive popular uprising in 1976—77, the imperialist powers now
have greater confidence in the long-term survival of the apartheid regime.
South Africa is the economic keystone of the sub-continent, and a jewel of
imperialism. The collapse of white rule in South Africa would provoke a
severe crisis for the economies of the imperialist powers; thus, when the
apartheid regime puts its survival on the line, they will always treat it with
kid gloves. Because the regime regards it as indispensable to its survival that
it preserve its tight economic and above all political hegemony over the
states on its northern borders, it has fiercely resisted the degree of political
liberation the West could live with in Zimbabwe and Namibia. Since 1978,
the South African regime has been mounting an increasingly aggressive
campaign of its own to 'restabilise' its periphery on its own terms. In the

129

case of Namibia, this means a fierce resistance to the Western proposals. And the evidence is that the imperialists are once more swinging behind the apartheid regime, attacking and isolating the liberation movements in Namibia and South Africa and attempting to weaken the solidarity and support they receive from the frontline states.

Non the less, when in the late 1970s the Western powers became anxious to reach a settlement with South Africa on Namibia, they faced an awkward dilemma. On their own behalf they could easily reach an accommodation agreeable to both South Africa and themselves — as Britain had tried to do several times before with the rebel Smith regime. But no such bilateral settlement over Namibia would be recognised internationally unless it were acceptable to the U.N. And the Western powers had themselves endorsed the key Security Council Resolution 385 of 30 January 1976, which set out the principles and conditions to be observed in any transition to independence. Accordingly, when the imperialists made their move in April 1977, it was the five Western members of the Security Council (Britain, France, the U.S., Canada and West Germany) who took the lead. The actions of the so-called Contact Group — commonly known as the 'Gang of Five' — were entirely unilateral and carried no mandate from the U.N.; but since the Group was able to block any action by the U.N. itself, it has managed to keep the initiative.

The Group's strategy followed a predictable course. First, it formulated its own proposals for the transition to independence, which it claimed were in the 'spirit' of Resolution 385 but which in fact compromise the U.N.'s sovereignty in important respects. Then it attempted to negotiate their acceptance by both South Africa and SWAPO — implicitly acknowledging that no settlement would be acceptable without SWAPO's endorsement — pressing the latter throughout to acquiesce in the presence of the illegal occupation regime during the transition. Only in mid-1978, when it had secured the agreement in principle of both sides, did the Group allow the Security Council to act, and then only to implement what it had already negotiated.

This strategy has created the illusion that agreement is both possible and near; but it has so far foundered on the harsh reality that South Africa is only prepared to allow a transition process which will guarantee that its own puppets will take power at independence. In practice, the Contact Group's role is to block effective U.N. action indefinitely and thus protect its South African ally — unless and until the U.N. endorses a plan acceptable to the occupation regime. For its part, SWAPO remains unflinchingly committed to upholding the democratic principles enshrined in U.N. resolutions on Namibia, and until the U.N. is able to exercise its sovereignty in Namibia will continue the struggle for national liberation by all possible means. Whatever its legality, the substance of imperialist domination in Namibia is colonial oppression, from which the people have an inalienable right to liberate themselves by their own efforts.

South African Colonialism in Namibia: From Annexation to Neo-Colonialism

South Africa's Stake in Colonial Rule

The imperialist offensive, however short-lived it may prove to be, did provoke angry disagreement between South Africa and its Western allies, and thereby brought into sharp relief the crucial differences between Western and South African interests in Namibia. South Africa's interests — political, economic, military — overlap at several levels. Together, they give the apartheid regime a powerful motive for maintaining its colonial rule in Namibia.

The direct economic stake of the South African Government and the 'national' capitalists with whom it is closely allied is considerable (see Figure 23). The South African treasury makes a comfortable surplus on current account* from the Territory, and, more importantly, benefits from a net inflow of foreign currency to the tune of R380 million a year. Several state corporations and Afrikaner-owned companies have invested in mines, either to supply raw materials to South African industry or for export. The fishing industry is also a fiefdom of Afrikaner capital. Most or all of this will be lost once Namibia is liberated. So, too, will the protected market for South African food and manufacturers (worth about R300 million a year) and the artificially cheap food supplies (saving South Africa about R40 million) which Namibia is forced to supply to the South African home market. Because an independent Namibia will find cheaper imports and higher-priced markets for its exports elsewhere, South Africa can expect to lose most of its trade very quickly on purely economic grounds, reducing its exports by about R250 million and adding about R150 million to its import bill. It will also expect to have to provide for most of the settler population, in particular for thousands of displaced ranchers. The only South African-owned interest able to stand outside this prospective scenario is Consolidated Diamond Mines.

* This cannot properly be discounted against capital spending which, because the state in question is foreign, counts as 'foreign investment'.

Publisher's Note

The Publisher, Zed Press, would like to point out to the reader that the text of this book, including the preceding pages analysing the strategy of the Western powers in Southern Africa, were prepared and approved by the relevant agencies in SWAPO *before* the liberation of Zimbabwe in April 1980. What the victory of the Patriotic Front forces in that country in the elections held near the beginning of that year did show was that the mobilisation of the people of Zimbabwe was too widespread to be halted, no matter what strategems the Western powers might resort to.

Figure 23 — South Africa's economic stake in Namibia, 1977–78.

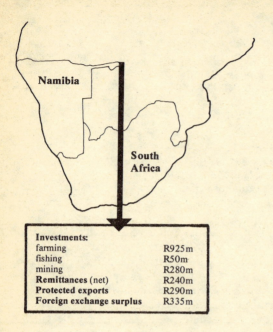

Investments:	
farming	R925m
fishing	R50m
mining	R280m
Remittances (net)	R240m
Protected exports	R290m
Foreign exchange surplus	R335m

None of these losses would do irretrievable economic damage to South Africa: the extra imports would add only 2% to South Africa's import bill; foreign currency earnings would decline by about 4.5%; and South Africa has its own base minerals in profusion and uranium as a by-product from its gold mines. But the consequences would still be serious, both for the particular interests concerned, and generally for an economy which is very fragile.

In reality the apartheid regime stands to lose a great deal more — nothing less than its military and economic hegemony over the entire sub-continent. Although the regime could probably survive such a collapse in the short term, it knows very well that the liberation of its captive periphery will herald the final stage in the people's struggle to overthrow racial oppression and imperialist domination in Southern Africa.

Economic and military factors are closely intertwined in the South African assessment. At present the transport networks of not only Zimbabwe and Namibia but also landlocked Botswana and Zambia all hinge upon outlets through South Africa. Were Zimbabwe and Namibia to be liberated, both these countries could build up good alternative trade routes and South Africa's power of economic blackmail over the sub-continent would be at an end. Indeed, Botswana has already commissioned a plan for a trans-Kalahari railway link with Walvis Bay, so as not to lose a moment when the Namibian people win their independence. In addition, South African industrialists today still have a captive market at their disposal which stretches as far north as Zambia and Malawi and includes Zimbabwe. Because under apartheid most South African blacks live in dire poverty, South African industry has a limited home market and desperately needs its economic hinterland. It is this, amongst other interests, which the South African armed forces have been guarding on the northern Namibian and (until recently) northern Zimbabwean borders.

In purely military terms, South Africa also has good reason for keeping its main defence line far to the north of its national boundary. In the case of Zimbabwe before liberation in 1980, it needed only to supply the arms and the cash and its settler allies did most of the fighting on its behalf. From its military bases in northern Namibia, it can mount military incursions far into Angola and Zambia and can keep the whole of Central Africa under surveillance. Ultimately, it is their own survival which is uppermost in the minds of the apartheid regime's strategists. Although the Orange River boundary between South Africa and Namibia may be easier to defend in purely military terms than the land frontier with Angola, they need the buffer zones in order to stop South African freedom-fighters and their supplies before they even reach the border. For once across, they will reinforce a long-established armed liberation movement and an oppressed people who have courageously demonstrated in recent years their commitment to revolutionary change. Thus Namibia is a vital element in South Africa's defence strategy. It is also a training-ground for the repressive forces which are already engaging South African freedom-fighters on their own soil, and a useful means of militarising and indoctrinating white youth to fight to the end for white supremacy.

Although military domination is the key to South Africa's stranglehold over the sub-continent, the apartheid regime has long recognised the need to dress it up in a political formula short of outright colonial rule. After the collapse of colonialism in the rest of Africa in the early 1960s, it floated the idea of a Southern African 'common market', in which neighbouring African states would be grouped with 'independent' bantustans as economic vassals and political hostages of an all-powerful South African metropolis. The Portuguese coup, the failed invasion of Angola and the Soweto Revolt pushed the regime for a time on to the defensive, but since 1978 it has revived the concept, this time with greater emphasis on achieving an agreed political framework.

At the same time, South Africa pushed strongly for 'internal settlements' in Namibia and Zimbabwe which would keep pliable puppet governments in power. To back this up, it has markedly stepped up its military aggression against Zambia, Angola and Mozambique with raids and air attacks. It gives training, arms, supplies and propaganda support to counter-revolutionary forces in all three countries, which are dedicated to the overthrow of the people's revolution and the role of democracy. It also unleashed the armed forces of the rebel Rhodesian regime, over whose strategy it had complete control, not only against Patriotic Front guerrilla bases and refugee camps but also to wreck the economies of Zambia and Mozambique by destroying their transport system. The South African threat to the black nations of Southern Africa rings ominously clear: end your support for the liberation movements and join us in building a 'confederation' of states, or we will destroy you economically and politically. The Western powers, which had earlier been pushing for a more liberal form of neo-colonialism, now seem to be adding their weight to the South African offensive.

Map 5 – South African aggression against Angola: attacks and airspace violations by South African land and air forces, April 1976–June 1979.

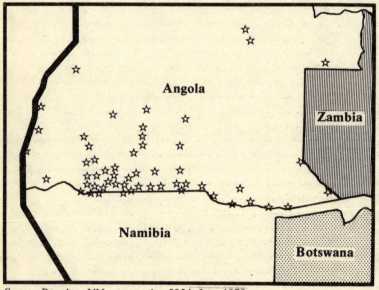

Source: Based on UN map number 3054, June 1979.

Namibia is an integral part of the modified South African strategy. However limited the power it now plans to devolve to its Namibian puppets, even its willingness to do so is a U-turn from the intransigence of the 1960s. Whereas then it seemed hell-bent on incorporating Namibia as a fifth province of South Africa, now it acknowledges the right of the Namibian people to constitutional independence. Whereas then it spurned all outside attempts to intervene, now it bargains with the Western powers and concedes that the U.N. has a necessary part in any settlement.

The Apartheid Strategy and the Turnhalle Conference
South Africa's methods of political control have in fact changed several times in the course of its 60-year occupation. For the first decade after the conquest (1915–25), all power was in the hands of the army, police and civil servants. Then, in 1925, it granted the vote and a substantial degree of

control over their own affairs to the white settlers, who could now elect both town councils — with authority over whites *and* blacks — and a territorial Legislative Assembly. Black Namibians, of course, were denied the right to vote. In the reserves they were ruled by all-powerful white officials and selected puppet 'chiefs' and 'headmen', in the towns by all-white municipalities and the Department of Native Affairs. Pretoria kept control of Police and Native Affairs, but in practice delegated most of its powers to the colonial administration in Windhoek. In appearance, Namibia was a cross between a province of South Africa and a typical colony.

South African troops returning from a cross-border raid into Angola, May 1978

The victory of the National Party in 1948 marked the beginning of a trend towards the incorporation of Namibia into South Africa. First, the white settlers were given the right to elect six M.P.s to the South African Parliament. Then, in 1954, the Department of Bantu Administration moved control over most aspects of 'native administration' to Pretoria. In the 1960s, the occupation regime began to impose its apartheid policy — its 'answer' to the rising militancy of the black nationalist opposition at home — on Namibia as well. Its blueprint was the report of the Odendaal Commission (1964), which proposed to divide the Namibian people into 12 'population groups', each only having political rights in its own 'homeland'.* In reality, the bantustans amounted to little more than the existing reserves. Economic-

* In fact, the regime has designated only 10 bantustans and the 'white area' — as in South Africa, it has no idea what to do with the 'Coloureds'.

ally, as we have shown in Chapter 4, the regime's objective was to turn all black workers in Namibia into faceless peasants and migrant labourers. Politically, it sought to strip black Namibians of all civil and political rights outside the bantustans and, by promoting the politics of tribalism, to divide the growing movement for national liberation. These so-called 'political rights' amounted to little more than the right to participate in a hollow farce stage-managed from Pretoria. In each bantustan the apartheid authorities planned to set up their hand-picked 'chiefs' and 'headmen' as 'natural political leaders', with all the constitutional trappings but none of the powers of independent government.

After initial caution, South Africa took the I.C.J.'s non-verdict in 1966 as a green light and proceeded rapidly to execute its apartheid masterplan (see Figure 24). New laws in 1968 and 1969 set the framework for constructing the bantustans and transferred many of the powers and most of the revenue from the Legislative Assembly into the hands of central government departments. Bantustan governments were set up and slowly evolved towards 'self-government'; by late 1977, only the Herero and Nama did not have a bantustan authority of some description. Pretoria was taking direct charge to execute its grand design, a white heartland surrounded by a cluster of helpless, 'independent' tribal mini-states — and the white settlers would, naturally, have the right to unite their 'homeland' with their South African fatherland.

But already things were going wrong for the South Africans. First, the decisive I.C.J. ruling of June 1971 made it clear that any violation of Namibia's territorial integrity — such as declaring a bantustan 'independent' — could never be recognised internationally, even by South Africa's Western friends. Then the great contract workers' strike at the end of 1971 and the total boycott in August 1973 of the bantustan election in Ovamboland, South Africa's show-piece 'homeland', completely destroyed the credibility of the bantustan programme, while the Portuguese coup in April 1974 brought the prospect of a powerful armed liberation struggle suddenly much closer. Prime Minister Vorster's 'Advisory Council' of bantustan puppets, created in 1973 as a sop to the Western powers who had to defend themselves at the U.N., did not win over even the most conservative of black political leaders. Clearly some formula was needed which would preserve territorial unity, keep open the possibility of national independence, stand a chance of winning at least a modicum of black support and, above all, buy time for South Africa and its imperialist friends to fix up a solution.

Accordingly, on 24 September 1974, the South Africans, in the guise of the National Party in Namibia, announced a conference of 'ethnic groups' to discuss constitutional options for Namibia. It was nearly a year before the conference actually met, in the old Turnhalle drill hall in Windhoek, and another year before it got around to serious discussions about a constitution. Its eleven delegations ('Kaokoland' merged with the Herero delegation) comprised the selfsame puppets whom the regime was setting up in the bantustans, augmented by a handful of conservative black politicians and a few renegade nationalists enticed back from exile. During 1975 and 1976 SWAPO brought all significant political groupings into a united opposition front and effectively destroyed the credibility of the Turnhalle Conference, even before it got to grips with its ostensible task.

Figure 24 — The imposition of the apartheid masterplan, 1968–77.

Key: Stage 1 ✹ advisory boards and councils
State 2 ✰ legislative councils with conditional legislative/administrative powers.
Stage 3 ● legislative assemblies with limited powers of internal 'self-government'.

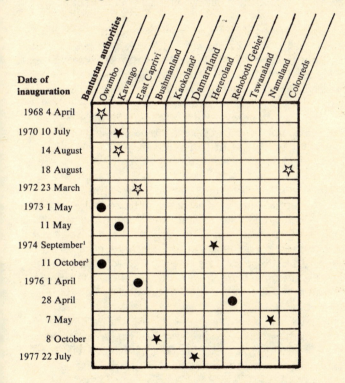

Notes: [1] Two 'Community Authorities' covering a minority of Hereros.
[2] The Kaokoland delegation was merged with that of the Hereros soon after the start of the Turnhalle Conference in September 1975.
[3] Revised constitution.

At this point South Africa's position began to worsen rapidly. Late in 1975 its big gamble, the invasion of Angola, failed disastrously; six months later its own cities erupted into open revolt, and the imperialist powers, losing confidence in the stability of the apartheid regime, began to intervene much more strongly in Southern Africa. Belatedly, between August 1976 and

March 1977, the regime got its Turnhalle Conference to produce an interim constitution which, with minor admendments, was clearly intended to be the basis of an 'independent' Namibia. In reality, the constitution did little more than confirm the existing local authorities and bantustan governments, with a third tier tacked on at the national level, composed entirely of nominees from each ethnic group and having extremely limited powers to change the *status quo*. With the exception that individual bantustans could not now become separately 'independent', this was little more than the Odendaal Plan in another guise. Indeed, the regime was rushing to get bantustan authorities installed for all remaining ethnic groups that did not yet have them.

Clearly this was not a package the Western powers could hope to sell at the U.N. and internationally. Acting in concert, they rapidly formed their so-called Contact Group and in April 1977 intervened strongly with Vorster to stop him declaring the Turnhalle Conference an 'interim government'. By June, South Africa had been forced to agree to appoint an Administrator-General (A.G.) with full legislative and executive powers — in effect a colonial-style governor — and to negotiate with the Contact Group on the terms of Namibia's transition to independence. From that point on, the Contact Group set itself up as the unofficial intermediary of the U.N. Security Council between the occupation regime and SWAPO. Its purpose, on the one hand, was to find a formula which could at least be loosely reconciled with the definitive framework of Resolution 385 which reaffirmed U.N. sovereignty and U.N. supervision and control of elections leading to independence, but a formula which would also guarantee the South Africans a powerful presence on the ground during the transition process. For, above all, the occupation regime needs to have the means at its disposal to intimidate the Namibian people so that its chosen puppets hold state power when independence finally dawns. On the other hand, the Contact Group had to force SWAPO to accept such a deal, and to that end began to bring pressure to bear on its allies in the frontline states.

Between mid-1977 and March 1979 a protracted series of negotiations gradually whittled down the areas of disagreement between South Africa and the U.N. On 2 February 1978, the Contact Group produced its own general framework for the transition to independence, which eventually both South Africa (25 April) and SWAPO (12 July) accepted in principle. However, the Western proposals left the practical arrangements for their implementation open — of necessity, for these remain the responsibility of the U.N. as sovereign authority. Accordingly, U.N. Secretary-General Waldheim sent out a special team to Namibia and, on 30 August 1978, laid his proposals before the Security Council. Because these would in large measure determine the balance of power during the transition process, it was to be expected that the South Africans would resist them strongly — and in the months following that is precisely what the occupation regime set out to do. By March 1979, it had forced a stalemate in the negotiations which not even the wiles of the Western diplomats could overcome.

138

Figure 25 – The profitability of colonialism: investment, output and profits per black worker in mining, fishing and farming, 1977.

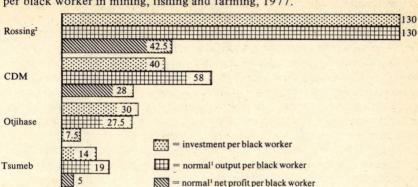

This lengthy diplomacy has masked a subtle but important shift in South African tactics. The main objective is unchanged: to ensure that at independence a client regime, dependent on South African military support, is firmly in power. But the means are different. Instead of dictating the precise mechanism of transition and the terms of independence – on the lines of the 'interim' government's constitution – the occupation regime now seeks only to be assured that its own men are in power at the crucial moment, knowing that it can rely on them to devise a constitution and follow policies which will protect its essential interests. Thus it can accept the U.N. formula – a national election, constituent assembly and so on – so long as it has the power to coerce the Namibian people into electing a majority of its own puppets. To prepare for this crucial test it has needed time – time to bolster the image of its puppets and to perfect its techniques of coercion while giving the appearance of an open democratic process.

In the second part of 1977, the new Administrator-General decreed a series of limited reforms to apartheid legislation designed to buy him credibility. In November 1977, the Turnhalle Conference dissolved itself and immediately reformed as a political party, the Democratic Turnhalle Alliance (D.T.A.).

During 1978 the D.T.A., with seemingly limitless funds at its disposal and backed by massive official intimidation, went on a nation-wide political crusade to win support. In December 1978, the South Africans forced through a national 'election', a carefully rigged farce in which people were forced to vote at gun-point and which predictably gave the D.T.A. a massive majority in the resulting Constituent Assembly. On 21 May 1979, this was renamed the National Assembly and given broad powers of internal legislation. The whole two-year process has been nothing less than a dummy-run for the real thing: the occupation regime now has a 'government-in-waiting' equipped with legislative powers to build its credibility, and a well-oiled and tested machinery of coercion to secure the election result it wants.

But the South Africans have still to resolve one crucial contradiction. They have failed miserably in their repeated attempts to break the will to resist of the Namibian people and their unity of purpose behind their liberation movement, SWAPO. It was precisely at the height of the regime's campaign of repression in the early months of 1979 that the liberation war, as the occupation army itself admitted, reached new peaks of intensity and even wider geographical scope, and the largest ever political demonstration in support of SWAPO occurred in the capital Windhoek. It is this, above all else, which drives the South Africans to hold out for terms even more biased in their favour, for they cannot now be sure that even their sophisticated apparatus of intimidation will deliver them the electoral result they need so desperately.

The Political Economy of Decolonisation

No exploiter will voluntarily give up his right to exploit. When, however, the exploited start to fight back, and more particularly when it seems they have some chance of winning, then those exploiters with greater room for manoeuvre may start to break ranks in order to salvage at least some of their interests. Conversely, as the tempo of the struggle heats up, there may be small groups amongst the oppressed who have more to lose than their comrades-in-arms and who may therefore weaken in the thick of the battle. With the liberation struggle now at an advanced stage in Namibia, it is worth outlining where these weaknesses and strengths are likely to lie.

We have already shown how the class of exploiters in Namibia presents extreme contrasts. Some are hugely profitable and powerful on a world scale; others are no more than individual proprietors whose profits yield a moderate family income by colonial standards. The colonial ruling class in Namibia divides broadly into the following groups: transnational corporations (T.N.C.s); South African and sometimes local manufacturing and processing companies; ranchers; small businessmen and professionals; and management, white-collar employees and artisans. Of these, the T.N.C.s are overwhelmingly the dominant force in the economy, and most of the companies are concentrated in one small enclave industry (fish processing), while the businessmen, white-collar employees and artisans are largely tied to the consumption needs of the settlers and to the colonial administration and the mining companies.

The great disparities between these groups are reflected in their capital assets and profitability. The T.N.C.s in mining control 40% of all productive investment (excluding public utilities) in Namibia — indeed, four of these (C.D.M., Rossing, T.C.L., and Otjihase) control a full third between them, which gives them enormous bargaining power in the Namibian economy. Not surprisingly, they also have by far the highest investment ratios: R13,500 per black worker at T.C.L.'s four mines, R30,000 at Otjihase, R40,000 at C.D.M. and a phenomenal R130,000 at Rossing. This compares with R6,000 in the fish canneries and R20,000 on the ranches (R10,000 of it in land). In fact, farming is much weaker than it appears, because its capital is far less productive than the more mechanised factories and mines. Each year, the big mines produce goods equivalent to the entire value of their investments,* and with C.D.M. and the fish canneries it is twice as much, whereas in stock-farming the proportion is little more than a seventh (see Figure 25).

Figure 26 — Subsistence wages and the profits squeeze.

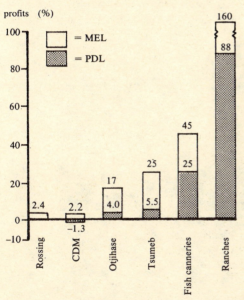

profits (%)

= MEL
= PDL

Note: 'wages' include payments in kind as well as in cash, and 'profits' are assessed at the average for the best years of the company or industry concerned. Also, the Poverty Datum Line is a theoretical bare minimum at which few working-class families could hope to survive without suffering. If wages were to be paid entirely in cash, not only farmers but also the fishing companies and even some base mineral companies might find their bloated profits severely trimmed by the enforcement of a national minimum wage.

These two factors, capital intensity and its productive yield, give the transnational corporations a vastly higher rate of profit than other capitalists in Namibia. T.C.L.'s profits, if maintained at the level of the 1960s and early 1970s, would amount today to an annual R5,000 for each black worker that it employs. In 1978, C.D.M. made a cool R30,000 per black worker — 15 times the average black wage in cash and kind. By contrast, the fish

* This ratio assumes full production at 1978 prices — in practice, Rossing achieved only two-thirds of its rated capacity, Otjihase was shut down, and the canneries had very little fish to process.

companies at their mid-1970s peak were making only some R3,000 per black
worker, and the ranchers are currently getting no more than R1,200 per
worker. Put another way, whereas one company alone (C.D.M.) generated
23% of Namibia's 1978 G.D.P., with only 2% of the total black work-force,
5,100 ranches produced only 10.5% of the G.D.P. with 21% of black workers.

Clearly, some capitalists can afford to lose more than others. Wage
differentials strongly reflect this pecking order: already C.D.M. pays its black
workers average wages (estimated cash and kind) 50% higher than the base
mineral mines, four times those in the fish factories* and five times those on
the ranches. Were the C.D.M. average (which anyway barely exceeds the
urban poverty line for the average family) to be enforced as a national minimum wage, it would reduce T.C.L.'s profits in its best years by about 10%,
in fishing it would halve them, but in ranching it would more than wipe them
out altogether. Since the least that Namibian workers will expect after
liberation is a living wage, the weaker sections of the colonial ruling class
rightly fear for their ill-gotten gains. At present, even the base mineral mines,
faced with low market prices, and the fish-processing companies, with ruined
fishing grounds, would see their profits disappear if forced to pay a living
wage (see Figure 26).

The Contact Group

Small wonder, then, that, as the liberation struggle has advanced,
Namibia's colonial class has begun to break up in dissension. The settler

---

* Since they work a six-month season, a year-round rate would be double.

farmers have bitterly opposed the slightest change in the colonial forced labour regime. When, during the 1971–72 contract workers' strike, the big mining companies engineered the abolition of SWANLA, the farmers fought even this minimal concession tooth and nail and soon formed their own monopoly recruiting organisation to ensure that the wages of contract labourers were kept down. In 1976, when the Turnhalle Conference was indulging itself by recommending some cosmetic reforms, it was the farmers' voices which were raised loudest against the concept of a national minimum wage. In the latest phase, it is they again who have been the backbone of the white political opposition to the D.T.A. For this sector any easing in the apparatus of labour oppression, however, limited, is seriously damaging. And if they flee, they will of necessity have to leave most of their assets behind and, despite the grandiose settlement schemes in Bolivia, New Zealand and elsewhere suggested at various times in imperialist circles, they know they have little chance of getting alternative farms outside Namibia.

The ranchers have found some support amongst white government employees and small businessmen, who have good reason to fear the transfer of some of their jobs and businesses to Namibians, even under the tamest of client regimes. But in general this group is confused and demoralised. In 1979, growing numbers of white employees joined the extreme racist parties and terror groups, in particular the H.N.P. ('Purified National Party') and the W.W.B. ('White Resistance Movement') in an attempt to block reforms of any kind by means of direct action. But many small urban businessmen, especially Germans, are not bothered about the colour of their customers so long as they have a cast-iron guarantee that their capitalist property rights will be safeguarded. These, consequently, have been amongst the D.T.A's most ardent supporters. Lastly, it should be noted that only a handful of professionals (lawyers, doctors and the like) have recognised that their skills will be needed after liberation and consequently have thrown in their lot with the liberation movement.

Of the foreign companies the fish factories are the most vulnerable. They have a convenient escape hatch, because their main assets are located in Walvis Bay, which South Africa claims as part of its national territory and adamantly refuses to decolonise except in a deal with an 'independence' government of its own choosing. For the mining transnationals, it is another matter: obviously they cannot export their assets and, consequently, they have a vital interest in the form of decolonisation. Even so, except for C.D.M., their Namibian operations, although sometimes large in themselves, are neither a major part of their world-wide investments nor sources of profits strategically vital to the marketing of their main products. Consequently, they can afford to take a risk in keeping a colonial or neo-colonial regime going as long as possible, and have proved themselves to be powerful backstage promoters inside Namibia of the D.T.A.

On the other hand, they have great confidence that they will be able to retain at least a proportion of their investments in Namibia after liberation. T.N.C.s have considerable experience in manipulating Third World governments, even those committed to breaking the imperialist stranglehold on their economies. Because the T.N.Cs have huge financial resources, managerial expertise and a monopoly of mining technology, they can often blackmail such governments, to whom colonial and imperialist exploitation has denied these essential requirements, into favourable deals by threatening to close down the mines. Even nationalisation or partial state ownership is not the end of the world for them, since they can still force lucrative management, marketing and service contracts on the government concerned. So the T.N.Cs in Namibia will be confident that they can survive after liberation, even if their profits are reduced, no matter what they do beforehand. In the meantime they will not try to hasten the end of the colonial or neo-colonial regime which benefits them so hugely. So while their senior executives have in several cases held exploratory talks with SWAPO, they still allow their mine managements actively to coerce their black workers to support the D.T.A. and systematically to persecute SWAPO members and supporters.

The one exception is C.D.M., which supplies over 20% of the group profit of its parent, de Beers, and an even higher proportion of its gem diamonds. Because de Beers depends absolutely on maintaining a world monopoly of diamond sales, if C.D.M.'s output were sold independently it could well bring de Beers' entire marketing system crashing down in ruins. Not surprisingly, therefore, C.D.M. has tried to take some precautions to ensure its survival after liberation. It has ostentatiously refused to back the D.T.A. and has allowed SWAPO to organise amongst its work-force. It has invested a small proportion of its profits in technical training for black workers and in mineral prospecting in Namibia. No doubt it will readily enter into a deal with a people's government (as it has already done in Botswana) which allows the state to take a large share of the profits and the ownership. But in the meantime, even C.D.M. is not actively seeking to subvert South Africa's neo-colonial design and is busily sucking out as high a profit as it can. Harry Oppenheimer, boss of C.D.M.'s ultimate owner, the Anglo American Corporation (he was a strong backer of the Muzorewa clique in Zimbabwe) has recently strongly implied that he thinks South Africa should be given every chance to make its D.T.A.-type 'independence' stick.

Central to the task facing the liberation movement in Namibia is the fact that the power structure is colonial in character. Most of the white settlers have other countries which they regard as 'home', to which they know they can return in the last resort, and which will in fact receive them and treat them well. About 60% of them are Afrikaners and nationals of South Africa; another 25% are German-speaking, of whom some are old-time colonials but as many as half hold West German passports; some 10% are English-speaking South Africans; and the remaining 5% are expatriates of other Western countries. When the Namibian people take over state power and the colonial administration departs, over half of all white employees and most of the other Afrikaners will lose their jobs and go, no doubt to be absorbed into government employment in South Africa. Most of the ranchers, three-quarters of whom are Afrikaners who would find it difficult to tolerate even a neo-colonial settlement, will follow them, taking as much of their stock, vehicles and machinery as they can. Many of the Afrikaners and Germans in commerce will also follow their bank accounts back to their colonial homelands, though perhaps more slowly than the farmers and bureaucrats. Only the artisans and technicians, supervisors and managers, administrators and scientists, largely employed in the factories and mines, are likely to stay on — and whether they do will depend a great deal on the policy decisions of the people's government and the level of support it gets from international agencies and friendly governments.

Historically, however, imperialism has always sought an alternative to true liberation when colonialism has reached the end of the road: neo-colonialism. To maintain a combination of political independence and economic dependence, a neo-colonial regime requires indigenous class allies of imperialism who hold sufficient political and economic power to establish a stable government without depending on imperialist military power to keep it going. Such conditions do not already exist in Namibia: there is no potential neo-colonial class of any strength amongst black Namibians. So extreme has colonial oppression and apartheid been that there are no more than a tiny handful of small black businessmen, urban shopkeepers, rural traders, lorry owners and the like. Virtually the only commercial farms and luxury houses owned by black Namibians are those with which the occupation regime has rewarded its Turnhalle puppets. A few Namibian cattle-owners and traders are quite wealthy, but in no way could they become a national ruling class, holding the reins of power on their own. Nor are they strong enough to provide a political facade for those settlers who want to keep their economic power by setting up a neo-colonial regime.

This is a principal reason why in recent years South Africa has dressed up its puppets in elaborate neo-colonial clothes — parliamentary debates and all. Knowing that the imperialist powers want a neo-colonial solution, the occupation regime is doing its best to give them the illusion of one, complete with a national 'election' by universal suffrage. Some of the imperialist powers have chosen to be impressed with the results — the British Conservatives sent out an observer to the December 1978 'election' who afterwards declared it to be valid. The regime has also seized every chance to try and turn different experiences of colonial oppression amongst the Namibian people caused by the artificial racial segregation, into major political antagonisms.

But the South Africans know that they cannot deliver the substance of a neo-colonial solution for a long time to come. Their policies have meant that there are very few trained black bureaucrats or white-collar workers, the class of functionaries who might possibly have been subverted to support a conservative neo-colonial settlement. Any D.T.A.-based regime would need not only the South African army, but also the entire South African-provided machinery of repression for many years to come. And in their more lucid moments the Western powers have recognised this hard fact. This is why they have insisted on including SWAPO in any solution, while doing their best to ensure that, should the liberation movement seize state power, it will be in a straightjacket and forced to dance to the tune of the big corporations. They have also spared no effort to infiltrate the ranks of the liberation movement itself with political tendencies in line with their own interests.

The truth is that both the occupation regime and the Western powers have reached a dead end. Neither possesses the means to create a viable neo-colonial regime. And any chance of imposing a fraudulent settlement through rigged elections has been destroyed in advance by the high level of mobilisation which SWAPO has achieved amongst all sections of the Namibian people and which in the last decade has defeated each new twist in colonial and imperialist strategy. The South Africans know that their puppets cannot win an election unless they can rig it; the Western powers know that they could never sell such a phony 'independence' internationally. As a result, the Western powers throw up their hands in helpless impotence; the occupation regime hangs on by means of increasingly desperate military repression; and slowly, grimly, with great sacrifice, the liberation struggle advances towards ultimate victory.

The Illegal Rossing Uranium Contract

Typical of the multinationals' arrogant disregard of the interests of the people of Namibia has been the greed with which the British-based mining giant Rio Tinto Zinc has exploited the huge deposits of uranium in the Namib Desert, to which it bought the rights in 1966. In flagrant defiance of international law, in particular the U.N. General Assembly's termination of the Mandate in 1966, the World Court's Advisory Opinion of 1971 and the UN Decree on Natural Resources of 1974, R.T.Z. signed long-term contracts with the British and other governments for the supply of Namibian uranium. Since 1976 it has been mining and exporting uranium ore from Rossing. The largest of these contracts was with British Nuclear Fuels for the supply of 7,500 tons between 1977 and 1982. As the following statement makes clear, SWAPO has repeatedly declared its categorical opposition to this wanton pillage of the nation's natural resources:

It is our view that foreign investment in

Namibia is one of the major factors contributing to the continuing presence of South Africa's illegally occupying forces . . . The development of the uranium mine at Rossing, jointly by Rio Tinto Zinc and the Industrial Development Corporation of South Africa, represents the largest single investment in Namibia . . . Foreign companies such as R.T.Z. are taking advantage of the immediate political situation in Namibia, and it is therefore necessary to emphasise, to them and to all foreign companies investing in Namibia, that all mining titles and temporary prospecting rights granted after 1966 are illegal, and that they constitute, moreover, a criminal exploitation of irreplaceable natural resources which rightfully belong to the people of Namibia . . .

In this situation there can be no question of trying to maintain a position on the fence. Those who have relations with the illegal South African regime in Namibia and actively contribute, by trade and revenues, to the regime, are helping to perpetuate the illegal occupation of Namibia and South Africa's cruel exploitation of our people.

We also condemn the pretence by the British Government that this blatant violation of international law . . . should be justified by a totally fictitious claim to the right which belongs only to a future lawful government in Namibia, namely whether or not to extract uranium from Namibian soil . . . We wish to remind the British Government that, in terms of the 1971 Advisory Opinion of the International Court of Justice, it is obliged to cease all dealings with the illegal occupation regime in our country.

We call upon the British Government to recognise the 1971 Opinion and to terminate the contract between British Nuclear Fuels Ltd and Rossing Uranium immediately.

Extracts from SWAPO Dept. of Information and Publicity Aide-Memoire, 8 March 1977

SECTION 2
The People's Resistance

6. Traditions of Popular Resistance: 1670–1970

Traditions of Popular Resistance: 1670–1970

The Undermining of Namibian Independence 1670–1890

The record of popular resistance to foreign intrusion in Namibia stretches far back. Over the years it has taken a variety of forms — not only military but also diplomatic, political and economic. In the present armed struggle for national liberation it has but found its latest and most advanced expression.

Shielded by the formidable Namib Desert, nearly two centuries passed between the earliest contacts and the first tentative initiatives to colonise Namibia. However, the people soon had a foretaste of what was to come. The expanding Dutch colony at the Cape sent shock-waves far into the interior of Southern Africa in the late 16th and 17th Centuries as Khoisan people migrated away, rather than become the serfs of the Afrikaner trekboers who were usurping their best lands and waterholes. The first recorded meeting between Namibians and an aggressively expanding European civilisation took place at the mouth of the Kuiseb River near Walvis Bay in 1670. Seven years later, the crew of an exploration ship from the Cape encountered a group of Namas at the same spot. An attempt to barter for cattle with them ended in misunderstanding and suspicion, and the Namas drove the landing party from Namibian soil. In this first symbolic encounter the pattern was set for future relations between the people of Namibia and the agents of a world-wide commercial capitalism.

The Orlams who migrated across the Orange River between 1810 and 1870 had been more intensely affected by settler colonialism. Escaping from Boer farms, from mission settlements or from rapidly shrinking pastures many could speak Afrikaans, had been affected by evangelical Christianity and possessed guns, wagons and horses. Free once more, but robbed of their economic resources, they organised themselves into semi-nomadic bands under leaders, and raided both neighbouring Namibians and encroaching colonists for their subsistence.

Most famous of the new leaders was Jager Afrikaner. His life history is typical of the manner in which the self-reliant fighting traditions of the Nama people were born. His father's clan, forced out of Tulbagh in the Western Cape in the 1790s, settled hundreds of miles inland near the present

Calvinia. Even here, the onward march of Boer colonisation soon encroached and, after his father's death, Jager found himself the servant of a despotic farmer. Goaded by the man's cruelty, Jager and his community rebelled, seized the farmer's cattle and guns, and migrated north to the Orange River with a government price on Jager's head. Here, by the time of his death in 1823, he had built a substantial following and a formidable military reputation. His son Jonker (1798–1861) was to become the dominant figure in mid-19th Century Namibia. When, in 1830, severe drought brought the Herero herds far south into Nama pastures, the leading Nama ruler called upon Jonker for protection, promising land in return. Exploiting his monopoly of firearms and horses, Jonker established himself strategically in the central highlands, alternative his capital between Windhoek and Okahandja. He wielded control over large parts of Central Namibia for more than three decades.

But the seeds of destruction were already being sown. By the 1840s, traders and missionaries were penetrating every corner of the land, seeking to secure their interest by bending tribal leaders to their influence. Plying first Jonker and later the Nama *kapteins* with arms, the traders incited them to pay their debts with Herero cattle by using their new weaponry for plunder. In this manner, the pressure of the traders turned the intermittent raiding by the Nama and Orlam leaders, whose pastures had long since become overcrowded, into prolonged years of warfare with the Herero.

In the end Jonker became an obstacle to traders and missionaries alike. Although he built the traders a road to Walvis Bay — a remarkable feat of engineering — and enforced safe-conduct for them over wide areas, he also attempted to fix prices, ban permanent trading posts and restrict missionary activity. Above all, he controlled and taxed the traffic between Hereroland and the Cape cattle markets. After his death in 1861, the traders, enthusiastically supported by the German missionaries, exploited the Herero struggle for emancipation (1863–70) to destroy the Orlam state. Henceforth, despite a decade of uneasy peace (1870–80), the struggle for survival degenerated into a pattern of endemic warfare. Nama and Orlam raided traders, each other and, above all, the vast Herero cattle herds; while the Herero retaliated by sending expeditions deep into Namaland. The social order of the central plateau was temporarily disrupted.

Rapidly acquiring insight into an increasingly threatening outside world, Namibians exploited all possible sources of information in the long struggle to preserve their independence. They used missionaries, who were familiar with the workings of colonial and imperial governments, diplomatic intermediaries and arbitrators, and carefully tapped missionaries, traders and explorers for up-to-date information on the activities of the colonisers. They sent their sons to mission schools to learn the ways and skills of the imperialist forces of which these intruders were the harbingers, and they equipped and retrained their fighting forces with modern arms.

Despite their relations with missionaries and trade suppliers, Namibian leaders retained tight political and economic authority over their activities.

Accounts of the period are rife with the fulminations of the white intruders against Namibian rulers who rejected their advice and curtailed their freedom to pursue their disruptive interventions. In the north, the Ovambo kings did not permit permanent trading stations at all. Indeed, as late as 1911, the Kwanyama King Mandume, although beset on all sides by hostile colonial forces and economic boycotts, expelled all traders from his territory for exploiting the prevailing famine and fixed the rates of exchange himself. The rulers of pre-colonial Namibia were all too aware of the predicament caused by their lack of resources in the face of a growing world imperialism.

The economics of underdevelopment divided Namibians tragically against each other. First the Cape Government (in the 1870s), the German merchants and officials (in the early 1880s) exploited the political intervention of missionaries and traders and the fears and rivalries of local rulers to bind them piecemeal with separate treaties. When, in the early 1890s, the Germans moved into Namibia in force, they were quick to apply divide-and-rule tactics. The Herero had never acknowledged a 'paramount chief', so the Germans recognised Samuel Maharero as ruler of all Hereroland and then used their patronage of him to crush all Herero opposition to colonial hegemony. Hendrik Witbooi, the great Nama leader, fought the Germans alone at this stage and was defeated. For the next ten years (1894–1904), he held power only as long as he supplied military contingents to aid the Germans in suppressing resistance elsewhere to their rule. The German Governor Leutwein (1894–1905), as he later admitted, used his 'best endeavour to make the native tribes serve our cause and to play them off against each other.'

Nevertheless, far-sighted Namibians came to understand the forces which trapped them, and attempted to transcend them by building a broader front of resistance to foreign intrusion. As early as 1858, ' Jonker Afrikaner, most of the important Nama and Orlam and some Herero leaders had come together at Hoachanas in a great peace conference to attempt to settle their differences. Their deliberations produced historic treaty – ironically entitled the 'League of Nations' – which amongst other provisions bound the parties to settle disputes by arbitration on pain of collective punishment. The Treaty also outlawed mining concessions and land sales to Cape colonists without the prior agreement of all, promised military support and extradition rights to the Griquas, and called for a general assembly of the parties to be held each year. This first attempt at forging a broadly based alliance collapsed before Jonker's death three years later, but it marked the beginnings of a tradition of consultation and negotiation amongst Namibian leaders.

Peace Treaty of Hoachanas

In the name of the Holy Trinity, the Father, the
Son and the Holy Ghost, we the undersigned have
resolved to unite in the following treaty:

Article 1: No chief with his people will have the
right, should a dispute arise between him and
another chief of standing, to pursue his own
vindication, but shall be pledged to bring the case
before an impartial court.

Article 2: When the case has been examined by
the impartial chiefs, the guilty party shall be
punished or a fine shall be imposed upon him.
Should he be unwilling to comply with the judgement and should he attempt to dispute the issue
by force of arms, then shall all the treaty chiefs
be pledged jointly to take up arms and punish
him.

Article 3: No chief is permitted to send or allow
to be sent a raiding party against the Herero unless
the Herero have given legally valid cause for so
doing. Should a chief's man disobey and launch
such a raid, should he attempt to punish them and
pass sentence but find them unwilling to submit
themselves thereto, and should he lack the means
to enforce the punishment, then shall the neighbouring chief come to his aid to ensure the
sentence is carried out.

Article 4: No chief may allow a sub-chief or
official, or the son of a chief, to dispose of important matters without the chief informed thereof. No-one shall have the right himself to take
back arbitrarily something owed to him.

Article 5: No chief may permit copper being
mined in his territory without the knowledge and
agreement of all other chiefs, or to sell a farm or
site within his territory to a white person from the
Cape Colony. Whoever despite this makes such
a sale shall be heavily fined, and the purchaser
himself will have to bear the cost if he has been
acquainted with this law beforehand.

Article 6: We resolve also to close our bond and
treaty with all Griqua chiefs. Should they need us
in any major war which may befall their country,
then we are ready to come to their assisrance.

Article 7: We the undersigned resolve further that
fugitives from Griqualand who enter our country
in order to hide will be handed over by the chief
in whose territory they are found, should the
Griqua chief request this. The same responsibility
will rest with the Griqua chiefs.

Article 8: No chief shall allow himself solely on
account of rumours to become mistrustful and be
prepared to take up arms without getting written
proof thereof. Should this provision nevertheless
be broken, the chief responsible will be heavily
fined by the other chiefs.

Article 9: No chief shall have the right to settle
murder cases alone and to judge and execute the
guilty party. The trial must be held in the presence
of two or three important chiefs, who together
will have the responsibility of passing sentence and
carrying it out.

Article 10: It is also resolved that each year a day
and date will be agreed to consult together for
the welfare of the land and the people.

Article 11: Every citizen, on appearing before his
chief, whether on account of his own misdeed or
of a complaint which he brings before his chief or
government, has the right, should he see or believe
that he has been done an injustice, to set his case
before other Treaty chiefs. These will thereupon
examine the reasons for his dissatisfaction, and if
the impartial chiefs determine that he has been
unjustly treated, then he shall be given justice. But
if his case is not substantiated, he shall accept
the verdict.

Article 12: Should a chief or chiefs ill-treat a
citizen or unlawfully use force against his property
or act unjustly towards him in any other manner,
then that citizen has the right to take his complaint before the court of the Treaty chiefs. His
case shall thereupon be investigated. If it is
established as a result of the inquiry that the
said chief is guilty, then that chief shall be

> punished after the Treaty chiefs have declared their verdict upon his guilt.
>
> Discussed, approved and unanimously adopted by us the undersigned chiefs:
>
> | | |
> |---|---|
> | Cornelius ‖Oasib ǂKarab | Willem Swartbooi |
> | Jager Aimab | ǂHuiseb |
> | Hendrik Hendrikes | ǂGarib |
> | !Nanib | Piet Kooper ǀGamab |
> | Kido Witbooi ǂA-Ileib | Amraal ǂGai-Inub |
> | Jonker Afrikaner | David Christian |
> | ǀItara-mûb | ‖Naichab |
> | Paul Coliath | Tjamuaha* |
> | ǂHobechab | |
>
> Also present: Andries van Rooi**
>   Maharero
> * represented by his two sons.
> ** a Griqua, formerly Commandant of Andries Waterboer and elected chairman of the Conference.

The German Colonial Regime

Resistance to Colonial Intrusion (1878–1903)

During the 1870s and 1880s, growing colonial interference provoked increasingly cohesive resistance throughout Namibia. Yet unity was still only possible on a regional basis and tactics differed. Maharero sought to guarantee Herero rights and limit colonial intrusion by entering into 'protection treaties', first with the Cape Colony, then with Germany. The victim of deception and vacillation by the British and Cape Governments, Maharero was to comment sadly: 'The British flag flew here. It waved this way and that; we attached ourselves to it, and we were waved backwards and forwards with it.' In 1888 he told the German Commissioner: 'It seems strange that whenever you big people come to me you always bring strife.' Hendrik Witbooi expressed the reservations of many when he said: 'You will not understand the German laws and the works of Dr. Goering [the German Commissioner] because he will not bend himself to your customs, but you will have to bend to his customs.' And on another occasion: 'This giving of yourself into the hands of the whites will become to you a burden as if you were carrying the sun on your back.'

In the south, at this time, many of the Nama leaders resisted signing protection treaties. 'Protection, what is this protection?' protested Witbooi. 'Everyone under protection is the subject of the one who protects him.'

In the end, Witbooi's view proved more accurate than Maharero's. But the cost of the defiance in the interim was piecemeal conquest in a series of short, bloody wars against a colonial power with vastly superior resources.

Hendrik Witbooi

Hendrik Witbooi was one of the outstanding leaders in the Namibian people's resistance to German colonisation. A man of deep religious inspiration, he came to the conviction in the early 1880s that he should unite the Nama people under his leadership against the Herero. But in the growing power of German colonialism he soon came to perceive a more serious threat. He attempted, without success, to play off the German, Cape and British Governments against each other and to ally the Herero to the anti-colonial cause. In 1893, he turned his legendary skill as a guerrilla commander against the German troops. 'If you kill me for my country and my independence without transgression on my part,' he wrote to his enemy Governor Leutwein, 'that is no disgrace and loss to me because then I die honourably in the cause of that which is mine.'

In the far north the Ovambo kings were defending their territory with equal vigour against attacks from two colonial powers. The first Portuguese military expedition had invaded the territory of the neighbouring Nkhumbi as far back as the late 1850s. Although short-lived, it was followed at intervals by other expeditionary forces as the Portuguese sought to extend their control inland from the Angolan coast. Each attack was uncompromisingly, and usually successfully, resisted by the Ovambo kings, who often combined forces to confront the invaders. Experiencing massed fire-power for the first time, they rearmed rapidly and extensively with modern European firearms, and built up a formidable military deterrent. On 25 September 1904, Ombadya forces won a resounding victory, putting to flight a 2,000-man Portuguese column, killing 305 of the enemy and capturing large quantities of arms, including cannon. But gradually the Portuguese closed in, conquering all the outer kingdoms until only Ukwanyama remained independent on the Angolan side of the frontier.

At first, the Ovambo kings regarded Portuguese and German colonialism with equal suspicion. When Governor Leutwein tried to visit him in 1896, Kambonde, King of Western Ondonga, replied that 'what Leutwein had written was all very well but that he, Kambonde, did not wish at any time during his lifetime to see Leutwein, for the Germans came with friendly words, but when they arrived, they wanted to rule, and that he could do himself.' The same year, secret overtures established an understanding between Samuel Maharero and the southern Ovambo kings. During the national uprising eight years later in 1904, the Eastern Ondonga King Nehale attacked the German border post at Namutoni, and he and other kings gave aid and refuge to Herero refugees.

The Ovambo kings came to understand the long term threat from European colonialism and exploited the rival ambitions of the Portuguese and German regimes. When, however, it became clear that the Germans were too pre-occupied with their brutal suppression of the Herero and Nama to invade Ovamboland, most of the kings, with Portuguese forts ringing their northern borders, agreed to sign 'protection treaties' with the German regime in 1908.

Thus began a fatal compromise. For the Germans, soon perceiving the divisions in Ovambo society, began to turn them to their own advantage. Pre-colonial penetration by traders and missionaries had made the kings dependent on imports of arms and luxury goods. To clear their debts, they were increasingly forced to tax their people heavily in cattle. A parasitic autocracy of state functionaries emerged, on whom the kings depended for their incomes. Beset by the blandishments of labour recruiters, they collaborated with the German regime in forcing thousands of their men to labour on the railways and mines as migrant workers, taxing their hard-earned income heavily on their return. It was a simple matter for the South African regime after 1915 to incorporate the tribal autocracies as willing collaborators into the colonial administration. The kings themselves — those that survived — held aloof for a while, but their power had been fatally usurped.

The War of National Liberation (1904—8)

The ending of Namibian independence in the central and southern parts of the country, however, was bloody and traumatic. Goaded beyond endurance by unscrupulous traders, encroaching settlers and the degrading cruelty of the colonial police and courts, the Herero leaders decided to throw off the colonial yoke. Samuel Maharero, sensing the prevailing mood, moved decisively to unite the Herero people under his leadership. The Herero chose their moment with care. In October 1903, the Bondelswarts had renewed their protracted guerrilla struggle in the far south, tying down the entire colonial garrison. On 11 January 1904, the day before the uprising, Maharero sent messages to Hermanus van Wyk, the Rehoboth leader, and to Hendrik Witbooi. To the former he wrote: 'It is my wish that we weak nations should rise up against the Germans. Either we destroy them or they all will live in our country. There is nothing else for it.' He challenged Witbooi: 'Let us rather die together, and not as a result of ill-treatment, prison, or all the other ways.' But tragically, Maharero's call for national unity never reached Witbooi, for van Wyk handed over his letters to the Germans.

Maharero's war directive was clear and principled: women and children, non-German Europeans, missionaries, friendly traders were all to be spared. 'Only German men were regarded as our enemies,' the Herero Chief Kariko later explained. Even without Witbooi's assistance, the Herero forces kept the Germans at bay for several months, using both orthodox and guerrilla tactics. But the German Imperial High Command, its honour at stake, despatched reinforcements under the extremist Lieutenant-General von Trotha. The turning point came with the battle of Waterberg on 11 August, after which the Hereros were fighting in retreat. They were forced into the *omaheke*, the waterless sands of the Kalahari. Little more than a thousand survivors, including Maharero, reached sanctuary near Lake Ngami in Botswana. On 2 October, von Trotha issued his notorious 'Extermination Order'. 'I believe,' he explained to his superiors, 'that the Herero must be destroyed as a nation.' For more than a year, until an armistice was signed on 20 December 1905, the imperial army waged war by genocide, poisoning waterholes and machine-gunning survivors — a 'final solution' quite as deliberate as Hitler's a generation later.

The genocide had hardly begun when at last the south, too, rose in revolt. Nama soldiers attached to the German forces deserted and reported to Hendrik Witbooi both the ruthlessness of German repression and that many Hereros had escaped from the Waterberg. In July 1904, three key leaders of the Bondelswarts returned from exile and began to recruit for a new campaign against German colonialism, even as German reinforcements were disembarking for service in the south. On 3 October 1904, Witbooi declared war on the Germans and rallied most of the Nama people to the cause. Then followed years of desperate and protracted guerrilla warfare as the Nama irregulars, skilled and mobile marksmen, took on a vastly superior German force in difficult terrain. Witbooi himself died in action in October 1905, but other leaders prolonged the struggle to the end of 1906. In its final phase, several leaders retreated across the Cape and Botswana boundaries and continued to harass the Germans in cross-border raids. Not until February 1909 was the final treaty signed with Simon Kooper in Botswana. One of the last to fall (he was killed by Cape police in collusion with the

German military on 20 September 1907) was Jacob Morenga, truly a distinguished fighter. Little is known of his early life, but his leadership in the Bondelswarts uprising late in 1903 was sufficiently powerful for the Germans to outlaw him in the peace settlement of January 1904. Six months later, he returned to Southern Namibia. Establishing an inaccessible base in the Great Karras Mountains, he rapidly built up a formidable fighting force. Morenga was unusual amongst Namibian leaders of the time. Lacking any hereditary title, he nevertheless became the strongest and most durable of the major commanders in the south. He united both Herero and Nama in his following, which grew from a mere 11 in mid-1904 to over 400 six months later. Fluent in English, French and German, he was sharply aware of the workings of imperialism and unflinchingly committed to national liberation. Asked later whether he knew that Germany was one of the mightiest military powers in the world, he answered: 'Yes, I am aware of it, but they cannot fight in our country. They do not know where to get water and do not understand guerrilla warfare.'

Of this, Morenga was a master. Supplying his force from settler farms and captured arms, he held the initiative in the south for fully 20 months before finally retreating across the Cape border in May 1906 in the face of a large-scale offensive. Harassed and imprisoned by the Cape authorities, his escape from surveillance shortly before his assassination 'had the effect of an electric shock' amongst the Namibian people, according to the then Governor. 'The excitement amongst the natives was noticeable everywhere' and volunteers began to gather around him once more. The Germans poured troops into the south, and the Cape Government, wholeheartedly collaborating with the colonial regime, sent out patrols. It was one of these which, on 20 September 1907, gunned Morenga down in cold blood. Morenga's death marked the end of a significant phase in the struggle against colonialism in Namibia, but not of the people's will to resist. Upon his internment in May 1906, Morenga was asked whether the war could continue much longer. 'Yes, certainly,' he replied, 'as long as there is a man in the field.'

In the far north, the ending of Ovambo independence was delayed by a decade. In the last years, Mandume, the powerful King of Ukwanyama (1911–17), symbolised Ovambo resistance to colonial hegemony. When, upon the outbreak of the First World War, the Portuguese retreated and the Germans turned to face a South African invading force, Mandume attempted to unite the separate Ovambo kingdoms and destroyed the Portuguese forts surrounding his territory. But a Portuguese expeditionary force, arriving in mid-1915, decimated his army and people by scorched earth tactics, taking no prisoners. Forced to cross the border into Namibia with the survivors at the height of the worst famine ever known in the region, he had no option but to submit to South African authority.

The intrusion of colonialism established a new political and economic system on Namibian soil. Once brought under its political authority, Namibians were transformed from independent cultivators and pastoralists into forced labourers and rightless peasants enslaved by imperialism to the

interests of international capital. The conquest complete, their only option
was to struggle within the system to resist oppression, improve their conditions of life and, ultimately, to unite in struggle for the overthrow of colonialism itself.

Jacob Morenga

The Aftermath of Genocide and Forced Labour (1905–15)
The cost of the colonial conquest to the Namibian people was devastating.
Of the entire black population in the war area more than half perished.
Fewer than 20,000 out of 80,000 Herero survived the holocaust. In the
aftermath of the war, blacks in Central and Southern Namibia found themselves stripped of all rights in the land of their birth. The regime banned
all tribal leadership and executed any leaders it could find. It dispersed the
people around the country far from their homes, some thousands of them
into prison camps on unhealthy offshore islands where they died like flies.
The grim struggle to live became the most urgent priority for the survivors.

Despite the extremity of their oppression the people's will to resist was not broken. For years, many of the Herero refused to submit to the German yoke, some taking the dangerous escape route to Botswana, others leading a precarious existence in the open veld. The people in the countryside, whether forced labourers or diehard resisters, repossessed the cattle herds which had once been theirs, but were taken, along with the land, from them in war. Some, driven to desperation by starvation and brutal floggings on settler farms, escaped to the towns, where conditions were marginally better. Others, dispersed to all corners of the territory by a regime determined to destroy the last vestiges of social cohesion, deserted the labour camps and farms and returned clandestinely to their ancestral lands. In urban locations and on the farms, the surviving leaders, disguising their true identity, regrouped a shattered people and gradually forced the authorities to recognise their power. The missionaries themselves acknowledged that their mass baptisms and packed churches were no more than a cover for a movement of the Herero and Nama people towards communal solidarity.

The South Africans Take Over

Resisting the Conquest (1915—24)

Little more than a decade after the national uprising, the First World War brought an abrupt end to German colonialism. Deceived by the imperialists' rhetoric of 'freedom', Namibians rose against the colonial regime in support of the invading South African forces. A good number of German settlers abandoned their farms. Others were forced to leave as the Herero and Nama people, many of whom had already regrouped, took control of their ancestral lands and the livestock of which they had been robbed. The Governor-General of South Africa toured the country, promising the people their 'old freedom' and wealth; military tribunals sat in judgement on German atrocities; and a government commission took evidence on the brutalities of German rule.

But the people's hopes of a new dispensation were quickly dispelled. Far from restoring to the people their former lands, the new colonial regime, with few exceptions, simply confirmed the German expropriations. With feverish haste and lavish financial support, the land was parcelled out to farmers from South Africa or handed back to its former German owners. At the same time, the new colonial police, as brutal as their predecessors, drove the people into subjection under a battery of repressive legislation. The crowning insult came in 1922 when, with vast areas of prime grazing land still unoccupied, the regime announced its plans for 'native reserves': for the Nama, little more than the pitifully small German treaty areas; for the Herero, large stretches of waterless sandveld — the very *omaheke* on which the flower of their nation had perished in the war of freedom.

During the first decade of South African rule (1914—25), the whole of Namibia was in turmoil. In the north, such was the prestige of the Kwanyama

King, Mandume, that the Portuguese and South African regimes only felt safe once they had jointly disposed of him in 1917. In the central region, the Herero flouted the authority of farmers and colonial police alike as they repossessed their ancestral lands. The missionary influence disintegrated as the sacred fires flamed anew. In order to preserve the tradition of their epic resistance to the full might of German imperialism, the Herero formed a military-style association, meticulously organised, symbolically, by German rank and uniform. When Samuel Maharero died in exile in Botswana, his burial at Okahandja on 26 August 1923, in the grave of his forefathers Maharero and Tjamuaha, became the occasion and venue each succeeding year for a full-scale military parade where the Herero commemorated their fighting traditions. It was on this anniversary to the very day, 43 years later in 1966, that the national liberation movement SWAPO was to launch the armed struggle for the liberation of Namibia from colonial oppression.

Samuel Maharero

As it became clear that South African colonialism differed from the German only in style and minor detail, Namibians turned to the black opposition in South Africa and the United States for inspiration and assistance and began to build new forms of resistance. For a time, the influence of Marcus Garvey's Pan-Africanism, with its slogan 'Africa to the Africans', was strong, particularly in the central part of the country. Branches of his Universal Negro Improvement Society were started in Windhoek and Luderitz. Jacobus Christian, the Bondelswarts leader, sought assistance from

the radical Griqua leader Le Fleur. Coloured immigrants from the Cape
formed a branch of the African Political Organisation in Windhoek. A South
West African Native Association appeared at Luderitz. The Industrial and
Commercial Workers' Union (I.C.U.), fast becoming a mass labour movement
in South Africa, took root amongst workers in the same town. Ovambo contract workers on the diamond fields formed a benefit society whose chief
object was to indemnify strikers against the inevitable fines in the colonial
labour courts. For the first time, modern political organisations arose alongside the traditional leaderships; the masses of peasants and workers moved
into action on their own initiative. But this early militant phase of black
resistance to colonialism could not survive the ruthlessness of South African
repression. The different regional groupings, the many strands of political
and economic activism, were still too disunited.

Occasionally, the heavy hand of repression drove the people to open
defiance. In the south, there were two last episodes of open resistance to the
colonial regime. Both are notorious for the brutality with which the South
Africans crushed them. Once more the Bondelswarts were in the forefront
of the struggle. This proud section of the Namibian people had risen three
times in ten years against German rule (1896, 1903 and 1904) and was one of
the last to surrender in the national war of freedom. It had produced a series
of courageous and resourceful fighting leaders — notably Jacob Morenga,
Jacobus Christian and Abraham Morris. After its defeat, the Germans had
confined the people to a small, arid reserve. No longer able to find pasture
for their stock, they became skilled hunters with packs of dogs. To force
them out as wage-labourers for the surrounding farmers, the colonial regime
imposed a dog tax, and in 1921 raised it to prohibitive levels. This, on top of
a severe drought, pushed them to the verge of starvation. They came to the
bitter realisation that the South African regime had not the slightest intention of returning their lost lands.

Goaded beyond endurance by stock controls, low wages and degrading
treatment on the farms and heavy-handed police repression, the people
responded readily when their exiled leaders returned from the Cape (Christian
in 1919 and Morris in April 1922). When the police suddenly demanded that
Morris be handed over, the people refused and grouped defensively on a hill
called Guruchas. Instead of negotiating, the colonial regime mounted a full-
scale military attack. Aircraft bombed the hill, killing women and children
as well as men. By the end of the short campaign 100 Bondelswarts had been
killed, including Morris, and 468 wounded or taken prisoner.

Two years later, the colonial regime clashed with the Rehoboth community. The Rehobothers had secured recognition for their pre-colonial territorial rights in the Gebiet, and also a constitution and an elected council (*Raad*)
in a 'Treaty of Protection and Friendship' with the Germans in 1885, which
allowed them local autonomy. However, this did not prevent the colonial
regime from encroaching upon their rights, and in 1915 the Rehobothers
expressed their frustration by siding with the South African invading force.
After the Mandate had been granted to South Africa, they assiduously

petitioned the League of Nations and the British and South African Governments, seeking to retain their status 'as an independent people under the
Union Jack'. In 1923, however, the South African regime persuaded the
Raad to be incorporated into the Administration. Incensed, the Rehobothers
repudiated the *Raad* and elected an unofficial council pledged to independence. After a year of deadlock, the regime suspended the 1923 agreement,
imposed a magistrate on the Gebiet and demanded that the people brand
their cattle as a token of submission to South African authority. When the
leader of the unofficial council was summonsed, all his followers demanded
to be taken into custody as well. The regime's response was a massive show
of force. Martial law was declared in the Gebiet, and three war-planes were
dispatched. On 5 April 1925 the village of Rehoboth itself was surrounded,
most of the men (638 in all) arrested and disarmed, and the 'ringleaders'
imprisoned.

In Ovamboland there were two last confrontations with the colonial
authorities. In both cases they were deliberately provoked by the South
African regime, which was anxious to replace the more popular of the former
kings with councils of government-appointed headmen. Inevitably,
Mandume was the chief victim. South African and Portuguese representatives
met to plot his suppression. On the pretext of alleged border violations, the
South African authorities demanded that he come to Windhoek to explain
his actions, something forbidden by the strict rule that no king was permitted
to leave his territory, and vetoed in any case by his advisory council. A
South African military expedition thereupon marched into Ovamboland.
Ordered to surrender, Mandume breathed defiance to the last. 'If the English
want me, I am here and they can come and fetch me. I will fight till my last
bullet is spent.' In the ensuing battle Mandume's forces were defeated and he
himself killed.

This action had its sequel in 1932 when the colonial regime used a flimsy
pretext to depose the Kwambi King Ipumbu, who after Mandume's death
had become the new symbol of Ovambo defiance. Making a deliberate show
of force, the South African regime sent in a column of armoured cars and
planes which razed Ipumbu's headquarters to the ground. Ipumbu, who had
never put up armed resistance, was captured and exiled.

The brutal repression of these scattered revolts in the early years of South
African rule did not crush the determination of the people to struggle for
freedom. It did, however, drive home the lesson that isolated acts of direct
resistance could no longer succeed against an entrenched colonial regime.
Ultimately, this realisation was to give birth to a liberation movement representing all sections of the subject people and dedicated to the overthrow of
colonialism itself.

The Dark Years (1925–45)
These last isolated flickers of revolt heralded a dark period for the Namibian
people. The South African regime cynically flouted its obligations under the
Mandate and exploited its possession to the full. It was now that the dogged

persistence of the traditional leaders played its part in preserving the spirit of resistance. The Herero waged an unremitting struggle, one which continues to the present day, against their removal from the few areas of good farmland they had secured to the dreaded sandveld. Having been granted good grazing land around Orumbo by the Germans in 1913, the Herero were ordered by the South Africans to make way for white farmers. In the words of Festus Kandjou, a principal Herero spokesman in the 1940s:

> The people at first refused to leave Orumbo, but then they came from Windhoek and set our houses and gardens on fire. Although the houses were burned, we remained at Orumbo for some time. But most of our cattle were on the other side of the fence, and they were not allowed to return to Orumbo. So in this way, in the end, we were obliged to leave.

At every move, Chief Kutako and other traditional leaders throughout Namibia confronted the officials of the regime, exposing its self-seeking exploitation and making clear the sufferings of the people. In 1924, the government offered the Herero unoccupied land near Epukiro. But when Herero delegates inspected it and reported it to be of good quality, the regime promptly appropriated it and drove the Herero further east into the sandveld around Aminuis.

> Within six months the cattle began dying in hundreds and thousands. I then took a sample of the grass and the number of the cattle which had died to Windhoek . . . 'Perhaps,' they said, 'the cattle disease will die out' or 'the cattle will get used to the district', or I must 'learn to master the disease'.

With supreme cynicism, upon each removal the government handed over to white settlers boreholes and reservoirs which the Herero had erected out of their own hard-saved community funds, and refused any compensation. The testimony of Herero, Damara and Nama leaders, then and later, demonstrates that such tenacious defiance of the regime's exploitative land police was common to all Namibians.

The Formative Phase of Nationalist Resistance (1946–60)

The Second World War marked a turning point in the Namibian people's struggle for freedom. Thousands of auxiliaries returned battle-hardened and victorious from the frontline, their eyes opened to a new dimension of co-existence and freedom. The late 1940s and the 1950s were the formative phase in the building of the modern national liberation movement in Namibia. Opposition to colonialism emerged in four main fields of active resistance: within the traditional leadership, in the churches, amongst educated people and intellectuals and workers in the main urban and mining centres. During this period (1946–60), the stragety of struggle was transformed from weak and localised attempts at self-defence against the excesses of colonial oppression to a widespread commitment to national liberation by revolutionary armed struggle.

Traditional Leaders and the U.N.

Traditional leaders, especially amongst the Herero, provided an invaluable link between the early resistance to colonisation and the rise of the national liberation movement. After 1945, it was the courage and determination of men like Hosea Kutako and David Witbooi which gave the anti-colonial movement its initial impetus. Despite constant intimidation by the colonial regime, they held consistently to the democratic aspirations of their people. In the consultations which preceded the Herero's first petition to the U.N., no decision was taken until the issue had been fully debated in Maharero and Kutako's advisory councils, by delegates from other reserves and the urban locations, and by the people themselves at a series of meetings.

Later, building on their initial success at the U.N., Kutako and other leading Herero formed a Council of Chiefs to watch, publicise and protest each new act of oppression by the colonial administration. The Council, although mainly concerned with Herero interests, tried to link with other traditional leaders and co-opted advisers from the small but growing number of educated Namibians. Each instance of colonial oppression which came to its attention led to a deputation of protest or a petition to the U.N. exposing the nature of South African rule. By 1960, 120 petitions a year were reaching the U.N.

When, in 1946, the South African regime organised a farcical 'referendum' in support of its claim for annexation, the Herero took the lead in bringing the opposition of the people to the forum of the U.N. To their Chief, Frederick Maharero, exiled in Botswana, came an urgent plea early in 1946: 'The heritage of your fathers' orphans is about to be taken from them . . . We are being asked that our land be joined to the Union, but we have refused . . .' On behalf of the Herero, Hosea Kutako demanded that the U.N. itself should conduct the referendum. The regime rejected his request, then refused him permission to send four delegates to the U.N. to put their case. In desperation, on 18 March 1946, Kutako cabled the U.N. direct: 'We want our country to be returned to us', and a little later: 'Please let the United Nations be informed again that in South Africa and in Bechuanaland we would like to be under the British Crown; that we deny the incorporation of the country into the Union of South Africa.'

Refused representation by the regime, Maharero and Kutako briefed the Rev. Michael Scott to lobby on their behalf at the U.N. Other Namibian leaders supported the Herero position. As David Witbooi, son of Hendrik, told Scott, 'the Herero people and I fought many battles against one another. But . . . we have now made peace. Since then and up to today we live as brothers.' In his petition to the U.N., he spoke for the Nama people: 'We ask and entreat, let us be the subjects of the United Nations Organisation. . . . We

167

do not want to be incorporated into the Union.' And the Ovambo although, deliberately deceived by the officials conducting the referendum, implicitly rejected South African rule. A leading Ovambo reported that 'they had said ... that their country should fall under the British Government, not that it should fall under the Union ... Nothing was mentioned about the incorporation into the Union of South Africa.' And the Damara replied to the South African officials: 'Our country will not be joined to yours. We shall only wait until our children are educated, then we shall see whether they do not bring us freedom ... You say you would like to be the trustee of this country. We say we should like the big nations to be the trustee.'

After 30 years of South African rule, the people's rejection was unanimous. In solidarity came representations from Chief Tshekedi Khama of Botswana and Dr. A.B. Xuma of the African National Congress of South Africa, who cabled: 'We have long experience of South Africa's policies [and] would not like hundreds of thousands more innocent victims to be brought under South Africa's race- and colour-dominated policies.' This first intervention at the U.N. was instrumental in defeating South Africa's attempt to secure sovereignty over Namibia by annexation.

The Emancipation of the Churches

The first stirrings of nationalist anti-colonial sentiment were also beginning to penetrate popular ideology and culture. The people's early efforts to take control of their own cultural life prefigured and later reinforced the political drive towards national liberation. Prominent in this field of struggle was the movement for religious autonomy and democracy.

Although missionaries were amongst the first to penetrate Namibian society and their ideological influence was powerful, pre-colonial Namibian rulers had been careful not to surrender complete control to them. When their resident missionaries overstepped the mark, both Jonker Afrikaner and Moses Witbooi, father of Hendrik, took over their religious functions themselves. The great Hendrik Witbooi saw himself as divinely appointed, a prophet figure with no need of foreign missionary help. Indeed, few Herero or Ovambo adopted Christianity before the colonial conquest.

After colonisation, Christianity rapidly became the mass religion of all sections of Namibian society. Henceforth, the focal point of struggle was to be local autonomy. Two missionary societies had secured a near monopoly, in the centre and south the Rhenish Mission Society (R.M.S.) and in Ovamboland the Finnish Mission Society (F.M.S.) In the south, black church assistants formed the Nama Onderwysers en Evangelistebond at Maltahohe in 1926. The stubborn refusal of the R.M.S. to allow blacks to train as pastors caused rising tension. When in 1946 the Society seemed prepared to hand over to the pro-apartheid Nederlandse Gereformeerde Kerk (N.G.K.) rather than set up an independent church, more than a third of its members and two-thirds of its black assistants in the south seceded and joined the black-controlled American Methodist Episcopal Church (A.M.E.C.), which had already started a small mission in Windhoek. With bitterness the people saw the churches and schools which they had built with their own hands taken from them as the R.M.S. asserted its legal rights to the property. With unremitting self-sacrifice the people built and ran new schools for their children, braving the implacable hostility of the South African administration.

Amongst the Herero, dissatisfaction was also stirring. When, after the South African invasion in 1915, they repossessed their stolen lands and cattle, the influence of the R.M.S. had simply melted away. As the full weight of South African repression bore down on them, the Herero pinned their faith on the prophecies of the Garveyite movement. Soon disillusioned, however, they turned once more to the religion of their forefathers in an effort to preserve their communal solidarity. The R.M.S. made a partial comeback, but gradually its autocratic colonial spirit pushed the Herero towards a decisive break. Finally, on 25 August 1955 (the eve of their national day), Hosea Kutako declared the formation of an independent 'Church of the Community' (*Oruuano*). In contrast to the Nama secession, however, some Herero evangelists remained loyal to the mission and the break was a movement of the people, supported by their traditional leaders, to harmonise their adopted religion with their cultural and political aspirations. 'We knew that our church belonged to the people. That gave us heart . . . This church has not been imported from Europe, it has arisen on African soil. It is a church for the indigenous population of Africa.'

Shaken by these body blows, the mission began tentatively to decolonise themselves at last. Relentless pressure from Germany forced the R.M.S. missionaries to give their church local autonomy in 1957 as the Evangeliese Lutherse Kerk (ELK). Ten years later, it became fully independent. In Ovamboland, the F.M.S. had largely safeguarded itself from secession by training black pastors (the first seven were ordained in 1925, and by 1942 there were as many as 31 in the field). In 1956, the mission became the independent Evangeliese Lutherse Owambokavangokerk (ELOK). In 1960, the synod elected its first black leader, Bishop Leonard Auala, who has played, and continues to play, an important role in the liberation struggle.

The superior resources and training of the ELK enabled it to survive its crises and recover. After the first flood of enthusiasm, the breakaway Nama and Herero churches declined or fragmented as the energies of the people and their leaders were increasingly channelled into the drive for national liberation. As early as 1956, some Herero pastors of the R.M.S. had opposed the formation of a separate Herero church on a principled basis: 'We are *one* church in *one* land amongst *all* black peoples.' In 1963, the ELOK and the ELK combined their theological training at the latter's seminary in Otjimbingue, renamed the Paulinum — a symbol and an inspiration to the fostering of national consciousness. Further co-operation between the two leading black churches followed, and church leaders began to speak out against colonial oppression.

Early Nationalism and Trade Unionism
By the early 1950s, the changing political climate was turning the handful

of educated Namibians into political militants. Inspired by the 1952 Defiance Campaign in South Africa, when blacks in their thousands openly courted arrest in protest against unjust laws, a group of Namibian students in schools and colleges in South Africa formed the South West African Student Body (S.W.A.S.B.). In Namibia and South Africa, young militants canvassed the possibilities for transcending the old sectional divisions in an aggressive and popular nationalism. In 1955, they formed the culturally orientated South West Africa Progressive Association (SWAPA), 'a small club of teachers, clerical workers and other intellectuals in Windhoek'. For a short period in 1959 until it was banned, they published the *South West News*, the first black newspaper to appear in Namibia.

The activists argued their position with the traditional leadership. Indeed, one of them, Jariretundu Kozonguizi, was co-opted on to the Council of Chiefs in 1954, and in early 1959 was chosen as its petitioner at the U.N. But despite the sympathy of the Council, the plan for a national independence movement was still no more than an aspiration in the minds of small groups of activists. It lacked both a platform and a mass base.

It was the Namibian working class which was to provide that base, and in particular the most deeply exploited section of Namibian society, the contract labour force. Collective action had long been a well-tried tactic amongst contract workers. Even official reports made regular mention of strikes, walk-outs and go-slows at the mines and processing plants in which contract workers were concentrated. But the savagely repressive labour code, which made breach of contract a criminal offence for all workers, whether or not a written contract had been signed, allowed little chance of success to this tactic in isolated plant-based struggles. At the first sign of trouble employers would call in the colonial police, who, if they did not beat the workers into submission, would arrest and charge them for striking, or deport them to the appropriate reserve, there possibly to receive further punishment at the hands of puppet tribal authorities. To take but one instance: when several hundred contract workers went on strike at Walvis Bay in June 1962, 55 were arrested and 54 were sentenced to R60 (a full year's wage for an average contract worker) or three months' imprisonment.

In such a hostile environment, trade unionism never took root in Namibia. The Luderitz I.C.U. (Industrial and Commercial Workers Union) branch lasted only a few years in the early 1920s, and the occasional benefit society which sprang up did not usually last long. A tame railway union, the Non-European Railway Staff Association, formed in 1949, claimed a majority of black railway workers as members. But it was clearly a tool of the management. 'The Association co-operates to the best of its ability in combatting absenteeism,' explained the Railway Welfare Officer. 'There are no standard grievances . . . but numerous petitions and minor complaints have been brought to the notice of the Railway authorities and could in most cases be remedied.' Not surprisingly, the Association sank without trace.

Unionism of a wholly different order brought about the first real test of a trade union-based strategy in the early 1950s. In 1949, the militant Cape-

based Food and Canning Workers Union sent its president to organise the
fish canning workers at Luderitz. He was followed in 1952 by the redoubt-
able Ray Alexander. A branch was formed, and union officials probed pay
and conditions and pressed for protective industrial legislation. The regime's
response was brutal. No sooner had the Union negotiated an agreement
than police attacked and dispersed the branch meeting. A witness testified:
'I was present there and they ordered me out of the place and terrorised the
workers, our committee members and shop stewards, and forced us to break
up the branch . . .' Alexander was banned, and contact between Luderitz
and Cape Town was throttled. The contract workers mounted large strikes
in 1952 and 1953, in the second of which police opened fire, killing three
workers. The regime's reaction to genuine trade unionism was massive repression, and the lesson was not lost on the contract workers. Isolated struggles
could be picked off one by one; and an open local leadership could be
hounded into ineffectiveness.

> Even without formal trade unions, time and again,
> contract workers proved well able to mount large-
> scale actions and strikes and to articulate clear
> demands. One such instance at Tsumeb shows dra-
> matically the spirit of militant solidarity amongst
> the workers. On the morning of 17 October 1954
> the police raided the compound, supposedly in a
> drive against home beer-brewing. The workers
> defended themselves, and when the police returned
> in the afternoon forced them to flee, though not
> before they had shot dead one of the workers. The
> next day the whole work-force came out on strike,
> and only agreed to return when the management
> undertook to pay the fines of those who had been
> arrested and to transport them back from the
> magistrate's court. The workers also won improved
> rations and an increase in basic pay.
> *Rundle Commission, 1955, pp.3–7*

By the 1950s, contract workers from the north, who as prisoners of
SWANLA were the most deeply exploited section of the black workers,
were beginning to organise against SWANLA itself. In November 1952, a
letter to a colonial newspaper from an Ovambo worker laid the blame for
the deepening poverty and underdevelopment in Ovamboland firmly at the
door of the contract labour system. 'The whole Ovambo tribe is a fixed
property of SWANLA (a human trade firm) and are the cheapest labourers
for all the employers . . . The Ovambo tribe has not got a mouthpiece to
interpret its unsolved problems.'

One of the workers' chief grievances was that at the police road-block at Namutoni all the workers returning to Ovamboland were searched and many were systematically robbed by the colonial police. This was a particularly vindictive practice, for the workers' possessions usually represented their entire savings, carefully scraped together from pitifully small wages. In January 1954, a pioneer workers' leader, Eliaser Tuhadeleni (now imprisoned on Robben Island) made written protests to the police, to no avail. A few months later, in April 1954, a courageous Anglican priest, Theophilus Hamuntubangela, collected evidence from hundreds of workers about this persecution and sent off a letter of protest to the U.N. In 1955, the authorities put him on trial in an attempt to destroy his persistent exposure of South African oppression. But the people whose cause he championed turned out in their thousands in his support. As soon as the trial began the crowd lifted him shoulder high of 'this is our hero . . . this is our fighter'; there were shouts and the crowd thundered its applause. The trial judge, who had been imported from Windhoek, hastily withdrew, returned to Windhoek and persuaded the Anglican bishop to transfer Rev. Hamuntubangela there. Even then the priest's spirit was undaunted and he began to hold regular political meetings with Sam Nujoma and other political leaders. In 1958, although he was by then a sick man, the colonial regime was forced to deport him back to Ovamboland once more. Leadership of this calibre and the mass response it evoked were but a foretaste of what was to come; the time was right for a more concerted drive against the structure of colonial repression.

OPO, SWANU and the Windhoek Massacre

When activists began campaigning in 1959 for the abolition of the contract labour system itself, they met with a ready and immediate response amongst contract workers. The plan was born amongst a group of Namibian workers and students in Cape Town, whom in 1957, Herman ja Toivo had organised into the Ovamboland People's Congress, renamed in 1958 Ovamboland People's Organisation (OPO). They were given support and assistance by members of the Communist Party, the Liberal Party and the African National Congress.

Although it was decided that the contract labour system was the most immediate and burning campaign priority, the founding group was by no means exclusively Ovambo, and from the outset had the wider cause of national liberation in view. Ja Toivo himself already had vast experience of working under Namibian and South African conditions, as a serviceman in the Second World War (rising to the rank of corporal) as a Rand gold miner, as a clerk on a manganese mine, and as a railway worker in Cape Town. Late in 1958, ja Toivo smuggled out to the U.N. a tape containing oral evidence of South African oppression. The South African Special Branch tracked him down and ordered him to leave the country within 72 hours. The time had come to launch the new organisation in Namibia itself. In December 1958, ja Toivo travelled north to Ovamboland, briefing and consulting Nama, Herero and other leaders on the way. Despite house arrest and periodic imprisonment after his arrival in Ovamboland, ja Toivo campaigned and recruited tirelessly for the new organisation.

Herman ja Toivo.

In April 1959, Sam Nujoma and Jacob Kuhangua launched OPO in Windhoek. Membership was open to all Namibians who agreed with its aims. The experience of the Walvis Bay branch gives some measure of the explosive impact of the campaign to abolish the contract labour system. A successful go-slow and strike in a fish cannery in January 1959 had raised the confidence of contract workers in their collective power and had thrown up a grassroots leadership. On 25 June, Sam Nujoma came down to Walvis Bay and addressed mass meetings in the main compounds. 'Almost everybody came out. The word got around fast and the men were eager to hear.' Nujoma explained the reasons for the formation of OPO and its main objective, the abolition of the contract labour system. He urged the workers to build a strong branch in Walvis Bay. 'We must work together — you, me, all of us — to end our oppression.' When he finished some of the comrades spoke up, generally expressing strong approval, though a few had fears and doubts. 'We are encouraged to know where OPO stands,' said one worker. 'I think most of us would join OPO right now.'

Three months later, according to the Branch Secretary, Vinnia Ndadi, 'we had a membership of several thousand [the vast majority of the contract work force] and had collected over £800 in subscriptions.' The branch was organised into compound committees, with branch meetings of delegates from each at regular intervals. Despite employer and police harrassment, from the outset the branch soon developed an effective and representative leadership structure. Discussion groups formed on the factory floor and in

the compounds. 'We discussed politics whenever we could; talked about day-to-day problems, news from Windhoek and the rest of Africa, and our dreams of freedom in Namibia.'

Painstaking organisation and recruitment rapidly established OPO branches in many locations and contract worker compounds throughout Namibia. In its early days, OPO's principal task was to consolidate its position in the ranks of the contract workers on whom its national campaign was centred. By this time, however, other political forces were also entering the field. On the eve of ja Toivo's expulsion from South Africa in December 1958, Kozonguizi approached him suggesting that OPO be merged into a wider nationalist organisation based on regional congresses in the south, centre and north of Namibia. Notwithstanding his departure into exile two months later, Kozonguizi was involved in the formation in May 1959 of the South West Africa National Union (SWANU), an alliance between urban youth and intellectuals and the Herero Chiefs' Council. In September, the entry of several leaders from OPO and other organisations to its executive broadened its national character.

The new united front was soon to receive its baptism under fire. For some time, the Windhoek City Council had been preparing to remove the entire black population of the 'Old Location' to a new apartheid-style township named Katutura — a monstrosity of social engineering in which residence was to be ethnically zoned and every aspect of life subject to rigid control. The residents of the Old Location, already on the borderlines of poverty, faced crippling increases in rents and transport costs. In the face of total official intransigence, OPO and SWANU leaders mounted a joint campaign, organising deputations and meetings through which people could express their frustration and bitterness.

Finally, the people's patience snapped. The decision was taken to boycott municipal services, including the buses and the beer hall, a prime source of municipal profits. Women in the Location took the initiative in mobilising the inhabitants. On 9 December, a procession of women marched from the Location and, defying police tear-gas, demonstrated in front of the residence of the Administrator, the regime's top official in Namibia. On the morning of the 10 December, pickets were out in force — from the start the boycott was completely effective. The Location Superintendent responded by calling in the South African Police and military units with armoured cars. With supreme arrogance, municipal officials and police refused to negotiate, demanded that the boycott end by the following day and provocatively arrested three pickets. Angry crowds gathered in the streets. Then, without warning, a police unit opened fire. The people defended themselves, but stones and bottles were little use against sten-guns. At least 11 Namibians were killed that night and 54 wounded, two of whom later died. Notwithstanding this brutal repression, it was not until August 1968 that the last element of resistance was broken and the remaining inhabitants compelled to move to Katutura.

The Windhoek shootings — Namibia's 'Sharpeville' — transformed the

perspectives of liberation in Namibia. In the clearest possible terms the
occupation regime had shown that it would ruthlessly crush all attempts
at peaceful persuasion and popular mobilisation. In the aftermath of the
shootings, police intensified their repression of the nationalist leadership.
Kuhangua was deported to Angola and Nujoma to Ovamboland, but the
latter escaped to lead the liberation movement from exile. Louis Nelengani,
Nathanill Mbaeva and many other leaders of the emerging nationalist organisation were imprisoned, banned or restricted.

Figure 27 – Apartheid in practice: residential apartheid in Windhoek.

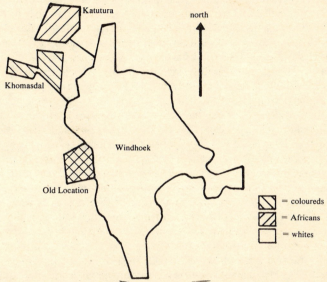

Note: Between 1959 and 1968 the apartheid regime systematically destroyed the multi-racial Old Location
and threw nearly all blacks living in Windhoek into separate ethnic ghettoes. In Windhoek proper the
30,000 whites live in spacious suburbs with generous amenities. In the locations the 15,000 'coloureds' in
Khomasdal and 40,000 'bantu' in Katutura live crammed together in tiny municipal houses with few
facilities of any kind.

Source: Derived from Pendleton 1974, map B.

The fragile national alliance of opposition forces did not long survive
the confrontation. The Chiefs' Council distrusted the radicalism of the
younger men who formed the nucleus of SWANU. Largely an outgrowth of
S.W.A.S.B. and SWAPA, SWANU itself possessed limited and sectional
support, principally in the centre of Namibia and from students and teachers.
OPO, however, had already developed a mass base amongst workers and a
party organisation on a national scale; nor, despite the priority of its contract
labour campaign, did it lack support in membership or leaders from outside
the contract work-force. Its leadership recognised that the abolition of the
contract labour system could not be achieved outside the wider national
struggle for independence from colonial oppression.

Building the National Liberation Movement (1960–70)

The Formation of SWAPO and the Launching of Revolutionary Armed Struggle

On 19 April 1960, OPO was formally reconstituted as the South West Africa People's Organisation (SWAPO). Its central objective was the liberation of the Namibian people from colonial oppression and exploitation, and to that end the organisation was broadened into a national united front. SWAPO continued to allow tactical co-operation with separately organised political tendencies, but it was now for the first time unequivocally the leading political force in Namibia, and the only one to be nationally organised and representative. The organisation's solid roots in the Namibian working class enabled it both to survive the difficult years of repression in the 1960s and to emerge as the authentic liberation movement of the Namibian people.

SWAPO's principal concern in the early 1960s was to build the party structure nationally and to channel the grievances and aspirations of workers and peasants into political commitment to the struggle. In Ovamboland, party organisers drew hundreds to their first mass meetings in the middle of 1960. The peasants responded enthusiastically to the two cardinal rallying points of SWAPO's campaign: national unity and self-reliance in the struggle for independence. At every turn SWAPO cadres exposed the oppressive policies of the regime and its tribal lackeys. Since the authorities had failed to provide adequate relief for the prevailing drought, SWAPO bought and distributed grain to those in need. By acting as local advisers in place of the headmen, who had forfeited the people's trust by collaborating with the regime, SWAPO cadres won the confidence of the peasants for the party and its programme. Soon a network of cadres and committees was established throughout Ovamboland and much of the rest of the country.

In the aftermath of the Windhoek massacre, the inability of U.N. resolutions to change South African policy in the slightest degree deepened the disillusionment of the Namibian people. In the words of its leaders, 'SWAPO had come to the realisation that to rely on U.N. intervention to liberate Namibia was to leave this liberation to mere chance.' SWAPO decided that political and military efforts in pursuit of national liberation were not contradictory, but, rather, that they were complementary and should be pursued concurrently. Accordingly, at a national congress at Windhoek in 1961, it was resolved to prepare for the eventual armed struggle. In succeeding years, hundreds of cadres were recruited and sent abroad for military training. Activists inside the country began to establish a supporting infrastructure for the coming struggle. In 1964–65, the first militants returned as trained guerrillas to set up rural bases for training the local people. In October of that year, the Caprivi African National Union (CANU) merged with SWAPO, closing a regional gap and expanding the base of popular support in a hitherto isolated area.

The World Court's failure to deliver a judgement, made public on 18 July 1966, finally removed the last pretext for holding back the launching of the

armed struggle. That same day, a statement from SWAPO's external Headquarters in Dar-es-Salaam declared that the Court's inexcusable refusal to
act 'would relieve Namibians once and for all from any illusions which they
may have harboured about the United Nations as some kind of a saviour in
their plight . . . We have no alternative but to rise in arms and bring about our
liberation.' The first military engagement took place on 26 August when
SWAPO fighters from the Omgulumbashe base camp in Ovamboland engaged
South African forces in battle. A month later, on 27 September, a guerrilla
unit attacked the large government administrative complex at Oshikango
and burned it to the ground. Other targets were the puppet chiefs and their
bodyguards and government installations in the populated areas along the
northern border and the Caprivi Strip. Fighting units penetrated deep into
the white farming area around Grootfontein, causing a degree of panic
and confusion amongst the hitherto complacent settlers.

The launching of the armed struggle brought new problems for the
liberation movement in both the military and political fields. The logistical
difficulties in supplying and communicating with the frontline were
formidable. Most of Namibia's northern border was occupied by the
Portuguese colonial regime in Angola, whose close collaboration with South
Africa was notorious. In addition, all the inhabited areas of Namibia except
the Eastern Caprivi were separated from the nearest friendly base area in
Zambia by hundreds of miles of dry, sparsely populated country. Thus, new
recruits and returning guerrillas faced a long and dangerous journey through
territory constantly scoured by the enemy's Western-equipped air power.
Their equipment consisted only of what they could carry on foot; and
communications with base areas were at best tenuous.

Under these conditions, the first phase of the armed struggle necessarily
took the form of small-scale guerrilla warfare. Equipped only with light arms,
bazookas and land mines, the small, highly mobile fighting units of SWAPO
ambushed South African patrols and convoys, mined military roads and, less
frequently, raided enemy posts. Despite usually having to restrict military
activity each year to the rainy season in order to render enemy trackers
ineffective, the level of sustained campaigning has always been higher than
South African propaganda has cared to admit. In one year (October 1971 to
September 1972), SWAPO forces estimated that they killed or wounded
between 150 and 200 South African troops. Highly effective landmining
combined with well-planned raids in strength enabled the guerrillas to retain
the initiative.

Tactical experience in battle was translated into improved fighting
methods. Early setbacks; in which a number of freedom fighters were
captured, exposed the vulnerability of large, permanent base camps in the
war zone. As a result, SWAPO freedom fighters began to locate arms
caches separately, made only temporary transit camps and changed the
sites of both at frequent intervals. Arms and equipment captured from the
enemy were put to effective use.

Because of logistical problems the freedom fighters depended from the start on the active support of the people amongst whom they were based. It was, moreover, SWAPO policy to integrate the military and the political arms of the struggle in the war zone. In selection, training and the conduct of the armed struggle, the motto has been 'it is always politics which leads the gun.' SWAPO's freedom fighters have always been first and foremost armed political militants.

In the fighting zones, cadres returning from training abroad integrated into the local population. Some were assigned to enter the political organisation, to penetrate areas beyond the frontline, or to recruit and train local volunteers. Many lived indistinguishably from the local peasantry. The freedom fighters were largely dependent on local party cells and sympathisers to organise the provision of their everyday supplies. The people were also their eyes and ears, shielding them from the occupation forces and providing them with essential military intelligence. But this was a reciprocal relationship. Some freedom fighters were also assigned to provide civilian services which the regime did not provide adequately, in particular medical assistance and literacy teaching.

The extent to which the local population responded to the SWAPO campaign was evident in the increasingly repressive measures which the occupation forces imposed on the Namibian people, particularly along the northern border. In the face of their refusal to inform on SWAPO cadres, the South African Police and their tribal collaborators stepped up their harrassment, interrogation and torture of the civilians in the war zone. Along the Okavango River, a number of 'security villages' were set up into which villagers were forcibly herded under curfew. In the Caprivi, massacres of villagers were reported on several occasions. In October 1968, after a successful SWAPO attack on a South African military camp in the Eastern Caprivi, South African troops took savage reprisals on nearby villages, killing 63 peasants and rounding up hundreds more for interrogation and torture. As a result, some 4,000 peasants sought refuge in Botswana and Zambia late in 1968, and others followed at regular intervals.

The increasingly widespread tactics of harrassment and terror employed by the occupation regime only served to sharpen Namibians' commitment to the struggle and their perception of its priorities. The repression of all anti-colonial political activity repeatedly drove home the necessity for armed revolutionary struggle. This issue, above all others, exposed the political colours both of other professed anti-colonial groups and of the regime's tribal collaborators in the reserves and bantustans, whose whole-hearted defence of South African colonialism aroused the special hatred of the people they oppressed. At the trial of freedom fighters in July–August 1969, the first to be held in Windhoek, crowded public galleries testified to the keenness with which blacks followed the course of the liberation war — so much so that the next trial, in 1970, was held in secret.

The move to armed struggle, together with escalating oppression, changed the conditions of political mobilisation, both in and outside the war zone.

Right up to 1966, SWAPO continued to function openly with local branches and and a public leadership. But the repeated arrest and imprisonment or restriction of leaders, particularly after the first guerrilla attacks, hampered on-going political work inside the country. And the clamp-down on public meetings from 1963 largely cut out the principal means of mass mobilisation and information. After the World Court ruling in July 1966 the regime progressively applied South African security legislation to Namibia as well. As a result, SWAPO was increasingly compelled to operate underground. But even after 1966, the regime did not dare to ban the party formally. SWAPO has therefore continued to exploit every opportunity to function openly as well, in order to inform and mobilise the people and to expose the workings of colonialism in its dying days.

The Tanga Consultative Congress
At the end of 1969, unable to hold its Annual National Congress inside Namibia because of the forced exile of many of its leaders, SWAPO called together a Consultative Congress at Tanga in Tanzania. It brought together delegates from all the organs of SWAPO, including the cells and branches inside Namibia. Meeting between 26 December 1969 and 2 January 1970, the Tanga Congress reviewed the progress of the struggle, made changes in policy and organisation, replaced or re-elected the leadership and strengthened its dedication to the liberation of the Namibian people from all forms of oppression and exploitation. To give effect to the Tanga strategy and programme of action, the party reformed and broadened its organisation. Structures were created or reactivated to give expression to the struggle against particular forms of exploitation alongside the general movement for national liberation. The Youth League, open to party members between the ages of 6 and 35, was to play a vanguard role in the struggles which erupted during and after the contract workers' strike in 1971–72. The Elders' Council provided for liaison with traditional leaders, symbolic representatives of the people's long record of resistance to colonialism and exploitation. The Women's Council sought to assist the struggle of women against their double oppression, not only as the group most deeply exploited by colonialism but also as victims of male domination. SWAPO's military wing was re-organised and in 1973 renamed the People's Liberation Army of Namibia (PLAN).

By the start of the 1970s, SWAPO was poised to take the struggle into a higher phase. Out of the long series of encounters and painful new beginnings which had characterised the 1960s, it had emerged battle-hardened, its commitment to liberation undaunted and its strategy clearly formulated.

On 18 July 1970, Hosea Kutako died at the age of 104. Kutako's lifetime had spanned the entire epoch of colonialism in Namibia. In 1904, he fought as an officer in the Herero army and was taken prisoner by the Germans. His leadership of the Herero became a national symbol of the people's resistance. The people of Namibia were fortunate to have had a leader such as Chief Hosea Katjikururume Kutako during this early period of the liberation struggle. He not only provided a sound and courageous leadership for the

179

The 'Terrorism' Trial 1967—68

South Africa's response to the launching of the
armed struggle was to stage the first of its political
show trials of SWAPO leaders and members. After
the first armed clashes in Ovamboland, the occupation regime poured in troops and rounded up
hundreds of Namibians, amongst them many
SWAPO cadres, for torture and interrogation. On
7 August 1967, 37 Namibian patriots, including
founder-member Herman ja Toivo and pioneer
workers' leader Eliaser Tuhadeleni, were put on
trial in Pretoria, far from the land of their birth,
under the notorious Terrorism Act. This evil law
had been enacted only a few days previously and
made retroactive to 1962 specifically in order to
convict the Namibian patriots. The trial itself was
a complete mockery.

All the prisoners had been tortured for months
on end in South African prisons to compel them
to sign 'confessions' — so severely in fact that one
of the 37, Ephraim Kamati Kaporo, died in
hospital before the end of the trial. Ja Toivo himself suffered such systematic and repeated beatings, sleep deprivation and 'statue' torture that
after some weeks he lost his memory. Yet it was
on these 'confessions' and the evidence of witnesses similarly tortured that the South African
kangaroo court convicted 34 of the Namibians.
On 8 February 1968 it sentenced 20 of them to
life imprisonment, nine to 20 years' hard labour
and five to five years suspended.

These patriots, together with many others
imprisoned since then, remain to this day incarcerated under inhuman conditions on Robben
Island. But if the apartheid regime thought that
it could terrorise freedom-loving Namibians into
submission by humiliating and gaoling their
leaders, it was sadly mistaken. Rounding on their
gaolers and torturers, the patriots explained in
clear terms why SWAPO had taken up the armed
struggle and they also rededicated themselves to
the cause of total liberation in words which have
given inspiration to a whole generation of free-

Johannes Nankudhu

Kaleb Tjipahura

Petrus Kamati

Kambua Kashikola

Malakia Ushona

David Shimuefeleni

Betuel Nunjango

Lazarus Zachariah

dom-inspired Namibians.* In the words of Eliaser
Tuhadeleni:

'I came to realise that we could expect no progress
from those who ruled us and that my children
could expect no better life than I had. A peaceful
struggle was not possible. We of SWAPO were not
allowed to hold meetings and our leaders were
victimised. I believe that we must take up arms
for the freedom of my people, to liberate them from
poverty and ignorance. And so I went into the
forests with the others. Our struggle against South
Africa is an unequal one. I have seen the power
of South Africa at Omgulumbashe, but David
slew Goliath because he had right on his side, and
we Namibians have faith that we, too, have right
on our side.'

* We reprint Herman ja Toivo's speech from the dock
in an appendix.

Striking contract workers mass at the compound gate in Katutura

Herero people for whom he was the traditional head, but boosted an early alliance of anti-South African forces, in which he himself took a central role, incorporating ethnic and community representatives from most parts of Namibia. Through tireless petitioning of the U.N., dogged resistance to South African land robbery and constant exposure of South African misrule, their joint action forced a unity of purpose amongst the Namibian people in the crucial formative phase of their liberation struggle.

It was Kutako who inspired the early appearances at the U.N. and who provided a rallying point against the regime's first attempts to extend its notorious policy of apartheid to Namibia. Kutako's prayer at the grave of former Herero chiefs at Okahandja expressed the heartfelt cry of all the Namibian people: 'Oh lord, help us who roam about. Help us who have been placed in Africa and have no home of our own. Give us back our dwelling place.'

Tributes to Kutako came from far and wide. In London the SWAPO Representative for the U.K. and Western Europe, Peter Katjavivi, organised a memorial service which was attended by British supporters of the Namibian liberation struggle, and all Namibians living in Britain united in this moment across party affiliations. Nothing captured Kutako's commitment to national unity more appropriately than his request that he be buried, not in the grave of his forefathers, but alongside the great 19th Century Nama leader, Jonker Afrikaner. Although he did not live to enjoy the freedom for which he unflinchingly fought in his lifetime, at his passing the Namibian people were on the threshold of a new era of struggle.

7. From Tanga to the General Strike: A Revolutionary Turning-Point, 1970–71

The dawning of the 1970s marked the high tide of South Africa's imperialist ambitions in Africa. Kissinger's 'tilt' towards the white south and the election in 1970 of a Conservative Government in Britain pledged to resume arms sales to South Africa assured the minority regimes of the active support of two of the major Western powers, while the third, France, was skilfully orchestrating the subversion of pan African unity through 'dialogue'. South African emissaries attempted to buy off African support for the liberation movement with fulsome promises of economic 'aid', and pro-government intellectuals championed the dream of a Southern African 'common market'. The new-found self-confidence of the South African Government expressed itself in open aggression towards its 'buffer states'. In the same year that Vorster was feted by Banda in Malawi (May 1970), the apartheid regime interfered in the internal affairs of Lesotho in support of Chief Jonathan; maintained its garrison in Zimbabwe to prop up the illegal settler state; tried to stop Botswana's plan for a lifeline bridge across the Zambezi to Zambia; and openly threatened to raid neighbouring states if this was in its military interests.

In Namibia, South African legislation in 1968 and 1969 had prepared the ground both for the full-scale implementation of apartheid in the territory and for its virtual incorporation into South Africa as a fifth province. But the decade of the 1970s had also opened with the Tanga Congress and the fruits of SWAPO's revised strategy began to filter through. The rainy season of 1970–71 witnessed a marked escalation of the guerrilla war. SWAPO freedom fighters were not only active throughout the Caprivi Strip, but regularly ambushed and mined the supply lines of the South African occupation forces along and to the south of the Okavango River. Their most notable victory was the complete destruction in December 1970 of the South African army camp at Andara.

On the international front, the U.N. Security Council was at last moving into action. In 1969, it endorsed the General Assembly's revocation of the Mandate in 1966; and when South Africa refused to comply with its order to withdraw from Namibia, referred the issue in July 1970 to the International Court of Justice (I.C.J.) for an Advisory Opinion which would in effect test the legality of U.N. authority over Namibia. This time, the

Namibian people themselves, through SWAPO, were actively involved in determining their own destiny. South Africa's massive legal, diplomatic and propaganda effort met a resolute Namibian response both inside and outside the I.C.J. As the SWAPO journal *Namibia News* commented afterwards, 'If the people had not, through the armed struggle, shown such a strong determination to fight for freedom, would the outcome at the International Court of Justice this time have been the same?'

The World Court Ruling and the Mass Upsurge

The Advisory Opinion of the I.C.J., announced on 21 June 1971, was a complete and decisive vindication of the U.N. position. At last, after 25 years of equivocation, the rights of the U.N. as the lawful governing authority in Namibia had been put beyond legal doubt by the world's highest judicial body. The outcome was a seminal political event in the history of the struggle for national independence, because it destroyed the last vestige of legitimacy which South Africa could claim for its colonial administration. Namibians have never acknowledged the right of their colonisers to rule and exploit them. Now, throughout the country, the people responded with a massive show of support for the I.C.J.'s ruling. In towns and villages, at schools and churches, Namibians staged demonstrations and held meetings to demand the end of the South African occupation. In this new phase of mass mobilisation three sectors took a leading role: the churches, high school students and contract workers.

The principal Namibian churches responded to the patriotic aspirations of their members by taking, for the first time, a public stand against the continued occupation of their country by South Africa. Thinking to use them as propaganda tools against the U.N., the South Africans approached the leaders of the two Lutheran churches, Moderator Gowaseb of E.L.K. and Bishop Auala of E.L.O.K., between them representative of the vast majority of Christians in Namibia, for their opinion on the World Court's ruling. On 30 June, they got their answer, in the form of an Open Letter to the Prime Minister, signed by the two leaders on behalf of their Church Boards. They declared unequivocally: 'We believe that South Africa in its attempts to develop the country has failed to take cognizance of Human Rights as declared by the United Nations in the year 1948 with respect to the non-white population.' The letter listed a series of damning examples, and concluded:

> The Church Boards' urgent wish is that in terms of the declarations of the World Court and in co-operation with the United Nations, of which South Africa is a member, your government will seek a peaceful solution to the problems of our land and will see to it that Human Rights be put into operation and that South West Africa may become a self-sufficient and independent state.

Simultaneously, the Church Boards issued a pastoral letter, stating in clear language their opposition to apartheid.

> True peace does not allow people to hate each other. But we observe that our people are caught up with fear . . . In our opinion this fateful development is caused and upheld by the policy of apartheid. We believe that a false impression arises when it is stated that peace reigns in our country. The peace is maintained by forceful measures . . . Our purpose is to stand for the truth and for a better future for our people and races, even when it involves suffering for us.

The pastoral letter was read in every Lutheran church in the land. In a country, 80% of whose black population is Christian, its impact was profound. The two other major churches, the Anglicans and the Roman Catholics, gave their full and public support to the Lutherans' stand. 'The Christian Church, as the conscience of this nation, must now speak out with clarity and without fear,' stated Bishop Colin Winter on 25 July. 'Apartheid must be denounced as unacceptable before God.' Attacked in the colonialist press, Bishop Auala and Moderator Gowaseb, strong in the knowledge that they expressed the will of the people, replied:

> We find that our non-white congregation understand us well because we have referred to the true facts . . . Our own people who experience the actual conditions every day are grateful that the Church Councils have intervened on their behalf. We can, therefore, only stand by the words which we have released. . . We can do no other than to see South West Africa with all its ethnic groups as a unit . . . We must all of us together be independent in one country. This is what we asked of the government.

On 18 August, the two leaders, with members of their Church Boards, confronted the Prime Minister face to face in Windhoek. Unflinchingly, they expounded a searing indictment of apartheid in Namibia and re-affirmed their commitment to national unity and independence. This was courageous and inspiring leadership, and it brought the churches into the mainstream of the national liberation movement.

Nowhere was the mass upsurge of popular resistance more strongly expressed than in Ovamboland, South Africa's show-piece bantustan and the lynchpin of the notorious contract labour system. In January 1971, South Africa had offered the I.C.J. a plebiscite on its rule in Namibia, confident that the puppet tribal officials, with suitable police backing, would deliver a massive 'yes' vote from an area which contained nearly half the total population. A few days before the IC.J. gave its ruling, the authorities laid on a guided tour of Ovamboland for selected foreign pressmen, who duly produced glowing reports on the 'development' of the area and the political contentment of the 'tribesmen'.

The people did not waste much time in shattering that illusion. When the South African-nominated 'Chief Councillor' of the puppet bantustan government of Ovamboland claimed on the local propaganda radio that the people of Ovamboland were '100%' for the continued occupation of Namibia by South Africa, he was confronted in Ondangwa on 28 June by a delegation of Ovambo leaders in protest. 'We deplore your statement . . .', their declaration read, 'and your disregard of the World Court decision is non-acceptable to the entire Ovambo tribe.' Having spelt out in uncompromising detail the degradation of human rights under South African rule, it concluded:

> Ovambos pertinently want to bring it under the attention of the South African Government that they completely agree with the decision of the World Court that South Africa's continued presence in South West Africa is illegal. The Ovambos do not want to be guilty of recognising an illegal government of South Africa. Ovambos would rather suggest to Vorster and his company to create *whitestans* for Germans, Afrikaners and English — but not in Namibia.

The Chief Councillor was left speechless. At the same time, leaflets distributed in Katutura called on all Ovambos to reject the Chief Councillor's claim. 'There will be no justice under the present South African Government,' they stated, and added that 'these aims can only be achieved through the United Nations'.

Above all, it was students from the high schools who took the lead in the popular protest in Ovamboland. Students were active elsewhere in Namibia as well (and indeed 70 were expelled in September from the Augustineum Training College in Windhoek), but it was in the north that their militancy was especially marked. As *Namibia News* reported:

> The pupils in several of the schools, both mission schools and government schools, write 'Namibia' on the blackboard before lessons each morning. They refuse to learn Afrikaans because this is necessary only for working for South Africans. There have been strikes in many schools and in one school a letter was addressed to the United Nations which began like this: 'We welcome the World Court's decision, therefore we appeal to the United Nations to intervene in Namibia, because the South African Government is still continuing its apartheid in the territory.'

Schools throughout Ovamboland were in turmoil, with regular expulsions and police reprisals. On 2 August, 500 students from Ongwediva and the Anglican High School at St. Mary's, Odibo, marched through the centre of Ondangwa to present a letter to the Bantu Affairs overlord in the territory, Commissioner-General de Wet. In it, they protested against apartheid and the widespread violations under South African rule, and supported the World

Court ruling. When they took their procession into the contract workers' quarter, over 1,000 local people joined in, 'singing songs and carrying a large banner expressing support for the United Nations'. When the Minister of Bantu Education opened the new Ongwediva Training College with full pomp and ceremony four days later, a number of school choirs boycotted the event. By 10 August, a full-scale student boycott had closed down Ongwediva completely. When it reopened a month later, a large meeting of the students' parents charged the South African authorities with bringing guns and tear-gas with their education and demanded that all students be reinstated. Defying the united opposition of students, parents and black teachers, the authorities expelled those they considered to be 'ring-leaders'. Their reprisals were to help escalate the level of popular mobilisation into a new dimension of struggle.

The General Strike

The Struggle Against Contract Labour
It was the massive general strike of contract workers, launched in mid-December 1971, which consolidated the gains of this period of mass upsurge and propelled the liberation struggle irrevocably into a higher phase. From decades of bitter experience, contract workers had developed a strong tradition of collective solidarity and sophisticated methods of struggle.

The major industrial centres and mines, with their huge, grim bachelor compounds, were the storm centres of this relentless conflict between contract workers and the employers and their police allies. It was Walvis Bay which provided the setting for an outstanding example of the workers' ability to sustain a united stand by means of underground collective action: the campaign, launched early in 1968, for proper overtime pay. That this was a burning issue can be seen from Vinnia Ndadi's vivid description of conditions in the canneries a decade earlier. Shifts were not fixed, but started as soon as the first boats returned in the early hours and ended only when the last of the day's catch had been processed.

> The first ones usually returned around 2 a.m. The watchmen then came to wake us up shouting 'cannery, cannery, cannery, cannery, cannery'. Which meant: 'The boats are in, get to work!' We quickly dressed and ran the 50 yards to the factory. Then we worked until the fish were finished. If, say, five boats came back full we'd work from 2 in the morning until 5 in the next evening. Sometimes even till 9 p.m. — and without a single break! . . . The machines were kept going continuously, belts full and moving all the time. Many men got swollen legs and feet from standing for so long. Eighteen hours! It's just too much for a human being . . . We worked seven days a week throughout the fishing season. We got overtime for anything more than 13 hours a day, but it amounted to only 6d an hour.

Manifesto of the SWAPO Youth League 1971*

Under Boer rule, a Namibian does not matter, did not matter and will not matter as long as the Boers remain in power. An African is regarded as a thing rather than a human being, and his place in white society is tied to the work for which he sells his labour as a commodity . . .

To understand why Namibia is still a colony, one should first and foremost understand the question of property ownership and exploitation of both the raw materials and labour of Namibia and the Namibian people by the monopoly capitalists. Being a system of ruthless exploitation, and a system whose directors exist at the expense of the sweat, blood and death of thousands of our people, colonialism, an auxiliary of capitalism, is aimed at:

1. Exploitation of the raw materials and the labour of the African people;
2. Making Namibia a market for sale of poor quality manufactured goods at a very high price;
3. Making Namibia a new sphere of capital investment and for surplus manufactured goods;
4. To have military bases in our country to protect these property and economic interests and to suppress the national liberation movement of the Namibian people.

Namibia, like so many countries in Southern Africa, is a very rich country in minerals and other land and sea riches. But its people are the most poverty-stricken — kept in hunger, ignorance and disease . . .

Youth and Students

Youth and students are the most courageous and fearless age group of our people. Composed of the people who have no property or family to care for at the time being, or belonging to a definite class of their own, this age group is one at the front of the struggle, particularly in the towns. Youths are ready to attack, provoke and challenge racism and its colonial and capitalist institutions.

When a Namibian youth is not fighting for a better education he is found engaged in a battle against the bosses, foremen and even boss-boys in the working place. He is also found either battling or running for his life in the streets, where the fascist police are harassing the population. When expelled from work, or from school a Namibian youth finds work for himself to survive, and most of his time is devoted to the struggle for the emancipation of his people . . .

Dear Compatriots, our country is passing through a difficult point in its history, and to participate in the struggle has become a must for every Namibian. None will ever come from Mars or Moon, or even from the U.N.O. or from the O.A.U. to do the fighting for us. It is we, and only we in our own country who will fight for our own liberation, our own independence and for our own future. We may not always be successful, but through our hard work, and determination to free ourselves, victory will surely be on our side, on the side of justice. Let us work in Solidarity, for Freedom and Justice! We have nothing to lose, except our suffering!

Long live the Namibian people!

Long live SWAPO, the glorious vanguard of our revolution!

Long live the people of Africa!

Down with imperialism and Vorster's neo-fascism!

EVER ONWARD TO VICTORY!

* This Manifesto was issued after the Tanga Congress but well before the I.C.J. Opinion was delivered in June 1971. Its call to action was in many respects prophetic of the way in which students, the intelligentsia and workers were to take the lead in the latter half of 1971.

Not only the cannery workers, but also many of those in the docks were tied to this gruelling daily cycle.

In July 1968, workers in the canneries started an overtime ban, demanding that all work after 5 p.m. be paid at overtime rates; and dock labourers soon joined them. The South African authorities imported puppet chiefs and headmen to cajole them back to work, and when this failed, brought in strike-breakers from Ovamboland. The workers stood firm, and the first batch of supposed strike-breakers joined their ranks immediately on arrival. Eventually, after nearly a month of deadlock, the South Africans deported some 650 workers back to Ovamboland. The outcome of the workers' action was not reported, but seven months later, in February 1969, dockers employed by South African Railways and Harbours (SAR & H) reimposed an overtime ban on unloading ships. Again the colonial press failed to report the outcome, but in mid-October 1970 the ban was in force once more. The employers imported scab labour from Southern Namibia, not daring to try to use Ovambo workers again as strike-breakers.

Despite this, by January 1971 other dockers had joined the ban and the stevedore companies and SAR & H were outbidding each other to come to terms with the workers. The tenacity of their three-year campaign had paid off, a remarkable achievement under so brutal a labour regime. An incident at the height of this campaign highlights the unity and militancy of the workers. When, on 15 January, a black railway policeman attempting to arrest an African stevedore shot him, his fellow-workers walked out in solidarity. The next morning, the entire stevedore work-force met in angry protest to demand a meeting with the police. However, following their usual practice, the police staged a confrontation and broke up the assembly — but not before the workers had defended themselves vigorously with stones, and demonstrated their unbreakable mutual solidarity.

In Katutura too, the 6,000 workers who were forced to live in the contract compound had built up a high level of autonomous struggle. By early 1971, they had made their barrack-like quarters a night-time 'no-go' area for the local police after their return from work each day at 5 p.m., as the police themselves admitted. Numbers of them operated a bulk-buying food co-operative and market which served the whole location, bypassing the expensive location stores and the degrading canteen food. The compound offered a haven for those trying to evade the repressive labour controls, above all the hated pass laws. Confronted by such a wall of solidarity, the police resorted to periodic mass raids (one in March, another on 11 June), encircling the compound with armed police and arresting hundreds of workers on technical offences. After the June raid, the authorities built a check-point designed to allow only workers with valid passes to enter or leave — in effect making the compound a concentration camp. Five months later, on the night of 11 November, workers mounted a well-organised attack which completely destroyed the check-point and offices. Four days later came the inevitable police retaliation: a massive dawn raid in which police combed the workers' quarters, confiscating and destroying personal property and arresting over 200 people. It was virtually open warfare. Contract workers had transformed their compounds, designed to serve the same func-tion as prison camps, with barbed wire and glass-topped wall perimeters, into revolutionary enclaves within colonial society.

The Contract Workers Organise
Contract workers had long understood the workings of the system which oppressed them. We have already described the first stirrings of revolt in

Ovamboland in the 1950s and the formation of OPO, pledged to fight the
contract labour system. But as yet, concerted collective action had been
limited to particular factories, towns or compounds. The idea of a national
strike to abolish the system of contract labour altogether had been discussed
in general terms in SWAPO's ranks at least as far back as the Tanga Congress.
Now a group of ex-students, including Thomas Kamati and other future
leaders of the SWAPO Youth League, took up the proposal once more. Some
of them had recently been expelled from Ongwediva and Odibo for their part
in the demonstration and boycott in August. Others had recently returned
from contracts at the fish canneries in Walvis Bay, and it was there that most
of the group returned to canvass support for their plan.

By September 1971, all had secured jobs at Walvis Bay and other centres.
Those at Walvis Bay established contact with students and activists in other
towns and mines, and within two weeks of their arrival held a joint meeting
with students from Windhoek and SWAPO members from Walvis Bay to
discuss the proposed strike. Crucial to the success of their strategy was the
presence of long-established SWAPO branches and the battle-hardened
experience of local cadres. According to one of the organisers, SWAPO
militant Hinananje Nehova:

> Just about every student was a SWAPO member even though you
> couldn't come right out and say it. We all attended regular SWAPO
> meetings twice a week. Soon we began to organise. We would approach
> one or two workers in each factory, in the railways and building
> companies. We only talked to those we trusted. All agreed that some-
> thing had to be done about the contract labour system.

When, on 27 November, Commissioner-General de Wet denied the church
leaders' criticism of contract labour as 'slavery' since workers came forward
voluntarily for recruitment, the activists put his statement to effective use in
their mobilisation campaign.

> We used this article to tell our fellow-workers: 'See, the South Africans
> are saying that we are pleased with this system, so we should do some-
> thing to show them that we really don't want it. If we break this
> present system with a strike we could have the freedom to choose our
> jobs and move freely around the country; to take our families with us,
> and to visit our friends wherever they are.' Everyone supported these
> ideas.

By early November, the organisers were strong enough to call a mass
meeting. 6,000 workers attended, the vast majority of the contract work-
force in Walvis Bay. The speakers denounced the contract system, SWANLA
and the puppet bantustan leaders. 'The reaction after the speeches was overwhelming and support for the strike swelled.' The meeting endorsed the plan
to strike and return to Ovamboland until the contract system was abolished;

and voted to send delegates or letters to other centres throughout the country to seek national support for the strike.

The organisers at Walvis Bay had also written to SWANLA, de Wet and the bantustan 'government' of Ovamboland, 'explaining our disagreement with the article which the Commissioner-General had written. We told them that they would soon witness our true feelings about the contract labour system'. Already alerted by the mass meeting in November, the South African Police had arrested 14 of the organisers, leaving only Nehova, Kamati and a few others at large to operate underground to rally the workers. The police continued to question and intimidate the workers about the coming strike. In Katutura, the police mounted a show of force on 7 December and tried to disrupt the handwritten notices ('letters') which militants posted up at strategic places to communicate with the mass of the workers. The diary of Leonard Nghipandulwa, one of the Katutura organisers, records that 'though the superintendent of the compound and the black messengers tried to destroy the letters, instead of these letters decreasing they increased in number. The letters were read from 5–11 December, when they decided to meet in order to discuss the abolition of the contract.' A meeting of delegates and activists on Saturday 11 December in Katutura endorsed the strike call, and took their decision to a mass meeting of thousands of workers the following afternoon, which gave its overwhelming support. The strike was to start the next day, Monday 13 December, and that night pickets were posted at the compound gates.

Realising that the workers were determined in their resolve, the South African regime desperately played its last card and brought its puppets down from Ovamboland to dissuade the workers from striking. Mr. White, the Chief Native Affairs Commissioner for South West Africa, called a mass meeting at Walvis Bay on Sunday 12 December. As well as the bantustan puppets, Bishop Auala, who was on holiday nearby, was called to the platform. It was a dramatic confrontation. When White and the headmen tried to speak, the crowd shouted them down.

> Only Bishop Auala spoke, saying that, in his way, he too was trying to change the system. Someone spoke from the crowd: 'Look, our brothers have been arrested and now the white administrators are trying to stop our strike. . . They are cheating us! All they really want to do is arrest our leaders and continue the system.' 'Al right,' he answered, right in the presence of the Special Branch, 'then you have no choice but to go on strike.' The crowd burst into shouting and applause, breaking up the meeting with SWAPO songs. Those who had passes then burnt them in further protest against the system.

Launching the Strike

By now, the workers' leaders in Walvis Bay knew that support for the strike was growing on a national scale. 'The delegates we had sent to Windhoek, Tsumeb, Swakopmund and elsewhere returned with reports from all over the country that the news had been received with great enthusiasm. The workers in Windhoek and some mines in that area had decided to join the strike immediately.' That Monday the workers gave notice to their employers that they would be returning to Ovamboland the next day. The South African attempt to call the workers' bluff, by threatening deportation to Ovamboland (their ultimate deterrent, short of violence, against localised labour action) was turned by the workers into their main mobilising tactic. Armed police stood by helplessly as contract workers from all over Walvis Bay gathered in the compound that night for solidarity, packed their belongings and began leaving for the north the next morning in their thousands.

In Windhoek, the strike was already on. Although the gates were open and workers passed freely in and out to buy food (they had also decided to boy-cott the detested compound canteen), the stoppage was total. The authorities made one last desperate intervention. In the words of Nghipandulwa:

> The Commissioner of Windhoek, Mr. White, came and begged that the Ovambo people should start working. Although he tried very hard the people refused. They had decided that if the contract was withdrawn it is only then that they will go to work. If it is not withdrawn they will wait. The day it is withdrawn then we will go to work. The Commissioner found it difficult to persuade the people because the reasons given him were extremely good. He said the people must choose their spokesmen — there should be 8 or 10 of them — whilst he would get in touch with the bigwigs in Ovambo, who were in Walvis Bay due to similar disturbances.

The strikers elected a committee, which met for three hours and formulated their demands. Early the following morning, White arrived with the three bantustan puppets (Elifas, Kaluvi and Iipumbu). Confronted with the workers' indictment of the contract system and their demand for its abolition, the bantustan men had no answer, and could only plead helplessly for a return to work on the promise of future discussions. White laid down his ultimatum: end the strike, or be deported back to Ovamboland. The workers' leaders stood firm. 'When it was announced through the loudspeakers, all the people gathered outside the office where the consultations took place. The whole meeting thanked them with applause. The entire meeting decided to return to Ovambo.'

This time the police did not stand idly by, but sealed off the compound and set out actively to intimidate the workers. They drove the pickets away from the gates and used loudspeakers to call on all those who wanted to work to come out under police protection. They refused to allow anyone to enter or leave, arresting outside visitors who had been trapped inside. Leonard Nghipandulwa wrote a graphic account of what it was like to be inside the compound during this testing period:

When Commissioner White left with the guests the Boer police started encircling the compound on 13 December. They started to hurt the people badly and the gate was closed. We could not go out to buy food. We could not withdraw money from the bank or fetch our clothes from the dry cleaners. At dawn on 14 December the police started knocking on the roofs and also threw stones at the windows, and were also beating up people as well as breaking the radios at the windows. The police started setting fire to the rooms occupied by the people. Then people had to leave the rooms and sleep outside. These events lasted from 14 to 17 December. The people could not sleep, and the leaders started taking the numbers of the police so that they could give them to the Chief of Police; but the Chief of Police said that was nothing to do with him.

Armed police encircling the Katutura compound during the strike

But the unity and morale of the workers was unbreakable. Their dignity and massive solidarity in the face of violent police provocation impressed even white observers. One newsman, watching the exodus from Katutura, reported that 'as they filed into the buses, they started singing. It was low and mournful and sounded like hymns.' The workers were still 'singing and chanting' as the crowded train edged out of the station. In Walvis Bay, too, 'some started singing hymns as the train pulled out.'

By the end of the week, most of the 6,000 contract workers in Windhoek and some two-thirds of the 3,000 at Walvis Bay (it was by now the fishing industry's closed season and several thousand had already departed in the preceding weeks) had left for the north. On Tuesday 14 December, the General Manager of Tsumeb declared: 'All our Ovambos are working and there is no sign of unrest.' Three days later 3,800 contract workers, 90% of the black work-force at the mine, stopped work and returned to Ovamboland. Within a week of the launching of the strike, over 13,000 contract workers at six major centres (the two largest towns and four mines) had joined in. Whereas on the 10th de Wet was confidently claiming to have a reserve of contract workers ready for Walvis Bay, by the 17th recruitment at Ondangwa had stopped altogether and by the 22nd pickets were closing the border with Angola to incoming recruits. Within the space of a fortnight, the workers, despite their lack of a trade union organisation of any kind, had made their national general strike totally effective.

In a remarkable demonstration of organisational skill and national solidarity, contract workers had by the end of 1971 brought most of the major industries of the country to a halt and prevented the large-scale recruitment of strike-breakers from Namibia and Southern Angola. The regime scoured Southern Africa for black replacements, but neighbouring black governments refused to co-operate, and in the end it found less than a thousand prepared to scab on their Namibian comrades.

This was a major landmark in black solidarity throughout Southern Africa. In Walvis Bay, the authorities' importing of a 'large alternative labour force' from South Africa before the strike began, in order to break the workers' resolve, was, as Nehova relates, 'a total failure. The work was too hard for them, and they didn't have the necessary skills either. They were also intimidated by the other workers. Some of the employers even refused to hire them. After a while, most simply asked to be returned to where they came from.' Other black Namibian workers, and even a few of the foreign white technicians and managers, supported the strikers. 'There was great solidarity among the African people. In Walvis Bay, many of those living in the town entered the compound. Even people not working under the contract system came to stay in the compound. Others gave food to the workers going on strike.' In Windhoek, domestic servants and workers living in town gave refuge to leaders hunted by the police.

Over the next three weeks, contract workers in towns and mines in every corner of the land joined the strike or demonstrated their solidarity, most returning to Ovamboland. Many simply waited until their next pay-day before leaving. This caused problems for some whose pay had been kept in arrears, as in Walvis Bay — some being owed up to three months' back pay. Even at C.D.M., which paid the highest contract wages in Namibia and guaranteed virtually permanent employment to its workers,the 4,000-strong work-force downed tools for several days, making clear their complete solidarity with the strike and extracting a commitment from the general manager to work for a revised system. 'I have received a deputation from the Ovambos here, who made it clear to me that they are against the contract system and asked me to put forward their views to the government officials.

I have done so.' Even so, some 10%, mainly domestic rather than production workers, did join the strike early in January. A few days later, C.D.M., to stop the strike spreading, granted a 10% flat-rate increase to all its contract workers.

Even on the farms, a substantial number of workers who heard of the strike by word of mouth or on the radio deserted to join their comrades, defying extreme brutality in order to do so. 'On one farm in the Grootfontein district nine contract workers went on strike, according to a report towards the end of December. 'The farmer said he did not wish to employ two of them, who he regarded as "agitators". They were sent back to Ovamboland. The remainder were beaten, and were then asked if they would return to work, and six of them again refused.' According to the farmer, 'my kitchen-Ovambo heard about the strike on the radio, told the others about it, and they all went on strike.' In Ovamboland itself, 600 workers on a canal construction project came out in solidarity with the returning strikers in early January (1972).

By the middle of January, 13,500 contract workers had been transported to Ovamboland by the government alone; many others returned on their own initiative. Counting the 3,000-odd fishing industry workers whose contracts ended in the weeks before the start of the strike, some 22,500 contract workers from towns, mines and work-camps — probably more than 25,000 if farm-workers are included — had taken strike action, of whom about 18,000 had returned to Ovamboland. In other words, well over half the recorded 43,400 contract workers and over 70% of those employed outside farming joined the strike against the contract system. Most of the 23,000 who came from Ovamboland participated; and an appreciable number of the 17,400 from Angola, a large proportion of whom worked on farms and were therefore cut off, 'returned home with the same intentions as those in Ovamboland,' according to Nehova, himself one of several rank-and-file organisers to have come originally from Angola. It was a devastating blow against the hated contract labour system and the regime of apartheid which legitimated it.

Closing the Ranks

The South African regime and the capitalists it served may have expected that by deporting the strikers back to their 'homeland' it would quickly break their unity. They were mistaken. The complacency of one building employer was revealed in this remark: 'There are many thousands of Ovambo to choose from, and when they are hungry they will return to work.'

Ultimately, this remains true while contract labour and apartheid last: workers from peasant families in the northern bantustans cannot escape in the long term from their forced dependence on wage-labour for at least part of their and their families' subsistence. But in the short term, it was to take more than simple hunger — a daily experience for most workers whether or not they had jobs — to drive the strikers back to work. An observer reported in February that 'it seemed to be a matter of pride among the few Ovambos whom the writer spoke to that there was enough food in Ovambo. The suggestion that the Ovambos might be starved into submission was dismissed as propaganda.' The strikers were turning their bondage to their own tactical advantage. With such low wages, they could not save enough to stay out for more than a few days in the compounds; by returning to the land they could eke out an existence for months on end. Indeed, early in January the strike leaders in Ovamboland urged them to 'go back to the land and raise as big a crop as possible' during the harvest season (then about to begin); and the rains allowed the people to harvest a fair grain crop that year.

But mere survival would not win the strikers' cause: it required organisation and leadership to defend their unity and represent their demands. In the crowded compounds, workers and leaders could communicate easily and meet to take decisions collectively. But on their return to Ovamboland in the second half of December, the strikers had dispersed to all corners of the reserve. The workers' leaders, linking up with an already militant local opposition, wasted no time in establishing a grassroots organisation. Delegates to a 'contract committee' were elected on a regional basis, and met on 3 January 1972 under the chairmanship of Johannes Nangutuuala, a member of the delegation which had protested to the Chief Councillor the previous June. They decided that any agreement reached without the consultation and endorsement of the strikers themselves should be rejected. They passed a series of resolutions setting out the workers' rejection of the contract system and demands for its replacement. They circulated these in the form of a pamphlet and presented them to a mass meeting of 3,500 strikers on 10 January at Oluno-Ondangwa. The meeting passed them unanimously and elected a delegation to represent them at any future negotiations.

Thus, within a month of the start of the strike and a fortnight after the return of most of them to Ovamboland, the strikers had a coherent set of demands, an elected leadership, a form of grassroots organisation and clearly defined tactics: no end to the strike without their endorsement of any revised labour code, no recruitment of any kind, pickets to turn back incoming recruits at the Angolan border, and representation through their elected leaders alone, not the bantustan collaborators with whom the South Africans chose to 'negotiate'.

The South African regime launched a two-pronged attack to crush the strike. First, it brought forward a meeting with the large employers to discuss the contract system, which had been arranged before the strike, to 19 January. The meeting, held at Grootfontein, the headquarters of SWANLA, agreed to abolish SWANLA itself, but replaced it with regulations which allowed only minor changes in the contract system. In effect, the reform simply brought Namibia into line with the Labour Bureaux system in force in South Africa, transferring the administration from SWANLA to the puppet bantustan government. The Ovambo 'cabinet' rubber-stamped the agreement the next day with little discussion. The cosmetic effect was the important thing, and South Africa launched a major propaganda drive, especially through its mouthpiece Radio Owambo, to sell the 'new deal' to the strikers as a major change. They scored an important coup when the Chairman of the Strike Committee, Nangutuuala, was tricked into calling for an end to the strike over Radio Owambo. It was a tragic error of judgement, which, together with the weight of South African propaganda, undoubtedly confused thousands of workers and damaged their hard-won solidarity.

Nevertheless, it is clear that the great majority of the strikers did not break ranks. Two thousand of those who did turn up at Ondangwa for registration in the last week of January walked out rather than undergo the degrading medical examination whose abolition their manifesto demanded. Others were press-ganged into signing contracts. One worker caught this way described the process: 'They broadcast on Radio Owanbo that the factories want boys . . . We go there and find ourselves rounded up. They force the people to be recruited . . . What is said on Radio Owambo is not the same as happens at Ondangwa. We don't see any change in the system. The government is trying to blind us.' At the end of January, less than 1,000 workers had been registered for contracts, and a month later, little over 6,000, a fair number of whom were neither strikers nor Namibians. As late as 7 July, it was reported that the number in the Katutura compound had only just reached 4,000, still a third down on its pre-strike total. Many of those who did sign new contracts came determined to exercise the new 'freedoms' promised them in government propaganda. When they discovered that the old system remained in force in all essentials, many hundreds stopped work once more at scores of work-places, some electing to return to Ovamboland for a second time.

The Peasant Uprising and the Reign of Terror

There was in fact good reason for the remainder, even though bitterly disillusioned, to stay at work in the south. For the South African regime launched a reign of terror against the population in Ovamboland, the second prong in its attack on the strikers' solidarity, and soon the major one. The South Africans realised that not only was the workers' morale undaunted by their mass deportation but that they were now organising in Ovamboland to defend their unity. On 12 January, after a couple of attacks on the homes of headmen and two days after the strikers' mass meeting, contingents of South African Police infantry were flown in from Pretoria. As the Deputy Commissioner of Police stated succinctly, 'the police are not moving into Ovamboland because of any trouble. We are merely augmenting the established force there because we haven't broken the back of this strike yet. We must take measures to guard against any internal flare-up.' Five days later, the pliable Executive Committee of the Ovambo 'Legislative Council' banned all public meetings and requested the police to break up all 'illegal gatherings'. This was the signal for an indiscriminate armed attack upon all strikers' meetings, the focal points of mobilisation, at which workers could gather local support, exchange information and take collective decisions.

Contract Workers' Manifesto

Firstly the meeting discussed the report of the elected Contract Committee which met on 3 January 1972. The resolutions of the Contract Committee follow.

What is the contract system? Contract means an agreement between at least two parties. When the word 'contract' is used that an Ovambo is on contract, it should mean he is on an agreement with his employer. But this contract system used by SWANLA in Ovamboland has no agreement between the employer and the employee. That agreement is just between SWANLA and the employer. SWANLA sells Ovambos to the employers and so the Ovambos have come to be slaves of SWANLA and employer, and because of this wrong and bad system this agreement has been changed into wire instead of the contract.

Evils of the Contract System
a. This system makes use of forced labour such that a person has no right to do a job of his choice;
b. It has meagre wages, and because of these our people are forced to leave a job with the intention of getting better paid jobs;
c. It breaks up the family life and spoils the upbringing of the children;
d. Because of this system the employee and his family have no right to visit each other;
e. This system caused the Ovambos to be looked down upon by the other Africans in Namibia and is causing hatred among the blacks of Namibia;
f. What is the purpose of the anal examinations for blacks when they are going on contract? Do the whites also undergo this anal examination when they come to Ovamboland on contract? . . .
g. Because of this evil system the employer values the work done by an Ovambo instead of the person who does the work;
h. Because of this system an Ovambo is not under

the protection of the law.

The Contract System is a Form of Slavery

a. All people irrespective of race and colour are
created by God with the same human dignity
and are equal before him. This system under-
mines the God-given human dignity of an
Ovambo worker;

b. The so-called homelands have become the
trading markets where blacks are bought and
in this trade SWANLA has become richer and
richer and the blacks poorer and poorer;

c. This slavery brought about the erection of the
compounds with surrounding walls on top of
which sharp pieces of glass were built. In
compounds workers sleep on hard beds made
of cement and bricks which cause lameness
and death . . .;

d. This system brings ill-treatment throughout
the contract period.

The Favourable System of Looking for Labour

a. We Ovambos do not want any improvement of
or new name for wire. But we want to do away
with wire, and to have a contract in the true
meaning of the word.

b. We totally reject any form of buying and selling
people because of their colour.

c. We want an agreement with the following rights;
i) freedom to do a job of his choice with the
corresponding salary according to his skill;
ii) freedom to leave an unwanted and low-paid
job, and to look for another job of his choice
without police interference;
iii) freedom to have his family with him, and to
visit or be visited by his family;
iv) his salary must be according to the work
done regardless of his colour, irrespective of
where he is working in Namibia.
[A series of detailed demands followed.]

*Extracts from the minutes of the mass meeting of
striking contract workers at Oluno-Ondangwa, 10
January 1972.*

201

But by this time, the workers' cause was merging with a more general rising on both sides of the border against the institutions of colonial rule themselves. There had been several attacks on the property of headmen in the first half of January, and the house and store of Headman Kaluvi, a member of the bantustan delegation at Walvis Bay and Windhoek and from 1 January 'special representative' for the urban areas, were burnt to the ground by arsonists. The public meetings began to raise explicitly peasant demands as well: the removal of the colonial border fence, the destruction of stock-control kraals, and the expulsion of the oppressive white bureaucracy. On the night of 16 January, over 100 km of the border fence between Angola and Namibia was cut, and this action was repeated during the next fortnight. The fence was destroyed, explained a letter from Ovamboland at the time, because it was erected 'unconstitutionally and undemocratically and prevents our cattle from reaching the grazing areas now at Angola.'

The people, defending themselves against police attacks as best they could with home-made weapons, retaliated by attacking the property of tribal collaborators and informers, destroying some 140 government stock-inspection kraals and fences, as well as government offices. For a few days, government transport in Ovamboland was forced off the roads, and on 22 January white women were evacuated from Oshikango. Attacks took place on both sides of the border, and the Portuguese hurriedly sent in troops. The confrontation had become a popular uprising by the people of Ovamboland against Portuguese and South African rule. On 4 February, the occupation regime clamped emergency regulations on Ovamboland (R 17–72) which gave the police and army complete licence to do their worst. Even before this, eight Africans had been killed by the police, four in an unprovoked massacre of a group attending church. Police and troops poured into the area, which was sealed off from the outside world. Hundreds of people were arrested indiscriminately and herded into barbed-wire concentration camps, where many were tortured and held for months without charge or trial, and numbers of houses were burnt down. It is not surprising that under such a reign of terror the strikers' grassroots organisation was suppressed and that some sought to escape by taking contracts in the south. It is more remarkable that under such conditions the majority continued to hold out for months to come.

In formal terms this year of open mass confrontation brought few immediate tangible gains. On the contracy, the South African regime reacted with typical violence, intensifying its harrassment of political activists throughout the country, unleashing an indiscriminate reign of terror in Ovamboland and, despite some superficial tinkering, hardening its methods of labour repression. Nevertheless, it transformed the basis of popular struggle being transformed and immesurably strengthened the liberation movement as a whole. For the first time, new and powerful forces were brought into the mainstream of popular resistance, above all the students and youth and the churches. The national character of the struggle and the principle of national unity were brought into sharp focus, both in mass activity and in the anti-colonial campaigns of leaders at all levels. The people's experience of nation-wide mobilisation generated a new and militant national consciousness. Abov Above all, that experience infused a consciousness, which has never been lost, that ultimately the power to shape their own destiny lies in the hands of the people themselves, that victory to the popular movement is certain in the end end. This period of mass resistance transformed the character of the movement inside the country from sectional and localised resistance to sustained mass action on a national scale.

SWAPO Intensifies the Liberation Struggle

The existence of an experienced and principled liberation movement was an essential condition of this transition. It was SWAPO's crowning achievement at this time that the explosion of mass resistance was not allowed to dissipate in defeatism and disillusionment under the full fury of South African repression, but was conserved and channelled into long-term forms of struggle, into lasting gains for the movement as a whole. It is the nature of such mass up-surges that their form is largely spontaneous and popular, breaking out in many different places and circumstances. The general strike was a product of heightened militancy amongst all the people of Namibia and of the emergence of an effective rank-and-file leadership amongst contract workers themselves. In this sense Nathaniel Mahuilili, acting President of SWAPO and constrained under a South African banning order, was accurate in describing the strike on 4 January 1972 as 'entirely spontaneous'.

But in a more fundamental sense the existence of SWAPO was a necessary precondition for the successful emergence, both in popular consciousness and in rank-and-file leadership, of such forms of mass struggle. Through the liberation movement, workers had access to a tradition of resistance to the tyranny of contract labour stretching back to the early days of OPO. As Theo-Ben Gurirab, the SWAPO Representative at the United Nations, stated to the Council for Namibia, 'the subsequent broadening of the aims and objectives of SWAPO has not made it deviate from the initial fight against the contract labour system.' The workers and their representatives could also draw on the experience and resources of a leadership at branch level which had survived over 10 years of South African repression. Many of the strike organisers were already SWAPO members and participated actively in the local branches; and at Walvis Bay (to take the best-known instance) the local party branch was involved in the planning of the strike from the outset. After their return to Ovamboland, the strikers could call on the resources of a regional organisation and leadership which Herman ja Toivo's pioneering work and SWAPO militants had rooted strongly amongst the people. Abroad, SWAPO's tireless international campaigning was instrumental in alerting neighbouring black governments to South Africa's attempts to recruit strike-breakers and mobilised world-wide popular and trade union support.

The Youth League rally in Windhoek, 12 August 1973

The general strike was the spectacular culmination of a period of mobilisation which touched every corner of Namibian society. As *Namibia News* stated early in 1972:

> The overall struggle for our freedom has many facets, and the strike by our workers is a major one. SWAPO has been accused of counteracting the strike as a gigantic non-violent operation by linking it with the armed struggle. To us Namibians there is only one struggle, of which the strike, the guerrilla activity, school children's demonstrations and churchmen's pastoral letters all are a part. However, SWAPO is the umbrella under which all these different forms of struggle for independence and human rights take place.

'SWAPO's military, political and diplomatic activities abroad,' declared Theo-Ben Gurirab, 'are functionally and dialectically complementary with the political actions of the masses at home.'

The dominant influence of the liberation movement was reflected after the World Court ruling at all levels, from diplomatic lobbying to grassroots organisation. The local SWAPO leadership moved rapidly into action to mobilise and organise the growing popular resistance to South African colonial rule. As early as August 1971, their influence was sufficient to alarm the stooges on the Katutura Advisory Board. In the press report of their monthly meeting, one claimed that 'people from outside' were moving into the township and were holding meetings. 'It needs only a spark to cause a blaze . . .' According to another, 'already the "fore-runners" of those instigating were busy with secret meetings and writing documents. It had gone so far already that even in small incidents these men saw a chance to thwart the authorities . . . Katutura's residents were listening to these men, who were usually educated.' The people were indeed in revolutionary mood, and SWAPO, the instrument of their struggle for liberation, was in the vanguard of the popular movement.

It was in the translation of the short-term gains of spontaneous mass struggle into a permanent strengthening of the liberation movement that SWAPO faced its most important test. SWAPO leaders cautioned the people to be self-reliant in their fight, and not to pin their hopes on outside agencies such as the U.N. An official statement in Lusaka on the day after the I.C.J. judgement of 1971 declared: 'SWAPO is pessimistic, while welcoming the ruling of the Court, as to whether it will ever be effectively carried out by the Security Council.'

Inside Namibia, SWAPO worked actively to unite the broadest possible range of anti-colonial forces in a popular front, and was instrumental in launching the National Convention of Namibia in November 1971, a loosely-knit nationalist front comprising a variety of political parties and other groups, all opposed to South African rule and its bantustan schemes for Namibia. For this, the Tanga Congress had prepared the ground well. As the phase of mass mobilisation reached its climax in the uprising in Ovamboland in the early months of 1972, it was the structures and the strategy launched two years earlier, above all the People's Liberation Army of Namibia (PLAN) and the Youth League (Y.L.), which were to carry it forward into sustained mass struggle.

8. 'The People are SWAPO': Sustained Mass Struggle, 1972–79

The nation-wide demonstrations of support for the World Court ruling and the contract workers' strike together inaugurated a period of popular struggle against South African rule which has continued to this day, undiminished in vigour or dedication to the goal of final liberation. The past decade has seen the application of the Tanga strategy of intensified political and military struggle. This policy entailed, on the one hand, the extension of the role of PLAN's military cadres into social and political spheres of action, and consequently a closer co-ordination between the political and the military party structures. On the other hand, it led to the setting up of coherent forms of organisation to lead the political mobilisation of different sectors of the population. This initiative eventually resulted in the establishment of the National Union of Namibian workers (N.U.N.W.) as an affiliated body alongside the Youth League, Women's Council and Elders' Council. Furthermore, i it required the formation of a revitalised parallel leadership inside the country to take strategic command of the anti-colonial campaign within the areas of political activity still allowed by the occupation regime.

Since early 1972 the struggle has passed through three broad phases. During the first (January 1972 – April 1974), the apartheid regime proceeded remorselessly to implement its bantustan programme, using savage repression in an attempt to crush all opposition. In the face of full-scale repression, contract workers, youth and peasants in the north, with strong church support, launched a sustained and courageous campaign to destroy the political credibility and institutions of apartheid, especially South Africa's bantustan puppets and the so-called 'reforms' to the contract labour system.

The collapse of Portuguese colonial rule in Angola heralded a second phase (April 1974 – June 1977), in which South Africa tried to devise and impose a neo-colonial settlement on Namibia which would safeguard all essential features of its apartheid plan. Before its chosen instrument, the Turnhalle Constitutional Conference, had even met (September 1975), SWAPO had rallied all political tendencies of any significance into a united front of opposition to South Africa's tribal circus. Throughout the northern zone, guerrilla units of PLAN rapidly extended and intensified the attack on the occupation regime's repressive forces, particularly after the defeat of South Africa's invasion of Angola (late 1975). As students mounted a boycott of apartheid education (late 1976), a number of groups which had hitherto held aloof, particularly in the south, dissolved themselves and joined the ranks of SWAPO in a determined and massive demonstration of national solidarity against the Turnhalle Conference. Such was the level of popular mobilisation generated by SWAPO's campaign that the imperialist powers had no option but to compel South Africa to shelve its plan to make the Turnhalle delegates into an 'interim government'.

South Africa's reluctant agreement with the U.N. in mid-1977 to negotiate Namibia's transition to independence marked the beginning of a third phase in the struggle. Although appearing to abandon its plan for a unilateral 'internal settlement', by mid-1979 the occupation regime had set up its Turnhalle puppets as an internal 'government'. At the same time, it relied on its imperialist allies to force SWAPO and the U.N. to accept conditions which would turn any U.N. election into a stage-managed farce and win the D.T.A. puppets the international recognition South Africa desperately needs.

As the occupation regime has turned the full force of its machinery of repression against SWAPO's political structures, so party organisation has gone largely underground and armed struggle has increasingly taken the leading role. While willing to keep negotiating through the U.N. so long as there is the slightest chance of an agreed settlement, SWAPO has mobilised all its political and military resources for the revolutionary liberation war to drive out the occupation regime.

The Struggle Against the Bantustans (1972–74)

The regime's reaction to the militant action of 1971–72 was unambiguously brutal — rapid and repeated repression through violent attacks, imprisonment and torture in response to every manifestation of opposition. But the spectacular scale of popular resistance, reinforced by SWAPO's sustained publicity and lobbying abroad, could no longer be ignored. When, therefore, in February 1972 the U.N. Security Council met to consider how to compel South Africa's compliance with the World Court ruling, its Western members felt obliged to embark on an exercise in dialogue, and the South Africans yielded just enough to give it credibility. In February 1972, even as South African troops were pouring into Ovamboland to smash the resistance of the strikers, the Security Council authorised Secretary-General Waldheim to initiate contacts with all interested parties towards securing South Africa's withdrawal from the territory. Two years of fruitless negotiation and deliberate prevarication by the South African Government were to follow before the talks were finally called off.

When Waldheim himself visited Namibia in March 1972, on a brief tour organised by the South African authorities, Namibian leaders in both Ovamboland and Windhoek tore aside the veil of secrecy with which the authorities surrounded him to remind him forcefully of the strength of opposition to South African rule. His special emissary, Dr. Alfred Escher, sent to Namibia in October 1972, found virtually unanimous support amongst the various political parties and groupings and from the National Convention of Namibia for the U.N. demand that South Africa withdraw. Not only in the big towns but also in the smaller locations the delegations meeting Escher on his 26-day tour were accompanied by crowds of several hundreds carrying banners demanding independence — in Walvis Bay alone, 700 had gathered before the authorities panicked and diverted Escher's entourage elsewhere.

The Brussels International Conference

The mass popular upsurge and the forthright public demonstrations which greeted Waldheim and Escher were strongly reinforced at an international conference on Namibia convened by SWAPO in Brussels on 26–28 May 1972. 'The conference was attended by just over 540 delegates,' reported *Namibia News*, 'delegates from governments, particularly from the African Continent, from 32 international organisations, from a variety of widely representative national organisations, and a large number of personalities of international renown. Both from the point of view of attendance, in fact, and in its overall impact, the Namibian International Conference was a success far surpassing the hopes and expectations of SWAPO . . . ' The Conference's principal aims were 'to publicise the generally little-known situation of Namibia in the West in particular; to pass resolutions to be forwarded to the O.A.U. and the U.N. to be of assistance in their debates on Namibia; and to solicit support for the legitimate struggle of the people of Namibia as represented by SWAPO.' 'This conference,' stated the final declaration, 'accordingly recognises that the initiatives, methods and conduct of their struggle lie with SWAPO, the authentic voice and fighting organisation of the people of Namibia . . . Since the future of Namibia can only be determined by its people, any action affecting the future of Namibia should be with the consent of SWAPO. All negotiations and dealings with the occupying power must be conducted with their consent and proper participation. Towards this end the

conference calls for the recognition of SWAPO
as the true and legitimate representative of
Namibia and demands that it be accorded formal
status in all international forums and institutions
concerned with Namibia. The Namibian conflict
has been internationalised not only by the world
community's historic responsibility for her fate
but also by the close economic, political and
military links between SA and her allies . . . This
conference considers that the response to this
crisis must lie in the forging of an alliance
between the combined forces of all antagonists
of imperialism and the freedom forces of Namibia.
This alliance-in-action will require a multi-level
approach to support and solidarity action which
on the one hand will render effective moral and
material assistance to the struggle of the
Namibian people, and on the other, will
combat the growing complicity of Western
powers and interests.'
Namibia News, Vol 5, Nos. 6 & 7, 1972.

These forthright popular demonstrations were reinforced by the renewed
commitment to the cause of freedom in Namibia by many African governments represented at an international conference on Namibia called by
SWAPO in Brussels in May 1972. Although the South African Government
had not the slightest intention of yielding its colonial grip on Namibia, it
was forced to pay lip-service, albeit in highly ambiguous language, to some
of the U.N. demands. For the first time 'self-determination' and 'independence' were put on the agenda for Namibia. In discussions with Dr. Escher
and in a written submission in April 1973, the South African regime stated
that the constitutional form of self-determination and independence would
be for the Namibian people themselves to decide, that it did not envisage
bantustans becoming independent and that all political parties should have
freedom of speech and assembly, 'subject to the requirements of public
safety'.

These promises were, however, disregarded even as they were being made.
In the centre and south, the police tightened up pass law controls, backing
them up with regular dawn raids on the urban living quarters of the workers,
especially the contract workers' compounds. In the north, from March 1973
South African Police paramilitary units started to hand over to regular
troops. A costly road was built from Grootfontein to Katima Mulilo in the
extreme north-east of the country, and tens of millions of Rand were set
aside for the building of other military roads. The South African military

base at Katima Mulilo, where the Defence Forces had been operating for nearly a decade, was strengthened. The base at Grootfontein was expanded, and sophisticated and permanent army and air force facilities installed. And a chain of military posts was built along the Okavango and Caprivi border.

Implementation of the bantustan programme was speeded up. An amending Act of February 1973 empowered the South African State President to bypass Parliament and grant self-governing status to 'homelands' in Namibia. Two months later Ovamboland, still in the vice-like grip of the R 17 Emergency Regulations, was proclaimed self-governing, and in June elections were set for 1 and 2 August. At the same time, in an attempt to hoodwink the U.N. into believing that a representative national authority was being established, South African Prime Minister Vorster called into being an Advisory Council, a body with no powers of its own and composed of handpicked nominees from the ranks of South Africa's tribal puppets. It was to meet only twice, in March and August 1973, before being consigned to oblivion.

But the Namibian masses refused to be intimidated by this latest onslaught, and their militancy carried forward the momentum of popular resistance on a broad front. Its leading sectors were contract workers, peasants in the northern bantustans and youth throughout the country.

The chairman of the original Strike Committee in Ovamboland, Johannes Nangutuuala, was soon leading a small locally based party (DEMKOP), found founded on a platform similar to SWAPO's in a campaign of active opposition to the further extension of bantustan legislation in Ovamboland. Although public expression of opposition was illegal under the emergency regulations, local activists, amongst whom the SWAPO Youth League played an increasingly important part, mobilised a series of mass demonstrations, which were suppressed by the South African Police with considerable violence and the arrest of a number of leaders.

When SWAPO called a boycott of the bantustan elections, the Youth League held meeting after meeting throughout Ovamboland and in the main centres of contract labour in the centre and south — including Windhoek — to unite the people in opposition. Despite mounting harassment by tribal and South African Police, who had detained over 300 people by election day, popular enthusiasm began to grow. The boycott was a spectacular success, an important landmark in the liberation struggle. Only 2.5% of the registered electorate of 50,000 — itself less than a third of those qualified to register — cast their votes. Most of these were members of the tribal administration whose very livelihoods depended on their loyalty to the South African regime.

The election boycott was a shattering blow to South African policy in Namibia. This and the naked repression which followed were the major factors which compelled the Western members of the Security Council to agree to the ending of two years of dialogue with South Africa on 11 December 1973, and a few days later to allow the U.N. General Assembly to appoint Sean MacBride as U.N. Commissioner for Namibia and to recognise

SWAPO as 'the authentic representative of the people of Namibia'.

The S.A. Police – a threatening presence at every SWAPO meeting

The victory of the election boycott gave inspiration to all Namibians. 'There was a feeling of exuberance among the people after the elections victory,' reported *Namibia News*. 'Political meetings were held in many parts of Namibia.' SWAPO leaders were in the forefront, and especially the SWAPO Youth League. The young men were determined to speak out, to act, to encourage the Namibian people to fight against the oppressors. On Sunday 12 August, 3,000 people marched on the Ondangwa Magistrates Court in Ovamboland where three prominent leaders, arrested after protests against bantustan self-government, were to be put on trial. That same day, another 3,000 gathered at a militant Youth League rally in Windhoek.

Alarmed by the success and strength of SWAPO's mobilisation campaign, the South African Police swung into action in a nation-wide crackdown on SWAPO activists and supporters. Paramilitary police indiscriminately charged the Ondangwa demonstration; attacked a SWAPO meeting on 16 August; and, when contract workers in Windhoek launched a general strike four days later, broke it up in a brutal attack on the workers in their compound. The police began a massive manhunt for leaders of the Youth League, particularly those who had spoken out so courageously at the 12 August rally. Three Youth League leaders were later tried and each sentenced to eight years' imprisonment. Addressing the South West Africa National Party Congress on 21 August, Vorster threatened: 'If it is trouble they are looking for, they are going to get it.'

In Ovamboland the tribal police, trained and armed by South Africa, launched an indiscriminate series of detentions and beatings, under the close direction of the South African Security Police. Hundreds of men, women and children, including many prominent leaders, were rounded up and interned in a concentration camp at Omidamba. Most were eventually brought before tribal courts and sentenced to savage and degrading public floggings. The object was to attack and suppress every manifestation of support for SWAPO. 'People were flogged,' reported *Namibia News*, 'for singing SWAPO songs, calling our country Namibia, and in any way associating themselves with SWAPO.'

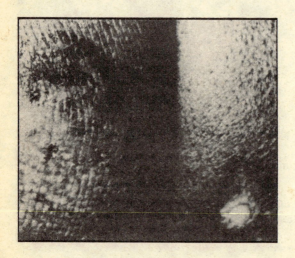

Despite the floggings, harassment and arrests, SWAPO's power and support continued to grow. At a three-day national conference of SWAPO delegates in Walvis Bay at the end of December 1973, National Chairman David Meroro, capturing the uplift in morale which followed the U.N. decision earlier that month to recognise SWAPO, called on party members to join hands' in the struggle for freedom in Namibia. The conference resolved to launch a campaign of nation-wide popular mobilisation through meetings and demonstrations and to extend the party organisation in outlying regional centres.

The South African response was to try even more systematically to take SWAPO apart, attacking every level of the party leadership from ordinary members to the National Executive itself. During January 1974, the police used the pass laws and mass raids to get hundreds of Namibians sentenced for trivial offences, some of whom were 'repatriated' to Ovamboland for further brutal punishment by the tribal police. They combed houses and newspaper offices for documents, and in early February picked up ten top

SWAPO leaders, including Meroro, to be held in solitary confinement under the Terrorism Act.

At the series of trials of SWAPO leaders arrested between August 1973 and February 1974, SWAPO members packed the court in defiant solidarity. Two key SWAPO witnesses, Shihepo Imbeli and George Itenga, savagely tortured by the police into giving fabricated evidence for the state, came from gaol and in the witness box turned on their torturers and supported their comrades in the dock. The leaders, on trial for their commitment to the cause of freedom, remained calm and resolute under the sneering cross-examination of the prosecution, and by their articulate defence and their exposure of the torture to which they had been subjected, turned the proceedings into a trial of their accusers. The three Youth League speakers at the August rally who were put on trial in November 1973, Jerry Ekandjo, Jacob Nghudinua and Martin Kapwasa, demanded a lawyer from the U.N., and then conducted their own defence and refused to recognise the right of the illegal court to sentence them. A fourth, Eliakim Andreas, tried in January 1974, contempt-uously tore up his identification papers in the witness box, declaring that he 'was not born with a pass and will not carry one,' and condemned 'Vorster's slavery' — an act which got him an extra three months in gaol.

One of the Western diplomats compelled by the pressure of SWAPO's international campaign to attend most of these political trials said, after watching Youth League Chairman Ezriel Taapopi stand up to cross-examina-tion for two days at his trial in July 1974: 'I don't understand much of what he said. But I would follow him anywhere.' As Taapopi and Youth League Acting Secretary Joseph Kashea were led from the dock, sentenced to two years' imprisonment, they paused at the top of the stairs leading down to the cells and turned to the black gallery, which stood in tribute. Prisoners and gallery saluted one another with a raised thumb for freedom. A Youth League rally on 28 July gathered thousands in protest, and two days later, as sentence was passed, SWAPO militants took their defiance of South African oppression to the steps of the Supreme Court itself, raising placards and fists in solidarity. Far from being 'broken', as a National Party news-paper had triumphantly claimed in February, SWAPO leaders and militants were repeatedly asserting the true calibre of their commitment to liberation.

In their general election campaign in April 1974, the South West Africa National Party issued a manifesto promising to promote closer ties with South Africa and to push apartheid to its 'logical conclusion' of ethnic independence whereby 'the whites will have their own areas where they alone will rule.' In an election address in Windhoek, Vorster himself pledged that the future of whites in Namibia would be determined solely by the all-white Legislative Assembly, that South Africa would stay as long as its presence was needed, and that any ethnic group, including the whites, could seek separate independence or refuse to join a federation. It was a message of arrogant defiance towards the U.N. and the people's demand for freedom: the Odendaal apartheid programme was to be relentlessly imposed to the end.

On 24 April, the National Party won a clean slate of seats in the Legislative Assembly and the South African Parliament. On the same day, the Chairman and Acting Secretary of the Youth League, Ezriel Taapopi and Joseph Kashea, were charged with inciting SWAPO to murder. Next day, 25 April 1974, the Portuguese armed forces overthrew their fascist regime, and the liberation movements in the Portuguese colonies began their final drive towards independence. Suddenly the strategic perspective of white rule in Southern Africa had been transformed.

The Drive for National Unity Against the Turnhalle (1974—77)

South Africa Recruits Its Tribal Circus

The 25 April Coup was greeted with enthusiasm by militants inside Namibia. Now, after long years of hardship and painstaking organisation, the edifice of colonialism in Southern Africa was beginning visibly to crumble before the expanding armed liberation struggles of its oppressed peoples. At a SWAPO rally in Katutura a few days after the Coup, 1,500 Namibians greeted the fall of the fascist dictatorship with the slogan 'Caetano yesterday, Vorster tomorrow'. In June and July, several thousand young men and women crossed the Angolan border to volunteer for the armed struggle.

The months following the Coup were full of suspense as the South Africans reassessed their strategy towards Africa. In Namibia the authorities marked time. Not that the severity of the political repression was eased in the slightest. All SWAPO leaders caught in the ongoing series of arrests were subjected to long periods of solitary confinement and to cruel and sadistic forms of torture, and South African judges refused to put a permanent ban on the barbaric and arbitrary floggings in Ovamboland. Nevertheless, no new major arrests were made after April, and the authorities suddenly lost their enthusiasm for mounting show trials, repeatedly postponing hearings and even allowing some of the accused, including Chairman David Meroro, out on bail.

From mid-1974 onwards, the revised South African strategy was gradually revealed. To Africa, Vorster offered an apparent hand of friendship in a renewed diplomatic offensive, trying, through 'detente', to weaken the unity of African governments' opposition to white minority rule in Southern Africa. In Namibia, he made serious efforts to construct at least the pretence of an 'internal settlement', which his propaganda machine could sell abroad as an 'exercise in self-determination'.

The first official recognition of this new strategy came on 2 September 1974 in a parliamentary debate, during which Vorster reiterated the traditional South African position on Namibia but did concede that the ultimate choice belonged to 'the peoples of South West Africa.' In mid-September Vorster consulted with his 'Bantu Affairs' overlord in Namibia, Jannie de Wet, and the Executive Committee of the South West Africa National Party (SWANP). On 23 September, SWANP chiefs met in Windhoek. The following day, they announced an invitation to all 'population groups' in Namibia to discuss the territory's constitutional future. This was the birth of the Turnhalle tribal talks.

That very same day, South Africa's Ambassador to the U.N. was telling the Security Council that 'it is for the inhabitants of South West Africa to decide their own future'. South Africa's ten-year time scale for Namibian self-determination, arrogantly thrown in the face of the U.N. the previous April as no more than a remote possibility, was now, he admitted, no longer tenable. Three days later, Vorster's defunct Advisory Council was summoned to Cape Town to rubber-stamp the plan. On 5 November, in the course of his famous 'give us six months' speech, Vorster appealed to the world 'to give the people of South West Africa an opportunity to work out their own future for themselves'.

The central purpose of the South African plan was to create the illusion of a genuine process of self-determination. Behind this cover the regime could proceed as rapidly as possible to bring the bantustan programme to completion, while its allies at the U.N. would have a pretext for blocking any moves against South Africa in the Security Council. The trouble was that it had precious few black collaborators with any popular support to make its plan work. Consequently, it had little option but to use its existing bantustan puppets, attaching as many reactionaries and renegade nationalists as it could find to bolster their credibility. As only 'population groups' were to participate, nationally based political parties were automatically excluded, whatever their attitude towards the Conference. The only real shift in the South African position was that separate 'independence' for individual bantustans seemed now to be ruled out, although even this aspect was to remain ambiguous for more than two years.

The South Africans faced another problem too: their bantustan programme was only six years old and in most of them the installation of tribal 'governments' had hardly begun. Not surprisingly, the regime needed nearly a year to concoct its 12 ethnic delegations. Most of the regime's paid tribal administrators did as they were told and duly sent delegations to the Conference. Those who did not, such as the Damara Tribal Executive, soon found themselves bypassed. In fact, many traditional leaders in the Police Zone reserves were bitter opponents of apartheid, and some refused to have anything to do with the South African scheme. In several cases, Bantu Affairs officials and secret police agents were reduced to picking up people unknown even in their home areas in order to make up their delegations. Huge sums were put into the expense accounts of the Turnhalle delegates, into frequent foreign tours, into propaganda and bribery, even into buying up the only national English- and German- language newspapers as mouthpieces for the Turnhalle.

The regime did its best to give their puppets an aura of democratic legitimacy. Still smarting from their resounding defeat in Ovamboland in August 1973, only six days after announcing their plans for a constitutional conference the South Africans called another election for 13—17 January

1975. This time nothing was left to chance. The bantustan administration
gave itself a full three and a half months in which to try to destroy any
opposition and intimidate people to vote. SWAPO again called for a boycott,
but with many of its members detained or across the border, it did not have
the resources to inform or organise the people as effectively as in 1973, although it did circulate leaflets throughout the land. The authorities, on the
other hand, prepared massively, with relentless propaganda over the radio,
no fewer than 116 polling stations and troop reinforcements swarming everywhere. SWAPO meetings were attacked and broken up. Bantustan employees
were told they would lose their jobs if they did not vote, old people their
pensions, visitors their travel permits, contract workers all future employment, and people generally their right to health services. And since all had to
carry a bantustan 'identity card' on which their voting record was marked,
there was no escape.

Even so, on the first day of voting only 2,000 turned out in Ovamboland
itself and hardly any in the south. Alarmed, the authorities resorted to direct
coercion, driving people to the polls with threats and beatings, and rigging
the result by forcing some to vote many times over. Under such conditions,
and with a full five days of systematic blackmail, it is surprising that as little
as 55% of the registered electors actually voted, although the South Africans
hailed the result as a tremendous victory. As in August 1973, amongst
contract workers in the south the boycott was solid.

Outside the ranks of their bantustan 'governments' the South Africans
found very few black politicians willing to go along with its scheme. One
source of recruitment was a small group of disaffected exiles, a few of them
formerly members of SWAPO. About a dozen did return, but as they no
longer had any standing in the liberation movement or any following outside
Namibia, their impact was barely noticeable except in the Western press, a
matter of deep disappointment to their paymasters. In fact, only a minority
had been active in the liberation struggle, and then only in its formative phase
and often mainly to advance their own reputations. A typical example was
Mburumba Kerina: a voluntary exile in the U.S. since the early 1950s and
briefly involved with SWAPO in 1960, he returned to Namibia in 1976 in a
blaze of press exposure to join the pro-Turnhalle publicity campaign. But,
like several others, the lavish South African funds put within his reach seem
to have been the main attraction, and his presence has hardly been noticed
since.

Inside Namibia the blandishments of the apartheid regime persuaded few,
even amongst the range of small political groups and parties which continued
to hold aloof from full commitment to the liberation movement. Since the
severity of the colonial forced labour regime had prevented the emergence of
any sizeable black petty bourgeoisie, most of the leaders of these groups held
their positions by virtue of tribal status, although some were conservative
members of the tiny educated elite. Nearly all resisted full incorporation into
South Africa's bantustan authorities, but a few were attracted by the ethnic
basis of the Turnhalle Conference.

The South Africans' only major coup was to detach Chief Clemens Kapuuo, conservative leader of the Herero people, from the National Convention of Namibia (N.C.N.). Kapuuo's political importance stemmed not from his national representative status (his support was exclusively tribal) but from his succession to the Herero tradition of resistance to German and South African colonialism, an inheritance to which he now turned traitor. Having supported the N.C.N.'s demand for independence and having resisted strong pressure from local white politicians towards the end of 1973 to join Vorster's Advisory Council, fear that SWAPO's growing national power would diminish the political weight of his tribal base and South African promises of 'self-determination' led him in 1975 to become a whole-hearted advocate of the South African Turnhalle plan. On 27 September 1973, Kapuuo had held secret discussions with Dirk Mudge, a senior SWANP politician who was to become Vorster's chief white pace-setter in Namibia. The result was a joint statement rejecting 'violence' and supporting dialogue with the occupation regime. In July 1974, he pursued this policy further and tried to promote the N.C.N. internationally as the sole representative of the Namibian people, attempting to usurp the recognition won by SWAPO after 15 long years of liberation struggle. When, on 7 January 1975, he issued a statement denouncing SWAPO as a solely Ovambo organisation and accepting that Namibian politics should be ethnically based, his break with the anti-colonial front was complete.

The National Convention of Namibia had in any case been largely moribund for over a year. On 17 January 1975, SWAPO announced its withdrawal from it, pointing out that 'when SWAPO members have been arrested, flogged, tortured, killed or gaoled, it has failed to voice any protest against the illegal South African administration which committed these atrocities.' The N.C.N.'s silence had been at its most conspicuous during the wave of repression exclusively directed at SWAPO in late 1973 and early 1974. It had anyway lost its cohesion, and therefore its purpose, as Kapuuo and his allies had begun to work actively inside it to undermine SWAPO.

SWAPO Unites Anti-Colonial Forces Against the Conference

Despite persistent provocation, SWAPO, although by far the strongest political party in Namibia and the only one nationally representative, retained its membership of the N.C.N. until the last possible moment. Its policy has always been to co-operate as far as possible with other nationalist forces in order to provide a common forum and united front against the divisive tactics of the enemy. Having left the N.C.N., SWAPO wasted no time in working to bring about a regrouping of genuinely anti-colonial organisations, and was the driving force behind the formation, in March 1975, of the Namibia National Convention (N.N.C.) on a platform of militant opposition to South Africa's bantustan programme and the Turnhalle Constitutional Conference.

In a wide-ranging policy statement issued at a press conference in Windhoek on 17 January 1975, SWAPO declared its position on the Turnhalle talks: 'We refuse to have anything to do with the currently proposed multi-racial talks because they are tribally oriented and do not involve the true leaders of the Namibian people.' SWAPO rejected the Turnhalle in its entirety and consistently refused to have any dealings with it. 'South Africa has decided that the best way to keep Namibia as a colony is to pretend to let it go', the January statement continued. 'It is using every means to find allies, internal and external, to help it in this cynical but doomed venture.'

Throughout the run-up to the Conference SWAPO concentrated on mobilising nation-wide support for its platform of opposition. Although during late 1974 and much of 1975 most SWAPO public meetings were banned, and although those that were allowed to start were often violently broken up, SWAPO nevertheless managed to hold several large and success-ful rallies: 1,500 people attended in Katutura in December 1974, 3,000 at Tsumeb and 900 at Gobabis in mid-January 1975, 2,000 in early February in Katutura again and 1,500 at Walvis Bay three months later.

When on 16 August 1975, a fortnight before the Turnhalle Conference was due to open, the hated Chief Filemon Elifas, the so-called 'Chief Minister' of Ovamboland, was gunned down by an unknown assassin, there was rejoicing among contract workers throughout the country. The following day, a Sunday, crowds of people, including large numbers of young people, marched through the streets of the Ovambo residential quarter in Katutura. But the assassination was used as a pretext for a nation-wide wave of repress-ion on the part of the regime, surpassing even the arrests and atrocities in early 1972, August 1973 and January–February 1974 after previous triumphs in the people's resistance. Police arrested demonstrators in Katutura, and hired thugs — followers of Chief Kapuuo — broke into the homes of top SWAPO officials in Windhoek and handed them over to the police. Only David Meroro, forewarned, was able to escape and cross the border to safety. A Namibia National Convention rally in Katutura was attacked by police with batons and dogs, and all the speakers were arrested. During the last fortnight in August, virtually the entire leadership of SWAPO, the Youth League and the Regional Executive in the north, together with scores of militants (more than 200 in all) were detained and held in solitary confine-ment.As usual, many were beaten and tortured, and in Northern and Central Namibia hired thugs of the Turnhalle puppets harassed SWAPO supporters and in some cases destroyed their homes. Most of the leadership was released in early October, but those arrested in Ovamboland were not, and it soon became clear that the occupation regime had decided to implicate SWAPO directly in the assassination by means of a 'terrorism' trial of two SWAPO leaders (National Organiser Aaron Mushimba and Hendrik Shikongo) and four other SWAPO members.

The victimisation of Mushimba and Shikongo was to become a trial of strength between the occupation regime and the liberation movement. By constantly detaining SWAPO leaders for long periods in inhuman conditions and subjecting them to severe torture, the occupation regime has hoped to break their will to resist and to disrupt the cohesion of SWAPO's organisation. In this it has failed utterly, such has been the courageous resolve of those imprisoned and the unbreakable bond of solidarity between the leaders and the people. It has also attempted to use trials under the Terrorism Act to pin criminal responsibility for PLAN's guerrilla operations on the activists of SWAPO's political structure inside Namibia. The prosecution of Mushimba and Shikongo in 1975−76 under a death penalty clause of the Act, alleging indirect involvement in the assassination of Elifas, was clearly intended as a precedent whereby the occupation regime could imprison and kill any Namibian who supported the liberation struggle in whatever form.

The Trial of Mushimba and Shikongo

When the regime has resorted to its armoury of repressive laws to persecute political leaders and freedom fighters, the spirit and unflinching dedication of SWAPO militants has transformed the trials into impressive acts of solidarity with the accused and turned the illegal South African courts into a searing indictment of the occupation regime. Throughout the first session of the trial of Aaron Mushimba and Hendrik Shikongo and their four co-accused, on 1−2 December 1975, 200 people picketed the Windhoek Supreme Court, signing SWAPO songs and paying tribute to exiled and imprisoned leaders of the liberation movement. Their placards captured the challenge of the hour: 'SWAPO is sure for victory − freedom now, now. . .' 'Illegal regime has no right to try the just cause!' and 'We are suffering for a free and united Namibia'. At one stage, the judge ordered the main doors of the courtroom to be closed to shut out the sound of the freedom songs. When the trial restarted in February 1976, the vigil resumed, and police stormed the crowd of over 200 with batons and dogs. With extreme courage Axel Johannes and Victor Nkandi, who were savagely tortured in an attempt to make them turn State's Witness, refused from the dock to testify against their comrades, and publicly exposed the crimes of their torturers.

On 12 May, after a farcical trial in which the only so-called evidence consisted of propaganda against SWAPO, Mushimba and Shikongo were sentenced to death. It was the first time in the history of the liberation struggle in Namibia that a death sentence had been passed under the Terrorism Act. In this case it was for only the most tenuous association with the alleged crime, even if the trumped-up state evidence were to be fully believed. The trial had clearly been staged in order to get a death sentence and the judge only confirmed this by refusing leave to appeal. As Mushimba and Shikongo left the dock, they turned to salute their comrades with clench fists. 'South Africa, remember: what the evil men do lives after them. So be it with you,' proclaimed one placard held by the defiant crowd outside the court.

But the colonial regime had over-reached itself. Both inside Namibia and abroad, a sustained solidarity campaign exposed the murderous intention of the South African Government and the mockery of 'justice' it had perpetrated. Alternative judicial avenues were found and an appeal was set in motion. Eventually a South African court was forced to declare a mistrial because police spies had infiltrated the defence team and passed information to the state before and during the trial. Not daring to mount another show trial, the regime finally released the two men on 17 March 1977, ironically just one day before the Turnhalle Conference ratified its ill-begotten constitution.

Demonstrators outside the Swakopmund Supreme Court during the trial of Aaron Muchimba and 5 other SWAPO members in 1976

Their release was greeted with jubilation throughout Namibia.

A crowd of over 2,000 gathered in Windhoek singing, shouting and weeping when they saw the two men. 'SWAPO was condemned to death; now it has risen again' and 'The struggle continues: SWAPO will win' were the slogans of the hour. People waited for hours to see them, to touch them, to make sure that they were really there. A truck carrying the two patriots and crammed with SWAPO members and supporters, fists clenched in salutes, led a procession of over 70 cars from Windhoek Central Prison where they had been held. People followed on foot shouting 'Long live SWAPO' and 'Power, power'. They phoned up from all over the country just to hear Aaron and Hendrik speak.

The celebrations lasted through the night and the next day, when a similarly jubilant procession followed the car in which Anna Ngaihondjwa and Rauna Nambinga, the two SWAPO women who had been tried with them, travelled from the airport.

Shortly after his release Hendrik Shikongo returned to Windhoek Central Prison armed with a large number of SWAPO membership cards to sign up all those in prison who had decided after discussion with Aaron and Hendrik to join.

It was thus in the midst of a nation-wide crackdown on the political organisation of the liberation movement that on 1 September 1975 the Constitutional Conference began its first session in the old Turnhalle drill hall. It closed less than a fortnight later with a vaguely worded 'Declaration of Intent' in which it gave itself three years to work out a constitutional solution. One of the leading white delegates, Eben van Zijl, told the all-white Legislative Assembly with evident satisfaction that the Declaration 'had excluded the principle of one man one vote or a unitary South West African state . . . '

In October, the South Africans sent a 34-man Turnhalle group on a month-long tour of Britain, the U.S. and West Germany to drum up Western support. It was clear to all that for the apartheid regime the Turnhalle Conference was little more than a propaganda exercise — indeed, South African diplomats at the U.N. were circulating the draft of the Declaration days *before* it had been voted on in Windhoek. But SWAPO's sustained campaign in the preceding months had discredited the Conference even before it had started and denied it any significant political support inside Namibia. On 29 August, a few days before it was due to begin, SWAPO upstaged its deliberations by issuing a detailed and carefully thought out Discussion Paper on a constitution for an independent Namibia. Abroad, an active diplomatic and publicity offensive ensured the Turnhalle delegation a hostile reception, even from Western government circles, and it had to return home without achieving the breakthrough its masters expected of it.

The Triumph of the Angolan Revolution
But by now other events were overtaking the political campaign against the Turnhalle Conference. The struggle for freedom in Namibia, indeed in the whole of Southern Africa, was rapidly approaching a major turning-point, in which Angola was to be the decisive battleground. As 1975 wore on, the South Africans had watched with alarm the increasing successes of PLAN and the growing strength of the popular forces in Angola under the leadership of the M.P.L.A. On 9 April, PLAN fighters took control of a South African military camp in the Eastern Caprivi; on 18 July, they destroyed a four-vehicle military convoy; and on 24 July, engaged in what a source from the front described as 'one of the fiercest battles ever fought by SWAPO freedom fighters'. In each case, a number of enemy soldiers were killed and NATO weapons captured.

The possibility of SWAPO having military bases in Angola if the M.P.L.A.

took control enormously increased the potential of PLAN activity in the near future. The South Africans were well aware of this. When, therefore, the M.P.L.A. proclaimed 'generalised popular resistance' on 26 July and rapidly took control of most of the centre and south of the country, the South Africans made their own preparations for intervention. At the end of July and in early August, South African troops and Portuguese mercenaries crossed into Angola without warning, driving out M.P.L.A. garrisons and attacking PLAN units and camps. The South African Minister of Defence claimed later that their only objective was to protect the Ruacana hydro-electric scheme, but their real purpose was to control the far south of Angola and prepare a springboard for the much larger military intervention which was to follow.

In October 1975, in an operation carefully co-ordinated with the C.I.A., the reactionary elements in Zaire and the imperialist surrogates F.N.L.A. and UNITA, South African and mercenary columns swept in towards Luanda from the south and north in order to try to prevent the formation of the People's Republic of Angola under the leadership of the M.P.L.A. on Independence Day, 11 November 1975. It was to no avail. Timely assistance from Cuba and other socialist countries enabled the guerrilla formations of the M.P.L.A. to fight a conventional war alongside their allies. The offensive was halted on both fronts, the M.P.L.A. proclaimed the People's Republic, and then launched a counter-offensive which first smashed the F.N.L.A. in the north and then, in January—February 1976, forced the South African invaders to retreat across the border, leaving UNITA to disintegrate as a military force. When the acid test came none of the imperialist powers which had egged on the South African advance dared to commit open military support on its side.

PLAN Escalates the Armed Struggle

South Africa's large-scale invasion of Angola was to transform the situation for the operational area of combat between SWAPO and the occupation troops. On 6 August, only ten days before he was assassinated, Chief Elifas had gone to Pretoria in a blaze of publicity to meet Vorster, who afterwards announced that the South African army and police had been given *carte blanche* to remain in Ovamboland indefinitely 'to assist in the maintenance of law and order'. For a time the Bantu Affairs boss, Jannie de Wet, actively promoted the idea of a 'Greater Ovamboland', incorporating part of Southern Angola into an 'independent' Ovambo bantustan. But very soon the South Africans were on the defensive, even as their invasion force was sweeping north into Central Angola.

In late October, the authorities began clearing a 'free-fire zone' at least one kilometre wide along the entire 2,250 km Ovamboland/Angola border — an exercise which entailed uprooting some 20,000 peasants from their land and homes. At the same time, South African instructors equipped the trigger-happy tribal police with automatic weapons and began 'counter-insurgency' training. In December 1975, a large unit of South African paramilitary police, hand-picked for their experience in anti-guerrilla warfare, was flown up from Pretoria with instructions to wipe out 'terrorist infiltration'. 'We are going to clear Ovamboland,' threatened the South African Minister of Police, 'It is a fairly strong group we are sending.'

The South Africans were getting edgy, for their military escalation was not only reaching stalemate in Angola but was also failing to achieve its second immediate aim, to pre-empt the extension of SWAPO's guerrilla campaign. Despite air attacks, SWAPO fighters had engaged South African troops in a five-day running battle in Southern Angola in September 1975, shooting down three helicopters. A month later, in two actions on 11–12 October, PLAN units carried the battle into Ovamboland, killing eight collaborators, including six armed tribal police. As the South African forces extended their raids and atrocities through Southern Angola, the fighting intensified and PLAN soldiers inflicted a mounting toll of casualities, only some of them officially admitted, amongst the white South African troops. For the period July 1975 to April 1976, the occupation regime admitted a total of 59 military clashes with SWAPO fighters, two of them south of Ovamboland. The South African offensive had failed disastrously in Namibia too.

In February 1976, the invasion army withdrew rapidly from Central Angola and by the end of March all defence force units had retreated across the border. It was the signal for a massive build-up of South African military power inside Namibia, overwhelmingly concentrated along the northern border. From 16,000 in January 1976, the size of the occupation army had reached 50,000 by the end of August, including 19,000 frontline troops, a squadron of Mirage fighters and several helicopter squadrons. On 6 March, a full session of the Turnhalle Conference repeated the blanket endorsement of the military occupation which the Ovambo 'government' had given the previous August. New regulations under the emergency law (R 17–72) on 5 and 19 May not only imposed the full weight of martial law but also extended it to the whole of the northern zone, covering over 55% of the Namibian population. Major additions to the fixed army and air-force installations at the Grootfontein military base were completed in February, and a string of bases and camps was built throughout Ovamboland. Henceforth, troops of South Africa's army of occupation were to be the main instruments of repression in the north.

Ovamboland was now the major zone of confrontation between SWAPO's rapidly expanding liberation army and South Africa's garrison of occupation. Where formerly it had primarily been political cadres of SWAPO's local party organisation confronting the bantustan agents of the colonial state — particularly the tribal police, backed up by South African police and soldiers at times of crisis — now PLAN freedom fighters were locked in deadly combat with the might of the occupation army with its sophisticated NATO-made equipment. Throughout 1976, continuing right through the dry season (when conditions are difficult for guerrilla tactics), PLAN sustained a high level of attacks on the occupying forces. Indeed, the regular mining of

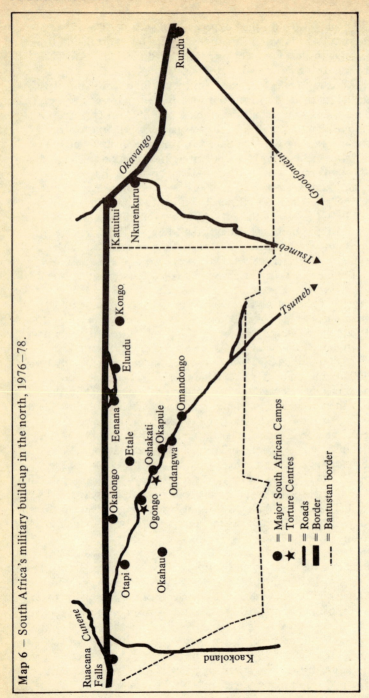

Map 6 – South Africa's military build-up in the north, 1976–78.

Ruacana Cunene Falls

Otapi

Okahau

Okalongo

Etale

Eenana

Ogongo

Oshakati

Okapule

Ondangwa

Omandongo

Elundu

Kongo

Katuitui

Nkurenkuru

Okavango

Rundu

Grootfontein ▼

Tsumeb ▼

Tsumeb ▼

Kaokoland

● = Major South African Camps

★ = Torture Centres

▮ = Roads

▮ = Border

┄ = Bantustan border

military roads and ambushing of South African patrols soon considerably restricted their mobility. Larger formations of freedom fighters mounted surprise assaults on South African camps and bases with considerable success: the helicopter base at Oruno in June 1976 and again with heavy arms in early November, destroying helicopters and vehicles; the Omboloka training camp for UNITA mercenaries on 2–3 June, shooting down three helicopters; the Epinga base on 4 September, overrunning and destroying it completely – these were only the more dramatic of a series of successes which took a heavy toll in South African casualties, 76 being killed in the three months up to June alone. By the end of 1976, PLAN combatants were moving freely into the central and southern regions of Namibia, though their missions were mainly political and intelligence-gathering rather than military.

The South African answer to their increasingly desperate military plight was to escalate their repressive practices into a systematic reign of terror over the entire civilian population of the north. Many of the sons and daughters of the local peasantry who had fled earlier waves of repression were returning as trained freedom fighters, confident in their cause and in ultimate victory. The people were welcoming them with open arms, giving them shelter, food and intelligence about enemy movements. As a SWAPO fighter commented on his own experience, 'the population is really in harmonious relation to our fighting cadres', valuing the protection they were increasingly able to provide against the routine searches and interrogation by South African patrols. A South African conscript soldier who later fled the country described one part of the South African retaliation, a systematic sweep across Central Ovamboland in which every single adult man was hauled in for torture and interrogation at army and police camps.

But quite apart from special operations such as these, rape, beatings and atrocities against civilians were matters of daily routine for South African patrols whose enemy was the entire black population. Most South African military camps had their own detention centres for the 'suspects' they rounded up, in addition to the corrugated iron jails for SWAPO members which had existed since 1973. Many civilians and SWAPO supporters have died or simply disappeared – one mass grave was found alongside Onuno, one of the torture centres. The South Africans turned the whole of the densely populated north into an armed camp. But the escalating and sadistic violence of their methods of repression was simply a measure of their desperation and their conspicuous failure to detach the people from the freedom fighters. Contrary to South Africa's propaganda claims, morale and efficiency among its conscript soldiers has never been high. Constantly caught on the defensive by SWAPO attacks (about which the local population gives no warning, despite systematic round-ups and savage torture), the occupation troops lashed out with random brutality against the very people whose 'hearts and minds' their spokesmen cynically claimed they were winning over. The peasants of the north were suffering grievously but they were also tasting for the first time the freedom of partial liberation and the ability to hit back at their oppressors.

South Africa's aggression against the Angolan revolution collapsed in ruins, but confronted by the Angolan people's solidarity with their Namibian comrades-in-arms, the occupation regime refused to abandon its aggressive designs. UNITA resistance in Central and South-east Angola did not long survive the withdrawal of its South African ally, and thousands of its troops and supporters soon followed the South African troops across the borders into Namibia. Henceforth UNITA was to be the occupation regime's principal subversive tool against the M.P.L.A. Government in Angola. It established a string of camps across the north of Namibia where it trained and armed thousands of UNITA mercenaries, and deepened its commitment to UNITA's subversive campaign inside Angola, financing, arming and supplying its operations.

The damaged South African army barracks at Katima Mulilo after a successful PLAN assault in August 1978

But the South African defence force also had another use for UNITA refugees — as mercenaries in its intensified anti-SWAPO drive. By the middle of 1976, it was sending them into action against the Namibian liberation struggle, posing as PLAN cadres in atrocities against civilians and attacking SWAPO camps in Southern Angola. A favourite tactic was to send bands of UNITA troops disguised in PLAN uniforms across the border to terrorise Angolan villages and drive hundreds or even thousands of civilians into Namibia as 'refugees', who could then be presented in a blaze of publicity to selected journalists as victims of SWAPO's 'barbarity'. Once inside UNITA camps, some were even forced to train as UNITA mercenaries for use against

PLAN soldiers arrive at a village burnt down by South African troops

SWAPO. UNITA itself has declared war on SWAPO. Their leader, Jonas Savimbi, has accused the West of selling out Namibia to the Soviet Union, 'represented' by SWAPO. He has vowed to continue to fight SWAPO and said that he will get the Angolan so-called refugees to vote illegally for the Turnhalle. Savimbi and his lieutenants have visited South Africa and Namibia on several occasions to consult with the South African Government, and it is clear that the latter has a strong influence on UNITA strategy and tactics.

SWAPO Builds a Wall of National Unity

The 18 months following the failure of the invasion of Angola saw a more serious attempt to conjure up an 'internal solution' which would both safeguard South Africa's essential interests and at the same time win the tacit support of its imperialist backers. Unfortunately for the apartheid regime the failure of its military adventurism had seriously weakened its standing in the eyes of Western strategists and had given a great boost to the morale of the liberation movement throughout Southern Africa. The national uprising in South Africa's own cities, which began in Soweto in June 1976, caused a serious crisis of confidence in the West in the ability of the apartheid regime to safeguard imperialist interests in Southern Africa. Above all, the

regime had utterly failed to break the united front of opposition to its plans
which SWAPO had organised and led, first through the N.C.N. in 1971—74,
then through the N.N.C. in 1975—76.

At first, the South Africans were fully preoccupied with their massive
military campaign in the north. The Turnhalle Conference met only in-
frequently and spent most of its time discussing economic and social issues
and not constitutions. But in August 1976, the regime was brought face to
face with its weakened position. SWAPO's intensive lobbying and the victory
of the M.P.L.A. in Angola had forced the imperialist powers to allow through
a crucial U.N. Security Council Resolution (S.C. 385 of 30 January 1976),
which set out in clear terms the conditions which South Africa was to observe
in withdrawing its illegal administration. It threatened to take 'appropriate
measures . . . under the Charter' unless South Africa took steps by 31 August
to withdraw its occupying forces and to allow free national elections for
Namibia as a single political entity, to be held under U.N. supervision and
control. In February 1976, SWAPO's international campaign had borne
further fruit when the nine foreign ministers of the European Common
Market declared for the first time their endorsement of the right of the
Namibian people to self-determination and independence and to free
elections under U.N. supervision and control, and condemned South Africa's

continued occupation.

With the August deadline fast approaching, the South Africans had to pull something out of the bag to buy time from the West. The Turnhalle's 'Declaration of Intent', adopted in September 1975, had promised completion of a draft constitution within three years, 'if possible'. But on 18 August, with the U.N. deadline looming and the South Africans anxious to head off the possibility of sanctions being imposed on them, the Turnhalle Conference committed itself to 'independence', set 31 December 1978 as a target date and promised to establish a Turnhalle-based 'interim government', if possible by 31 March 1977. This was sufficient pretext for Britain, France and the U.S. to cast a triple veto in the Security Council on 18 October, saving the regime from punitive action under Chapter VII of the U.N. Charter as a threat to world peace.

At last the Turnhalle set about its ostensible task — constitution-making. After months of haggling and informal discussion, during which at one point Vorster even had to summon them to Pretoria to lay down the law, the tribal delegations finally delivered the goods on 18 March 1977, a draft constitution for an 'interim government'. It envisaged a three-tier structure, the first two comprising the existing local bantustan authorities, the third being a federal assembly of bantustan nominees in which each bantustan would hold a fixed quota of seats. Since decisions were to be taken not by majority vote but by consensus, it was abundantly plain that the whites would have a veto on any changes in the apartheid *status quo*. If anyone still had doubts, white leaders made it clear that such was their design and that this was their model for the 'independence' constitution which the so-called federal assembly was to produce. Statements by leading white politicians, including the arch propagandist Dirk Mudge, to the effect that an independent Turnhalle government would continue to depend on South African economic aid and military assistance for some years to come, clearly exposed the hollowness of the so-called self-determination exercise. So slight was the real power which this constitution planned to transfer to the 'interim government' that it can hardly be described even as 'neo-colonial'. Even elections would be staged on an ethnic basis and thus fail to provide a vehicle for posing a genuine alternative to South Africa's contrived solution.

But it was already far too late for such a plan to have the slightest popular appeal. The Namibian people, inspired by the Angolan revolution and and the mass protests in South Africa, were powerfully on the move once more, as they had been in 1971–72. The momentum of popular resistance built an immoveable wall of national unity under the leadership of SWAPO. A national congress of the party convened at Walvis Bay on 29–31 May 1976 confirmed SWAPO's rejection of the Turnhalle Conference, restate restated the principles on which it would negotiate with the occupation regime and in clear terms reaffirmed the unity of the SWAPO leadership, whether working inside or outside the country.

During the second half of 1976, most of the groups which belonged to

the N.N.C., but which had remained outside the ranks of the liberation movement, disbanded and joined SWAPO *en masse*. On 17 August, the Rehoboth
Volksparty, habitually the majority party in the Gebiet, was the first to
declare its resolve. It was followed in October by the four most influential
groups in Southern Namibia, headed by Pastor Hendrik Witbooi (grandson
of the great resistance leader Hendrik Witbooi); on 27 November by NAPDO,
Namibian African People's Democratic Organisation, and in April 1977 by
the 17,000-member Herero Royal House. In December 1976, seeing no
further purpose in retaining its membership of the N.N.C., most of whose
members had already joined its ranks, SWAPO announced its withdrawal
and the N.N.C. — like its predecessor — faded into oblivion. The only
non-Turnhalle political groups which still held aloof from the liberation
movement were SWANU and a handful of small, regionalist organisations
with little popular support.

This period was the climax of a great drive for national unity. Responding
to the challenge, Pastor Witbooi declared on behalf of the leaders of the
south: 'Today we have arrived at this crossroad and our choice is clear: we
join unconditionally in the genuine nationalist platform of SWAPO created
by our fellow-countrymen and not Turnhalle, the platform created by our
enemy, the South African Government.' The Rev. Karuaera, former Chairman
of the Royal House, underscored earlier statements by others who had joined
SWAPO when he said: 'Only by unity can we strengthen the struggle of the
oppressed people in Namibia.'

The last months of 1976 saw the pace of mass activity quicken on all
fronts. Contract labourers took the initiative among the workers in organising
a nation-wide general trade union under the banner of N.U.N.W., holding
meetings and discussions in the main towns and mines. In November, high
school students launched a campaign against 'Bantu Education' by refusing
to sit end-of-year exams. The boycott gained total support in the centre and
south of the country. Many refused to return to government-run schools
in the New Year, and hundreds left the country to become freedom fighters.
The majority of university students who had come home after the closure
of the black campuses in South Africa also refused to return and joined the
liberation movement as SWAPO members. On 10 November, the entire body
of Nama teachers came out on strike against racial discrimination in salary
scales, and stayed out for 74 days in a protest which galvanised mass support
throughout Southern Namibia and won nation-wide solidarity from black
teachers generally.

During the latter part of 1976 and into 1977, the south became an
intensely mobilised part of the country where militancy ran high. People
greeted each other as 'comrade', the Youth League organised the students and
young workers, the Women's Council began to make great inroads in mobilising women and gave concerts to raise funds. Many of the songs which were
being sung in the south were the liberation songs composed during the
1904–8 war against German colonialism. As one local SWAPO member put
it: 'The south is like a liberated area, and we haven't even fired a shot!'

Not only in the south but also in the central reserves of Rehoboth, Damara-land and Hereroland, the concerted attempts by the occupation regime to impose its bantustan scheme during 1976 and the first half of 1977 aroused angry mass demonstrations and sustained opposition amongst the local peasants. And in the north, the armed struggle was making solid and perman-ent gains despite the intensity of military repression. The revolutionary commitment of the Namibian masses was something neither the imperialists nor even the South Africans could afford to ignore.

At the same time, the occupation regime launched a recruiting drive for the tribal armies it was creating in furtherance of its apartheid plans. Towards the end of 1976, the head of the South African Army visited Namibia to promote the drive and in December the Turnhalle set up a defence committee to liaise with the South African Government. Recruiting announcements and meetings started in the southern reserves — some people were recruited under false pretences and later managed to escape. By the end of the year, some 500 men in the Ovambo and Kavango battalions were serving on the northern border under South African command and it was clearly the regime's inten-tion to take some of the pressure off its own demoralised conscripts by localising the war on a tribal basis.

In August 1977, the operation moved into top gear when the entire command structure in Namibia was centralised in Windhoek, and training began of ethnic contingents from the Damara, Nama and Coloureds, with another Herero to follow shortly. Nevertheless, most of these recruits would take a year to train and even then provide only a fraction of the frontline troops which South Africa's colonial war required. PLAN's relentless guerrilla attacks, supported constantly by growing recruitment and better arms, including heavier weapons such as rockets and mortars, were progressively sapping the morale of the white conscripts, both in the field and back home, where white youth were becoming more sharply aware of what awaited them in a bloody and unwinnable colonial war.

South Africa Prepares Its 'Internal Settlement' (1977—79)

From 'Interim Government' to the U.N. Transition Plan

On 18 March 1977, after much haggling over the crumbs of power South Africa was throwing their way, the Turnhalle delegates finally ratified their constitution for an 'interim government'. But it was already too late. The Namibian revolution was too far advanced for the imperialist powers to ignore its vanguard movement, SWAPO. Throughout 1976, the Americans in particular, under the direction of Secretary of State Henry Kissinger, had tried to get South Africa to include SWAPO in the Turnhalle Conference. Great pressure had also been put on SWAPO to attend the Conference, but it steadfastly refused to do so. Likewise, South Africa refused either to negotiate directly with SWAPO or to convene the Conference in a form which would allow SWAPO to participate in co-operation with the U.N. Accordingly, on 7 April the five Western members of the Security Council (the three permanent members, the U.S., Britain and France, together with Canada and West Germany) confronted Vorster in Cape Town with the message that the Turnhalle constitution was unacceptable.

But they also offered him a way out which would neither commit South Africa to any particular solution in advance nor force it to acknowledge the sovereignty of the U.N. over Namibia: namely, for the Western five to set themselves up as mediators. That way, the South African regime would not have to negotiate directly with either the U.N. or SWAPO, and could simply shelve its plan for an 'internal settlement', not abandon it. The resulting diplomacy could also be spun out for as long as it liked because it would always have a veto, thereby keeping the hands of the U.N. tied because the Western five — the Contact Group — would block any strong move against South Africa while 'negotiations' were in progress — in other words, the perfect delaying tactic. On 7 July, after three months of negotiations with the Contact Group, the South African Government accepted the Western proposal. On 1 September, an Administrator-General (A.G.) was installed in Windhoek, empowered to rule by decree, whose task was ostensibly to prepare for elections to a constituent assembly which would frame an independence constitution.

This direct imperialist intervention, which marked the end of a behind-the-scenes role in the Namibian struggle, was invited by neither the U.N. nor SWAPO, but the former was forced to recognise its powerlessness in the face of the Western veto, and the latter, true to its principle of exhausting every possible peaceful road to independence, decided to participate in the process while reaffirming its commitment to revolutionary armed struggle. Reduced to essentials, the West needed two things for the 'internationally acceptable' settlement it wanted: South African agreement to go through the motions of free national elections based on adult suffrage, so as to meet the formal U.N. criteria for the transition to independence; and SWAPO participation in such elections, so as to commit the liberation movement to the terms of any negotiated settlement. In entering into negotiations with the Contact Group, the South African regime implicitly agreed to postpone any unilateral granting of 'independence' and accepted the need for national elections — U.N.-sponsored if the West insisted.

In no way, however, had South Africa's determination to hold on to Namibia weakened, and it was soon clear that it would only endorse a settlement which guaranteed it the power to rig the election in its favour. Only a client regime as obedient and dependent as its Turnhalle puppets would be acceptable as an 'independent' government, and the regime set out to stall the negotiators until it got its way. Consequently, the full weight and skills of Western diplomacy were directed towards persuading the U.N. and SWAPO to water down the principles laid down in Resolution 385 to ensure free national elections under U.N. supervision and control. That the Namibian people should get a chance to choose their own leaders in a fair and democratic manner is of scant concern to the imperialist powers who have profited so hugely from the South African occupation over the years.

The South Joins SWAPO

The following statement was issued in October
1976 by four of the principal, popular leaders of
the south:
'. . . Now there are only two platforms left:
the national movement SWAPO or Turnhalle.
We asked ourselves: Who repressed, persecuted,
humiliated, liquidated and betrayed us; was it
SWAPO or the Boers and their allies?

'In the present, Turnhalle is nothing else than
a desperate time-gamble of Big Baas Vorster, but
what is the whole sense behind it for the future?
How does it come about that the members of
Turnhalle who would like to be cunning like
jackals behave foolishly like baboons? They
must expect something. The rich man has many
friends, if he is prepared to slaughter the stalled
ox. The Turnhalle is nothing less than a very
comfortable training centre for a black minority
which aims at a neo-colonial solution. That means
for them a rise in economic and political privileges,
but for the mass of people only an increase of
their sufferings. We are neither fools nor simple
ones, we can hear and read what has happened in
most of the African countries since they got
independence as a poisoned gift from their
colonial masters about 15 years ago.

'SWAPO, on the other hand, has grown in the
last few years to the genuine platform of *all*
Namibian people organised by *themselves* in spite
of all the attempts of the allies of the South
African Government to disturb this development,
in spite of all the persecution by the South
Africans who forced many of its militants into
death, captivity or exile. Furthermore, it is
supported by states and organisations all over the
world who have never tried to oppress us, exploit
us or let us suffer. We heard in the last U.N. debate
the words of the Foreign Minister of the People's
Republic of Mozambique, Mr. Chissano, who
asked all those groups and individuals who up till
now have resisted separately to join this platform
and solve their common problems together. We

took this challenge for unity especially seriously
because he is the representative of FRELIMO, a
movement who lived through the same experiences
and sufferings in the last 15 years as we have
done, and still do, and whom we see therefore as
a true friend of a genuine independence in
Namibia.

'Today we have arrived at this crossroad and our
choice is clear: We join unconditionally in the
genuine nationalist platform of SWAPO created
by our fellow-countrymen and not Turnhalle,
the platform created by our enemy, the South
African Government. We also ask seriously all
other groups in a similar position to make the
same step so that we — as a united and democratic power — can master this stormy period
ahead of us.

'We know that unity and the genuine independence of Namibia has strong enemies: SA colonial
rule and its imperialist allies who have just vetoed
down our cause again in the U.N. and that they
have strong military, economical and political
weapons to fight us. But united by a correct
political line and guided by our fundamental
interests, the Namibian people will be able to
crush any aggressor, however powerful he may
be. The glorious examples of the people of
Vietnam and Mozambique give us courage.

'When we join SWAPO, we don't say all our
people are prepared to follow us at this particular
moment or that there are no problems on this
platform. We will tell no lies, nor will we claim
easy victories. We can't count the heads of our
forces in an oppressive situation like today but
we are sure that we can prove our strength in
numbers in a free election under U.N. supervision. Then it will be seen that the overwhelming
majority of the southern population will take the
same choice as we did now on the ballot box.
With this historic decision we honour the heroic
sacrifices of our fathers . . . and all the others
who already started to build a nation through
active resistance against German colonial aggression and who were only defeated because they were

not united enough . . .

' . . . Now we know that we waited too long for
salvation from outside, first from the British, then
from the Volkerebond [League of Nations] and
finally from the U.N. Now we will look ourselves
for the new water. We will rely on our own forces.

'The watchwords for the next period will be:
Rely on your own forces; Prepare yourself for all
possibilities; SWAPO is the People and the People
are SWAPO; Toa tama !khams ge.'

Signed: Pastor H. Witbooi (Gibeon)
Mr. J. Stefanus (Vaalgras)
Mr. S. Isaks (Keetmanshoop)
Mr. H. Noeteb (Hoachanas)

Inside Namibia, the occupation regime rapidly prepared the ground for
a rigged election. The Administrator-General, Justice Steyn, promulgated a
flurry of decrees within three months of taking office which removed some
of the most grotesque 'petty apartheid' discrimination and eased the worst
restrictions on freedom of movement and assembly. The Turnhalle
Conference quietly dissolved itself on 7 November, only to reappear
immediately as a political party, the Democratic Turnhalle Alliance (D.T.A.),
with the apartheid 'interim government' constitution as its programme for
an 'independent' Namibia. The new party, with heavy-handed police, army
and employer backing and seemingly limitless funds at its disposal, began
a nation-wide campaign of bribery and intimidation to build up the illusion
of popular support, which it totally lacked in reality. Turnhalle membership
cards were distributed throughout the country, with card-bearers being
promised preferential treatment and those without threatened with dire
consequences. Pensions, jobs, medical treatment, education — all were refused
to those who would not take out Turnhalle cards. In Ovamboland it was
taken for granted that anyone not carrying a card was a SWAPO supporter.
People there knew only too well what that meant: if unable to produce such
a card to a South African patrol they would be hauled off to an army detention camp and automatic torture as a 'terrorist suspect'.

Mass Mobilisation and Violent Repression
SWAPO meetings were violently broken up, members and supporters beaten
and their homes and property destroyed, increasingly by the tribal armies
and hired thugs of the Turnhalle rather than by the South African security
forces themselves. Chief Kapuuo's small and solely Herero based
party, the National Unity Democratic Organisation (NUDO), played a major
role in leading these attacks.

On 26 August 1977, Namibia Day, and the 11th anniversary of the launching of the armed struggle, celebrations were nevertheless marked by a mood of militant festivity throughout the country, and one strong theme was the clear identification of the people with the armed struggle. In the words of SWAPO Secretary for Education and Culture, Pastor Hendrik Witbooi: 'Someone who is against the armed struggle is like someone who wants the rain without thunder or the sea without waves.' In Katutura a crowd of 2,500 massed at a SWAPO rally which for the first time commemorated the armed struggle in public. But the meeting was attacked by about 50 NUDO thugs, fighting broke out and several SWAPO members were seriously injured. SWAPO changed the meeting place to a large open field, and the crowd swelled to 6,000 people. After the meeting it was discovered that the NUDO thugs planned to return in greater strength the next day and attack the houses of SWAPO supporters. But their sinister design was thwarted; road blocks were set up by SWAPO throughout Katutura and all cars entering and leaving the location were searched. A series of confrontations followed, during which one person was killed and several more injured.

In order to demonstrate its commitment to democratic principles, SWAPO sought to take advantage of the new political freedom supposedly introduced by the new Administrator-General by holding public meetings throughout the country, particularly in the north. The South African reaction was once again a series of violent attacks on SWAPO meetings and supporters. On 19 October, SWAPO held a public meeting at Oshakati, the notorious centre for interrogation and torture and a South African Defence Force stronghold. The emergency regulations prohibiting public meetings in the north had just been lifted, but permission still had to be sought from the Administrator-General under Proclamation AG 9 which replaced them. At the last minute permission was granted, but SWAPO Deputy Chairman Daniel Tjongarero was not allowed to attend. Stringent conditions were laid down by the regime and SWAPO was to be held responsible for any damage, although the safety of SWAPO property was not guaranteed.

Over 6,000 people flocked to the meeting in spite of heavy supervision by the South African troops and police and the tribal Ovambo army. But that night three SWAPO cars were damaged, and SWAPO speakers were threatened with bayonets and had bottles thrown at them and at the house where they were staying. On 16 December, South African soldiers and tribal troops violently broke up another SWAPO rally held at Oluno, the black township of Ondangwa, in Northern Namibia. The 8,000-strong crowd was shot at with tear-gas and live bullets. Many were injured and ten required immediate medical treatment. On 4–5 February, a SWAPO meeting at Katimo Mulilo in the Caprivi Strip, its first open demonstration there for many years, was violently dispersed in the same way. Clearly the regime had decided that SWAPO could not be allowed to demonstrate its popular support by peaceful assembly.

SWAPO leaders also came in for increased harassment. In another sinister development, the regime distributed 'black propaganda' purporting to come from SWAPO which singled out particular SWAPO leaders for slander and misrepresentation. On 2 December, Deputy Chairman Daniel Tjongarero, National Treasurer Tauno Hatuikulipi, Secretary for the Women's Council Martha Ford, Secretary for Legal Affairs Lucia Hamutenya, six other SWAPO members, and B.B.C. correspondent Justin Ellis were arbitrarily detained under Regulation A.G. 9 while on their way to a seminar in the north, organised by the ecumenical Christian Centre of Windhoek. Daniel Tjongarero was subjected to extreme physical and psychological intimidation. He was kept for hours on end in isolation in a corrugated iron hut (where the summer heat rapidly becomes unbearable), then taken to see the bodies of two Namibians who had recently been killed in a landmine explosion, and told that he too would be killed and his death blamed on PLAN. The South African interrogators eventually extracted a statement from him renouncing SWAPO, but which he repudiated immediately on his release.

The campaign of intimidation even encompassed the killing of selected SWAPO officials in cold blood. On 26 December, while on his way with a friend on a social visit, Abnel Amwama, SWAPO Regional Treasurer in Swakopmund, was stopped and shot by senior Special Branch officers – a 'Christmas present', they said. He died soon afterwards.

The South Africans watched with growing alarm the tidal wave of national resistance and the mobilisation of the people achieved by SWAPO, even under the severely limited freedom allowed by the Administrator-General since October 1977. Clearly the D.T.A., despite its massive secret funds, its government-issued arms and its powerful backing from all organs of the colonial state, was failing disastrously not only to drum up a semblance of public support but even to develop the illusion of such support so vital to the South African propaganda machine abroad.

In desperation the regime resorted to its well-tried tactic of brute repression. This time it used its new instrument, the D.T.A., to prepare the ground. By early 1978, the severe recession in South Africa, worsened by a government fiscal policy of tight money and high unemployment, had dragged the Namibian economy with it into stagnation. The grim consequence was rising unemployment amongst black workers. Some 12% of 'permanent' black workers were out of work in Windhoek, and over 1,000 in the small town of Swakopmund alone. At the same time, thousands of unemployed workers previously trapped in the reserves, particularly in Ovamboland, were taking advantage of the relaxation of the pass laws to flood the towns in a desperate search for jobs. Far from attempting to ease the social distress caused by its economic policy, the authorities increased their persecution of the jobless and homeless, and unscrupulous employers began to replace local workers with people from the north, who in sheer desperation would work for half the going wage-rate.

It was in this explosive situation that the regime tried to turn the social tensions its apartheid policy aroused into a sectarian bloodletting of Herero against Ovambo and then into a general assault on SWAPO members and their homes. On 28 February, a false message planted at a D.T.A. meeting in Katutura, presumably by South African agents, provoked a D.T.A. attack on SWAPO supporters which left two dead and 41 injured. The police were ready at hand to tear-gas the SWAPO supporters and, in the words of one witness, 'turned the searchlights mounted on top of the riot-wagons into the eyes of the SWAPO fighters'.

It was the signal for a campaign of widespread violence by Turnhalle thugs, at the instigation of the occupation regime, against SWAPO members and supporters throughout Central Namibia. In the course of one month 18 people were killed, over 200 wounded and many others detained. Trucks and buses were put at the disposal of the thugs to move from town to town. Windhoek, Okakarara, Otjiwarongo, Khorixas and Omaruru were the worst hit. Men, women and children were brutalised, their houses burned and their properties destroyed. The police aided and abetted the thugs by providing searchlights at night to identify the houses of known SWAPO supporters and sympathisers, and, when the fighting intensified, by arming them with sub-machine guns. At all times SWAPO members had only sticks and stones with which to defend themselves.

Katutura, in particular, became a battlefield as the police brought in hundreds of Kapuuo's supporters from the reserves, armed them with guns and gave them a general licence to go on the rampage. And the blood spilt was that of SWAPO members and supporters, who were even refused treatment at the state hospital in Windhoek. Only when 4,000 contract workers went on strike in protest, demanding an end to the violence, the release of those who had been detained, the arrest of the murderers and a guarantee that they themselves would not be victimised for their action, did the Administrator-General intervene to try to restrain the D.T.A. and NUDO bands.

By using NUDO thugs in this way, the occupation regime tried to create a conflict that would appear to be inter-tribal — most of those attacked were contract workers from the north. The whole episode had been deliberately organised by the South Africans to cause tension, violence and confusion, in the same way that at the height of the Soweto uprising in South Africa itself in 1976—77 they had incited and tricked migrant workers in the so-called bachelor hostels into attacking the homes of those location residents who were in the forefront of opposition to apartheid repression. The campaign reached its climax on 27 March when Chief Klemens Kapuuo was killed by unknown assassins. The regime immediately pinned the blame on SWAPO, but SWAPO has emphatically denied any part in it, and the timing was so convenient to the general South African strategy that suspicions remain that the hands of the regime itself were not untainted. Indeed, eye-witnesses saw armed white policemen in a church tower overlooking Kapuuo's house at the exact time of the killing. And it gave the regime the pretext it was looking for to abolish the limited freedom it had introduced six months earlier with so much fanfare and international propaganda.

In the weeks that followed, a massive round-up of SWAPO leaders and officials at national, regional and branch level took place. On 18 April, the

Administrator-General reintroduced indefinite detention without trial
(A.G. 26). Members of the National Executive Committee were detained,
along with others. Some were held 'in connection with the death of Chief
Kapuuo', but others were never charged with any offence. Administrative
Secretary Axel Johannes, who had spent 32 months between January 1974
and September 1977 in detention, was again badly tortured, as were many
of the others. The Security Police made strenuous efforts to pin responsibility for Kapuuo's murder on senior SWAPO leaders, as they had done in the
case of Elifas, but courageous resistance even under torture led the South
Africans to release them piecemeal in the latter half of 1978.

These new detentions marked a turning point in South African repression.
It became increasingly clear that the occupation regime was no longer going
to risk the adverse publicity of public show trials of SWAPO members.
White SWAPO member Peter Manning, who had worked in the Information
Department in Windhoek collecting and exposing details of torture and
UNITA's activities in Namibia, and who was detained in January 1978 and
then charged under the Official Secrets Act, was released on 20 April and all
charges against him dropped. Victor Nkandi, who had been re-detained
immediately on his release in March 1977 and later charged 'in connection
with the death of Chief Filemon Elifas', was acquitted on 1 May 1978. But
while the show trials were stopped, the torture, detentions and intimidation
escalated.

The U.N. Negotiations
It was against this background that the Contact Group of the Western powers
continued to negotiate with SWAPO and South Africa on the terms of
Namibia's decolonisation. SWAPO's position on negotiations with South
Africa, constantly deliberately misinterpreted by South Africa and the
Western powers alike, was expressed categorically in a policy statement
issued over two years before, on 17 January 1975: 'We wish to make it
absolutely clear . . . that SWAPO of Namibia, despite everything, is not
opposed to talks with the South African Government on the future of
Namibia — provided such talks can be meaningful.' The South African
Government, however, has always adamantly refused to negotiate with
SWAPO on any terms.

SWAPO, having learnt from bitter experience that Vorster was not to be
trusted, laid down certain conditions for any settlement under discussion.
These were restated in six points in the new Political Programme adopted by
the Central Committee at its meeting in July—August 1976. They entail
South African acceptance of the right to independence, absolute territorial
integrity, the release of all political prisoners, the free return of all exiles, a
commitment to withdraw its occupation army and police and U.N. supervision and control of elections.

Early on in the negotiations the strategies of the West and of South Africa
became clear, and it was evident that the interests of the Namibian people
did not appear in their calculations at all. The apartheid regime had not

slackened its commitment to install the D.T.A. in power; it had merely
been forced to accept a mechanism for doing so — national elections —
which would prove more difficult to manipulate unless it had tight control
at all stages of the transition. Its objective was therefore to secure the
minimum conditions to guarantee success. Until it did, it would spin out
the negotiations indefinitely, all the time building up the image of the D.T.A.
and attempting, through insidious propaganda, to discredit SWAPO as the
authentic representative of the Namibian people and sow doubts about its
commitment to a negotiated solution in the minds of the Western powers
and even black African states. In this manner, it hoped to be well placed to
install its puppet regime either by deceiving the U.N. into sponsoring rigged
elections or by regaining tacit imperialist support for a unilateral and phony
independence.

The West, on the other hand, while recognising the need to fulfil the
formal U.N. requirements, set out to bend their practical implementation
so far towards South African requirements that it could both head off a
South African 'internal settlement' and render virtually impossible any
chance of the liberation movement winning full political power through
free elections.

The Contact Group's soundings lasted more than six months. Then, on
9 February 1978, it convened the so-called 'proximity talks' in New York,
at which SWAPO and South African delegates were present but, because
of South Africa's refusal to deal with SWAPO, not face-to-face. A few days
previously, the Contact Group had put its own proposals before both sides.
Although ostensibly in line with Resolution 385, the Western proposals for
the transition period to independence were a major retreat from the U.N.'s
constitutional rights as laid down by the I.C.J. in 1971 and in subsequent
Security Council resolutions. Far from calling for the withdrawal of the
South African administration from Namibia, the proposals provided for the
continuing presence of the entire repressive apparatus of the colonial state
and even part of the occupation army right up to the moment of independence. 'U.N. supervision and control' would therefore depend entirely on a
small U.N. monitoring force, and the conditions under which it was to
operate were left deliberately vague, an open invitation to the South Africans
to drag out the negotiations in order to extract further concessions.

Nonetheless, the proposals did contain the *possibility* for effective U.N.
supervision and control of free elections. Accordingly, at the 'proximity
talks' SWAPO made far-reaching and substantive concessions. These included
the acceptance of 1,500 South African troops to remain in Namibia throughout the electoral process, and the confinement and surveillance of PLAN
forces by the proposed U.N. peace-keeping force. Stunned by these moves,
South African Foreign Minister Pik Botha abruptly left the talks for Pretoria
to seek a further mandate on South Africa's position. There followed two
months of intensive and heated exchanges within the South African Cabinet
which was increasingly split between those hard-liners who still wanted to
try to smash SWAPO politically and militarily, and others who recognised that

SWAPO must somehow be included in any transition process — however
rigged the election — in order to win international recognition. The outcome
was a continuing compromise: South Africa would accept national elections
while in reality continuing to repress opposition to the D.T.A., its chosen
successors in Namibia.

On 25 April 1978, South Africa formally announced its acceptance in
principle of the Western proposals. A week earlier, having already rounded up
most SWAPO leaders inside Namibia, it had decreed indefinite detention
without trial. Then, on 4 May, its troops poured across the Namibia/Angola
border and brutally massacred Namibian refugees in a settlement at Kassinga,
150 miles inside Angola. Out of 3,000 people living there, 867 were killed,
464 wounded and over 200 taken prisoner and hauled off to concentration
camps in Namibia. It is by far the worst atrocity yet in a brutally repressive
war. Most of these camp residents were women, children or old people.
Many had only very recently left Namibia to escape the South African
reign of terror. South Africa's claim, in spite of testimonies to the contrary
by SWAPO, the Government of Angola, Western journalists and a joint
mission of the U.N. High Commission for Refugees and the World Health
Organisation, was that this was SWAPO's military headquarters.

The timing of this genocidal raid and the strident propaganda offensive
which accompanied it, as well as the round-up of SWAPO leaders and the
violent intimidation of SWAPO supporters during March and April, were
clearly designed to make it difficult for SWAPO to endorse the Western
proposals. Indeed, the Kassinga attack came just before President Nujoma
was due to meet the foreign ministers of the Contact Group. Shortly afterwards, South Africa raised a tremendous hue and cry over Walvis Bay,
demanding that its purported annexation of September 1977 be recognised
as a condition for continuing the negotiations. Once more SWAPO's leadership kept a cool head. Walvis Bay has always been regarded as part of
Namibia's national territory: although originally annexed by the Cape
Colony rather than Germany, the fact that South Africa administered it from
Windhoek for nearly 50 years has compromised any legalistic claim it might
have. In the end, SWAPO agreed to allow the issue to stand over until after
independence on the understanding that the West would endorse a Security
Council resolution explicitly recognising Walvis Bay as Namibian territory.
Confronted with this stand, the occupation regime's threats disappeared like
so much hot air.

On 12 July 1978, SWAPO's leadership declared itself satisfied with the
clarification it had received, and it accepted the Western proposals in
principle. The U.N. swung quickly into action. Mandated by the Security
Council, Secretary-General Waldheim dispatched Commissioner for Namibia
Ahtisaari as his special representative to prepare a plan for the transition
process. Ahtisaari and a group of experts visited Namibia during August
and reported back to Waldheim, whose final proposals were approved by the
Security Council on 29 September (Resolution 435). The Waldheim
proposals, which have since provided the definitive framework for the

The South African massacre at Kassinga

Refugees at the camp a month before the raid

One of several mass graves after the racist regime's atrocity

243

transition to independence under U.N. supervision and control, specify a
four-stage process lasting a year:

— Ceasefire, partial demobilisation of the South African forces and
restriction to base on both sides;
— Repeal of all discriminatory and politically restrictive legislation; the
release of all political prisoners and the return of refugees and exiles; followed
by free national elections after an agreed campaigning period;
— The convening of the resultant national assembly to frame and adopt
an independence constitution;
— Enactment of the constitution and achievement of independence.

To oversee the whole process and assure the cardinal principle of U.N. supervision and control, the proposals envisage a Transitional Assistance Group
(UNTAG), comprising up to 7,500 troops and 1,200 civilians.

Such an orderly and democratic procedure was clearly going to be too
much for the occupation regime to swallow. On 20 September, Vorster
announced South Africa's rejection of the Waldheim plan in his last act as
Prime Minister. And his successor, P.W. Botha, the man who as Defence
Minister had ordered the invasion of Angola in 1975, defied the foreign
ministers of the Contact Group when they confronted him in Pretoria on
16–18 October. During the rest of 1978 and 1979, the regime dragged out
the negotiations to little purpose. Its one major outstanding difference with
the U.N. has been the disposition of military and paramilitary forces in the
northern border zone.

The issue at stake is in fact far from technical. In order to rig the U.N.
election successfully, the regime needs to be able to intimidate the populous
north, where nearly three-fifths of the population live, as it did in the Ovamboland bantustan election of January 1975 and the Turnhalle election of
December 1978. To do this it needs to have its repressive forces (police, tribal
militia, as well as army units) thick on the ground and SWAPO's freedom
fighters demobilised and confined to bases well outside the country. Hence
its strident demand not only that its paramilitary police forces be allowed
to operate unhindered throughout the country and retain bases inside Ovamboland, but also that SWAPO be denied any bases inside Namibia for its
fighting cadres stationed there and that, on the contrary, all these be withdrawn under close guard far into Angola.

The imperialist powers, now more confident that South Africa can survive
to carry out its role as overlord of the sub-continent, have been content to
side with the apartheid regime and let the negotiations drag on inconclusively.
Led by Britain, the Contact Group's mid-1979 interpretation of the suggestion of a demilitarised zone either side of the northern border, which had
originally been put forward by the late President Neto of Angola, would
allow the occupation regime's armed forces virtually unhindered control of
all parts of Namibia, losing the people even the protection that PLAN freedom fighters are currently able to give them over substantial areas of the north.

Imperialism and South African Aggression

The governments represented in the Contact
Group have been persistently conspicuous by their
silence on the repeated persecution of SWAPO
cadres inside Namibia, on South African military
terrorism in the war zone and on South Africa's
frequent aggressive incursions into Angola and
Zambia. This silence is tantamount to condoning
the barbaric practices of the occupation regime,
for when the Western powers really do get tough
— as they did to stop the installation of the
'interim government' in 1977 — the apartheid
regime will usually play along and can be deterred
from its most bloodthirsty excesses. Time and
again SWAPO has been able to predict the occupation regime's aggressive plans in advance and has
called on the Western powers to restrain their
South African client; time and again the West
has pretended that our warnings are not to be
taken seriously. The massacre at Kassinga is the
most notorious example to date. As early as mid-
January 1978, a source inside the S.A.D.F.
revealed that since September 1977 the army had
been planning a large-scale military operation
timed for May/June 1978 whose likely target was
inside Angola:

'Large numbers of tanks and large amounts of
ammunition are being shipped to Namibia for use
in this campaign. Barracks are being built in key
positions to accommodate ever increasing numbers
of troops, highly trained and in peak condition.
3,000 are already waiting in Bloemfontein to be
flown to Namibia. From this evidence it is quite
clear that the South African regime is not only
planning not to withdraw its troops from Namibia,
but is going to escalate its armed aggression against
the Namibian people. No deceitful or any other
political gimmicks can disguise this fact any
longer.' (SWAPO Press Statement, Lusaka, 29
January 1978).

Concerned by the occupation regime's military
preparations, President Sam Nujoma referred to
South Africa's aggressive designs in his address to

the U.N. General Assembly's special session on Namibia on 24 April:

'We have gathered irrefutable evidence through our own sources inside Namibia and from combatants of PLAN of an extensive enemy military build-up and activities in Namibia. For example, the regime has embarked on a reinforcement of its already huge army in Namibia. Concurrently, it is deploying new types of heavy and sophisticated armaments. This scheme involves the shipment of a large number of tanks, combat aircraft, artillery pieces and large quantities of ammunition. To facilitate this ever expanding military build-up in Namibia, new bases, barracks and military airfields are being built in strategic areas in the country for offensive purposes against SWAPO and the Namibian revolution . . . The strategic aspect of this show of force, which entails hegemonic ambitions of the racist regime, is to undermine the stability, peace and territorial integrity of the neighbouring independent African states. It has, continuously, used Namibia as a springboard to commit wanton aggression against the People's Republic of Angola and the Republic of Zambia.'

This warning came just 10 days before the Kassinga raid. But still the West refused to take it seriously, perhaps because just one day later (25 April) they got what they wanted: South African acceptance in principle of their unilateral settlement proposals. Yet our sources indicate that throughout April the South African Cabinet was deeply split on whether to allow the raid to go ahead, and a firm intervention by their Western masters might well have forced them to abandon it altogether. That intervention was not forthcoming. The Namibian blood shed at Kassinga stains the hands not merely of the occupation regime itself but also those of its imperialist allies which continue to arm, protect and condone its aggressive designs.

Intensified Military Rule
Events inside Namibia have, in any case, changed for the worse the situation

which both the Waldheim and the Western proposals were designed to meet. On both the military and the political fronts, the South Africans have proceeded remorselessly with their preparations, regardless of the U.N. negotiations, so that by the latter half of 1979 they were poised to install their client regime in power in an 'independent' Namibia as well through 'UN' elections as through a unilateral 'internal settlement'. The regime has pushed vigorously ahead with the militarisation of its occupation forces, a plan first conceived in 1976 and put into full operation after mid-1977, when the Western-sponsored negotiations began. The key element of this strategy has been the creation of a 'SWA Defence Force' (S.W.A.D.F.). In August 1977, all South African Defence Force (S.A.D.F.) formations were subordinated to a new 'SWA Command' with its headquarters in Windhoek and directly answerable to Pretoria. A new Commanding Officer, Major-General Jannie Geldenhuys, was appointed and charged specifically to recruit Namibians into the occupation army. The S.A.D.F. strengthened its command structure, expanded its military bases and training facilities, and scoured the reserves and bantustans with threats and blandishments to seduce black Namibians into betraying their country. The number of 'bantustan armies', first started in 1974 on an exclusively ethnic basis, was rapidly increased and a new supposedly multiracial unit was created as the nucleus of the future S.W.A.D.F.

By September 1979, the Namibian component of the S.A.D.F. consisted of one multi-racial unit (the 41st Battalion, first formed in 1977) and separate ethnic units of Ovambo (the 35th Battalion, June 1975), Kavango (the 34th Battalion, June 1975), East Caprivians (the 33rd Battalion, 1975), 'Bushmen' (the 31st Battalion, 1974) and Herero (1978). Whites are conscripted into the 41st Battalion and the all-white sections of the S.A.D.F. In addition, there are separate reservist and part-time units for Herero, Rehobothers, Coloureds, Ovambo and whites. These troops, together with bantustan and Coloured units from South Africa itself, have been pushed into the frontline of the regime's repressive war against the liberation movement. In this, the South Africans are faithfully copying the tactics of former colonial powers (including present members of the Contact Group) in trying to divide the colonised people against each other in order to spare the skins of their own white soldiers. The D.T.A., South Africa's mouthpiece, is now threatening to extend compulsory conscription from whites to all black Namibians as well.

Despite this rapid expansion in the recruitment of Namibians, the S.A.D.F. continues to provide all the sophisticated and deadly military hardware, most of the manpower and all of the command structure of the occupation army. It is becoming clear, however, that the regime is trying to bypass the demand that it withdraw its armed forces by localising as many of them as it can. Already it hopes to exclude them from some of the controls with which 'South African' units would have to comply under the terms of a ceasefire. Most of the whites living in Namibia, whom the regime can now define as 'Namibian', are of course South African citizens and members of the exploiting colonial class. In September 1979, in introducing new 'S.W.A.D.F.'

uniforms, South African military commanders stated that S.A.D.F. units wearing these uniforms could be seconded to the S.W.A.D.F. after 'independence' if the new 'government' requested it. This is music to the ears of D.T.A. leaders like Mudge and Ndjoba, who have repeatedly called for South African troops to remain in Namibia for many years to come. In other words, the South Africans fully intend not only to bypass any ceasefire but also to use the D.T.A. to legitimise the presence of their massive occupation army, whatever constitutional form 'independence' might take.

For the Namibian people this can only mean further hardship and suffering. In recent years, the role of the South African armed forces has extended far beyond military engagements to affect and even control wide areas of civilian life. Armed soldiers now run most of the schools, clinics, hospitals and technical services throughout the war zone in the north. With the extension of martial law in May 1979 and the reintroduction of the pass laws a few months later, they mount road blocks and identity checks in the reserves, farms and towns of the whole of Northern and Central Namibia; launch large-scale raids and attacks on locations and contract workers' compounds; break into homes in the dead of night, terrorise the inhabitants, destroy or steal their property, and whisk away anyone they please into detention for interrogation and torture, sometimes never to be seen again. Whatever the formal constitutional procedure which South African propaganda presents to the West, it is abundantly plain to Namibians that the regime intends to impose its client regime on the Namibian people under conditions of systematic military and police intimidation.

The Occupation Regime Installs Its Puppets
During the same period the South Africans have carefully groomed their puppets to take over formal political power, whether through new elections or through a unilateral 'independence'. For most of 1977 and 1978, vast sums (at one point estimated at R0.5 million a month) poured into the coffers of the D.T.A. from the now disgraced Department of Information and from foreign, especially West German, business and political interests anxious to keep Namibia under South African control. The D.T.A. kept up a lavish nation-wide electioneering campaign, using hundreds of paid organisers, sophisticated equipment such as films and portable video machines, and with army trucks, planes and helicopters constantly at their disposal. Its message, backed up by a flood of leaflets, posters and forged SWAPO publications put out by South African agents, amounted to nothing less than a strident anti-SWAPO crusade. Not to turn out to D.T.A. rallies or possess a D.T.A. membership card meant running the risk of severe reprisals from the army, police and employers, as well as the loss of pensions, medical treatment and jobs.

In the second half of 1978, the South Africans decided to prepare the way for an 'internal settlement' — still the first prize if ever sufficient imperialist backing could be won — by staging a national election. This exercise was also to serve as a useful trial run in case a U.N.-sponsored election should become unavoidable. First, all adult Namibians were compelled to register as voters. Then, in open defiance of the U.N. (at the very time the Waldheim proposals for the transition period were being drawn up and discussed), the regime called an election for a so-called 'Constituent Assembly'. All its considerable resources of intimidation and coercion were mobilised to force as high a turn-out as possible, and it was the army that played the dominant role, especially in the north. Thousands of reinforcements were sent north during October and November, and soldiers were swarming everywhere before and during the election. Armed troops staffed many of the polling booths and scoured the countryside with mobile booths in their armoured vehicles to force people to vote — soldiers were briefed to break into any house at any time of the day or night to check that the residents had voted.

Armed guards herd Namibians into polling booths during the fraudulent South African-run 'election', December 1978

The regime had carefully spaced the voting over five days, so that when, by the end of the second day, it became apparent that few people were turn-ing out, these tactics of general intimidation were dramatically escalated. Gun-toting D.T.A. 'guards' policed the entrances to the main polling stations, and inside, soldiers filled in the ballot forms for the illiterate, who number some 70% of the black population. Many employers gave willing assistance by threatening to sack any worker who refused to vote, and some (notably farmers) even rounded up their work-forces and carted them in lorries to the polling stations. At Consolidated Diamond Mines, (the only large employer which did not use such intimidation) it is significant that less than 10% of the workers voted.

Throughout this period all organised opposition was severely repressed. Most of the SWAPO leadership, rounded up the previous April, was not released until October, after registration had been completed; and many were re-detained just before the December election. Any criticism or opposition to registration was explicitly outlawed by decree (A.G. 37). Under these circumstances,with the decisive U.N. election still to come, most Namibians saw open resistance to this stage-managed exercise as pointless and went through the motions of recording their votes. But the real political significance of this gun-point election was not the allegedly high turnout but the chance to perfect the intimidatory tactics which the occupation regime intends to use to deliver the vote in any U.N.-sponsored election to its puppets in the D.T.A.

Having given the D.T.A. an aura of democratic respectability, however illusory in reality, the South Africans proceeded to install them as an 'interim government', a move the imperialist powers had originally stopped in April 1977 but now, two years later, allowed to pass without so much as a word of protest. On 21 December 1978, the Administrator-General inaugurated the 'Constituent Assembly', in which the D.T.A. had 41 seats out of 50. Over the next few months, like the Turnhalle Conference before it, the Assembly spent its time debating a range of issues and minor reforms; but as a purely advisory body it could do nothing. Then, on 21 May 1979, the occupation regime delegated wide powers of internal self-government to the Assembly and renamed it the 'National Assembly'. Since then, South African propaganda has presented the D.T.A. as the legitimate democratic government of Namibia and it appears that the imperialist powers are increasingly ready to buy the confidence trick they are being sold.

White Settlers and Black Collaborators in Disarray

But the propaganda image has been founded on an illusion. Even the narrow political coalition of settlers and puppets is in disarray. Having stoked the fires of tribalist discord through its apartheid policy, the regime can now do little but try desperately to damp them down as they continue to smoulder, not in the ranks of the liberation movement but between the competing ethnic delegations inside the D.T.A.

More seriously, the South Africans have still not managed to forge a consensus among the neo-colonial and tribalist elements in Namibia. On the one hand, the limited reforms reducing racial discrimination and the D.T.A.'s multi-racial trappings have come as a shock to many whites and a deep sense of betrayal among them is widespread. The D.T.A. may have 'won' 80% of the national vote in the December election, but the rigidly pro-apartheid S.W.A. National Party (S.W.A.N.P.) and the even more rabidly white supremacist Herstigte Nationale Party (H.N.P.), deadly rivals of the white D.T.A. boss Dirk Mudge, gained the support of over two-thirds of the white settlers, whose political co-operation will be vital to the stability of the client regime South Africa plans to install. In September 1977, Mudge had failed to take over the leadership of the S.W.A.N.P. and was forced to form his own all-white Republican Party instead.

Since then, the S.W.A.N.P. has done its best to sabotage the D.T.A. at every turn, hankering as it does for a more crudely colonialist solution. But after the election, substantial sections of the white community, notably farmers, small businessmen and government employees, lost confidence in the S.W.A.N.P. and white terror groups have mushroomed, to whom the H.N.P. has openly offered its political backing. It was one of these groups which destroyed SWAPO's national headquarters on 5 May 1979, and death lists of prominent black opponents of colonial rule, including church leaders, are known to have been drawn up. The murder of a white freemason in mid-1979 reveals that the secret societies of the ruling elite have even taken to killing each others' members — a sure sign of the breakdown of settler morale. It was mainly to rally the settlers to the regime's political strategy that Steyn was abruptly replaced as Administrator-General by Gerrit Viljoen, head of the all-powerful Afrikaner secret mafia, the Broederbond.

On the other hand, so limited is the real power to be transferred under the Turnhalle programme that the D.T.A. has failed to attract to its standard even those black Namibian elements which support a neo-colonial solution. These are loosely grouped together in the Namibia National Front, a coalition of less than half a dozen small parties. Other small regionalist and reactionary groups, including Shipanga's SWAPO-Democrats, a band of SWAPO renegades, cannot find enough meaning in the D.T.A.'s version of 'inde 'independence' to join its ranks, even though the South Africans have set aside 15 extra seats in the National Assembly to accommodate them.

SWAPO Advances the Revolutionary Armed Struggle

The rock on which the South African design continues to founder is the invincible unity of the Namibian people. SWAPO has exploited every remaining loophole to mobilise the people against the designs of colonialism and imperialism on their future. However, so systematic has political repression been since April 1978, that there has been little scope for normal political activity. Toughened by two decades of struggle under conditions of severe repression, SWAPO's party organisation has remained resilient and effective underground. Despite the imprisonment of the entire national and regional leadership, tens of thousands of Namibians turned out in August 1978 to welcome U.N. Commissioner Ahtisaari and, also in Windhoek, in May 1979 to protest against the latest police round-up of their leaders.

Every move by the occupation regime has been exposed by the nation-wide distribution of leaflets and by meetings to inform the people and discuss tactics. And the party itself has survived the latest wave of police and army repression as it has survived all previous crackdowns. It continues to educate, to mobilise and to lead the people from the grassroots. It maintains effective links between the leaders in gaol, the local branches and the party organisation abroad, so that national unity is not merely an empty slogan but the vital practical embodiment of the party's commitment to national liberation. When at each major stage of the negotiations with the Contact Group SWAPO has confronted the imperialists across the conference table, its negotiating team has contained representative delegations from the internal as well as the external leadership.

SWAPO supporters in northern Namibia

In recent years freedom fighters of PLAN have escalated the armed struggle to the point that it now plays the leading role in the liberation struggle as a whole. This has meant increasingly close integration of the civilian and military wings of the liberation movement. In the combat zone in the north, PLAN cadres perform a whole range of political and welfare functions in addition to their fighting roles. In a number of areas they are one component of a whole underground structure of legal administration as the grip of the different organs of the colonial state on the daily life of the people is gradually loosened and cast off. Further south, PLAN cadres move the length and breadth of the country, carrying information, gathering intelligence, recruiting volunteers for training and executing missions against the enemy's troops and lines of communication. Their very role as armed political militants, central to SWAPO's conception of the liberation process, requires a close co-ordination with other forms of struggle.

Most Namibians have long accepted the necessity of taking up arms and have not been slow to demonstrate their practical solidarity with the freedom fighters. Two instances demonstrate this unity in struggle well. On 21 December 1975 and 16 February 1976 a two-man team struck at two white farms in the heart of the Police Zone, killing four members of the most hated section of colonial society. Although not endorsed by SWAPO, these acts aroused wide sympathy in the hearts of Namibians daily subjected to brutal and humiliating treatment by their white colonial masters.

Despite a huge police manhunt, both men were protected by the people and remained at large for four months. Eventually, in a shoot-out in Katutura on 19 April, one of the two, Filemon Nangolo, was shot and paralysed from the waist down. But the other, Kanisius Heneleshi, miraculously escaped and evaded capture for another five months. By the time he was gunned down in September 1976, Heneleshi had become a popular symbol of defiance against the brutal colonial police. Nangolo was illegally sentenced to death and hanged on 30 May 1977, and a crowd of over 1,000 gathered at his graveside in solidarity. 'We dismiss the notion that Nangolo's case is not a political one,' declared a SWAPO statement the same day. 'The illegal South African occupation of Namibia is founded on violence and repression and Nangolo's actions must be understood in this context. A regime that bases its control on terror cannot expect that the people it represses will remain passive.'

Internal militants responded equally powerfully in solidarity when in 1977 other freedom fighters were put on trial under the Terrorism Act. Benjamin Uulenga, a PLAN cadre from a unit operating far inside Central Namibia, was wounded and captured after betrayal by Kapuuo's supporters, and was tried with three other SWAPO members. On 3 May, the trial opened to freedom songs and chants from SWAPO demonstrators outside the court and in the packed public gallery. Their banners proclaimed: 'South Africa has no right to try the people', 'You are on trial, not SWAPO' and, when sentence was passed, 'You can imprison revolutionaries, but you cannot imprison the revolution'. SWAPO had demanded that its captured soldiers be regarded as prisoners of war in accordance with the Geneva Convention, to which SWAPO is party but South Africa is not. Uulenga's lawyer argued this position in court, to no avail. But demonstrators picketing the court asserted this demand in the face of the regime's police and judiciary, demonstrating their defiant unity and solidarity with the freedom fighters.

The fighting units of PLAN have achieved major advances since the first large-scale campaign in Ovamboland in 1975–76. Their forces have been strengthened by a steady flow of volunteers dedicated to the liberation of their nation from the stranglehold of colonialism and imperialist exploitation, and by the world-wide solidarity of progressive and socialist forces in the face of imperialist hostility. PLAN's rainy season offensive during 1978–79 once again caught the occupation army by surprise. The frequency of military engagements increased sharply and S.A.D.F. units found themselves under attack and unable to move freely across wide areas of the north.

PLAN forces repeatedly proved their ability to concentrate in formations of 100 or more and attack major South African bases with heavy arms, then disperse and vanish as the S.A.D.F., for all its sophisticated hardware and air superiority, searched in vain. Several times the main power line from Ruacana was brought down, on one occasion plunging most of Namibia into darkness for several hours. The freedom fighters were even able to subject the main South African military headquarters and air base in Ovamboland at Ondangwa to mortar bombardment. In the centre and south, several road and rail bridges and an oil depot were attacked by PLAN units.

It is plain, even from South African reports, that PLAN holds the whip hand over the regime's poorly motivated conscript army. The people themselves are the eyes, ears and protectors of the freedom fighters, while the South African soldiers lash out blindly against an adversary they hardly ever see and can rarely distinguish from the mass of the people. In desperation, in March and April 1979, the S.A.D.F. High Command moved tens of thousands of reinforcements to the border and once again resorted to large-scale armed incursions into Southern Angola, ostensibly in search of SWAPO bases and guerrillas. They found hardly any, and it was Angolan villagers who suffered their wrath. Even as the invasion force was scouring Southern Angola and Southwestern Zambia, a large PLAN contingent crossed the Okavango River and dispersed to its assignments in the rich farming country around the S.A.D.F. military complex at Grootfontein. Once more, the South Africans poured in their reinforcements, but made not a single contact.

Now many of the ranches north of Windhoek are under round-the-clock armed guard, farmers are beginning to pack their bags and run, and the South Africans are even resorting to mercenaries to bolster their sagging defences. Twenty years after the formation of SWAPO and 14 years after the launching of the armed struggle, the liberation movement is continuing to make powerful advances and to build on its solid achievements. The Namibian people have committed themselves to armed revolutionary struggle and have learnt through hard experience that liberation can be won only by their own efforts and sacrifice.

9. Forces of Popular Resistance

The Principles and Strategy of the National Liberation Movement

From the beginning, SWAPO has worked at every level and used every tactic which is consistent with advancing its ultimate goals — national liberation and ending the exploitation of man by man — and with the twin principles of national unity and self-reliance in the struggle. The movement's strategy has been formed in the very thick of the struggle and has been tailored to meet the specific conditions applying to Namibia. Since 1966, SWAPO has been committed to an armed revolutionary war as the main form of its drive for national liberation. It has also campaigned on two other fronts: internationally, to win the maximum world-wide support for its cause and to weaken imperialist backing for the South African colonial regime; and inside Namibia, through open political mobilisation.

On both these fronts, weaknesses in the hold of colonialism and imperialism over Namibia have given the liberation movement extra opportunities to build the freedom struggle. Disagreements amongst the victors of the First World War prevented South Africa, as the local representative of the British Empire, from annexing Namibia outright and forced it to submit to a League of Nations Mandate. After the Second World War, the imperialist powers replaced the League with the United Nations and the League's sovereign rights over Namibia passed to the new body. From the start the U.N. had a non-capitalist minority, and as the colonised peoples of the Third World won their independence that minority became an anti-imperialist majority. The imperialist club has been able to protect its position only by using the permanent veto which three of its most powerful members hold in the Security Council. Although the U.N. has been prevented by this Western veto from becoming a leading instrument in the decolonisation of Namibia, its potential usefulness as a means of weakening the imperialist hold over Namibia and as a source of support to the liberation movement has been considerable. SWAPO has therefore always worked actively within the forum of the U.N. to win backing for its cause and has sought to conform to the constitutional rights which are vested in U.N. sovereignty over Namibia.

Ever since the U.N. blocked its attempt in 1946 to annex Namibia, South Africa has regarded it as its deadly enemy. Nevertheless, it cannot afford to defy its imperialist allies completely, for they are its sole protection against executive action by the U.N. to enforce its sovereign rights in Namibia. The western powers have been forced to move closer to the majority view at the U.N. in order to safeguard their world-wide interests. Thus, even at its most aggressive, the apartheid regime has never quite had the confidence to do completely what it wanted. One consequence of this is that the regime has never outlawed SWAPO as a political party as it did the A.N.C. and P.A.C. in South Africa itself. Despite the relentless severity of the political repression it has suffered at the hands of the occupation regime, SWAPO has used this limited opportunity to operate in the open to maximum advantage in order to rally and organise the oppressed people of Namibia in the cause of liberation.

Thus SWAPO has operated as a revolutionary underground and as an open political party, has taken up arms to drive colonialism from Namibia, and has co-operated with the U.N.'s campaign to establish its sovereignty. These parallel areas of struggle, not contradictory but complementary, are determined by the particular conditions under which the liberation movement operates in Namibia. Advancement of the cause of freedom is the supreme test of their usefulness. Fighting on three fronts under a savagely repressive colonial regime naturally brings tactical problems in its train — such as co-ordinating underground and open activities under a single political organisation, or communicating between leaderships at home and abroad. But these are matters of detail, not of principle. In whatever field it operates, SWAPO remains a single party united around a common programme and a common dedication to the overriding task of national liberation — this the Namibian people understand well. The South Africans and their allies have repeatedly tried to divide its ranks by labelling different sections of the party as 'internal' and 'external' wings and then alleging serious policy differences between them, the former being 'moderate' and 'peaceful', the latter 'communist' and 'terrorist'. Not once in the 20 years of its existence has this manoeuvre had the slightest success; it is the Western news media, not the Namibian people, who have been deceived.

SWAPO recognises that colonial oppression and capitalist exploitation take a number of different forms and that each section of the oppressed people experiences these forms to varying degrees of intensity. It also recognises that mass popular struggle may erupt at any time against the conditions of oppression particular to each form and that the timing and scale of such struggle cannot always be predicted or organised in advance. The course of popular resistance has not been even, different sections exploiting into activity at different times. In 1971–72, contract workers struck against the contract labour system; in 1972–73, peasants in Ovamboland rose against their subjection to South Africa's bantustan plan; and in 1976–77, high school students boycotted classes in protest against 'Bantu Education'. It has been SWAPO's task to channel the popular energy released in sectional campaigns into the national struggle against the system of colonial exploitation as a whole. It has been SWAPO's achievement that in each phase the political consciousness forged in the heat of short-term confrontations has been successfully translated into lasting gains for the entire liberation movement.

> SWAPO is a national liberation movement rallying together, on the basis of free and voluntary association, all freedom-inspired sons and daughters of the Namibian people. It is the organised political vanguard of the oppressed and exploited people of Namibia. In fulfilling its vanguard role, SWAPO organises, unites, inspires, orientates and leads the broad masses of the working Namibian people in the struggle for national and social liberation. It is thus the expression and embodiment of national unity, of a whole people united and organised in the struggle for total independence and social liberation.
>
> *SWAPO Constitution, 1976*
>
> The tasks before SWAPO at present and in the immediate future are:
> 1. The liberation and winning of independence for the people of Namibia by all possible means, and the establishment of a democratic people's government;
> 2. The realisation of genuine and total independence of Namibia in the spheres of politics, economy, defence, social and cultural affairs.
>
> To these ends, SWAPO has resolved:
> 1. To persistently mobilise and organise the broad masses of the Namibian people so that they can actively participate in the national liberation struggle;
> 2. To mould and heighten, in the thick of the national liberation struggle, the bond of national and political consciousness amongst the Namibian people;
> 3. To combat all manifestations and tendencies of tribalism, regionalism, ethnic orientation and racial discrimination;
> 4. To unite all Namibian people, particularly the working class, the peasantry and progressive intellectuals, into a vanguard party capable of safeguarding national independence and of building a classless, non-exploitative society based on the ideals and principles of scientific socialism.
>
> *SWAPO Political Programme, 1976*

Guided by this strategic objective, the 1969–70 Consultative Congress at Tanga created, as was pointed out earlier, several organs of mass struggle to operate alongside the main party organisation: the Youth League, the Council of Elders, the Women's League and, later, the National Union of Namibian Workers. They each have a dual function: to provide a vehicle for campaigns against particular features of the structure of colonial and class exploitation and to link these spheres of action to the broader liberation struggle. The relationship between political leadership and mass struggle is always reciprocal. Political leaders may initiate campaigns and explain to the oppressed the causes of their oppression, but equally, mass struggle educates the leadership as to the needs of the people and the potential for political mobilisation amongst different layers of the oppressed. For this reason SWAPO attaches great importance to the role of its mass organisations, to broad representation of all sections of the Namibian people within its ranks, and to democratic participation at all levels of its party organisation.

In the 20th anniversary year of its foundation, SWAPO remains as it started, a broad front against colonial oppression and imperialist exploitation. It is not a vanguard party, nor is it the exclusive instrument of any particular social class. Over the years, it has brought together within its ranks a wide range of political views and a long list of regional and sectional groups. The shape of the future is for the people of Namibia themselves to decide, when the winning of independence allows them for the first time to install a government of their own choosing.

But equally, SWAPO is a single united party with a common programme, not a federal alliance of separate organisations. In the course of a long and bitter struggle it has come to identify more clearly the enemies of freedom and social progress and to accept the need to prepare for the formidable task of national reconstruction when the occupation regime is finally driven out. SWAPO is not neutral in the struggle for democracy and social justice. The overwhelming majority of its members are workers and peasants, producers by the sweat of their own labour. It is their interests above all else that SWAPO represents and holds dear to its heart. Since the policy of apartheid has systematically destroyed the independent economic base of the peasantry, it is the workers on whom the future of an independent Namibia mainly depends.

Namibian workers know full well that victory over colonialism will not of itself loosen the imperialist stranglehold over the nation's economy, and that the chief agents of imperialism are the big capitalist corporations which are sucking the country dry of profits and precious resources. They know that they cannot fully determine their own destiny while capitalists, whatever their nationality, own and control the means of production by which they transform their labour into goods. Conscious of the responsibility with which it is charged, at its Central Committee meeting in August 1976 SWAPO adopted a Political Programme which commits the party to a socialist transformation of Namibian society. In accordance with the principles laid down in the Programme, the party has begun to prepare contingency plans for economic and social reconstruction so that the Namibian people will have before them a strategy for achieving a self-reliant and liberated society when victory is finally won.

The People's Liberation Army of Namibia (PLAN)

Fifteen years ago the Namibian people, under the leadership of SWAPO, took up arms to liberate their country. SWAPO's forces were then relatively small in number; their activities were based mainly in the Eastern Caprivi Strip and along the Okavango River, and confined to small-scale local encounters with the South African armed forces.

Today, PLAN is an army of several thousands. It has units which are permanently based inside Namibia, whose activities extend deep inside the country, infiltrating the so-called white areas both north and south of the capital – and the sound of automatic weapons has been heard in Windhoek itself. PLAN units, no longer just armed with light weapons, but with rockets, anti-aircraft guns, bazookas and mortars, mount attacks in formations 80 to 100 strong, and stand their ground as well as using their former guerrilla hit-and-run tactics.

Through PLAN, SWAPO has developed real military strength in the north, made possible to a large extent by the support it receives from the local peasantry. There are areas of the north where South African troops will only venture if given extensive air cover, and even then only in large and heavily armed units. In one typical instance in such an area, members of a PLAN unit have told how a South African army patrol, which had rounded up a group of peasants for interrogation, discovered it was itself surrounded by a detachment of freedom fighters and withdrew without firing a shot. In these areas, the administration of the South African regime and its puppet tribal authorities has broken down and SWAPO, in effective control, has set up rudimentary structures of collective organisation, health care and educational facilities.

Until recently, PLAN units permanently based in Namibia relied upon the local population for food and shelter. The people – SWAPO members and supporters – are the eyes and ears of PLAN, and many of its cadres have lived and worked among the local population. Now the relationship is becoming more reciprocal. PLAN bases inside Namibia grow their own food which they share with the local population, and provide safe refuge for those unable any longer to stand the terror of South Africa's occupation. It is PLAN cadres who escort those wishing to leave, for military training or to study, across the border to freedom.

> SWAPO holds the conviction that armed resistance to the South African occupation of our country is the only viable and effective means left for us to achieve genuine liberation in Namibia.
>
> However, much as we are convinced that armed struggle must now be

The People's Liberation Army of Namibia in action

PLAN unit on a mission inside Namibia

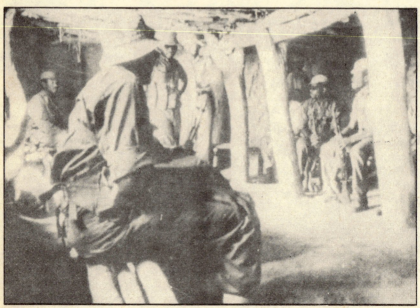

PLAN underground base inside Namibia

Cadres on parade

Medical unit holding a clinic for villagers in northern Namibia

the main form of our liberation activity, we do not beautify war as a purpose or regard it as a form of sport. We see war for what it is — an extension of politics by other means.

This quotation from SWAPO's *Political Programme* pinpoints the guiding principle that 'it is politics which leads the gun'. SWAPO freedom fighters are, first and foremost, armed political militants. It is the duty of each and every cadre, wherever he or she goes, to explain the aims and objectives of SWAPO so that people know why their sons and daughters are armed and fighting the enemy, why they are prepared to sacrifice their lives for the freedom of their country.

Moreover, each fighting unit, of whatever size, has a political instructor whose duty it is to educate the cadres before and after battle. A programme of classes is worked out in advance for each week and the political instructors lecture the cadres with the aid of books and pamphlets produced by SWAPO, as well as those from countries in support of our struggle. A strong internationalist flavour permeates these classes: the experience of other countries whose people have had to fight an independence struggle is discussed in order to develop an understanding of the forces against which SWAPO and the people of Namibia are fighting. They also include literacy training for those cadres who cannot read and write because of the lack of education provided by the South African occupation regime, and discussion of key issues such as relations between PLAN and the civilian population and SWAPO's policy and programme for a future independent Namibia.

PLAN is totally integrated into the overall structure and daily working of the party as a whole. It has the right to adopt its own rules and regulations governing its activities and administration, but these must be approved by the Central Committee, SWAPO's main policy-making body, which elects (as it does other Heads of Department) the Secretary for Defence, with overall responsibility for PLAN. There is concern for democratic structures and discussion within PLAN, subject to the framework necessary for maintaining a disciplined army. After battle, cadres will meet and discuss the operation, and it is through that discussion that experience and knowledge is forged as much as through the combat itself.

Within PLAN, cadres of both sexes receive equal training and there is no restriction on women cadres holding responsible positions of authority. There are in fact several women commanders. One of the purposes of political education is to teach the cadres not to regard women as confined to preparing food or child-bearing and rearing. Thus, although there is some division of labour within PLAN (with units responsible for food gathering, cooking, repairing and maintenance of weaponry and vehicles, etc.), it is not along sexual lines and all share in actual combat.

The Portuguese revolution of 1974 and the ensuing liberation of Angola heralded a new phase of SWAPO's armed struggle. Able to establish rear bases along the entire northern border of Namibia rather than just in the Caprivi Strip, PLAN was able to extend its field of activities ever further into Namibia. Now the existence of semi-liberated zones in the northern parts of the country enables PLAN to provide protection for the local population from the severe repression meted out to them by the South African occupation troops and police. These areas also now act as the rear bases for PLAN units who operate exclusively inside the country.

A Swedish film-maker, Per Sanden, who visited Northern Namibia with PLAN in March 1978, has described the liberated areas.* There are small bases on the outskirts with the main base holding 1,000–1,500 fighters, and a constantly shifting civilian population. These main bases include a hospital, a garage to repair the jeeps, trucks and ambulances, and small dwellings – all made out of traditional building materials. The bases grow their own wheat, maize and millet and rear cattle and goats. They are independent as far as food is concerned, although medicine and ammunition are brought to the bases from abroad.

Over the years, PLAN has pinned down increasing numbers of South African troops and paramilitary police units. It is a telling testimony to PLAN's effectiveness that South Africa now requires over 60,000 occupation troops to maintain any semblance of control. The past three years (1977–79) have seen a striking increase in SWAPO's military activity, in frequency, in size and, more significantly, in depth of penetration inside Namibia. A SWAPO War Report for January–February 1978* highlights major encounters between PLAN and the South African occupation troops, showing the range and scale of PLAN's operations:

2nd January
An enemy troop carrier was blown up by a landmine at Ohakafiya on the Nkongo-Onunu road, killing five and wounding several.

15 January
PLAN combatants ambushed a convoy of trucks carrying troops at Oidimba, northern region, using small and heavy calibre firearms. The enemy suffered heavy casualties, and a large quantity of their war equipment was seized or destroyed.

18 January
An enemy patrol unit consisting of Boers and Portuguese mercenaries was wiped out at Omalapalapa, northern region, and a quantity of war materials captured. Altogether, 14 enemy bodies were counted. PLAN suffered light casualties.

27 January
PLAN forces shelled an enemy position at a location between Onaimbungu and Oshinganda, northern region. 81 mortar shells, sub-machine

* *Namibia Today*, 2(1–2), 1978.
** *Namibia Today*, 2(1), 1978, p.13.

guns and thousands of rounds of ammunition were captured. Many
enemy soldiers were killed. On the same day PLAN attacked another
enemy base camp about 11 km west of Katima Mulilo, eastern region,
with mortar and rocket fire. Petrol drums and seven parked vehicles
were destroyed. The enemy suffered heavy casualties.

2 February
Two enemy companies consisting of South African and UNITA/FNLA
soldiers made an unsuccessful attack on one of our detachment bases
about 55 km north-east of Ondangwa, northern region, but were successfully repulsed.

3 February
At Oneengo, northern region, at about 15.30, PLAN combatants inter-
cepted two enemy trucks carrying 70 infantrymen. The two trucks were
destroyed and 63 occupants killed. Nine 60mm mortars, mortar shells,
four machine-guns and several rounds of ammunition were captured.

14 February
At 18.30, PLAN combatants attacked and temporarily occupied an
enemy base at Omafa, north-western region, killing 28 and capturing
many arms. The attack was carried out to put an end to enemy intru-
sions into, and harassment of civilians in SWAPO-controlled areas where
the enemy base was located.

18 February
PLAN units bombarded an enemy operative base with heavy mortar and
rocket fire for over 20 minutes. The base was severely damaged, about
30 enemy soldiers killed, and a large number wounded.
   On the same day, PLAN combatants attacked and overran an enemy
base camp at Eenghono/Elundu, northern region. 15 enemy soldiers were
killed and all their arms and other equipment captured. One enemy
soldier, Johan Van der Mescht, was captured and taken prisoner of war.
An enemy water supply installation was also destroyed.

21 February
In a vain attempt to recapture prisoner Van der Mescht the enemy,
supported by 155 mm artillery guns, attacked one of PLAN's major
bases in the northern region with mechanised units in A.P.S.s and A.P.Vs.
The attack was repulsed after three Armoured Personnel Carriers were
destroyed, and 21 soldiers killed, including a lieutenant.

27 February
A bridge and water pump were destroyed by PLAN sabotage squads in
the north-western region. Nine enemy guards were killed and many
others wounded. A quantity of war materials was captured.

In 1978 and 1979, PLAN stepped up its programme of strategic sabotage. Amongst a number of targets damaged or destroyed were the electricity line from Ruacana hydro-electric power station, railway bridges and track at Karibib and south of Windhoek, and a road bridge near Keetmanshoop. A major attack on the South African army base at Katima Mulilo in Eastern Caprivi in August 1978 caused extensive damage to the base and its installations, with many South African casualties. In February and March 1979, two other South African army bases were attacked (at Elundu and Ondangwa) by SWAPO, causing serious damage and loss of life to the South Africans stationed there. Major-General Jannie Geldenhuys, Commander of the South African army in Namibia, commented that SWAPO was 'demonstrating a spirit of arrogance unknown before . . . they have been attacking major military bases without hesitation.'

The armed struggle being waged by SWAPO is not only a battle for territory and physical control of Namibia, and its successes are not only military. The objective is also to use the impact of persistent military pressure to break the will and thus the spine of the South African occupation regime.

The effect of the prolonged and intensifying war on the morale of South African troops has been devastating. Most of these soldiers are young men called up to do their military service in a country which does not belong to them. Increasing numbers are beginning to realise that they have no place in Namibia and no right to be involved in fighting the Namibian people and preventing them from attaining the freedom which is their birthright. These young South Africans see the war as their Vietnam and, like their American counterparts before them, are rebelling, deserting, leaving the country or going underground to escape call-up. When a country is involved in a colonial war which has no relevance to those it calls upon to fight, it has already lost half the battle. The continuing war in Namibia is breaking the confidence and morale of South Africans. It is by this process also, as much as by every square mile of Namibian territory that is liberated, that PLAN's victories must be judged.

Workers

Sustained Labour Militancy

From the earliest days of nationalist resistance to colonial rule in Namibia black workers have been in the vanguard. As the most exploited and brutally treated section of the working class, contract workers from the northern bantustans and Southern Angola have always been militantly conscious of the structure of their oppression. They have been the solid core of SWAPO since its foundation, and their uncompromising dedication to the cause of freedom has been one of the strongest factors of bringing South African colonialism to the brink of defeat.

The contract workers' general strike in December 1971 struck at the heart of the economy. For most of 1972 and 1973, months after the strike ended, the official monopoly of the Labour Bureaux was largely ineffective.

The farmers, above all others, complained bitterly, for not only were many of their recruits simply failing to arrive, but those who did were asserting their rights and refusing to work such cruelly long hours or under such appalling conditions as previously. That this was not due to an overall drop in labour migration was perfectly clear: by October 1973, it was reported that there were queues of unemployed workers at the tribal labour offices in Ovamboland as the poverty of underdevelopment drove them off the land. During 1973–74, 30,000 Ovambo workers a year left on contract, making about 40,000 in the Police Zone at any one time – nearly 80% more than in 1971.

Worried at the workers' success in undermining their pass controls, the authorities began to tighten up. In September 1972, the municipality and police started checking up on employers and increasing pass checks on the streets. But in practice, their only effective weapon was to stage regular mass raids at dawn on the entire contract labour compound, surrounding the perimeter with armed police and armoured cars, and combing the compound for 'absconders'. On 11 December, for example, the police swooped on Katutura for the third time that year. As the compound police trucks drove off, hundreds of people standing outside raised their clenched fists in defiance, chanting 'Namibia, Namibia'. The arrested men (over 100 of them) taunted their oppressors as the police herded them away like so many cattle. Those brought to trial from this raid were fined, but it soon became the general practice to deport back to Ovamboland all those whose passes were not in order or who joined in collective action to better their conditions. By the end of March 1973, over 1,000 had been deported; during the whole of 1973, over 3,000, and in the first four months of 1974, another 700. Many of them were then subjected to further persecution by the tribal administration.

At the beginning of 1973, the regime launched a nation-wide drive to halt the massive evasion of the pass laws by contract workers. The police not only stepped up their raids on workers' compounds, but also searched living quarters and business premises in towns and intensified their harrassment of blacks on the streets. On 20 March 1973, the same day that the country's major employers and recruiting associations established a committee to eliminate wage competition, 'Bantu Affairs' Deputy Minister Jansen announced a policy of tougher action against 'absconders', including a blacklist which would deny future employment to anyone incurring the regime's displeasure, such as political activists, labour leaders and contract breakers. In February 1974, stricter checks were introduced at the Oshivello checkpoint, the entrance to Ovamboland, to stop workers bypassing the Labour Bureaux. And the police tried to turn the compounds into virtual prisons by checking the passes of everyone who entered and left – indeed, during 1973–74 nearly half the Katutura housing levy on employers of contract workers was spent on 'law and order'.

But this wave of repression was also a telling index of the regime's own failure to reimpose control. For despite the raids, the blacklist and the checkpoints, the police were still finding large numbers of workers to deport who had managed to escape their controls, and of course a good number of pass evaders took care that they were not caught. Since the Labour Bureaux soon made it very difficult for anyone to change jobs legally, most workers who decided to leave their employers did so without notice and went underground, invisible to officialdom until they were caught in a raid or check. Even being deported and put on the blacklist was not the end of the road; many Ovambo simply switched the ethnic identity with which the apartheid regime had labelled them and presented themselves at Okavango recruiting posts as 'Kavangos'.

In the many strikes during 1972–74, a minority of workers frequently opted to risk deportation and blacklisting rather than toe the management line. At one mine, for instance, 55 of the 200 who struck for a wage rise refused to accept the management's 15% offer and were deported to Ovamboland by the police as 'contract-breakers'. Inspired by the mass solidarity and political consciousness which the general strike had instilled in them, the whole body of contract workers redirected their campaign against the contract system into a sustained guerrilla attack on its central institutions of control, the pass laws. Their partial repeal late in 1977 was in large measure a belated admission by the regime that black workers had succeeded in making them impossible to enforce effectively.

Nevertheless, the price of resistance was high. Not only did workers attempting to 'beat the system' live in constant fear of detection, with the risk of permanent poverty and near starvation in the bantustans if they were blacklisted and could not escape to the south again, but they also constantly faced the routine brutality of the South African Police. In their worst atrocity yet, in April 1975, while entering the Katutura workers' compound in a routine search for 'loiterers and people without the necessary documents', the police opened fire without warning or provocation on a group of workers at the gate. The result was five workers dead, 13 wounded (most of them shot in the back) and 296 arrested and charged with committing public violence. The following day, the South African Police refused permission to SWAPO leaders in Windhoek to visit the hospital or mortuary to see the victims of the shooting.

But again and again, workers have proved themselves able and willing to bear the cost of resistance. The occupation regime has not been successful in quelling the continuing mobilisation of black workers, mobilisation which led to at least 70 strikes, some of them involving hundreds of workers, between June 1973 and June 1975 alone. These strikes have taken place in all sectors of the economy, in the mining and extractive industries, the fishing industry, on the big ranches and even among domestic servants.

Although contract workers have been in the vanguard of action on the labour front, other sections of the black working class have been by no means passive. On 1 May 1972, the South West African Fishermen's Union, formed 18 months previously, brought all 1,000 white and Coloured trawlermen at Walvis Bay out on strike for an improved landing rate for their fish, a demand which, within days, was substantially won. Five years later, in January 1977, black fishermen went on strike alone, demanding parity between black and white pay scales and terms of service and a minimum wage. White-collar workers have also often been in the forefront. The 74-day strike, between November 1976 and January 1977, by Nama school teachers to abolish apartheid pay scales was the most grimly fought campaign in Namibia since the general strike. Led by the Nama Teachers' Association, founded in 1970 to fight for pay equality with other black teachers in the racially divided education system and for better school provision, it galvanised mass community support in the south at a time of general mobilisation against apartheid and colonial rule, particularly amongst students.

Trade Union Organisation and the N.U.N.W.

Orthodox trade unionism as it is known in the centres of industrial capitalism has never been strong amongst black workers in Namibia. Official repression is the main reason for this state of affairs. Multi-racial trade unions have been as good as outlawed, and 'Bantu' unions were denied any legal rights or protection whatsoever — it was illegal for them to negotiate or conclude any agreement with an employer. The 1978 reform, which for the first time brought African workers within the definition of 'employee', makes little real difference, because it will be very difficult for any independent black union to qualify for registration, without which all its activities are illegal. Even if it does register, the legal restrictions on industrial action are such as to inhibit it severely from acting effectively in the interests of its members. Reform or no reform, workers have learnt from bitter experience the violent victimisation which employers and police are only too ready to hand out to 'open' trade unionism. They have therefore organised industrial unions only where particular skills or status gives them a degree of bargaining strength — in particular the Coloured Fishermen's Union amongst trawlermen, and the Nama, Black and Ovambo Teachers' Associations amongst teachers in Southern, Central and Northern Namibia respectively.

The main burden of organising and representing the interests of Namibian workers in recent years has fallen on the National Union of Namibian Workers (N.U.N.W.), an organisation affiliated to SWAPO, which of necessity has had to operate largely underground. It is particularly strong amongst contract workers and branches are firmly established in most of the big mines. It has an elected national and regional leadership structure and sub-divisions covering most of the different sectors of employment. Under the present conditions of struggle, the N.U.N.W.'s main function is to back up local worker campaigns and strikes rather than to lead from the front. It also plays a major role in getting plant-based shopstewards committees and, in the main towns, trades councils off the ground; gathering information about wages and conditions in the different sectors; in making available tactical expertise and common experiences of struggle to workers who might otherwise be isolated and divided by management manipulation; and in promoting the vital principles of unity and self-reliance as the foundation for a strong, united workers' movement.

> ## The National Union of Namibian Workers — Aims and Objectives
>
> a. Generally to organise and protect from exploitation and look after the interests of all workers in various job categories in Namibia.
> b. To create unity and solidarity among all workers in Namibia.
> c. To pave the way and prepare for a participation by the workers of Namibia in the government of an independent Namibia.
> d. To make the workers of Namibia conscious of the present system of labour and do everything in their power to strive for better and equal working and living conditions.
> e. Insofar as this is compatible with a Workers' Union to take part and contribute to a complete change in the present social, economic and political order, and do everything in their power to achieve this.
> f. To oppose all tribalism and ethnic grouping as well as types of discrimination among Namibian workers, and fight for the abolishment of all barriers of estrangement presently existing.
> g. To make a study in depth of all problems of the workers and find ways of solving them.
> h. To fight for the dignity of all workers.
> i. To do everything in its power to achieve economic equality in any future government of Namibia.
> j. To co-operate with other Workers' Unions having basically the same aims and objects.
> k. To fight for just wages, good working conditions and to protect the interests of all workers.
> l. To regulate relations, negotiate and settle disputes between workers and employers.
> m. To provide advice and/or obtain legal assistance where necessary for workers on matters affecting their employment.
>
> *Extract from draft constitution, Windhoek, 1977*

Since the contract workers' national strike, several of the larger companies have tried to defuse the militancy of the workers and their rank-and-file leaders by appointing personnel officers and toothless liaison committees. As a Walvis Bay worker explained, 'the appointment of such people like personnel officers is not because the company is really interested in the welfare of the workers. It's to keep the people at ease, to give them a sense of security. It gives them a sense that someone is representing them in the management.' Liaison committees are 'just to avoid trade unions being established. The works committees and liaison committees, they do not have much power. They can only recommend . . .' The management delegates 'have always got the veto right. If something dangerous [arises] they say "No, we cannot discuss." The N.U.N.W. has taken the leading part in exposing this divisive employer trick as a substitute for effective trade unionism.

Black trade union members are well aware of the problems they face in organising the workers and the tasks of the hour. 'I observe that the people are very, very advanced,' commented one member of a workers' committee, early in 1977, ' . . . especially in the compounds, groups are discussing only politics and what can be done and plans.' The problem is basically one of tactics. 'The people know what is wrong. Most know where they can hit and where they can kick. But what we need is the protection when they hit . . . The problem is the consequences of this.'

The basic difference between short-term mobilisation for a particular struggle — for which the crowded workers' compounds offer some scope — and ensuring lasting gains for the organised labour movement was stressed. 'If it's for a strike, then I think that the organisation of workers can be done very easily. . . . But for a trade union the real thing is that there must be someone who must organise the people, who must tell them exactly what are the advantages of a trade union.' Employers and police rigidly segregate the workers into ethnic ghettoes and company 'towns', so that it is often difficult for workers from a particular industry to organise together or even meet. On the farms, all meetings have to be kept completely secret, and workers establish comprehensive warning and intelligence networks so that migrant labourers can learn which farms to avoid at all costs and where to get refuge, food and news about jobs when they 'strike' — that is, leave particular farms as a group without notice.

In the Namibian political economy, workers are potentially the most powerful of the revolutionary forces ranged against the form of exploitation which colonialism safeguards in Namibia, and there is widespread consciousness of this amongst the rank-and-file. One SWAPO militant has expressed a common view: 'Once the workers realise how great their power is, they will automatically stop asking when the freedom fighters will be coming to free them.' In the general strike, contract workers experienced the power and the limits of mass labour action. It reinforced their commitment to national liberation as the essential prerequisite of their liberation as a class. It has also extended their consciousness of the necessity for unity not only in their own ranks but with all other sections of the oppressed in Namibia.

At a branch meeting in 1977, contract workers from Windhoek expressed the view of all working-class activists in Namibia in advancing the case for a nation-wide general union of all black workers.

I want to tell our fellow-workers that the weak point we have [to remedy] in order to change the system is unity and co-operation. And we must not distinguish whether some workers are sleeping in a compound and some are staying in the single quarters and some in the so-called locations. All of us who are exploited, we blacks, we must know that we are all workers. We workers want to be in unity. We workers in Namibia, we want to unite. It doesn't matter what kind of work he is doing, each and every worker should come into that union. After such unity and co-operation have been established, it is only then that it will be possible to campaign for better working conditions, for higher wages and to embark on any other action which will change the working conditions.

Once workers have organised and united, they will be able to form a union, they will try to make other workers aware of the conditions in which they are working. In such a union of workers, we are going to teach one another how people should respect one another and regard themselves as human beings. We know that if a person is starving he will become wise, he will learn something from that starvation. Because we are quite aware that we are being oppressed here in Namibia. It is only through a union that we will be able to force the Government to change the conditions under which we are working, and it is only through the union that we will be able to make an end to the exploitation of man by man.

Because we know that we can only force the Government if we are united. We, the workers of Namibia, we *have* to unite — all the workers in the country have to unite, then we will be able to embark on the kind of action that will force the Government to attend to our problems. If we cannot unite, then we will just continue to be exploited and oppressed.

We also want to teach other workers that the capitalists are busy robbing our country of its resources. All the workers should know that foreign investors are taking what we are producing to their countries overseas. Because when those foreign investors — monopolies — came to our country, they didn't come with anything. The wealth they are taking they found here in Namibia. We are dissatisfied with the fact that our mineral resources and other wealth are being exported. They are squeezing our country dry. Because it is a fact that this country is our country. We are in the majority in this country and we are the very people who are suffering, while the foreigners who have come from somewhere in our country are the ones who are giving orders and getting all the wealth of our country. Therefore we workers feel that we have to unite so that we can take action to end the exploitation of man

271

by man.

South African Labour Bulletin 1978, p. 42—4

Workers in the Vanguard of the Liberation Movement

The militancy of contract workers has long made their compounds in the towns and mines revolutionary enclaves for the liberation movement. But their commitment to national liberation extends to all areas of political life. This is reinforced by their strong ties, like all black workers, with other strata of the oppressed, ties cemented by the very system which oppresses them. Most also have close links to land and family in the north, and are thus intimately concerned with the resistance to bantustan repression and the degradation of rural poverty.

The workers' complete solidarity against the bantustans was nowhere more dramatically seen than in the effectiveness of their boycott of the two Ovamboland elections. In Windhoek, they refused even to register for these elections, and only four out of an eligible population of 3,000 voted in August 1973, three of whom were security police. In Walvis Bay, only nine workers out of thousands eligible voted. Similar results were reported for the election in Okavango. All in all, only 50 people voted at the 33 polling booths which were set up in urban centres outside the Ovambo and Okavango areas. This boycott was substantially repeated in the January 1975 bantustan election, during which it was only massive police and army brutality that drove most of their kinfolk inside Ovamboland to the polls.

Youth is another sector with which all black workers have a close association. The political integration between the two groups has been reinforced by the regime's repressive practices, since the frequent expulsions of high school and training college students for anti-colonial resistance threw many young activists into the workers' ranks, often in menial jobs. The organisation of the 1971—72 general strike was a vivid example of such collaboration between workers and ex-students in action, and the tradition has continued to hold strong.

During the period of mass mobilisation and heightened tension which followed the victory of the Ovamboland election boycott and the militant Youth League rally on 12 August 1973, the Youth League called a clandestine meeting of about 80 people on the night of 16 August in the Katutura contract workers' compound to teach them SWAPO songs. A police patrol hunting Youth League leaders raided the meeting and shot a SWAPO member dead. Immediately, the workers mobilised in angry mood, stoned a municipal building and burnt down the municipal police dormitory nearby. That same night, over 150 police, backed by the army with Saracen armoured cars, launched a massive pass raid, arresting over 300. The contract workers planned a general strike for Monday 20 August, but a Youth League rally that Sunday was banned and people who tried to assemble in defiance were twice attacked and broken up by the police. During that day and the next, a municipal policeman's house was attacked with petrol bombs and a cinema hall damaged. Only a violent assault by the police and 150 Portuguese mercenaries on workers in the compound that Monday thwarted the protest strike.

mercenaries on workers in the compound that Monday thwarted the protest strike.

At all times, workers have given protection to SWAPO militants on the run from the police or working underground. Many PLAN cadres have been able to use the migrant labour system to reach destinations in the centre of the country and to count on the solidarity of contract workers in all places and situations. Perhaps the most symbolic recent demonstration of the revolutionary commitment of contract workers came during the public celebrations of Namibia Day in Katutura on 26 August 1977. After the meeting was attacked by Turnhalle thugs, hundreds of workers from the contract compound set up the road blocks throughout the location. In spite of confrontations which followed, SWAPO remained firmly in control and the people were protected by this act of unity and solidarity. During the anti-SWAPO reign of terror launched by the police and gangs of D.T.A. thugs in March—April 1978, it was again workers, especially from the Katutura contract workers' compound, who put up a sustained defence at great cost to themselves, and eventually forced the issue by confronting the regime with a general strike.

Peasants

Peasants from the largest section of the oppressed population of Namibia. They are deeply exploited and forced to survive at levels of poverty well below subsistence. Since 1972, it has been the peasants in the north, where half the Namibian population lives, who have borne the brunt of the resistance to the occupation regime. Before 1974, the main front of the struggle was political and its target the imposition of bantustan tule. SWAPO's regional organisation in the north, together with the Youth League, mobilised demonstrations to greet Waldheim and Escher in 1972, despite the official secrecy imposed on the two visits. Their outspoken opposition to the tribal puppets' attempts to force the people to accept bantustan self-government aroused mass support amongst the peasantry. This sustained campaign and the mass popular response (a sequel to the peasant revolt of early 1972) led, as we have shown, to the successful boycott by peasants of the bantustan elections in Ovamboland in August 1973 — a shattering blow to the prestige of the apartheid regime.

But the mode of struggle was on the verge of a basic change. Since mid-1974, PLAN has been able to set up bases and supply lines which have permitted the extension of intensified armed struggle from the Caprivi to the whole of Northern Namibia. By the start of the 1975—76 rainy season (the rains usually last from November until March), PLAN was ready to strike. Guerrilla attacks on the occupation forces in Ovamboland rapidly escalated and have been continuous and active ever since. PLAN has increasingly been able to assure the peasants in large areas of basic protection from the worst excesses of the demoralised white soldiers and the brutal tribal police and soldiers. For several years, South African forces have been reluctant to enter certain areas in the border zone day or night, apart from occasional 'invasions' in overwhelming strength.

The peasants have indeed suffered greatly from the terror tactics used by the occupying forces to intimidate them into denying support to SWAPO cadres. But no matter how brutal, the regime has not been able to weaken the strong links of solidarity which have been forged between the rural population and the freedom fighters, links which have taken the concrete form of the militants providing basic health care to the peasants who in turn provide food for the militants when the latter are not able to provide their own. The freedom fighters are also trained to participate in the process of political education and mobilisation of the masses, and when they enter an area for the first time, they begin their work by telling the people about SWAPO objectives and programmes. The solidarity between the peasants and the freedom fighters — who may well be their own sons and daughters — is thus founded on understanding the necessity for armed struggle and the objectives of the Namibian revolution.

In the central and southern reserves, the main form of struggle has been resistance to the imposition of bantustans, resistance which intensified considerably during the two years to mid-1977 as the occupation regime speeded up its bantustan programme in the south to 'legitimise' its puppets at the Turnhalle Conference. The imposition of a bantustan-type constitution on the Rehoboth Gebiet in 1976 was met with an angry demonstration in Rehoboth itself and the rapid mobilisation of the local people into the ranks of SWAPO in the latter half of 1976. In July 1977, peasants again underscored their almost unanimous rejection of 'separate development' with massive protests against the inauguration of the Damara 'homeland' government at meetings in Khorixas and Outjo.

When the south went over overwhelmingly to SWAPO, the regime increased its intimidation of the local people. For instance, when boreholes for water broke down, the government no longer paid to have them repaired. As a result, the local people began to organise themselves for practical actions such as borehole repairs as well as for political action against the regime. Thus they are gaining the organisational and practical skills of self-reliance. This is a message and a principle which is being taken up in social consciousness and in small-scale local actions all over the country as people struggle to liberate themselves from the colonial mentality of dependence. It provides a pointer towards a new form of society based on co-operation and self-reliance.

Traditional Leaders

In most cases, the traditional leadership in Namibia has been abused and coerced by the occupation regime to serve the purposes of its apartheid grand design. Some are direct descendants of pre-colonial rulers; others

are artificial creations of the bantustan hierarchy. In the north, the traditional
leadership has sold out totally to the occupation regime. In the south, the
pattern has been more complex as traditional chiefs and headmen remained
partially responsive to their people's aspiration for freedom but felt
threatened by modern political parties organising for liberation on a national
and non-sectarian platform. Kapuuo and a few others, who formerly opposed
bantustans, gave in in the end when the South African Turnhalle plan
promised alternative means of preserving their ethnic power base. A few
more, such as the Damara Tribal Executive, have stayed outside Turnhalle
but have refused to join SWAPO. These have only small followings, usually
in the reserves where their influence is felt.

Hendrik Witbooi addresses a SWAPO rally in Southern Namibian during 1977

But some have committed themselves strongly to the cause of national
unity, and where they have identified with the popular movement have both
reinforced it with their influence and received recognition as true leaders.
In the south, it is actually the traditional leaders of the people who are
leading the struggle, and the dedication of such figures has been an important
counter to the propaganda which the regime makes out of its bantustan
puppets. The SWAPO Elders' Council — relatively inactive since the mid-
1960s when many prominent SWAPO leaders and cadres were arrested —
was revitalised with the appointment of a Secretary in March 1977. At a
seminar held three months later in Katutura, the Elders' Council issued papers
attacking the Turnhalle proposal to train 'tribal armies', and reaffirmed the

need for solidarity among the Namibian people. Men such as Pastor Hendrik Witbooi have proved effective and courageous articulators of the spirit of popular resistance. At a news conference on 4 November 1976, at which he announced the decision of thousands in the south to join SWAPO, Witbooi was pressured by a BOSS agent posing as a reporter to declare his attitude to 'violence'. Witbooi answered: 'The people in the south are like the venomous snake that lives there. If you leave it alone, it won't bother you. But if you bother it, then it strikes. But whose fault is it that the snake bites you?'

Youth and Intelligentsia

Youth has a special place in the ranks of the liberation movement. It is young people who have consistently been the powerhouse of radical ideas, the most courageous and outspoken activists, the pioneers of new forms of struggle against oppression. Their leading section has always been students at high schools or training colleges, a tiny fraction of their age group because of the discriminatory structure of the education system, but a powerful political force because of their clear understanding of the workings of the system of exploitation and their readiness to act as catalysts in other forms of struggle.

The point of conflict has regularly been repression by the police or school authorities of political activity by students in or outside the school. At the Ongwediva High School and Training College in Ovamboland, the entire student body of 500 organised a march and demonstration on 2 August 1971 in support of the World Court ruling six weeks previously, and a few days later boycotted the ceremonial opening of this show-piece establishment by the Minister of Bantu Education. Inevitably, most of the students were expelled, but they have aroused mass enthusiasm amongst the local popula- tion at Ondangwa and secured the support of their parents. Many soon joined the ranks of the migrant workers or became Youth League militants inside Ovamboland.

A similar sequence took place at the Augustineum College in Windhoek during the popular celebrations which followed the success of the election boycott in August 1973. When student leaders were expelled for trying to give support to the Youth League following its militant rally on 12 August that year, 250 students staged a mass walk-out on 17 August after refusing to comply with college regulations, and nearly all of them were expelled and refused re-admission. Six days later, 120 students, the great majority of the Martin Luther High School, boycotted classes for three days in sympathy with their Augustineum comrades.

It was in 1976 that for the first time students mounted a concerted attack on the institutions of their own oppression. In June, the students of Soweto (the network of black townships outside Johannesburg) touched off a spark which continues to burn to this day when they protested against Afrikaans as the medium of instruction. But the target was the whole apartheid system of which Bantu Education is only one part.

The spark came to Namibia later, but it did come. Beginning in early November, a boycott of end-of-year examinations began at Martin Luther High School in Omaruru in protest against Bantu Education and in solidarity with the youth and students of Soweto. Within three weeks, students throughout the country had joined the boycott. The regime responded quickly and harshly, and many students were arrested, intimidated and taken in for questioning. At Okakarara in Central Namibia, where police backed by troops with five armoured cars baton-charged a demonstration in which 70% of the students took part, one student died. Here, as elsewhere, attempts by the authorities to use their Turnhalle puppets to break the unity of the students failed completely. In several schools in the central parts of the country, including Okakarara, armed soldiers took over the teaching. This had already become standard practice in the northern bantustans, under the so-called 'hearts and minds' programmes of the S.A.D.F. : the message of a soldier in uniform teaching with his machine-gun on the table before he can hardly have been missed by the students.

As Namibian students have become increasingly articulate and united, the Namibian Black Students Organisation (NABSO) has played a leading role. Founded on 2 September 1975, it co-ordinated the students' boycott, exposed the authorities' repressive measures and articulated their position. 'The racist policy of apartheid, which is supported by Bantu Education, has failed,' declared its statement of 14 December 1976. 'Bantu Education is the foundation of racism and group identity; it is there to prepare black students for a third-class citizenship. It is a propaganda machinery of apartheid dehuminisation and discrimination.' Although the boycott ended at the start of the 1977 school year, a fair proportion of the students did not return to the government high schools. Some went to independent church-run schools such as Martin Luther, which adopted syllabuses from independent African countries like Botswana and Swaziland and dropped Afrikaans as a subject altogether. Others joined the ranks of workers as party activists. And several hundred, following the path laid down by thousands of their predecessors, left the country to join PLAN as freedom fighters. In the northern bantustans there have been repeated instances since early 1976 of whole schools crossing the border to join the armed struggle.

The SWAPO Youth League emerged, especially during 1973, as one of the most courageous, militant and uncompromising forces in the Namibian struggle. Large and militant mass rallies have taken place regularly in Ovamboland and Katutura where members of the Youth League — including teachers, students, nurses, and migrant labourers — took it upon themselves to articulate the feelings by the tribal authorities and frequent violent attacks in Ovamboland, at first against the imposition of 'self-government' on 1 May 1973 and thereafter against the August elections, holding meetings and rallies throughout the bantustan. These meetings had a shattering effect upon the authorities, as young men and women stood up and openly declared what had before been said mainly outside Namibia by SWAPO officials in exile. In speech after speech, the members of the Youth League declared their solidarity with the guerrillas and reaffirmed the necessity of armed struggle as an integral part of the larger struggle for national independence.

This upsurge of militancy was the dominant theme at the SWAPO Youth League rally, attended by more than 3,000 men and women, students and workers, in Katutura on 12 August 1973. In addition to being the Youth League's first official appearance in the southern part of the country, this rally was the climax of a powerful new initiative to confront the occupation regime. For the first time, speakers endorsed the armed struggle from a public platform. In the words of *Namibia News*, the SWAPO speeches were militant and direct.

The freedom is in your hands,' said David Shikomba, Secretary of the Youth League. 'Don't wait until tomorrow, start today'. 'Let us stand together and fight for freedom in the country in which God created us.' said Eliachim Andreas. Joseph Kashea talked about the hated 'Black Boers', the puppet chiefs and their henchmen. Several of them were mentioned by name and warned, among them the Chief Minister of Ovamboland, Filemon Elifas. And the freedom fighters who had given their lives for the liberation of their country were remembered. 'Hundreds have died and their blood is calling,' said one of the speakers. Youth League Chairman Jerry Ekandjo called a boycott of the South

African radio and instead urged the people to listen to SWAPO broadcasts from Zambia. And the crowd responded with the chant, 'We
shall fight until we die.'

Although this public outcry against South Africa's continued occupation
of Namibia resulted in widespread arrests, particularly of SWAPO Youth
League members, their trials became platforms for political protest with
courageous young Namibians challenging the legitimacy of the South African
courts to try them. The SWAPO flag and revolutionary salutes were
frequently displayed at these sessions. SWAPO songs were also sung. The
youth were determined, and their confidence in the struggle was aptly
summed up by one young SWAPO member when he said: 'If our leaders
are arrested, we shall elect new leaders. We are many. The police will have to
jail the whole of Namibia in order to break us.'

Thus from 1973 on, the SWAPO Youth League was instrumental in
mobilising both students and working youths, and in popularising and imple-
menting the task of combining armed resistance with political action.
Through the increased radicalisation of young people, the Youth League had
an important impact on recruiting volunteers for PLAN. It was factors such
as these which were behind SWAPO President Sam Nujoma's 1975 New Year
message to Namibian youth, in which he said;

> The militant activity of the SWAPO Youth League towards the imple-
> mentation of the party programme has been one of the most import-
> ant strides made by our movement . . . This youth section of our move-
> ment has affirmed in the anti-colonial activity one of our party's
> concepts that the youth are the blossoming flowers of the liberation
> struggle.

White-collar workers, many of whom gained their first experience of
political action and debate through student or Youth League circles, have
also played an important part in the liberation process, particularly in supplying leadership cadres. It was black teachers and government employees who
organised, led and articulated the opposition in Ovamboland to the imposition of the apartheid regime's bantustan policy and who made sure, despite
the efforts of South African officials, that Waldheim and Escher were confronted with the militant opposition of the peasants and workers during
their visits in 1972. By 1974, over 100 teachers had been sacked for their
membership of SWAPO, along with many other government employees.
When a large number of white-collar workers (teachers, clerks, nurses)
crossed into Angola after 1974, it was to contribute their skills to the armed
struggle. Those who remained have been active supporters of SWAPO despite
the brutal treatment they regularly suffer from the South African authorities.

In the south, the Nama teachers' strike in 1976—77 exemplifies the quality
of resistance from white-collar cadres. It was widely supported by the local
communities as well as the Black Teachers' Association, which represents

about 1,000 teachers in Namibia. Later, five Roman Catholic nuns, seconded to teach in the Nama schools in the south, withdrew from their duties in solidarity with their striking colleagues. The strike, however, ended without resolution when the government threatened permanent closure of the High School at Tses in Southern Namibia. But the militancy and determination of the teachers remains, and indeed, most teachers are an important and active section of SWAPO's membership in the south. By engaging in political work, these cadres are going against the regulations of the Department of Coloured Affairs under whose authority they fall. The Department has been unable to stifle this political work because the people are so united that if the Department attacks one, it quickly finds that it must fight against all.

Although university students are very few (only about 250 were studying in 1977), their intellectual skills have served the party well in recent years. When the black universities in South Africa closed down in 1976, most Namibians returned home and some resolved not to resume their studies. 'Back here,' explained one, 'I realised that the struggle is for the people, and we can start off an education which we can call a people's education.' This was but one part of a growing movement towards setting up alternative forms of education on a self-reliant basis outside the state system. This has been clearly expressed in the growth of correspondence study clubs and night classes, of workers' literacy classes and study groups, in the Nama teachers' plan for starting independent schools, and the decision of the major churches at the end of 1976 to go multi-racial, even at the expense of losing their government subsidies. Students at all levels of education have become fully engaged in the battle against ideological oppression. This has involved combating the inculcation of colonial attitudes such as subservience, deference to authority and elitist aspirations.

Asked if he and his friends often discussed political matters, one young SWAPO member had the following to say.

> Everything we talk about is political. If one of us sees a car and says 'Isn't that a beautiful car?' we immediately get a political discussion about what kind of consciousness is represented by the statement that a particular car is beautiful. We immediately get into a discussion about class and that some people can have a beautiful car while others can't. And we educate each other about the meaning of these attitudes and how the Boers encourage these attitudes to keep us divided.

Education and mobilisation: these are two of the main components of the work of SWAPO within Namibia, and youth have been and continue to be centrally involved.

The Churches

The churches play an important part in the cultural and political life of the

Namibian people. Over 80% of the population is Christian, and over three-quarters of these belong to the United Evangelical Lutheran Church (VELK), whose two principal components are the Ovambo-Kavango Church (ELOK) in the north and the Evangelical Lutheran Church (ELK) in the rest of the country. Although conceded self-government in the 1950s, the long presence of missionaries in Namibia, dating back to the beginning of the 19th Century, was a powerful ideological prop to colonial rule. It took time for the black Lutherans, along with the other main churches (the Roman Catholics and the Anglicans), to break through their conservative legacy which decreed that they should not intervene in political issues and should work within the existing social order. Before 1971, none had taken a public stand on the oppressive society in which most of their members lived and suffered, despite the growing persecution of their priests and staff by the occupation regime. But in 1964 and again in 1967, ELOK and ELK submitted joint memoranda opposing the Odendaal Plan, and in 1967, Bishop Auala of ELOK called for the reform of the contract labour system, only to be met with the answer: 'Change is impossible.'

The open letter of the heads of ELOK and ELK to the Prime Minister in 1971 supporting the World Court ruling was a watershed for the churches in Namibia. Their first major public statement on political matters, it had a powerful impact on Namibians throughout the nation and drew the support of the other main church leaders. 'It is vital that all Christian leaders in this territory make their views known also,' commented Bishop Winter of the Anglicans. 'The Christian church as the conscience of this nation must now speak out with clarity and without fear. Apartheid must be denounced as unacceptable before God.' The initiative provoked a critical self-examination by the churches of their attitude to social and political questions, a process reinforced by the influence of 'black theology' amongst their black compatriots in South Africa.

Since 1971, the churches' stand against the colonial regime has hardened and they have taken an increasingly activist role. Their repeated criticism of the oppression and injustices of colonial rule, in the face of constant South African intimidation, has made a valuable contribution to the freedom struggle, as have their efforts to expose the regime's repressive practices. In some instances they have gone further, actively defending the victims of South African persecution, especially in political trials.

The Anglicans have been the most outspoken and active. During the contract workers' strike it was they who publicised the workers' cause and exposed the atrocities of the South African Police and troops in Ovamboland, where, in one incident, police fired without provocation on a party of church-goers, killing at least four. Again, it was largely through the intervention of the Anglicans and ELOK that the tribal floggings after the August 1973 election first became public knowledge. Through church pressure, the Windhoek Supreme Court passed a provisional court order restraining tribal authorities in the north from further public floggings, although this order was lifted in February 1974 and floggings were not finally prohibited until a year later.

As the conflict intensified in the north and the brutality of South African repression escalated, the churches became actively engaged in the sufferings of the people. When hundreds bgean to cross the Angolan border in mid-1974, Bantu Affairs overlord de Wet asked church leaders to find out why. The leaders consulted their parishioners, and their findings were a searing indictment of South African oppression in the north.

> The people expect police to be defenders of peace, but the terrorism-like actions of the police, with their weapons, have frightened the people . . . The nation expects the government to change its methods and follow the will of the majority of the nation to give the people freedom and human rights.

There have been many allegations of widespread torture of detainees at the hands of the South African Police and military forces, allegations which were supported by the Anglican and Lutheran Churches. At a second meeting with Vorster on 30 April 1973, the Lutheran Church leaders again raised the issue and submitted 37 names of members who were prepared to testify that they had been tortured. Three months later, without troubling to investigate, Vorster issued a blanket denial, which the Lutherans adamantly rejected. 'We stand by our position that torture was and is practised,' they declared in July 1974. In May 1977, the main churches issued a statement on torture declaring that it had become a 'standard practice' in interrogation, and in June 1978, two churchmen published a booklet comprising a large number of sworn affidavits describing horrifying tortures. It was later banned by the regime and its authors, like many of their courageous colleagues who have spoken out in defiance of tyranny, were thrown out of the country.

The churches' alignment with the independence struggle has become more and more explicit in recent years. 'The desire for freedom and dignity can no longer be suppressed,' stated Lukas de Vries, head of VELK in September 1974. In January 1975, the Lutherans opened contacts with the nationalist parties in Namibia. In the same month, the Anglicans publicly supported SWAPO's boycott of the bantustan elections in Ovamboland. By now the Lutherans, and more cautiously the Catholics, were joining the Anglicans not only in supporting the position of the U.N., but also in recognising SWAPO as representing the aspirations of the great majority of Namibians, in opposing Turnhalle as a sham, and in demanding SWAPO's participation in any settlement. Shortly before Dr. Kissinger met Vorster in Europe in June 1976, the heads of the Lutheran and Anglican Churches in Namibia sent him a letter. South African policies, they wrote, 'have destroyed human dignity and bedevilled relationships with the family and community and totally alienated the black population . . . We are convinced that the vast majority of the black population of our country fervently desires that the South African Police; Army and Administration should rapidly leave their territory.' Shortly afterwards, in July 1976, the South African Council of Churches passed a resolution, moved by VELK, declaring 'strong support with all those

Christians and movements which are involved in the struggle for a free and just Namibia.'

Although the churches have been cautious in declaring outright support for the armed struggle, their statements have become progressively more sympathetic to its necessity. Exiled Anglican Bishop Wood defended the right of the oppressed to fight for their liberation in a letter to the London *Times* in October 1975. Early in 1976, the Anglicans withdrew their chaplains from the South African army of occupation while maintaining their clergy with exiled Namibians in Zambia, and both the Lutherans and the Catholics have kept up contact with their adherents abroad. Privately, many churchmen are more explicit in their support of the armed struggle. Some belong to SWAPO, as do many of their members; indeed church officers are strongly represented in the SWAPO leadership. One leader of the Lutheran Church in the north has put it this way: 'The freedom fighters are our children. Even people who are suffering still give them food because they know the freedom fighters are the people who come from us, who are fighting for our freedom — and we've got to help them. They're brave people.'

South African persecution of the churches has become more systematic and vindictive as their engagement on the side of the oppressed has become more explicit. Their main weapon has been to bar the entry of or to expel church officers who are foreign citizens, even those who have lived in Namibia for many years. In this way Anglican Bishops Colin Winter and Richard Wood, both British citizens, were deported, in 1972 and 1975 respectively. In Bishop Winter's case, he antagonised the South African authorities by his outspoken support of the general strike and of its leaders when they were brought up for trial in Windhoek in 1972. And Bishop Wood was outspoken in his condemnation of the brutal floggings of SWAPO men and women in Ovamboland in 1974, and was instrumental in exposing them.

Others have been banned from entering the northern zone under the security regulations — in this way the Anglican Church's headquarters was virtually cut off from most of its members in Ovamboland. Lay personnel such as nurses and teachers have been blocked as well, and church hospitals have even been shut down despite facilities for blacks being already desperately overcrowded. Police and soldiers regularly abuse local church officers in the north, some have been interrogated and at least one killed. Interference has been even more direct: in mid-May 1973, ELOK's R600,000 printing press at Oniipa in Ovamboland was expertly blown up in an act of sabotage which had the strong imprint of South African instigation. Undaunted, the Church rebuilt the press and two years later it was in operation once more. The churches have not, however, been intimidated from instigating practical projects such as a correspondence course, the Ecumenical Christian Centre and independent multi-racial education. Their courageous opposition to the barbarity and injustice of South African rule has not been diminished by persecution.

The Lutheran church's printing press at Oniipa in Ovamboland, destroyed by a bomb attack

Women

In recent years, women in Namibia have begun seriously to question the ideology which legitimises their double oppression. Traditional attitudes as well as all-embracing legal discrimination under colonialism have been responsible for the subjection of women. In order to imobilise women for full participation in the liberation movement, it is therefore necessary to struggle on both fronts.

Putuse Appollus, member of SWAPO's Central Committee has this to say on the position of women in pre-colonial times: 'Within African society women were long considered commodities and brought up as slaves for the men, told how to cook, bring up children, be loyal and friendly to the husband — not to speak badly of him but to bring him a nice plate of food.' Commonly men had control of the lands and cattle through their position as heads of the household, and dominated political life through the elders' and chiefs' councils. Generally speaking, the practices of initiation rites, polygamy and *lobolo* (bride-price) are the structures through which sex discrimination can most obviously be seen to be operating within tribal society, although *lobolo* was not widespread in pre-colonial Namibia. But because they shared with men the productive work — as field cultivators (in the north), food-gatherers and craft-workers — women retained substantial rights and a degree of social autonomy. It is capitalist colonialism which has systematically exploited such discrimination by using its system of migrant labour and influx of controls to exclude women from most wage-earning jobs outside domestic service, trapping them in impoverished rural ghettoes.

At their second conference in November 1976, the Organisation of Mozambican Women issued strong attacks on all three of these practices on the grounds that they institutionalised a view of women as objects of pleasure and sources of cheap manual labour. Initiation rites inculcate feelings of inferiority into a women, whereby she is prepared for three fundamental roles: to be submissive and resigned to her inferior status, to be an object of sexual pleasure and to be a child-bearer. The practices of *lobolo* and poly-gamy have a more obvious economic basis: 'The rationale for *lobolo* is that it is compensation for the transfer of labour power from one family to another . . . Under polygamy, as head and proprietor of the family, the husband acquires more wives to augment the labour force at his disposal.' That these views are current in Namibia, too, is illustrated by this comment from a man at a SWAPO meeting inside the country — also in November 1976: 'I pay *lobolo* for a woman according to tradition. Therefore she becomes my possession. I am her boss and she is my property. You don't expect me to be submissive to my own shirt, so why should I treat her differently?'

Traditional attitudes of this sort are, however, being strongly challenged by the younger people within SWAPO, both men and women. Another SWAPO man said this: 'By marrying a women we are confining her to a house to cook our food and look after our children . . . the protection we give women is a form of oppression.' A SWAPO Women's Council seminar held in Windhoek in April 1977 was attended by a large number of men as well as women. The following are comments made about this meeting by a married male SWAPO member, who is soon to be ordained as a pastor.

> In the meeting they said the black man, because he's oppressed by the white man, his boss, when he comes home he tries to do the same thing to his wife, and in this situation the man is oppressed and he's also oppressing the wife. This idea was the main idea of the whole meeting. The men at the meeting agreed with this.

A woman at the meeting explained the difficulty for older women in accepting these new attitudes. 'In the older generation, the man has his own work to do, such as chopping wood, and the woman has her own work, such as washing clothes and cooking. Therefore my mother can't understand my husband helping me.' The speech given at this meeting ended with a reading of a poem written by Samora Machel to his wife Josina Machel when she died, and with the slogan: 'The participation of women in the struggle will hasten our victory and will thus end the slavery of Namibians.'

The involvement of women in struggle has a long and proud history in

Namibia. Women are in some ways more accessible and easier to organise than men because their residence is not so transient or so rigidly controlled. Many men are shunted about by the contract labour system and find it difficult to stay in one place for any length of time. But women tend to be long-term residents in the place where they live, whether on peasant plots in the reserves, on white farms or in urban locations. In the towns, women live in houses rather than bachelor barracks and work for white 'madams' and small employers rather than in large factories or municipal work-gangs. Social and political ties between women therefore develop most strongly in their community context.

Women and girls have thus been vital communication links in all phases of struggle. This role has, ironically enough, been facilitated by the attitudes of male officialdom which to some extent have assumed that women are political, no matter how severely they may suffer under the political system. Apart from carrying messages and keeping channels of communication open, women have hidden combatants, guns and ammunition. They have even carried guns, disguised with baby clothes, in full view of the occupying forces, to their destination.

Women also play an extremely important role in the upbringing and education of children, for which they usually have sole responsibility because of the contract labour system. A leading SWAPO woman cadre has described the sort of questions which women are endlessly called upon to answer by bewildered children: 'I can't really understand. All the time my father is on contract. We can only be with him three or four months. The whites who are working on the road — they are together with their families but its not the same for us the blacks. Why?'

These activities, which may perhaps be regarded as traditionally feminine, because essentially supportive, are no less vital to the liberation movement. But from the earliest days of anti-colonial resistance women have also been prepared to initiate militant campaigns in their own right. After the genocide of their people by the German army in 1904—5, Herero women resolved not to bear children while German rule lasted in their homeland. Later, it was Herero women who took the lead once more in refusing — where they could afford it — to abase themselves by becoming 'nannies' for white families. In 1955, women were prominent in the Herero revolt against the apartheir-practising Lutheran Church in Namibia which culminated in the formation of the *Oruuano,* an independent community church. In 1958, it was the women who were responsible for the routing of government puppets from the Windhoek Advisory Board. They successfully organised against Boardman Mungunda, who had asked the government to apply corporal punishment to women pass law offenders.

One of the landmarks of women's resistance was the demonstration and boycott of 1959, which culminated in the Windhoek massacre, only months before the Sharpeville massacre took place in South Africa. It was the women of the Old Location who on 9 December marched in procession and demonstrated in front of the Administrator's residence. They took a leading part in organising the boycott of location services the following day. On the streets of the Old Location, women were prominent in the crowds which resisted the police attack, for all that their only weapons were rocks and bottles. One women was shot dead as she tried to set fire to a police can. Thirteen in all were killed that day and over 60 wounded. Putuse Appollus has said of the killings: 'They activated the hitherto patient forces embodied in the indomitable willpower of Namibian women.'

The illegal regime recognises the threat which the women pose. Between August 1973 and February 1974, over 3,000 people were forcibly expelled from the area around Windhoek, and sent to the northern region of the country. Two-thirds of this number were women and young people. They were all accused of furthering SWAPO aims and objectives in the urban areas.

SWAPO's emphasis is on women and men fighting the problem of women's oppression together. A woman SWAPO militant, speaking at several meetings in Namibia in 1977, analysed the political priorities for activists. 'Let us put it clearly that the oppression of women is not a matter between men and women but that the system which accommodates this evil should be scrutinised by both men and women in a common effort to understand it as comrades.' Closely related to this is the recognition that by confining women to the home,

> Half the manpower of the country is kept from full participation in the struggle. The man has become helpless in the house . . . When the wife is not at home to clean, cook, wash and iron, then in most cases the man is completely helpless. This dependence of the man on the services of the woman is in complete opposition to the idea of self-reliance. The man should thus be liberated from this dependence, and the woman from her self-sacrificing tendencies induced to keep her in slavery and thus from participation in the struggle for liberation . . . The woman should therefore refuse to give birth to slaves. This she can only guarantee by her full participation in the struggle.

At the many SWAPO meetings which take place almost every week throughout the country, and in the study groups which are developing in the secondary schools, the same preoccupations arise. Many men and women are becoming aware that they must fight against the traditional attitude that women cannot be leaders because they are inferior or too emotional. One woman tells a story about a meeting she attended where someone was explaining how women are excluded from political discussions in her community. 'She was so angry and bottled up about this exclusion that she began to shout her anger in the street . . . and everyone thought she was crazy.' But she felt that this experience was typical of the experience of many women, and that the anger was positive because it meant that women were beginning to ask questions about their role in society and in the liberation struggle.

During 1976, several meetings occurred around the country which dealt

Women fight alongside men in the Namibian revolution

Leaders of SWAPO's Women's Council address a rally during 1977

specifically with the problems facing Namibian women. Discussion centred on how to mount political education campaigns which would draw women more centrally into the struggle for liberation and which would also educate the men about the problems unique to women. In addition, at SWAPO public meetings throughout the country, Women's Council representatives are often among the speakers. There are also women's study groups in some of the secondary schools, aimed specifically at examining the problems women face in the struggle for personal emancipation and national liberation.

At the SWAPO Annual National Conference held in March 1977, the first Secretary of the Women's Council inside Namibia was appointed. Within one month, the first Women's Council seminars to occur inside the country took place in Katutura and Rehoboth, and plans were made to hold such seminars regularly all over the country. On 11–12 June 1977, there was a Women's Council meeting in Walvis Bay, and the following weekend there was a public meeting in Katutura organised by the women which was attended by almost 4,000 men and women, including many whites. At a meeting in Windhoek, April 1977, a male SWAPO member remarked:

> I think the Women's Council is just starting this year to really mobilise women as a whole. They are also trying to explain house by house, to meet everyone personally and tell them what's going on. And then, after the discussion, it depends on the woman whether she wants a SWAPO card or not. In this time, now more wives understand what SWAPO is and they come more and more to be SWAPO members.

Large numbers of women in SWAPO have now undergone military training and are fighting side by side with the men. The implications of this for personal emancipation of women from both traditional and colonial sources of oppression cannot be overestimated. There was an unprecedented number of women in the 1974 exodus, when thousands of Namibians trekked through Angola to Zambia. Many of them refused to stay at the refugee camps but insisted on going straight to the front to participate in the fighting. 'You have to have convictions to go and fight', says Putuse Appollus.

> Many of the girls say we can have education later, we want to go and fight with the others. But we only let women between the ages of 19 and 30 go. On the front all the work is shared without question. Everyone takes their turn in the hunting, skinning and cooking of the animals. They all wear the same uniform and it's interesting to see that the girls don't treat themselves as girls . . . It's a matter of 'comrade', a communal sort of life, without the sexist division. In fact, the women are so good at shooting that they often beat the men. The men tend to fear them for they are trained in judo and self-defence, of course. The men later won't want to marry them. They will think, 'If I beat her, she can just take a gun and shoot me.'

289

SWAPO's policy concerning women is that there is no difference as to the role either could or should play in the struggle and in decision-making. Both should be able to perform the same tasks. The biological difference between men and women should not lead to women having less privileges than men in society as a whole. SWAPO is waging a struggle against the exploitation of man by man, women by men, and vice-versa — to gain control over our own lives and to govern our country robbed from us by the South African regime and its dehumanising system of exploitation.

When one understands how the system which fosters exploitation operates and conditions the oppressed to accept their oppressive situation, one will also easily understand what has been the root cause of women being passive objects — trained and geared to please.

Before our country was colonised by the Germans and after them the Boers, there was already a division in the role of male and female in society. Women were looked at as objects of pleasure and convenience by men and were regarded as possessions by their husbands — the payment of *lobolo* (bride-price) is clear proof of this. Thus there are traditional customs which served to oppress women.

The colonisation of Namibia oppressed women further since now they were oppressed also by foreign masters as cheap labour. Furthermore, through the contract labour system, the woman was divorced from her husband for long periods and had to fend for her and the family by herself.

The Namibian Woman is realising that she should be actively involved in the national struggle for liberation to free her country from the yoke of colonialism and at the same time, free her and her male counterpart of the wrong practices and customs which served to keep them both 'un-liberated'. Thus she ensures that there is a revolution within a revolution.

Women are daily being harassed by the South African security police, but they face the Boers fearlessly and are continuing with their work showing that we cannot be intimidated into silence and passivity.

Women are educating their children into the political line of SWAPO and you see in towns and villages the power sign from toddlers who can hardly speak.

Male 'know-all' arguments at women's quest for self-assertion and independence are daily being swept away. Bastions of male dominance and reasoning of 'a woman's place' are being tumbled by a revolutionary wind so strong and a new woman so forceful that they have no choice but to accept a new reality.

We realise that what SWAPO fights for should be explained to the masses and should become part of them, therefore S.W.C. have seminars and discussions throughout the country attended by both men and women. In these seminars and discussions it is clearly explained why the liberation of women is necessary for the liberation of mankind as a whole.

The S.W.C. has the task of not only mobilising women to participate in the national struggle, but to make them conscious that they have the same right and obligation as men to make decisions concerning their nation's interest; that the woman should therefore develop herself to be a comrade in all aspects and not just a 'homemaker'; that both male and female should understand the system of exploitation and combat it as comrades.

We are still male dominated at the National Executive level and at branch level and would like to see a conscious effort at drawing women into the decision-making organs of our organisation. We have a long way to go but the struggle will continue.

Martha Ford, then Secretary of the SWAPO Women's Council inside Namibia

The participation of women in the struggle has stressed the need for them to have better education, and the time for this can often only be provided by making children a social responsibility. At the SWAPO Health and Education Centre in Zambia many of the women who come have some education or training, but many others do not. The supervisors at the Centre are responsible for seeing that there is enough food and medical supplies, and the children are all well fed and cared for collectively. School is organised at different hours according to age, and the women usually have their lessons in the evening. Even the young children are allowed to take part in political studies, and collective political discussion is central to the whole concept of education. Putuse Appolus says:

> Our job is to make comparisons between the Western countries and the socialist countries, and they have to decide what they want. It's for them to decide and not for you to force them: that way you don't get anywhere. For example, miniskirts: I always say to the boys, it's a sign of progress. Don't tamper with them. Let them wear what they want to wear. They have to decide what kind of society they want to build up for themselves and for their children to live in. In socialist countries there is at least the minimum, I won't say the maximum, equality . . .

Of course, there are problems to be overcome, Kokauru Nganjone, former Political Commissiar in PLAN commented on the position of women comman commanders:

> In the beginning some men were trying to disobey or get round their orders. In these cases we had stern discussions with the militants involved and told them that these women were given such responsibilities and powers by the party because of their intelligence and capacity. Through open criticism and self-criticism we are able to deal with these problems on an ongoing basis.

10. Towards Independence

National liberation movements are not always easy to characterise. Unlike political parties they are bodies which express not class or sectional interests but national ones, under conditions where these have been undermined by foreign conquest, domination or occupation. A national liberation movement holds together supporters from all sectors of the population – men and women, young and old, peasants, intellectuals and workers – forged into a cohesive whole in pursuit of the goal of national independence.

But mere mass support is not in itself enough. A sound organisational structure, a democratic decision-making process and a clear political understanding of the root economic structures and causes of oppression are vital to ensure that the movement does not become a loose populist one whose leaders could at some future time manipulate the masses. For true liberation, the attainment of state power is only the beginning. Africa has learnt to its cost that merely to unite national forces to get rid of a colonial power is not enough, because the structures of exploitation on which colonial domination is built have been systematically and deeply embedded in the colonised society.

SWAPO has faced these challenges. It has come to strength at a time when not only have the disastrous consequences of false decolonisation been revealed on the African continent, but also at a time when alternative directions are being taken by its neighbours in Southern Africa who share a similar tradition of a long armed liberation struggle against colonial regimes. More importantly, the specific conditions under which SWAPO has had to operate and the nature of the repression of the South African occupation regime have forced SWAPO to adjust both the form of its organisation and its political strategy.

These aims have not themselves changed much. What has changed has been an understanding of how to attain them. SWAPO has analysed the consequences of the apartheid regime's systematic social engineering, which has not only blocked the emergence in any strength of a neo-colonial elite of indigenous businessmen, professionals and managers, but has also destroyed the independent economic base of the peasantry. It has recognised the leading role of the black working class in building the future of an independent Namibia, and the fact that even when imperialist domination is overcome, capitalist exploitation may still persist. Today SWAPO is committed to a classless society and the social ownership of Namibia's natural resources and the means of production. In its Political Programme, adopted in 1976, SWAPO is committed to uniting 'all Namibian people, particularly the working class, the peasantry and progressive intellectuals, into a vanguard party capable of safeguarding national independence and of building a classless, non-exploitative society based on the ideals and principles of scientific socialism.'

PLAN cadres at a political education class

In 1960, SWAPO was confronted with two major tasks: to unite the Namibian people into one solid political organisation capable of confronting the South African occupation regime; and to mobilise world opinion at the U.N. and elsewhere against that occupation. Today SWAPO has achieved both these tasks. From its early days it has organised all sectors of the Namibian people to rally behind its call for national unity. From the 1964 joining of the Caprivi National Union to the tumultuous acclaim accorded SWAPO in 1976 and 1977, when so many thousands from all parts of the country and all sections of society joined SWAPO, the Namibian people have answered this call.

International recognition has come at the same time, growing in proportion to SWAPO's strength, for no nationalist body can claim credence internationally without clear proof of its base amongst the people it claims to represent. The SWAPO Conference in Windhoek in 1962 emphasised the importance of making Namibia's case known to the world. That of 1963 decided to establish external missions on the African continent and elsewhere, and to extend links outwards from Namibia on a high political level. That year saw the return of SWAPO President Sam Nujoma to Dar-es-Salaam where he established the Provisional Headquarters of the party. SWAPO's struggle for Namibian nationhood at the international level, as well as through armed struggle and mass mobilisation at home, led to its full recognition by the Organisation for African Unity in 1965 and by the U.N. in 1976 as the 'sole authentic representative of the Namibian people'.

Although the Namibian people have learnt that international support can only be a helpful auxiliary to the struggle for liberation conducted by the people themselves, the special status of Namibia as a Mandated Territory and, after 1966, as a Trustee of the U.N. itself has brought its own advantages. It has meant that South Africa stands condemned in international law for its failure to withdraw from the country. It has given the socialist and non-aligned majority at the U.N. a useful lever for preventing the West from condoning and legitimising any South African-inspired 'solution' which is not acceptable to the U.N. in terms of its basic principles of self-determination and political freedom. It has also meant that South Africa has never dared to ban SWAPO formally, as it has banned its own liberation movements. SWAPO has thus been able to organise inside Namibia, despite the repression, and be one with, and truly representative of, the broad masses of Namibian society. That there is not one other political organisation in Namibia today that can claim a truly national following is testimony to SWAPO's organisation and its representation of the aspirations of all Namibians.

It is the lessons of the past 20 years that have shaped SWAPO: the setbacks and the victories; the long hard years of sacrifice and determination. But it is the people who have made it and guaranteed its success. For a national liberation movement derives its strnegth and character from its supporters. It is no more and no less than the people who have brought it together. Today SWAPO and the Namibian people stand together: a national liberation movement poised on the brink of political power, a people poised on the bring of nationhood.

But the first day of political independence cannot be the first day free from imperialist domination. That is a daydream. Namibians are under no illusions that the occupation regime will prove graceful in defeat where it has been ruthlessly exploitative at the height of its power. It is to be expected that the retreating settlers and colonial state will leave considerable chaos and destruction in their wake, particularly in the farming sector, urban commerce and the administration and public services. Beyond the immediate aftermath of independence, the people's government will face a formidable take of national reconstruction and social transformation. Colonialism has left Namibians without the skilled manpower and technical resources to run the mines, the fisheries and a number of state organs, and it is precisely

here, as the experience of many newly independent nations has shown,
that imperialism is at its most subtle. Nationalisation alone has not always
broken the stranglehold of foreign economic domination, because the transnational corporations may still control the management, marketing, technical
expertise and know-how on big local operations such as mines, and imperialist interests still dominate the international sources of finance and credit.

SWAPO is fully aware that to mobilise the resources which will be required
to meet the basis human needs of Namibia's people and transform the
structure of the economy, the mines must be run, the fishing grounds fished,
the Kunene scheme transformed and completed. Most of the minerals and
fish will necessarily be exported. Certain expatriate personnel will be needed
until Namibians can gain the experience previously denied them. Political
independence thus marks the threshold of a new phase of struggle whose
objectives will be nothing less than the complete elimination of all forms
of imperialist domination and the transformation of capitalist exploitation
into genuine socialist democracy.

*SWAPO supporters greet Martti Ahtisaari, UN Commissioner for Namibia,
during his visit to Ovamboland in 1978*

In recent years SWAPO, in close co-operation with the U.N. Institute for
Namibia, has been actively engaged in detailed planning for the transition
period which will follow the winning of independence. Such planning is
essential to thwart the intrigues of the multinational companies and the
imperialist governments which are always ready to prey on the disruption
which inevitably follows victory through armed revolutionary struggle. It

is also important to resolve short-term emergencies in such a way that they do not block the road to long-term national reconstruction in accordance with the democratically decided priorities of the liberation movement. The best weapon in the hands of the Namibian people is their own mobilisation and their consciousness through struggle of the contradiction between the interests of imperialism and capitalism and their own aspirations to control all aspects of their own lives themselves and to enjoy to the full the fruits of their labour. In this task of political inspiration and leadership, SWAPO has and will continue to play the leading role. The words of Amilcar Cabral, revolutionary martyr to the cause of Pan-African liberation, speak powerfully to Namibians today:

> In the present historical situation — elimination of imperialism which uses every means to perpetuate its domination over our people, and consolidation of socialism throughout a large part of the world — there are only two paths for an independent nation: to return to imperialist domination (neo-colonialism, capitalism, state capitalism) or to take the path of socialism.

The United Nations Institute for Namibia

SWAPO views the establishment of the United Nations Institute for Namibia as a very significant and great achievement. To us this development is yet another expression that men of conscience and goodwill have continued to affirm and reaffirm their solidarity with the ongoing efforts of SWAPO to liberate Namibia and, essentially, that the world community has a particular responsibility to the Namibian people . . .

President Sam Nujoma at the opening of
U.N.I.N., 26 August 1976

U.N.I.N., which opened officially on Namibia Day 26 August 1976, currently has over 200 students, half of which are in their second year. The training programme is aimed at preparing a nucleus of cadres for the public administration of the government of an independent Namibia. It is estimated that 20,000—30,000 South African civil servants may have to be replaced after independence. Thus U.N.I.N. reflects the realisation that political independence without economic

---

independence is only a trap and that it is not
possible to build and run a modern state without
an effective, efficient and above all, indigenous
administrative infrastructure.

The two-year training programme is inter-
disciplinary and comprises 38 topics. Tuition is
in English. Continuing consideration of a third
year of training is obviously bound by the political constraints of developments in Namibia and
the coming independence. If necessary, the
students will receive either a third year of
academic training or will engage in in-service
training in Zambia or nearby African countries.

U.N.I.N. is not in any way a traditional training
college. Its Charter states that it is to undertake
research, training, planning and related activities
with special reference to the struggle for independence and freedom in Namibia. As an Institute
of applied research it is an integral part of the
political as well as technical training ground for
Namibia's future administrators. Its Charter
defines the primary function of U.N.I.N. as 'to
provide to Namibians the necessary education
and training so as to strengthen all their efforts,
including those at the political level, in the struggle
for freedom and equip them for the future planning of and participation in the organisation and
administration of various government departments and public services in an independent
Namibia.' Each division of U.N.I.N. — educational
and social; political, cultural and historical,
economics; agricultural and land resources; constitutional, legal and judicial — is fully engaged
in this programme . . .

SWAPO sees the Institute as just one facet of
the struggle for independence. The deliberate
neglect of education, job training and employment of Namibians by the South African occupation regime must be overcome and U.N.I.N. is
one vehicle. SWAPO cadres who are at the
Institute must maintain a link with the Party.
Some cadres were recalled from the Front and
from various other assignments to go to the
Institute. Others spend their free time, and the

students, their vacations, assisting with other
SWAPO projects, and especially the Namibian
Health and Education Centre in Zambia. The
struggle continues at all levels: all our cadres,
whether at the Front, in secondary school or at
the Institute or elsewhere, are contributing to the
development of a future united and independent
Namibia.

Namibia Today, Vol. 2 No. 1, 1978

Sam Nujoma, President of SWAPO

Appendix A: Chronologies

Namibia's International Status: a chronology of the colonial occupation

16 July 1866	Cape Colony annexes islands off southern coast.
14 December 1879	Great Britain annexes Walvis Bay.
7 August 1884	Walvis Bay islands transferred to the Cape Colony.
5 September 1884	Imperial Germany declares a Protectorate over the coastal zone between the Orange and Kunene Rivers. Germany's right to occupy Namibia is confirmed by the Conference of Berlin (1884–5).
1884–90	Namibia's present international boundaries are established by treaties between Germany and Portugal (1886) and Great Britain (1890).
1890	Germany declares its Protectorate a Crown Colony.
9 July 1915	German forces surrender to the invading South African army. South Africa imposes martial law.
28 June 1919	Treaty of Versailles: Germany renounces all rights over its colonies to the Allied Powers (Article 119).
17 December 1920	In accordance with Article 22 of the Treaty of Versailles, the Council of the League of Nations grants South Africa the right to govern Namibia as an integral part of its territory, subject to the terms of a class C Mandate and the supervision of the Permanent Mandates Commission.
1 January 1921	Martial law replaced by a civilian colonial administration (Act 49–1919).
1 October 1922	Walvis Bay transferred to the S.W.A. Administration (Act 24–1922).
October 1945	United Nations created.

April 1946	League of Nations disbanded.
1946	South Africa conducts a fraudulent 'referendum' in Namibia and demands the right to annex the territory at the UN General Assembly's first session. The General Assembly rejects this demand, but South Africa refuses to place Namibia under the Trusteeship System.
1949	The new National Party government amends the S.W.A. constitution to delete references to the Mandate and give whites seats in the South African parliament (Act 23–1949). The General Assembly refers the issue of sovereignty to the International Court of Justice (I.C.J.).
November 1949	For the first time the UN Fourth Committee hears a petitioner (Rev. Michael Scott) on behalf of the Namibian people.
1950	In an Advisory Opinion, the I.C.J. rules a) that the Mandate and its terms are still in force; b) that the UN has succeeded to the League's supervisory powers; c) that although South Africa was not obliged to submit Namibia to a Trusteeship Agreement, it was not competent by itself to alter the international status of the territory. South Africa refuses to recognise the Opinion and obstructs further negotiations.
4 November 1960	Ethiopia and Liberia, as former members of the League, apply to the I.C.J. for a binding judgement against South Africa on the grounds that it has flagrantly violated the Mandate.
1961	For the first time the General Assembly demands the termination of the Mandate and sets the independence of Namibia as its objective.
1964	In the Odendaal Report the colonial regime announces its plans for the fragmentation of Namibia into bantustans.
18 July 1966	On the casting vote of its chairman the I.C.J. refuses to rule on the substance of the Ethiopian/Liberian case on the grounds that the applicants have no standing in the matter.
26 August 1966	SWAPO proclaims the armed struggle for the liberation of Namibia and the first military engagements take place.
27 October 1966	The General Assembly formally revokes the Mandate

and assumes sovereign responsibility for Namibia (UNGA 2145).

19 May 1967 The General Assembly creates the Council for S.W.A. – renamed the Council for Namibia the following year – to bring Namibia to independence and to administer it in the interim.

1968–69 South Africa begins to impose its bantustan programme on Namibia (Act 54–1968) and transfers most important government functions to Pretoria (Act 25–1969).

1969 Security Council resolutions for the first time endorse the termination of the Mandate (SC 264 of 20 March) and recognise the legitimacy of the liberation struggle (SC 269 of 12 August).

29 July 1970 The Security Council requests the I.C.J. for an Advisory Opinion on the consequences for states of South Africa's continued occupation in defiance of UN decisions (SC 284).

21 June 1971 The I.C.J. rules a) that South Africa is under obligation to withdraw its illegal administration immediately; b) that other states are obliged to recognise the illegality of the occupation regime and to act accordingly in any dealings with South Africa.

1972–73 Negotiations between the Security Council and South Africa yield no result and are terminated.

December 1973 December 1976 The General Assembly recognises SWAPO as the 'sole authentic representative' of the Namibian people and appoints Sean MacBride as the first Commissioner for Namibia.

1974 The Council for Namibia enacts a Decree on Natural Resources, forbidding the exploitation and export of such resources without its authority.

1 September 1975 South Africa opens its so-called Turnhalle Constitutional Conference, which gives itself three years to draw up a constitution for 'independence'.

30 January 1976 The Security Council lays down the guiding principles for a South African withdrawal, demands that national elections be held under UN 'supervision and control', and orders South Africa to comply by 31 August 1976.

18 March 1977 The Turnhalle Conference produces an 'interim consti-

	tution' based on the bantustans. Western pressure forces South Africa to drop this and impose direct rule.
1 September 1977	South Africa appoints an Administrator-General with full legislative and executive powers and re-annexes Walvis Bay (Act 91-1977).
1977–79	The five Western members of the Security Council, acting without a mandate, form themselves into the so-called 'Contact Group' and begin negotiations with South Africa and SWAPO for an agreed transition process to independence. The Group produces its proposals (February 1978), which South Africa and SWAPO accept in principle.
August–September 1978	Authorised by the Security Council, Secretary-General Waldheim submits a report on arrangements for a UN-supervised transition process which the Council endorses (SC 435 of 29 September 1978), SWAPO accepts but South Africa rejects. The report requires the repeal of repressive laws, free elections, a constituent assembly to frame an independence constitution, and a UN Transitional Assistance Group to enforce the UN's authority.
1978–79	South Africa prepares the way for UDI, forcing through a rigged election to a puppet 'Assembly' (4–8 December 1978) and then creating a 'National Assembly' with wide legislative powers (21 May 1979). South Africa, with Western connivance, plays for time and blocks further progress in the UN negotiations.

Chronology of the People's Struggle for Freedom

1677	Namibians repulse a ship's landing party from the Cape Colony at the mouth of the Kuiseb River.
c1770–1870	Groups of Nama migrate across the Orange River rather than submit to the yoke of colonialism in the Cape.
1858	Leaders from southern and central Namibia sign a historic treaty, the 'League of Nations', which amongst other provisions outlaws mining concessions and land sales to Cape Colonists except by common agreement.
1859–60	The Ovambo kings repulse a Portuguese invasion force.

1877–78	Chief Frederick Maharero attempts to head off colonialist intrusions by negotiating a protection treaty with the Cape Colony, but the Cape government later backs off.
1883–94	Herero and some Nama leaders apply the same strategy to the invading German colonisers. Hendrik Witbooi begins to rally the south to armed resistance against colonialist aggression.
1891–94	Witbooi leads a grim rearguard defence, using guerilla tactics against German troops, but is eventually defeated by German reinforcements.
11 January 1904	Chief Samuel Maharero proclaims a general uprising against German colonial rule, Herero forces drive German troops and settlers out of Central Namibia.
28 January 1904	Nehale, king of Eastern Ondonga in Ovamboland, attacks Fort Namutoni in solidarity with the Herero, and forces its garrison to flee.
11 August 1904	German reinforcements under von Trotha defeat the Herero army at the Waterberg.
25 September 1904	Ovambo forces destroy an invading Portuguese column, killing 305 of the enemy and capturing arms, including cannon.
2 October 1904	Von Trotha issues his notorious extermination order against the Herero.
3 October 1904	Hendrik Witbooi declares war on the German colonial regime and leads the south into four years of bitter guerilla warfare against the colonial forces.
25 October 1904	Hendrik Witbooi dies leading his troops in battle, aged 80 years.
20 December 1905	An armistice ends the campaign of genocide, but four-fifths of the Herero population have already been killed.
20 September 1907	Jacob Morenga, the great guerilla leader, cold-bloodedly gunned down by Cape Colony police on behalf of the German regime.
1905–12	Gradual Portuguese encirclement and occupation of western and northern Ovamboland. German forces push up to the Okavango River and into the Caprivi Strip.
1914–15	After a clash between German and Protuguese forces at Naulila on the Kunene, the Portuguese evacuate. King Mandume of Ukwanyama attempts to unite

	Ovamboland in order to preserve its independence, and destroys all Portuguese forts in the region. Eventually a large Portuguese invading forces drives Mandume over the border into Namibia, using scorched-earth tactics and slaughtering the people indiscriminately. Simultaneously South Africa occupies southern Ovamboland.
1915	Behind the invading South African army, Namibians repossess their ancestral lands from the fleeing German farmers, only to be brutally suppressed by the South African police.
6 February 1917	The Portuguese and South African colonial regimes hatch a plot to eliminate King Mandume. A South African column invades Ovamboland and Mandume dies in battle.
29 May 1922	Having failed to drive the Bondelswarts into bondage through land robbery and taxation, the South African regime dispatches a military force with machine-guns and bombers. Over 100 of 600 Bondelswarts, including women and children, are massacred.
26 August 1923	Chief Samuel Maharero, exiled in Botswana since 1904, is buried at his death alongside his forefathers Tjamuaha and Jonker Afrikaner in a symbolic gesture of national unity.
1924–25	The Rehobothers defy the regime's attempts to remove their hard-won autonomy rights. In response the regime declares martial law, dispatches a large armed contingent and arrests hundreds of men (5 April 1925).
1932	The South Africans, deciding that King Ipumbu of Ukwambi is too popular with his people, send a military column with armoured cars and warplanes into Ovamboland. Ipumbu's residence is razed to the ground and the king himself sent into exile.
1946	The traditional leaders voice popular resistance to South African rule in the regime's fraudulent 'referendum' on incorporation into South Africa.
1946–49	Traditional leaders, inspired by Chief Hosea Kutako, petition the UN for the removal of the South African regime.
1952	Formation of the S.W.A. Student Body in South Africa.
1954–55	Mass demonstrations in Ovamboland against contract

	labour.
1955	Formation of the S.W.A. Progressive Association in Windhoek.
1957	Herman ja Toivo and others organise the Ovamboland People's Congress, renamed the Ovamboland People's Organisation (O.P.O.) the following year, amongst Namibian workers in Cape Town and in Namibia.
April 1959	The O.P.O. launches a national campaign against the contract labour system, led by Sam Nujoma in central Namibia and Herman ja Toivo in the north. The campaign gains massive support amongst contract workers.
May 1959	Formation of SWANU, the first nationalist party as such.
September 1959	SWANU's representativeness is broadened by the entry of several O.P.O. leaders into its national executive.
10 December 1959	SWANU, O.P.O. and the Chiefs' Council form a united front of opposition to the regime's attempt to drive the African population of Windhoek into a new apartheid-style ghetto, Katutura. Police fire on unarmed demonstrators, killing thirteen and wounding 52, and arrest black political leaders, forcing Sam Nujoma and many others into exile.
19 April 1960	The O.P.O. is relaunched as the national liberation movement SWAPO. With the united front now in disarray and peaceful protest fruitless, henceforth it is SWAPO which is to carry the main burden of the political struggle.
1962	SWAPO's leadership decides to prepare for armed struggle. Hundreds of recruits are sent abroad for training.
1964	The first cadres return to Namibia to prepare the ground for guerilla warfare.
26 August 1966	SWAPO's fighters engage South African troops at Omgulumbashe in Ovamboland in the first military clash of the war of liberation. Freedom fighters grouped in small, fast-moving guerrilla units attack South African positions throughout the northern border zone.
26 December 1969 – 2 January 1970	SWAPO's Consultative Congress meets at Tanga in Tanzania, bringing together delegates from all sections

of the party. The Congress restructures the Department of Defence and creates several new departments — the Youth League, the Women's Council, the Elders' Council — which are to play a leading role in the coming decade.

June — August 1971 Nationwide mass demonstrations and resolutions in support of the I.C.J. ruling (21 June 1971) that South Africa's occupation of Namibia is illegal and must end.

30 June 1971 The leaders of the influential Lutheran churches issue a pastoral letter declaring publicly their support for the I.C.J. ruling.

November 1971 With the active participation of SWAPO, the National Convention of Namibia (N.C.N.) is formed as a united front for all anti-colonial forces.

1 December 1971 Contract workers launch a national strike, demanding the abolition of the oppressive contract labour system. Within a month, over 20,000 workers are out, and the regime deports most of them to Ovamboland.

January — February 1972 In Ovamboland the peasants rise against the colonial administration and its hated tribal accomplices. The regime imposes a state of emergency (Resolution 17 of 4 February 1972) and sends in troops, which savagely repress all political opposition.

August 1973 Defying severe harassment, SWAPO organises a resoundingly successful boycott of the Ovamboland bantustan elections — less than 5% of those registered cast their votes.

December 1973 SWAPO's national conference at Walvis Bay launches a campaign of popular mobilisation to confront the wave of repression aimed by the regime at the party leadership and the Youth League in particular.

June — July 1974 Following the collapse of Portuguese colonialism in Angola, several thousand cross the border to volunteer for the armed struggle.

17 January 1975 SWAPO withdraws from the N.C.N., by now moribund because of Chief Kapuno's betrayal in joining the Turnhalle circus. Within two months SWAPO has taken the leading role in recruiting all genuinely anti-colonial elements in the Namibia National Convention (N.N.C.).

9 August 1975 South African columns invade Angola to forestall the victory of the M.P.L.A. In their rear PLAN rapidly extends and escalates its attacks on the regime's forces in Ovamboland and adjacent areas. The regime admits 59 clashes with freedom fighters between July 1975 and April 1976.

29 August 1975   SWAPO issues a detailed Discussion Paper on a constitution for an independent Namibia, thereby exposing the bankruptcy of the Turnhalle Conference which only begins constitution-making a year later.

29–31 May 1976   SWAPO's national congress, meeting at Walvis Bay, confirms its rejection of the Turnhalle circus and re-affirms the unity of the party leadership, whether inside or outside the country.

28 July – 1 August 1976   At its expanded Central Committee meeting in Lusaka, SWAPO ratifies the decisions of the May Congress and adopts a revised Constitution and a Political Programme. The Programme rededicates the Party to the winning of genuine independence, to armed revolutionary struggle, and to build a society free of all forms of exploitation. It also defines the tasks of the Party and its cadres and restates the terms on which negotiations with the racist regime can take place.

26 August 1976   Zambian President Kenneth Kaunda opens the United Nations Institute for Namibia in Lusaka, which is to provide a training ground for Namibian future administrators.

August 1976 – April 1977   In a great drive for national unity, most of SWAPO's partners in the N.N.C. disband to join SWAPO. SWAPO withdraws from the N.N.C. (December 1976), its usefulness now ended.

4 September 1976   In one of a number of increasingly large-scale attacks, PLAN units overrun and destroy a South African base at Epinga in the north. The occupation regime pours massive reinforcements into the border zone, building up its forces to over 60,000 strong.

November 1976   High School students boycott exams and classes and demand the end of 'Bantu Education'. Many dedicate their skills to the liberation movement at home and abroad.

10 November 1976   Nama school teachers strike against apartheid pay-scales, staying out for 74 days. Militant opposition to the occupation regime is intense throughout the south.

March – June 1977   Confronted by SWAPO's wall of national unity, the Western powers force South Africa to put its Turnhalle

	plan on ice, and the UN negotiations begin.
26 August 1977	At rallies throughout the country, Namibians openly commemorate the 11th anniversary of the launching of the armed struggle.
4 May 1978	In by far its worst atrocity yet, South African troops massacre Namibian refugees at Kassinga, many of them women, children and old people, killing over 600 and wounding over 400.
12 July 1978	SWAPO accepts in principle the Western proposal for a UN-supervised transition to independence.
29 September 1978	The UN Security Council endorses the report of the Secretary-General Waldheim on the implementation of the proposals — rejected beforehand by South Africa (20 September) and again in a confrontation with the Contract Group (16–18 October). SWAPO accepts the terms of the resolution.
November 1978– April 1979	PLAN's rainy-season offensive takes the occupation regime by surprise in its power and extent. PLAN units repeatedly prove their ability to concentrate in large formations against South African military bases, to avoid detection, and to execute missions in central and southern Namibia.
April 1979	The regime yet again sweeps almost the entire internal SWAPO leadership and hundreds of rank-and-file members into detention in a systematic effort to destroy SWAPO as a political party. Despite this, a rally in Windhoek (early May) draws the biggest turn-out yet seen.

Appendix B: Selected SWAPO Documents and Speeches

Statement from the Dock by Herman ja Toivo, Pretoria, February 1968

'My Lord, we find ourselves here in a foreign country, convicted under laws made by people whom we have always considered as foreigners. We find ourselves tried by a judge who is not our countryman and who has not shared our background.

'When this case started, counsel tried to show that this court had no jurisdiction to try us. What they had to say was of a technical and legal nature. The reasons may mean little to some of us, but it is the deep feeling of all of us that we should not be tried here in Pretoria.

'You, my Lord, decided that you had the right to try us, because your Parliament gave you that right. That ruling has not and could not have changed our feelings. We are Namibians and not South Africans. We do not now, and will not in the future recognize your right to govern us, to make laws for us in which we had no say; to treat our country as if it were your property, and us as if you were our masters. We have always regarded South Africa as an intruder in our country. This is how we have always felt and this is how we feel now, and it is on this basis that we have faced this trial.

'I speak of 'we' because I am trying to speak not only for myself, but for others as well, and especially for those of my fellow accused who have not had the benefit of an education. I think also that when I say 'we', the over-whelming majority of non-white people in South West Africa would like to be included.

'We are far away from our homes; not a single member of our families has come to visit us, never mind be present at our trial. The Pretoria jail, the police headquarters at Compol, where we were interrogated and where statements were extracted from us, and this court is all we have seen of Pretoria. We have been cut off from our people and the world. We all wondered whether the headmen would have repeated some of their lies if our people had been present in court to hear them.

'The South African government has again shown its strength by detaining us for as long as it pleased, keeping some of us in solitary confinement for 300 to 400 days and bringing us to its capital to try us. It has shown its strength by passing an act especially for us and having it made retroactive. One's own are called patriots, or at least rebels; your opponents are called terrorists.

'A court can only do justice in political cases if it understands the position of those that it has in front of it. The state has not only wanted to convict us, but also to justify the policy of the South African government. We will not even try to present the other side of the picture, because we know that a court that has not suffered in the same way as we have, cannot understand us. This is perhaps why it is said that one should be tried by one's equals. We have felt from the very time of our arrest that we were not being tried by our equals but by our masters, and that those who have brought us to trial very often do not even do us the courtesy of calling us by our surnames. Had we been tried by our equals, it would not have been necessary to have any discussion about our grievances. They would have been known to those set to judge us.

'It suits the government of South Africa to say that it is ruling South West Africa with the consent of its people. This is not true. Our organization, SWAPO, is the largest political organization in South West Africa. We considered ourselves a political party. We know that whites do not think of blacks as politicians — only as agitators. Many of our people, through no fault of their own, have had no education at all. This does not mean that they do not know what they want. A man does not have to be formally educated to know that he wants to live with his family, and not where an official chooses to tell him to live; to move about freely and not require a pass; to earn a decent wage; to be free to work for the person of his choice for as long as he wants; and finally, to be ruled by the people that he wants to be ruled by, and not those who rule him because they have more guns than he has.

'Our grievances are called 'so-called' grievances. We do not believe South Africa is in South West Africa in order to provide facilities and work for non-whites. It is there for its own selfish reasons. For the first 40 years it did practically nothing to fulfill its 'sacred trust'. It only concerned itself with the welfare of the whites.

'Since 1962, because of the pressure from inside by the non-whites and especially my organization, and because of the limelight placed on our country by the world, South Africa has been trying to do a bit more. It rushed the Bantustan Report so that it would at least have something to say at the World Court.

'Only one who is not white and has suffered the way we have can say whether our grievances are real or 'so-called'.

'Those of us who have some education, together with our uneducated brethren, have always struggled to get freedom. The idea of our freedom is not liked by South Africa. It has tried in this court to prove through the mouths of a couple of its paid chiefs and a paid official that SWAPO does not represent the people of South West Africa. If the government of South Africa were sure that SWAPO did not represent the innermost feelings of the

people in South West Africa, it would not have taken the trouble to make
it impossible for SWAPO to advocate its peaceful policy.

'South African officials want to believe that SWAPO is an irresponsible
organization and that it is an organization that resorts to the level of telling
people not to get vaccinated. As much as white South Africans may want to
believe this, this is not SWAPO. We sometimes feel that it is what the government would like SWAPO to be. It may be true that some member or even
members of SWAPO somewhere refused to do this. The reason for such
refusal is that some people in our part of the world have lost confidence in
the governors of our country and they are not prepared to accept even the
good that they are trying to do.

'Your government, my Lord, undertook a very special responsibility when
it was awarded the mandate over us after the First World War. It assumed a
sacred trust to guide us towards independence and to prepare us to take our
place among the nations of the world. South Africa has abused that trust
because of its belief in racial supremacy (that white people have been chosen
by God to rule the world) and apartheid. We believe that for 50 years South
Africa has failed to promote the development of our people. Where are our
trained men? The wealth of our country has been used to train your people
for leadership and the sacred duty of preparing the indigenous people to take
their place among the nations of the world has been ignored.

'I know of no case in the last 20 years of a parent who did not want his
child to go to school if the facilities were available, but even if, as it was said,
a small percentage of parents wanted their children to look after cattle,
I am sure that South Africa was strong enough to impose its will on this,
as it has done in so many other respects. To us it has always seemed that our
rulers wanted to keep us backward for their benefit.

'1963 for us was to be the year of our freedom. From 1960 it looked as
if South Africa could not oppose the world forever. The world is important
to us. In the same way as all laughed in court when they heard that an old
man tried to bring down a helicopter with a bow and arrow, we laughed when
South Africa said that it would oppose the world. We knew that the world
was divided, but as time went on it at least agreed that South Africa had no
right to rule us.

'I do not claim that it is easy for men of different races to live at peace
with one another. I myself had no experience of this in my youth, and at first
it surprised me that men of different races could live together in peace. But
now I know it to be true and to be something for which we must strive. The
South African government creates hostility by separating people and emphasi-
zing their differences. We believe that by living together, people will learn to
lose their fear of each other. We also believe that this fear which some of the
whites have of Africans is based on their desire to be superior and privileged
and that when whites see themselves as part of South West Africa, sharing
with us all its hopes and troubles, then that fear will disappear. Separation
is said to be a natural process. But whey, then, is it imposed by force, and
why then is it that whites have the superiority?

'Headmen are used to oppress us. This is not the first time that foreigners have tried to rule indirectly — we know that only those who are prepared to do what their masters tell them become headmen. Most of those who had some feeling for their people and who wanted independence have been intimidated into accepting the policy from above. Their guns and sticks are used to make people say they support them.

'I have come to know that our people cannot expect progress as a gift from anyone, be it the United Nations or South Africa. Progress is something we shall have to struggle and work for. And I believe that the only way in which we shall be able and fit to secure that progress is to learn from our own experience and mistakes.

'Your Lordship emphasized in your judgment the fact that our arms came from communist countries, and also that words commonly used by communists were to be found in our documents. But, my Lord, in the documents produced by the state there is another type of language. It appears even more often than the former. Many documents finish up with an appeal to the Almighty to guide us in our struggle for freedom. It is the wish of the South African government that we should be discredited in the western world. That is why it calls our struggle a communist plot, but this will not be believed by the world. The world knows that we are not interested in ideologies. We feel that the world as a whole has a special responsibility towards us. This is because the land of our fathers was handed over to South Africa by a world body. It is a divided world, but it is a matter of hope for us that it at least agrees about one thing — that we are entitled to freedom and justice.

'Other mandated territories have received their freedom. The judgment of the World Court was a bitter disappointment to us. We felt betrayed and we believed that South Africa would never fulfil its trust. Some felt that we would secure our freedom only by fighting for it. We knew that the power of South Africa is overwhelming, but we also knew that our case is a just one and our situation intolerable — why should we not also receive our freedom?

'We are sure that the world's efforts to help us in our plight will continue, whatever South Africans may call us.

'That is why we claim independence for South West Africa. We do not expect that independence will end our troubles, but we do believe that our people are entitled — as are all peoples — to rule themselves. It is not really a question of whether South Africa treats us well or badly, but that South West Africa is our country and we wish to be our own masters.

'There are some who will say that they are sympathetic with our aims, but that they condemn violence. I would answer that I am not by nature a man of violence and I believe that violence is a sin against God and my fellowmen. SWAPO itself was a non-violent organization, but the South African government is not truly interested in whether opposition is violent or non-violent. It does not wish to hear any opposition to apartheid. Since 1963, SWAPO meetings have been banned. It is true that it is the Tribal Authorities who have done so, but they work with the South African government, which has never lifted a finger in favour of political freedom. We have found ourselves voteless in our own country and deprived of the right to meet and state our own political opinions.

'Is it surprising that in such times my countrymen have taken up arms? Violence is truly fearsome, but who would not defend his property and himself against a robber? And we believe that South Africa has robbed us of our country.

'I have spent my life working in SWAPO which is an ordinary political party like any other. Suddenly we in SWAPO found that a war situation had arisen and that our colleagues and South Africa were facing each other on the field of battle. Although I had not been responsible for organizing my people militarily and although I believed we were unwise to fight the might of South Africa while we were so weak, I could not refuse to help them when the time came.

'My Lord, you found it necessary to brand me as a coward. During the Second World War, when it became evident that both my country and your country were threatened by the dark clouds of Nazism, I risked my life to defend both of them, wearing a uniform with orange bands on it.

'But some of your countrymen when called to battle to defend civilisation resorted to sabotage against their own fatherland. I volunteered to face German bullets, and as a guard of military installations, both in South West Africa and the Republic, was prepared to be the victim of their sabotage. Today they are our masters and are considered the heroes, and I am called the coward.

'When I consider my country, I am proud that my countrymen have taken up arms for their people and I believe that anyone who calls himself a man would not despite them.

'In 1964 the ANC and PAC in South Africa were suppressed. This convinced me that we were too weak to face South Africa's force by waging battle. When some of my country's soldiers came back, I foresaw the trouble there would be for SWAPO, my people and me personally. I tried to do what I could to prevent my people from going into the bush. In my attempts I became unpopular with some of my people, but this, too, I was prepared to endure. Decisions of this kind are not easy to make. My organization could not work properly — it could not even hold meetings. I had no answer to the question: "Where has your non-violence got us?" Whilst the World Court judgment was pending, I at least had that to fall back on. When we failed, after years of waiting, I had no answer to give to my people.

'Even though I did not agree that people should go into the bush, I could not refuse to help them when I knew that they were hungry. I even passed on the request for dynamite. It was not an easy decision. Another might have been able to say "I will have nothing to do with that sort of thing". I was not, and I could not remain a spectator in the struggle of my people for their freedom.

'I am a loyal Namibian and I could not betray my people to their enemies. I admit that I decided to assist those who had taken up arms. I know that

the struggle will be long and bitter. I also know that my people will wage
that struggle, whatever the cost.

'Only when we are granted our independence will the struggle stop. Only
when our human dignity is restored to us, as equals of the whites, will there
be peace between us.

'We believe that South Africa has a choice — either to live at peace with us
or to subdue us by force. If you choose to crush us and impose your will
on us, then you not only betray your trust, but you will live in security for
only so long as your power is greater than ours. No South African will live at
peace in South West Africa, for each will know that this security is based on
force and that without force he will face rejection by the people of South
West Africa.

'My co-accused and I have suffered. We are not looking forward to our
imprisonment. We do not, however, feel that our efforts and sacrifice have
been wasted. We believe that human suffering has its effect even on those
who impose it. We hope that what has happened will persuade the whites
of South Africa that we and the world may be right and they may be wrong.

'Only when South Africans realize this and act on it, will it be possible for
us to stop our struggle for freedom and justice in the land of our birth.'

The Declaration of the Central Committee of SWAPO of Namibia adopted by its Second Annual Meeting held at Gabela, People's Republic of Angola, 4—7 January 1979

Cognizant of the prevailing tension and the ever sharpening contradictions
between the forces of progress and liberation, on the one hand, and those of
oppression and exploitation, on the other, in the world in general and
Southern Africa in particular, the Central Committee critically and compre-
hensively analysed the current phase of the struggle of the Namibian people,
under the leadership of their vanguard Movement, SWAPO, at the military
political, diplomatic and other fronts and adopted new strategies and tactics.

On the basis of this analysis, the Central Committee is convinced that the
racists in Pretoria and their imperialist mentors are engaged in new and more
sinister manoevres, machinations and intrigues aimed at imposing a puppet
regime in Namibia with a view to perpetuating racist domination and
capitalist exploitation in our country.

Against this background, the Central Committee re-affirms that:

1.   The armed struggle is and remains the main method of liberating Namibia.
2.   The bulk of the human and material resources of the Movement shall
     be deployed in the intensification and prosecution of the armed
     liberation struggle.
3.   The Central Committee welcomed with enthusiasm the special

message from the SWAPO National Headquarters.

4. The Central Committee, fortified in the knowledge that the broad masses of the Namibian people are firmly behind SWAPO, will never accept any neo-colonial solution and will persevere in the struggle for genuine independence.

5. The Central Committee, thus, vehemently condemns and rejects the secret deal hatched up in Pretoria on 16th October, 1978 between the racist regime of Pretoria and the five imperialist powers led by the United States; this secret deal, allowing South Africa to conduct bogus elections in Namibia, was intended to legitimise and perpetuate the illegal occupation of our country through the imposition of a puppet administration in Windhoek.

6. SWAPO denounces and rejects with the same vehemence and with scorn any attempt or schemes aimed at undermining its hard-won national and international recognition and support by putting it on the same footing with the South African quislings.

7. The Central Committee re-affirms SWAPO's resolve to build a class-less, non-exploitative, non racial and just society which will assure the restoration of social ownership, control and management of Namibia's natural resources.

8. In pursuit of the objectives of overthrowing racist oppression and capitalist exploitation and construction of a socialist society, the Central Committee appeals to all progressive forces, especially the socialist community, to redouble assistance to the Namibian people, through SWAPO.

9. The Central Committee, furthermore, expresses its profound gratitude and appreciation to the OAU, especially the Front-line States and the Non-Aligned countries, Nordic countries and Holland for their continued material, political, diplomatic and moral support, and urges them to continue and increase the same.

10. The Central Committee, in the same vein, re-iterates SWAPO's commitment to the full and scrupulous implementation of the UN Secretary General's final and definitive report as endorsed by Security Council Resolution 435 (1978). In this context, the Central Committee commends the UN Council for Namibia for its persistent efforts in support of the just struggle of the Namibian people and pledges SWAPO's continued close co-operation with it.

11. The Central Committee pays its high tribute to the memory of the fallen Namibian patriots who have made ultimate sacrifices for the cause of the total liberation of Namibia.

12. The Central Committee salutes the People's Liberation Army of Namibia (PLAN) for its brilliant exploits and impressive victories scored against the enemy, and extols the gallant and heroic Namibian patriots to persevere in the struggle and to march forward in unity and in strength towards certain final victory.

13. The Central Committee expresses its profound thanks to Comrade Dr.

Agostinho Neto, President of MPLA-Workers' Party and of the People's Republic of Angola, the Party, Government and the people of Angola for making it possible to hold its Second Annual Meeting in the beautiful and scenic surroundings of Gabela and for all the facilities and arrangements provided.

14. The Central Committee re-affirms its militant solidarity with and extends revolutionary salutations to the liberation movements, namely, ANC (S.A.), Patriotic Front (Zimbabwe), Polisario (W. Sahara), PLO (Palestine), Fretilin (East Timor), in Asia and Latin America, and all other forces fighting for liberation, social progress and democracy.

Address delivered by Comrade Sam Nujoma, President of SWAPO, to the Ministerial Council of the O.A.U., 1979

Allow me to draw your attention to the daily sharpening confrontation between the forces of national liberation, on one hand, and those of racist oppression in Southern Africa, on the other.

'In Namibia and Zimbabwe, the liberation forces under the leadership of SWAPO and the Patriotic Front, are daily locked in combat against the fascist troops of South Africa and Rhodesia. In South Africa, too, our comrades are setting up the necessary network for a protracted people's war of liberation. Hardly a month passes without the racist regime of Botha admitting armed confrontation between its forces of repression and those of the African National Congress of South Africa.

'While the struggle for liberation in Southern Africa remains primarily a responsibility of the people of Namibia, Zimbabwe and South Africa, it is also an African problem. As such, the OAU must continue to play a major role. The African countries must never relegate their responsibilities to outsiders. The efforts and assistance from outside Africa should be welcomed. But it is the African people who must always have the final say as to what is the best way of solving the Southern African problem.

'Concerning the current developments in Namibia the situation remains complicated. The world has been witnessing intensive diplomatic efforts, initiated by the USA, Britain, France, West Germany and Canada to find a peaceful settlement to the Namibian problem. As the Hon. Ministers are aware, SWAPO has been participating fully in these diplomatic efforts. In participating in these diplomatic efforts, we proceeded from the conviction that political, military and diplomatic efforts are not contradictory but supplementary; and as such, they can be pursued concurrently. Moreover, SWAPO was never in doubt regarding the fact that South Africa intends and is determined to maintain its domination over Namibia.

'SWAPO was never taken in by any of Pretoria's pronouncements that

South Africa is ready to grant independence to the people of Namibia. Such pronouncements are only intended to mislead the world public opinion. In reality, however South Africa has been taking steps to consolidate its colonial and illegal domination over Namibia through its Turnhalle stooges.

'Pretoria has continued to carry out repressive measures against genuine Namibian patriots, and in particular, members of SWAPO, who are waging a struggle for genuine independence and true national liberation. At the same time Pretoria is spending vast amounts of money in an effort to prop up and popularise the myth that its own appointed puppets of Turnhalle are the true leaders of the oppressed Namibian people. But despite these neo-colonial efforts by racist South Africa to impose its quislings on the Namibian people, our people continue to rally behind their sole and authentic representative — SWAPO.

'In agreeing to participate in the diplomatic efforts initiated by the five Western powers, SWAPO proceeded from the assumption that these Western powers hold economic and diplomatic leverages by which they could genuinely pressure South Africa to relinquish her illegal and oppressive occupation of Namibia. It was on the basis of this assumption that we have been talking to the five who have been negotiating with South Africa.

'Twenty-two months, to be exact, have now passed since these diplomatic efforts began. Yet the prospects are far from being bright regarding a UN supervised and controlled transition of Namibia's independence. It is now time to take proper stock regarding these efforts. SWAPO considers such stock-taking essential because at times hopes might have been unduly raised too high and the enormity of the problem underestimated.

'As I have pointed out, Pretoria is bent on retaining its domination over Namibia. At the same time South Africa correctly recognised SWAPO as the obstacle to its neo-colonial design regarding Namibia. Therefore the diplomatic efforts have been running into difficulties. Racist South Africa realises that under conditions of genuine UN supervised and controlled elections its puppets would be soundly rejected by the Namibian people and that SWAPO would form a Government in Windhoek. These are frightening prospects for a regime that is based on racist domination and exploitation of the African people. It was against this background that Pretoria organised supervised and controlled bogus elections in Namibia last December.

'Again, racist South Africa is trying to put new conditions regarding the implementation of the UN plan as outlined in the Secretary-General's report. Among other things, this plan stipulates that a ceasefire should be concluded between South Africa and SWAPO; that the armed forces of both SWAPO and South Africa be confined to established bases in Namibia and being monitored there by the UN peace-keeping forces; that within three months from the date of ceasefire South Africa must withdraw all of its forces from Namibia except 1,500 who will be confined to bases at Groot-fontein and/or Oshivelo and who will be withdrawn from Namibia within seven days after the certification of the election. The plan has also stated that after the withdrawal and confinement of South African forces to bases,

Namibian exiles should be allowed to return to their homes without intimidation or arrest.

'As a result of a recent visit to South Africa by the Special Representative of the UN Secretary General, South Africa is now putting forth new conditions that are ridiculous and unacceptable. Pretoria is now proposing that SWAPO armed forces be confined and monitored at bases in the neighbouring territories during the transitional period. This, SWAPO totally rejects as being both unacceptable and contrary to the UN plan. SWAPO's position which is in line with the UN plan is that, first and foremost, SWAPO and South Africa must enter into a binding ceasefire agreement the instrument of which must be authenticated by the Secretary General of the UN to ensure that the agreement is scrupulously adhered to by the two parties concerned. SWAPO is therefore ready and willing to sign such a ceasefire agreement and honour all its provisions, provided that the South African regime is prepared to do the same.

'SWAPO is also ready to subject its geurrilla forces to confinement to bases *inside* Namibia and to be monitored by the UN peace-keeping forces. The People's Liberation Army of Namibia (PLAN) that has been born out of the historical necessity is a living reality, therefore, it has to be confined to bases in Namibia with all its arms, ammunition, and all its other equipments. As a guerrilla army, PLAN is a mobile army. It has no permanent structured bases. Its fighting units carry out their operations in the form of constant mobility throughout the country. Therefore, for the purpose of effective implementation of the ceasefire agreement, it has been agreed upon during the long negotiations between SWAPO and the five that specific bases will have to be identified *inside* Namibia to which SWAPO armed forces will be confined.

'Furthermore, contrary to the UN plan, South Africa is planning to set up concentration camps at several entry points along the Angola/Namibia and Zambia/Namibia borders under the cover of so-called 'reception centres'. This is a sinister plan designed to intimidate the returning exiles and to create psychological fear among our people that the kind of Namibia they are coming back to is still being controlled by the hated racist South Africa. This SWAPO categorically rejects.

'Mr Chairman, at this juncture I would like to make some brief remarks on the UN Secretary-General's proposals concerning the composition of the military component of the United Nations Transitional Assistance Group (UNTAG). In the considered view of SWAPO, the Secretary-General's list is heavily weighted in favour of racist South Africa's traditional allies, namely, the NATO countries which have massive economic investments in Namibia. Therefore, SWAPO totally rejects the inclusion of NATO countries such as Federal Republic of Germany, Canada, Great Britain, Australia, Denmark and Holland to the list of UN peace-keeping operations in Namibia.

'The Namibian problem being a colonial one, it is imperative that all those forces to be deployed under the UN transitional arrangements in Namibia must be genuinely interested in and sympathetic to the just struggle of the

Namibian people for national and social liberation and the achievement of genuine national independence. In this line, SWAPO has strongly recommended to the Secretary-General a list of countries for contribution of troops to UNTAG.

'I would, once again, like to call on Africa not to relinquish or allow its rightful role on the continent's decolonisation issues and processes to be subordinated to that of the outsiders.

'SWAPO regards the UN plan, as outlined in the Secretary-General's report, to be final and definitive. It also wishes to re-affirm its commitment to co-operate with the UN Secretary-General and his staff in the efficacious implementation of the plan. Our co-operation in this regard will always be based on our own objective judgement that there are not arm twisting. What is at stake is our own security and the destiny of our nation. As such we will be the final judge that conditions for fair, free and democratic elections are actually created.

'We, therefore appeal to you, Honourable Ministers, to call upon the five Western powers to see to it that South Africa is not allowed to create further obstacles regarding the decolonisation process of Namibia. The five must stop their fascist client from attempting to make new, ridiculous and unacceptable demands.

'In the same vein, we appeal to the OAU, the non-aligned movement and other progressive forces to vigorously condemn the move by the five Western countries to open up so-called joint offices of representation in the illegally occupied Namibia under the disguise of "observing the elections". Should this action be allowed or condoned, it will not only constitute a flagrant violation of the standing UN resolutions and decisions with regard to Namibia, but will also provide another serious obstacle to efforts towards speedy decolonisation of Namibia through free, fair and democratic elections under UN supervision and control.

'If racist South Africa and the five fail to abandon their efforts to obstruct progress, SWAPO will have no alternative but to continue with the intensification of the armed liberation struggle to its logical conclusion. In this regard SWAPO will request the OAU and all other progressive and peace loving forces to redouble material assistance to our people in their just and noble struggle for national liberation.'

Namibia Today, 3(4), 1979

Appendix C: Basic Namibian Statistics

1(a) Population by region of origin and race, 1960—80

Year	1960	1970	1977	1977	1980
Source	revised[1]	census	projection[2]	UNIN	UNIN[2]
Northern African[3]	320,000	427,732	532,500	735,000	802,500
Central/Southern African[4]	122,500	165,773	212,500	300,000	327,500
Coloured[5]	60,000	78,096	100,000	115,000	127,500
Total black	502,500	671,601	845,000	1,150,000	1,257,500
White[6]	73,500	90,583	102,500	102,500	(102,500)
Total	575,000	762,184	947,500	1,252,500	1,360,000

Notes:
1. The 1960 census is widely regarded as inaccurate. This column is a backward projection from the 1970 census assuming an average 2.9% growth rate.
2. Assumes growth rates of 3% for Africans, 3.5% for Coloureds (including immigration), and 1.75% for whites up to 1977 but static thereafter. Inclu Includes Namibian refugees outside the country.
3. For comparability we are forced to use the occupation regime's apartheid categories. This one refers to persons of Ovambo, Kavango and Caprivian ethnic origin, also some 20,000 Angolans.
4. Persons of Herero, Damara, Himba, Tswana and San ethnic origin.
5. Persons of Rehoboth, Nama and mixed race ethnic origin.
6. Includes expatriates, but excludes non-Namibian military personnel.

Sources: 1960 census, 1970 census, UNIN 1977.

1(b) Population by place of residence, 1977 (000s).

	blacks[2]			whites			total		
	male	female	total	male	female	total	male	female	total
[1]Northern zone[1]	278	327	605	1.2	0.8	2	279.2	327.8	607
Centre South: reserves	50	55	105	0.3	0.2	0.5	50.3	55.2	105.5
farms[3]	80	60	140	10	10	20	90	70	160
towns & mines[3]	177	123	300	41	39	80	218	162	380
	585	565	1150	52.5	50	102.5	637.5	615	1252.5

Notes:
1. Kaokoveld, Ovamboland, Okavangoland, Caprivi Strip. All other reserves are in Central/Southern Namibia.
2. Includes refugees outside Namibia. Nationals of Namibia are taken to be equally divided into males and females.
3. Includes 20,000 male Angolans.

Sources: UNIN 1977, own calculations.

2(a) Labour force, 1977: age and economic category (000s).[1]

	blacks				whites				total			
	male	female	total	%	male	female	total	%	male	female	total	%
children (12 and under)	261	259	520	46.0	13.5	13.5	27	26	274.5	272.5	547	44.4
students[2]	15	10	25	2.2	7	6.5	13.5	13	22	16.5	38.5	3.1
aged, disabled	31	39	70	6.2	3	3	6	6	34	42	76	6.2
total non-active	307	308	615	54.4	23.5	23	46.5	45	330.5	331	661.5	53.7
potential labour force	258	257	515	45.6	29	27	56	55	287	284	571	46.3
adults	304	306	610	54.0	39	36.5	75.5	74	342	343.5	685.5	55.6
total population	565	565	1130	100	52.5	50	102.5	100	617.5	615	1232.5	100

Notes (Table 2(a)):
1. Namibian nationals only, but including white expatriates.
2. Over 12 and in full-time education.

Sources: UNIN 1977, own calculations.

2(b) Labour force, 1977: class composition (000s).

	blacks				whites				total			
	male	female	total	%	male	female	total	%	male	female	total	%
workers[1]	172	73	245	45.8	19.5	7.5	27	48.2	191	81	272	46.0
migrants[1,2]	103	7	110	20.6	8	2	10	17.9	111	9	120	20.3
peasants[3]	100	158	258	48.2	–	–	–	0	100	158	258	43.7
capitalists and self-employed[4]	6	4	10	1.9	9	0.5	9.5	17.0	15	4.5	19.5	3.3
small[5]	6	4	10	1.9	2	0.4	2.4	4.3	7.5	4.4	11.9	2.0
medium[6]	–	–	–	0	6.9	0.1	7	12.5	7.4	0.1	7.5	1.3
large[7]	–	–	–	0	0.1	–	0.1	0.2	0.1	–	0.1	0
sub total	278	235	513	95.9	28.5	8	36.5	65.2	306.5	243	549.5	93.0
housewives[8]	–	22	22	4.1	0.5	19	19.5	34.8	0.5	41	41.5	7.0
total[9]	278	257	535	100	29	27	56	100	307	284	591	100

Notes:
1. Includes all salary and wage-earners, whether employed or unemployed. Does not distinguish between full and part-time workers. Includes 20,000 Angolan migrants.
2. Includes short-term white expatriates.
3. Assumed to be all adults (over 12) less full-time students and the aged and disabled.
4. Excludes those whose trade or service is mainly a supplement to their wage income.
5. Independent professionals and artisans, petty traders and contractors, cash-cropping small farmers.
6. Ranchers, family businesses and partnerships in commerce, service and processing.
7. Company proprietors.

8. Those engaged in housework and child-care in the home who are wholly without any other form of income.

9. This and all sub-categories include a nominal estimate of refugees outside Namibia.

Sources: Census 1970, S.A. Government Manpower Surveys 1971–5, Agricultural Census 1970/71, UNIN 1977, miscellaneous data and own calculations.

2(c) Labour force, 1977: regional distribution (000s).

	blacks				whites				total			
	male	female	total	%	male	female	total	%	male	female	total	%
workers[1] : ranches[2]	50	20	70	28.6	1	–	1	3.7	51	20	71	26.1
mines	18.5	–	18.5	7.6	3	0.5	3.5	13.0	21.5	0.5	22	8.1
†towns	95	51	146	59.7	14.4	6.8	21.2	78.5	109.4	57.8	167.2	61.6
reserves	8.5	2	10.5	4.2	1.1	0.2	1.3	4.8	9.6	2.2	11.8	4.2
sub-total	172	73	245	100	19.5	7.5	27	100	191.5	80.5	272	100
peasants : South/Central	10	19	29	11.2	–	–	–	0	10	19	29	11.2
Northern[3]	90	139	229	88.8	–	–	–	0	90	139	229	88.8
sub-total	100	158	258	100	–	–	–	0	100	158	258	100
capitalists & self-employed:												
small : farms[4] and rural	0.5	–	0.5	5	0.2	–	0.2	2.1	0.7	–	0.7	16.5
urban	1	0.5	0.5	15	1.3	0.4	1.7	17.9	2.3	0.9	3.2	3.6
reserves	4.5	3.5	8	80	0.5	–	0.5	5.3	5	3.5	8.5	43.6
medium/large : ranches	–	–	–	0	5	–	5	52.6	5	–	5	25.6
towns	–	–	–	0	2	0.1	2.1	22.1	2	0.1	2.1	10.8
sub-total	6	4	10	100	9	0.5	9.5	100	15	4.5	19.5	100
housewives[5] : ranches	–	8	8	36.4	–	5.5	5.5	28.2	–	13.5	13.5	32.5
mines	–	0.5	0.5	2.3	–	2	2	10.3	–	2.5	2.5	6.0
towns	–	9.5	9.5	43.2	0.5	11	11.5	59.0	0.5	20.5	21	50.6

reserves	−	4	4	18.2	−	0.5	0.5	2.6	0.5	4.5	4.5	10.8
sub-total	−	22	22	100	0.5	19	19.5	100		4.1	41.5	100
all economically active persons:												
ranches	50	28	78	14.6	6.2	5.5	11.7	20.9	56.2	33.5	89.7	15.2
mines	18.5	0.5	19	3.5	3	2.5	5.5	9.8	21.5	3	24.5	4.1
towns	96	61	157	29.4	18.2	18.3	36.5	65.2	114.2	79.3	193.5	32.7
reserves	113.5	167.5	281	52.5	1.6	0.7	2.3	4.1	115.1	168.2	283.3	47.9
total	278	257	535	100	29	27	56	100	307	284	591	100

Notes (Table 2(d)):
1. Includes 20,000 Angolans.
2. Includes c1500 working for small black farmers, the latter mainly Rehobothers.
3. All are now in bantustans: Kaokoland, Owanbo, Okavango and East Caprivi. The remaining parts of the Northern Zone are game parks or uninhabited.
4. Nearly all are black farmers in the Rehoboth Gebiet, where the land is privately owned.
5. This category is usually defined to exclude wives and mothers who do not work outside the home, thus concealing the fact that they are usually full-time workers in their own right. They have therefore been included here.

Sources: as in 2(b).

2(d) Labour force, 1977: 'permanent' and 'migrant' black wage-workers (000s).[1]

	ranches	mines	towns	reserves	total	%
migrants : from NZ reserves	10	18	27	−	55	14.3
from PZ reserves	15	−	20	−	35	22.4
from Angola	10	0.5	9.5	−	20	8.2
sub-total	35	18.5	56.5	−	110	44.9
permanent[2]	35	−	89.5	10.5	135	55.1
total	70	18.5	146	10.5	245	100

Notes:
1. These are categories created by the laws of apartheid. Many so-called 'migrants' are in real life long-term regular workers who are forced to return periodically to a reserve and to live in single quarters at their place of work.
2. A number are the wives and relatives of 'migrants', a few residing legally but many illegally with their menfolk. The remainder are those who qualify to reside permanently at their place of work.

Sources: UNIN 1977, own calculations.

2(e) Labour force, 1977: sectoral distribution of workers, (000s).

	blacks				whites				total			
	male	female	total	%	male	female	total	%	male	female	total	%
farming	48	19.5	67.5	25.3	1	–	1	2.2	49	19.5	68.5	21.9
mining	18.5	–	18.5	6.9	3	0.5	3.5	7.5	21.5	0.5	22	7.0
fishing & fish processing	7	–	7	2.6	0.8	–	0.8	1.7	7.8	–	7.8	2.5
other manufacturing and public utilities	7.5	0.5	8	3.0	1.4	0.1	1.5	3.2	8.9	0.6	9.5	3.0
construction	13	–	13	4.9	1	–	1	2.2	14	–	14	4.5
transport and communications	11.4	0.1	11.5	4.3	1.7	0.3	2	4.3	13.1	0.4	13.5	4.3
general government	12.3	4.7	17	6.4	5.9	5.1	11	23.7	18.5	9.8	28.3	9.0
commerce & finance	17	2.2	19.2	7.2	4.6	1.5	6.1	13.1	21.6	3.7	25.3	8.1
house-service[1]	15	45	60	22.5	–	–	–	0	15	45	60	19.1
sub-total	150	72	222	83.1	19.4	7.5	26.9	57.8	169.4	79.5	248.9	79.4
unemployed[2]	22	1	23	8.6	0.1	–	0.1	0.2	22.1	1	23.1	7.4
housewives	–	22	22	8.2	0.5	19	19.5	41.9	0.5	41	41.5	13.2
total	172	95	267	100	20	26.5	46.5	100	192	121.5	313.5	100

Notes (Table 2 (e)):
1. In private houses, flats etc. Those employed by ranchers (15,000) are entered not here, but under 'farming'.
2. Includes only those openly unemployed, omitting the large numbers of those underemployed and seeking jobs but for forced by apartheid laws to remain in the reserves

Sources: as in 2 (b).

2(f) Labour force, 1977: occupations and skill-levels of wage workers (000s).

	blacks				whites				total			
	male	female	total	%	male	female	total	%	male	female	total	%
managerial, administrative[1]	–	–	–	0	1.8	0.2	2	7.4	1.8	0.2	2	0.7
professional, technical	3	4.2	7.2	3.0	2.9	1.6	4.5	16.7	5.6	6.1	11.7	4.3
– teachers	2.5	2.3	4.8	2.0	0.6	0.7	1.3	4.8	3.1	3	6.1	2.2
– nurses	–	2.2	2.2	0.9	–	0.6	0.6	2.2	–	2.8	2.8	1.0
– others	0.2	–	0.2	0.1	2.3	0.3	2.6	9.6	2.5	0.3	2.8	1.0
clerical, secretarial	1	0.5	1.5	0.6	2.7	3.9	6.6	24.4	3.7	4.4	8.1	3.0
sales	1	0.8	1.8	0.7	1.2	1.3	2.5	9.3	2.2	2.1	4.3	1.6
supervision[2]	3	0.1	3.1	1.3	3.1	0.1	3.2	11.8	6.1	0.2	6.3	2.3
skilled[3]	1.4	–	1.4	0.6	4.5	–	4.5	16.7	5.9	–	5.9	2.2
semi-skilled[4]	29	1	30	12.2	3	0.3	3.3	12.2	32	1.3	33.3	12.2
unskilled[5]	118.9	6.1	125	51.0	0.3	0.1	0.4	1.5	119.2	6.2	125.4	46.1
house-service	15	60	75	30.6	–	–	–	0	15	60	75	27.6
total	172	73	245	100	19.5	7.5	27	100	191.5	80.5	272	100

Notes (Table 2(f)):
1. Senior and middle managers and civil servants.
2. Supervisors, foremen, guards and security personnel.
3. Artisans and apprentices.
4. Requires extended on-the-job experience.
5. Requires no previous experience or skills and little formal training.
Sources: as in 2(b).

3(a) Education: Students in full-time school education, 1977 (000s).

General note on Tables 3(a), (b), (c) and (d)
() = estimates or projections from data for previous years
* = no available data.

	Africans Northern	South/Central	total	Coloureds[1] total	all blacks total	whites total	total
primary: lower (sub A–B, St. 1–2)	28.8	88.5	117.3	10.0	127.3	8.8	136.1
higher (St. 3–5)	10.8	23.4	34.2	5.3	39.5	5.8	45.3
junior (St. 6–8)	4.0	5.1	9.1	2.9	11.9	5.3	3.15
senior (St. 9–10)	0.15	0.1	0.25	0.4	0.65	2.5	3.15
total	43.7	117.1	160.8	18.6	179.4	22.4	201.8

Notes:
1. Coloureds and Rehobothers only. The Nama, whose educational provision is similar to that for 'Africans', have been included with the latter

Sources: Melber 1979, tables 27, 36, 52, 69, 89.

3(b) Education: students in higher and technical education, 1977[1]

	Africans	Coloureds[2]	all blacks	whites	total
University: enrolled at S.A. Universities	79	(55)	134	1266	1400
taking Unisa[3] correspondence courses	63	(50)	113	722	835
teacher training: in Namibia	(630)	(10)	(640)	–	(640)
in S.A.	(30)	(217)	(247)	(500)[4]	(747)
total higher education	(802)	(332)	(1134)	(2608)	(3472)
craft and technical training in schools: in Namibia	(300)	–	(300)	(1000)	(1300)
in S.A.	–	(125)	(125)	(50)[4]	(175)
total	(1102)	(457)	(1459)	(3658)	(5117)

Notes:
1. Excludes those studying outside S.A. and Namibia.
2. 'Nama' included with 'Africans'.
3. University of South Africa, a national correspondence course institution.
4. Refers only to students sponsored by the government to teacher training in technical and high schools. Many more are privately funded of undertake training at University level.

Source: Melber 1979 .

3(c) Education: examination results, 1975.

	Africans no.	%	Coloureds[1] no.	%	Whites no.	%
Higher Primary Certificate (St. 5): candidates	4380[2]		1463		–	
passed	3040[2]	69.4	1022	69.9	–	
Junior Certificate (St. 8): candidates	452		499		(1475)	
passed	401	88.7	340	68.1	(1200)	(81.4)
Senior Certificate/Matriculation (St. 10): candidates	67		143		834	
passed	53	79.1	95	66.4	726	88.9
Univ. pass	39	58.2	50	35.0	520	62.4
Teacher's Certificate: Lower Primary	145		30		*	
Primary	68		10		*	
Secondary and above	–		11[3]		*	

Notes:
1. Here including Nama.
2. Figures for 1974.
3. Lower Secondary (1), Secondary (graduate) (7), Postgraduate degree (1), other (3).

Source: Melber 1979, tables 39, 40, 43, 57–9, 74–6.

3(d) Education: professional qualifications of teachers, 1976.

	Africans no.	%	Coloureds[1] no.	%	Whites no.	%
with teacher training and:						
Primary leaving certificate (St5)[2]	1668	50.5	–	0	–	0
Junior Certificate (St8)	357	10.8	359	47.5	–	0
Matriculation (St10)	46	1.4	194	25.7	–	0
University degree	11	0.3	16	2.1	1235	97.0
other	3	0.1	18	2.4	–	0
sub-total	2085	63.0	587	77.7	1235	97.0
without teacher training and:						
Primary or Junior Certificate	1212	36.6	121	16.0	–	0
Matriculation	10	0.3	39	5.1	–	0
University degree	3	0.1	–	0	38	3.0
other	1	0	9	1.2	–	0
sub-total	1226	37.0	169	22.3	38	3.0
total	*3311*	*100*	*756*	*100*	*1273*	*100*
with Matric or higher qualification	74	2.2	276	36.5	1273	100

Notes:
1. Here including Nama.
2. St. 6 was merged with St. 5 in the mid-1970s. Consequently the old St. 6 is equivalent to the present St. 5.
Source: Melber 1979, pp. 96–7, and Tables 49 and 67.

4.1(a) Economy: Gross Domestic Product (GDP) at current + constant (1938) prices, 1920–78 (Rm).[1]

	1920	1921	1922	1923	1924	1925	1926	1927	1928	1929
current	13	5.8	6.4	8.8	9.0	10.6	11.4	12.4	12.6	13.0
constant	7.3	3.7	5.1	7.25	7.5	8.6	9.0	9.6	9.8	10.1

	1930	1931	1932	1933	1934	1935	1936	1937	1938	1939
current	9.8	6.6	5.4	3.9	5.4	8.4	10.6	12.6	14.4	13.0
constant	7.9	5.65	5.0	4.1	5.8	9.1	11.3	13.1	14.4	12.7

	1940	1941	1942	1943	1944	1945	1946	1947	1948	1949
current	10.4	13.4	12.2	18.4	19.8	19.8	21.8/22.2	32.2	40.3	42.4
constant	9.7	11.9	10.25	14.8	15.1	14.4	15.55/15.8	21.8	25.4	26.1

	1950	1951	1952	1953	1954	1955	1956	1957	1958	1959
current	61.0	80.3	92.9	98.1	107.2	129.0	141.6	138.8	121.3	121.5
constant	35.55	43.4	46.9	46.8	49.1	56.1	60.15	56.9	48.3	47.5

	1960	1961	1962	1963	1964	1965	1966	1967	1968	1969
current	122.0/142	160	163	195	225	275	300	310	322	358
constant	46.8/54.4	58.9	62.3	73.4	82.8	96.6	106.4	106.0	104.0	107.9

	1970	1971	1972	1973	1974	1975	1976	1977	1978
current	348	355	440	580	600	674	755	830/1305	1455
constant	99.9	94.4	107.8	129.2	120.2	118.5	118.5	118.4/186.3	188.9

Note::
1. Based on official sources up to 1976 and hence underestimated, particularly in the 1970s. The more broadly based UNIN estimate for 1977 of R1135m has been adjusted to meet increases in the value of diamond and uranium output.

Sources: For GDP at current prices: 1920–46 – Krogh 1960; 1946–60 – Odendaal, 1964; 1960–75 – S.A. Reserve Bank as quoted in Thomas 1978, table D; 1976–7 – Thomas 1978, table D. At constant prices: 1920–69 (applying retail price index) – Odendaal 1964, p.317 Financial Mail 2.3.73; 1969–77 – Fragmentary data. The estimates for 1977–8 are based on UNIN 1977 and scattered sectoral data.

4.1(b) Economy: detailed breakdown of the GDP, 1977–8.

	1977 (Rm)	%	1978 (Rm)	%
primary:				
agriculture	157.5	12.7	172.5	11.9
commercial	137.5	10.5	150	10.3
peasant subsistence	20	1.5	22.5	1.6
forestry	2	0.15	2	0.14
fishing	40.5	3.1	30.5	2.1
commercial[1]	40	3.1	30	2.1
peasant subsistence	0.5	0.04	0.5	0.03
mining	545	41.8	645	44.3
diamonds	290	22.4	340	23.4
uranium	130	10.0	170	11.6
base minerals	125	9.6	135	9.3
sub-total	*745*	*57.1*	*850*	*58.4*
secondary:				
manufacturing	85	6.5	83	5.7
food processing	50	3.8	45	3.1
other commercial:				
large-scale	25	1.9	27	1.8
small-scale	7.5	0.6	8	0.6
peasant subsistence	2.5	0.2	3	0.2
construction[2]	60	4.6	65	4.5
electricity/water	15	1.2	17	1.2
sub-total	*160*	*12.3*	*165*	*11.3*

tertiary:

	amount	%	sub %	amount	%
(transport/communications/storage)	60	4.6		65	4.5
trade	110	8.4		120	8.2
accommodation	25	1.9		28	1.9
white	20	1.5	22.5		1.5
black	5	0.4	5.5		0.4
finance	85	6.5		95	6.5
social & personal services	50	3.8		55	3.8
domestic	15	1.2	16.5		1.2
other	35	2.7	38.5		2.6
general government[3]	70	5.4		77	5.3
sub-total	400	30.6		440	30.2
GDP (current prices)	1305	100		1455	100

Notes:
1. Value of processing included under 'food processing'.
2. Approximately two-thirds is government-sponsored.
3. State enterprises + consumption included under other heads. Over 80% of this category is wages and salaries.

Sources: UNIN 1977, as revised.

4.2(a) Economy: distribution of GDP, 1977 : between wage-workers, peasants and capitalists.

	amount (Rm)	%	R per person
capitalists + state[1]	945	72.4	(10,000)
workers[2]	330	25.3	610
peasants	30	2.3	44
total	1305	100	1,042

Notes (Table 4.2(a)):

1. R20m has been deducted from company taxation (R195m) and transferred to peasants (R5m) + black workers (R15m) as material income (medicines, food subsidies etc.) + services (health, education etc). Government services for whites are largely self-financed from the separate SWA Administration Account, which takes personal income tax. Most of the rest (R175m) goes into servicing the capitalists and repressing the workers and peasants they exploit.

2. Black and white and including Angolans.

Source: based on UNIN 1977.

4.2(b) Economy: distribution of GDP, 1977: between settlers and black Namibians.

	amount (Rm)	%	R per person
resident white businessmen and employees	315	24.1	3073
black peasants, workers[1] and small businessmen	145	11.1	126
total	460	35.3	367

Note:

1. Includes Angolans.

Source: based on UNIN 1977.

4.3(a) Trade: visible exports, 1963–78 (Rm).

	1963	1964	1965	1966	1967	1968	1969	1970	1971	1972	1973	1974	1975	1976	1977	1978
agriculture (Rm)	34.6	33.0	33.5	32.6	(32)	(37)	40	49	(67)	(80)	93	84	(100)	(115)	130	(140)
fishing (Rm)	22.5	34.2	45.0	49.3	46.0	(50)	(55)	56	40.1	56.8	89	110	(100)	(95)	65	(50)
mining (Rm)	65	99	122	142	137	127	138	120	106	150	244	238	(250)	(380)	645	760
total (Rm)	122	168	201	224	215	214	233	225	213	289	426	432	(450)	(590)	840	950
proportion of GDP %	62.6	74.7	73.1	74.7	69.4	66.5	65.1	64.7	60.0	65.7	73.5	72.0	6.8	74.5	64.4	65.3

agriculture (%)	28.4	19.6	16.7	14.6	14.9	17.3	17.2	21.8	31.5	27.7	21.8	19.4	22.2	19.5	15.5	14.7
fishing (%)	18.4	20.4	22.4	22.0	21.4	23.4	23.6	24.9	18.8	20.3	20.9	25.5	22.2	16.1	7.7	5.3
mining (%)	53.2	60.0	60.9	63.4	63.7	59.3	59.2	53.3	49.7	52.0	57.3	55.1	55.6	64.4	76.8	80.0

Sources: SWA Surveys 1967, 1974; Rijneveld 1977; Thomas 1978; UNIN 1977; sectoral data.

4.3(b) Trade: direction of trade 1977.

	to/from:SA		other countries		total	
	Rm	%	Rm	%	Rm	%
exports	160	19	680	81	840	100
imports: by point of entry	360	80	90	20	450	100
by country of origin	290	65	160	35	450	100
net balance	−130		+520		+390	

Sources: UNIN 1977, Barthold 1977, Thomas 1978, table 19.

4.3(c) Trade: balance of payments, 1974–7.

	1974	1975	1977(1)	1977(2)
visible trade:				
exports	410	425	570	840
imports	360	400	450	450
balance	+50	+25	+120	+390
invisible trade:				
service exports				10
service imports				50
balance				−40

remittances (state current account & private)	−150	−165	−180	−425
capital transfers (net):				
small savings				−30
company investments[1]	+50	+100	0	+65
state capital account[2]				+15
parastatal investments[2] [3]	+50	+100	+150	+25
balance	+100	+200	+150	+75
overall balance	0	+60	+90	0

Notes:

1. Mainly calls on foreign funds by RTZ + General Mining to finance the construction of their large uranium mines.
2. Calculated to reflect the approximate balance between total state expenditure + revenue − the R40m current account surplus is included in 'remittances'.
3. i.e. outside the state budget (SAR + H, Post Office, additional water + electricity infrastructure).

Sources: 1974—7(1) − Thomas 1978, table 19; 1977(2) − based on UNIN 1977 + sectoral data.

4.3(d) Trade: foreign exchange benefits to S.A., 1977.

net flows of currency between Namibia + third countries:[1]	*amount (Rm)*
trade balance	+520
services balance	−15
remittances	−167
capital transfers: small savings	−3
company investments	+45
currency balance	+380
S.A. imports from Namibia	+160
hidden subsidy element[2]	+ 20
estimated overall gain	+560
protected S.A. exports to Namibia	+290

Notes (Table 4.3(d)):
1. Because Namibia has no central bank, all foreign currency surpluses flow directly to the S.A. Reserve Bank for S.A.'s benefit. The calculations here take account of indirect flows to and from third countries through S.A. (transit trade, investment income etc.). The foreign exchange component of S.A.'s military expenditure in Namibia is excluded here because it would probably be spent on border defence anyway were Namibia independent.
2. Arising from the artificially low prices enforced by the state.

Sources: Fragmentary data.

4.4(a) Ownership and exploitation: distribution of means of production between the main export sectors, 1977–8.

	1977 Rm	%	1978 Rm	%
farming	1000	60	1000	55.0
assets	500	30	500	27.5
land	500	30	500	27.5
fishing	60	3.6	65	3.6
factories	40	2.4	42	2.4
fleet	20	1.2	23	1.2
mining	610	36.5	740[1]	41.0
total	1670	100	1805	100

Note:
1. This total includes mines under development but not yet in production.
Sources: a wide range of fragmentary data.

4.4(b) Ownership and exploitation scale of production units, 1977.

	no. of units	capital (Rm)	investment per unit (R000)	black workers[1]	workers per unit
ranches	5100	1000	200	50,000	·10
cattle			160		11
karakul			265		9
fishing					
canneries[2]	9	38	4,200	6,200	690
fleet[2]	80	20	250	800	10
mining	17	610	36,000	18,500	1100
CDM	1	200	200,000	5,000	5000
Rossing	1	200	200,000	2,000	2000
Tsumeb[3]	1	55	55,000	4,000	4000
Otjihase	1	62	62,000	2,000	2000
others[4]	13	94	7,250	5,500	425

Notes:
1. Workers in direct production only.
2. Excluding the smaller factories at Luderitz.
3. Tsumeb mine only – the Tsumeb Corporation also owns three smaller mines.
4. Small mines excluded, also those at development stage and not yet commissioned, notably Langer Heindrich and Elbe.

Sources: Fragmentary data and own calculations.

4.4(c) Ownership and exploitation: capital intensity + productivity, 1977.

	investment per black worker (R000)	ratio of normal[1] net profits to investment %	ratio of normal[1] output to investment %	ratio of normal[1] net profits to output %
ranches	20	6.5	13	50
fish canneries	6	75	200	25
mining	33	50	102	45
Rossing	130²	33	100	30
CDM	40	70	145	47
Otjihase	30	30	90	24
Tsumeb	14	30	135	30
others	17	25	65	35

Notes:

1. This criterion is used rather than the actual figures for 1977 because fish canning was already sliding to disaster, base mineral prices were depressed and Rossing was still under construction. For fish canning the period 1973–6 is taken as the norm for profits and output, for Rossing and Otjihase, full production, for the base mineral mines the mineral prices ruling in the 1960s and early 1970s. In the remaining instances (ranches, CDM), estimates for 1977 are employed. All values are corrected to 1977 current prices.

2. 1978.

4.4(d) Ownership and exploitation: rates of exploitation, 1977.

	net profits in normal[1] years (Rm)	profits per black worker (R000)	profits per unit (R000)	ratio of black wages to profits %
ranches	65	1.3	12.5	30

fish canneries	30	5		15
mining			3,350	
Rossing	275	15	16,200	10.5
CDM	85	42.5	85,000	3.5
Otjihase	137	28	**137,000**	8.5
	15	7.5	15,000	20
Tsumeb	20	5	20,000	25
others	18	3.3	1,400	37

Note:

1. See note 1 above.

Sources: fragmentary data and own calculations.

5.1(a) Base mineral production, 1969–77: volume (metric tons) and share of African output.

	1969	1970	1971	1972	1973	1974	1975	1976	1977	share of African output
copper:										
mine production (000 mt)	25.5	22.8	25.3	21.5	28.5	26.1	25.3	39.3	46.6	2
smelter (blister) (000 mt)	28.0	27.3	29.1	26.1	35.4	45.8	35.7	36.1	46.2	2.5
lead:										
mine production (000 mt)	75.7	70.5	73.2	59.0	63.3	51.3	48.3	42.2	40.8	29
smelter (refined) (000 mt)	69.3	67.9	68.4	64.7	66.7	64.2	44.3	39.6	42.7	51
zinc:										
mine production (000 mt)	38.2	46.1	50.6	41.9	33.9	44.9	45.6	45.5	38.3	14
cadmium (mt)	238	205	159	142	104	114	109	83	87	29
tin (mt)	680	720	700	660	700	1100	1117	1110		
silver (mt)	36	34	28	39	44	44	42.5	43	43	
salt (000 mt)					147	209				

Note (Table 5.1(a)): mt = metric tons.

Sources: Murray 1974, App. A, Murray 1978.

5.1(b) Diamonds & uranium, 1970—79: volume + value of output.

	1970	1971	1972	1973	1974	1975	1976	1977	1978	1979[1]
diamonds:										
output (m carats)	1.7	1.6	1.6	1.6	1.5	1.75	1.7	2.0	2.0	1.9
value (Rm)	59.9	56.8	97.0	149.7	123.6	170	215	290	340	380
uranium:										
output[1] (short tons)	–	–	–	–	–	–	771	3042	3800	6500
value (Rm)	–	–	–	–	–	–	30	130	170	220
combined value (Rm)	59.9	56.8	97.0	149.7	123.6	170	245	420	510	600
% of mineral output	49.8	53.6	64.5	61.3	51.8	57.6	65.3	77.1	79.1	80.0

Note::

1. Based on currently projected output + market prices. The 1978 uranium output figure is also approximate.

Sources: African Business, October 1978; Murray 1974, App. A; Murray 1978; fragmentary data.

5.1(c) Mineral production, 1964—78: value (Rm).

	1964	1965	1966	1967	1968	1969	1970	1971	1972	1973	1974	1977 (1)	1975	1976	1977 (2)	1978
diamonds	54.0	65.9	80.5	87.2	78.2	84.1	59.9	56.8	97.0	149.7	123.6	200	170	215	290	340
copper (refined)	19.8	27.5	36.0	27.8	28.6	28.8	28.8	20.8	21.5	44.5	44.6	40	50	50	40	42
lead (refined + conc.)	13.7	17.3	14.9	12.0	10.7	13.0	15.2	11.3	14.8	18.9	24.0	25	25	25	25	28
zinc	7.5	6.7	5.7	5.5	4.7	5.7	9.9	9.7	10.1	22.2	33.6	45	35	37	40	45

5.2(b) Agriculture: land availability.

	land (m.ha)	viable farmland (m.ha)	%	population (000s)	land per person (ha)	farmland per person (ha)	ratio white to black
rural whites	37.7	37.0	98	.20	1900	1850	1
blacks in reserves	32.6	7.5	23	710	46	10.5	175
Centre/South	21.7	5.3	24	105	205	50	37
North[1]	10.9	2.2	20	605	18	3.6	515

Note:
1. The Owambo, Kavango and East Caprivi bantustans.

5.2(c) Agriculture: livestock marketing : cattle and karakul pelts, 1965–78.

	1965	1966	1967	1968	1969	1970	1971	1972	1973	1974	1975	1976	1977	1978
cattle marketed (000s)	377	299	313	317	312	417	502	583	507	276		(328)	349	399
railed live to S.A. (000s)	244	177	240	259	241	312	353	435						
– slaughtered for local processing (000s)	103	94	46	31	47	75		(116)						
– slaughtered for local consumption (000s)	28	28	27	27	25	29		(32)						
karakul pelts marketed (millions)	2.24	2.98	2.90	3.42	3.64	3.48	3.4	3.9	(3.4)	3.3	3.4	(3.5)		

Source: fragmentary data.

silver	1.3	1.4	1.4	1.6	2.1	2.5	2.0	1.9	1.8	2.8	4.8	4	4	5	5	5
tin	0.9	1.3	1.8	1.7	1.8	2.4	2.7	2.3	2.8	2.6	3.9	4	4	5	5	5
vanadium	1.6	1.8	1.9	1.5	0.9	1.3	1.3	2.7	1.9	2.1	2.6	3	3	3	3	3
arsenic		0.2	0.2		0.4	0.2	0.4	0.4	0.4	1.5	1.3		2	3	2	2
other											4					
uranium													—	30	75	130	170
total	98.8	121.9	142.2	137.3	127.2	138	120.2	105.9	150.3	244.3	238.4	295	375	400	545	645

Sources: 1964—77 (1) — Thomas 1978, Table H; 1975—8 — UNIN 1977, projections based on fragmentary data and company statements.

5.2(a) Agriculture: distribution of land.

	area (m.ha)	%	reserves & bantustans (m.ha)	%	white farmland (m.ha)	%	proportion reserves %	ranches %	category other %	total %
Namib desert	12.9	16	3	9	0.5	1.5	23	4	73	100
Kalahari semi-desert	25.0	30	22.6	69	1	2.5	90	4	6	100
sub-total desert	37.9	46	25.6	78	1.5	4	67.5	4	28.5	100
plateau grassland	42.0	51	4.8	15	36.2	96	11.5	86	2.5	100
riverain and flood-plain	2.5	3	2.2	7	0	0	88	0	12	100
sub-total farmland	44.5	54	7.0	22	36.2	96	16	81	3	100
total	82.4	100	32.6	100	37.7	100	40	46	14	100

Sources: S.A. Government publications and maps.

5.2(d) Agriculture: farm costs and income, 1970/71 and 1977.

	1970/1 (Rm)		%	1977 (Rm)		(%)
recurrent costs and implements	25.2		34.5	45		30
gross fixed investment	15.3		21.0	15		10
interest on debts	(5.0)		6.8	10		7
sub-total	45.5		62.3	70		47
wages;						
whites	1.1		1.5	2.5		2
blacks	7.4		10.1	12.5		8
cash		4.7	6.4		7.5	5
kind[1]		2.7	3.7		5	3
sub-total	8.5		11.6	15		10
total costs	54.0		74.0	85		57
commercial sales	73		100	150		100
net surplus	19		26.0	65		43
per ranch (R)	3725			12,500		

Note:
1. Assumed here to be the cash cost to the farmer of food, building materials etc. In addition to this, some foodstuffs (e.g. karakul sheep carcases, maize) are often provided from the farms' own production, worth another R2.5m overall.

Sources: 1970/71 Agricultural Census, UNIN 1977, own calculations.

6(a) State budget: revenue and expenditure, 1974/5–78/9 (Rm)[1].

	1974/5	1975/6	1976/7	1977/8	1978/9
revenue:					
SWA Account	133.3	133.7	136.4	189.5	293.8
SWA Admin.	59.1	49.9	60.2	(66)	(71)
sub-total[1]	192.4	183.6	196.6	(256)	(365)
expenditure:					
SWA Account		120.0	141.4	153.3	(265)
SWA Admin.	95.5	104.5	119.6	(127)	(130)
transfer from SWA Account		50.9	48.9	53.9	((55))
sub-total		**224.5**	261.0	(280)	(395)
balance		−40.9	−64.4	−24	−30

Note:
1. These figures in no way provide an accurate picture of overall state revenue and expenditure. There is no proper published series of public accounts, and many categories are merged with the South African figures in government and state corporation statistics. Others, such as customs and excise on transit trade through S.A., simply disappear for lack of a Namibian central bank and border controls. Current and capital spending is not properly distinguished in the official figures. Much of the latter is anyway indirectly financed by loans, the interest charges on which will be paid from Namibian revenues — without its own central bank, Namibia has no separate public sector borrowing to finance its capital projects. A fair proportion of these are anyway no more than disguised defence spending. 'Roads', for example, would include the expensive tarred highway from Grootfontein to the Okavango River, built to carry SADF armoured vehicles and troop-carriers to and from the border. Thus what appears to be a large deficit is in fact no more than heavy spending by the apartheid regime of much of its rapidly increasing Namibian revenue on entrenching its occupation against the advances of the liberation movement.

Sources: Government data.

6(b) Sources of revenue, 1974/5—78/9.

		1974/5		1975/6		1976/7		1977/8		1978/9	proportion of all revenue (%) 1977/8	1978/9
taxation on companies:												
diamonds		57.1		43.1		51.5		73.1		163.0	28.6	44.7
mining	41.1		26.5		27.3		45.0		108.0			
profits	7.0		7.7		9.2		12.2		24.6			
export duty	9.0		8.9		15.0		15.9		30.4			
other mining		8.0		10.0		0.6		1.0		(4)	0.4	
non-mining		15.9		15.1		26.4		22.0		(20)	8.6	
sub-total		81.0		68.2		78.5		96.1		(187)	37.6	(51.2)
on individuals		8.5		12.0		26.5		26.5		(30)	10.4	(8.2)
customs and excise		22.1		27.9		36.0		37.7		(43)	14.7	(11.8)
total		110.6		108.1		141.0		160.3		(260)	62.7	(71.2)

Source: Calculated from official data.

Bibliography

(a) SWAPO Sources

Namibia News	SWAPO, UK and Western European Office, *Namibia News*, (London, 1968–76).
Namibia	SWAPO, Department of Information and Publicity (DIP), *Namibia*, (London, 1977).
Namibia Today	SWAPO DIP, *Namibia Today*, (Lusaka/Luanda, 1977–).
SWAPO	SWAPO, original *Constitution*, (1960s).
SWAPO 1971	SWAPO Youth League, *Manifesto*, (1971).
SWAPO 1972a	SWAPO, *Namibia Documentation*, (Brussels, 1972).
SWAPO 1972b	Papers submitted to the *Namibia International Conference*, (Brussels, May 1972).
SWAPO 1975	SWAPO, *Discussion paper on the Constitution of indepen independent Namibia*, (4th Revise, 1975).
SWAPO 1976a	SWAPO, *Constitution*, (Lusaka, 1976).
SWAPO 1976b	SWAPO, *Political Programme*, (Lusaka, 1976).
SWAPO 1977	SWAPO DIP, *Namibian War Diary 1977*, (Luanda, 1977).
SWAPO 1978a	SWAPO DIP, *Historical profile of SWAPO*, (Lusaka, 1978).
SWAPO 1978b	SWAPO DIP, *The People's resistance, 1976–7*, (Lusaka, 1978).
SWAPO 1978c	SWAPO DIP, *Namibian Political Prisoners*, (Lusaka, 1978).
SWAPO 1978d	SWAPO, *Massacre at Kassinga*, (Luanda, 1978).
SWAPO 1978e	SWAPO DIP, *Conference Reports, 1976–7*, (Lusaka, 1978).
SWAPO 1978f	SWAPO DIP, *Laws Governing the Namibian people's revolution*, (Lusaka, 1978).
SWAPO 1979	SWAPO, UK and Western European Office, *Applications of an 'internationally acceptable solution' to Namibia today today*, (London, 1979).
SWAPO 1979	SWAPO, *Constitution of SWAPO Women's Council*, (Luand (Luanda, 1979).

(b) Journals, digests, annual reports

Action on Namibia	Namibia Support Committee, *Action on Namibia*, (London, 1979–).
Focus	International Defence and Aid Fund, *Focus*, (London,

bi-monthly, (1974—   ).

Council for Namibia	U.N. Council for Namibia, *Annual Report,* (1967—).
Namibia Bulletin	U.N. Council for Namibia, *Namibia Bulletin,* (New York, 1973—).
Human Rights Commission	U.N. Commission on Human Rights, Ad Hoc Working Group of Experts, Annual country reports on violations of human rights in southern Africa, (1967—).
Objective: Justice	U.N. Office of Public Information, *Objective: Justice,* (New York, quarterly, 1969—).

(c) Books, articles, papers, theses

Amnesty 1977	Amnesty International, *Briefing on Namibia,* (London, 1977).
Aydelotte 1937	W. O. Aydelotte, *Bismarck and British colonial policy: the problem of South West Africa, 1883—5,* (Philadelphia, 1937).
Barthold 1977	W. S. Barthold, *Namibia's economic potential and existing economic ties with the Republic of South Africa,* (Berlin, German Devt. Inst., 1977).
Bley 1971	H. Bley, *South West Africa under German rule, 1884—1914,* (London, 1971).
Bruwer 1966	J. P. Bruwer, *South West Africa, the disputed land,* (Cape Town, Nasionale Boekhandel, 1966).
Carroll 1967	F. Carroll, *South West Africa and the U.N.,* (Lexington, 1967).
	scheme?', *Social Dynamics,* 2(1), 1976.
Christian Centre 1978	Christian Centre, *Report on the registration and election campaigning in Namibia,* (Windhoek, November 1978).
C.C.N. 1979	Council of Churches in Namibia, *Statements by churches in Namibia,* (Windhoek, 1979).
Christie 1976	R. Christie, 'Who benefits by the Kunene hydroelectric
Courtney/Davis 1972	W. Courtney & J. Davis, *Namibia: U.S. corporate involvement,* (New York/Geneva, 1972).
Cronje 1979	G. & S. Cronje, *The workers of Namibia,* (London I.D.A.F., 1979).
de Vries 1978	J. L. de Vries, *Mission and colonialism in Namibia,* (Johannesburg, Ravan, 1978).
Drechsler 1980	H. Drechsler, *Let Us Die Fighting,* (London, Zed Press, 1980).
Dugard 1973	J. Dugard, *The South West Africa/Namibia dispute,* (Berkel Berkeley, 1973).
Ellis 1979	J. Ellis, *Elections in Namibia?,* (London, British Council of Churches/Catholic Inst. of Internat. Relations, 1979).
Esterhuyse 1968	J. H. Esterhuyse, *South West Africa, 1880—94,* (Cape Town, 1968).
F.M. 1973	Financial Mail, *South West Africa: desert deadlock,* (special survey: Johannesburg, 2 March 1973).

First 1963	R. First, *South West Africa,* (Penguin, 1963).
First 1972	R. First, 'The bantustans: implementation of the Odendaal Report', paper submitted to the *Namibia International Conference,* (Brussels, 1972).
First/Segal 1967	R. First & R. Segal (eds), *South West Africa: travesty of trust,* (London, 1967).
F.A.O. 1977	Food and Agriculture Organisation, *Namibia: prospects for future development,* (draft working paper: Rome, 1977).
F.A.O. 1979	Food and Agriculture Organisation, *Ideas and Action, special issue on apartheid,* no. 126 (7/8, 1978), annex (Namibia & Zimbabwe).
F.A.A. Reports	Foreign Affairs Association, Pretoria, Study Reports (D. S. Prinsloo):
	No. 4. *South West Africa: the Turnhalle and independence,* (1976).
	No. 6. *South West Africa/Namibia: towards a negotiated settlement,* (1977).
	No. 8. *Walvis Bay and the Penguin Island: background and status,* (1977).
F.O. 1920	Great Britain, Foreign Office, Handbook No. 11, *South West Africa,* (London, 1920).
Fraenkel 1974	P. Fraenkel, *The Namibians of South West Africa,* (London, Minority Rights Group, 1974).
Freislich 1964	R. Freislich, *The last tribal war,* (Cape Town, 1964).
G.D.R. 1979	German Democratic Republic, Solidarity Committee, *From insurrection to organised liberation struggle,* (Berlin, 1979).
Gebhardt 1978	F. B. Gebhardt, 'The socio-economic status of farm labourers in Namibia', *S.A. Labour Bulletin,* 4(1–2), 1978.
Goldblatt 1971	I. Goldblatt, *History of South West Africa from the beginning of the 19th century,* (Cape Town, 1971).
Gordon 1975	R. Gordon, 'A note on the history of labour action in Namibia', *S.A. Labour Bulletin,* 1(10), 1975.
Gordon 1977	R. Gordon, *Mines, masters and migrants,* (Johannesburg, Ravan, 1977).
Gordon 1978	R. Gordon, 'Some organisational aspects of labour protest amongst contract workers in Namibia', *S.A. Labour Bulletin,* 4(1–2), 1978.
Gottschalk 1978	K. Gottschalk, 'South African labour policy in Namibia, 1915–75', *S.A. Labour Bulletin,* 4(1–2), 1978.
Graham 1971	A. Graham, *The response of African societies in Namibia to white administration, 1915–39,* (MA, SOAS, London, 1971).
Hamutenya/ Geingob 1972	H. Hamutenya & H. Geingob, 'African nationalism in Namibia', in C. P. Potholm & R. Dale (eds)., *Southern Africa in perspective,* (New York, 1972).
Horrell 1967	M. Horrell, *South West Africa,* (Johannesburg, S.A.I.R.R. 1967).
Hunke/Ellis 1978	H. Hunke & J. Ellis, *Torture: a cancer in our society,* (Christian Centre, Windhoek, 1978).

Imishue 1965	R. W. Imishue, *South West Africa: an international problem,* (London, 1965).
Innes 1978	D. Innes, 'Imperialism and the national struggle in Namibia', *Review of African Political Economy,* 9, 1978.
I.D.A.F. 1976	International Defence and Aid Fund, Fact Paper No. 3, *All options and none: the constitutional talks in Namibia,* (London, 1976).
IDOC 1973	IDOC Documentation Project, *Namibia now,* (Rome, 1973).
I.L.O. 1977	International Labour Organisation, *Labour and discrimination in Namibia,* (Geneva, 1977).
I.U.E.F. 1979	International University Exchange Fund, *Namibia Dossier,* (Geneva, 1979).
Jepson 1977	T. B. Jepson, *RTZ in Namibia,* (London, Christian Concern for Southern Africa, 1977).
Kane-Berman 1972	J. Kane-Berman, *Contract labour in South West Africa,* (Johannesburg, S.A.I.R.R., 1972).
Kiljunen 1978	K. & M-L. Kiljunen, *Report on a visit to Namibia,* mimeo, Brighton, 1978).
Kritzinger 1972	J. J. Kritzinger, *Sending en kerk in Suidwes-Afrika,* (PhD, Pretoria, 1972).
Krogh 1960	D. C. Krogh, 'The national income and expenditure of South West Africa', *S.A. Journal of Economics,* 20(1), 1960.
Landis 1972	Council for Namibia, *Review and digest of laws and practices established in Namibia by the government of South Africa which are contrary to the purposes and principles of the U.N. Charter,* (prepared by E. Landis, draft, New York, 1972).
Landis 1975	Council for Namibia, *Higher education in Namibia,* (prepared by E. Landis, draft, New York, 1975).
Lazar 1972	L. Lazar, *Namibia,* (London, Africa Bureau, 1972).
L.S.M. 1974	Liberation Support Movement, *Breaking contract: interview in depth with Vinnia Ndadi,* (Richmond, Canada, 1974).
L.S.M. 1976	Liberation Support Movement, *LSM News, special issue on SWAPO,* 1976 (11–12), (reprinted as book 1978).
Lissner 1976	J. Lissner (ed), *Namibia 1975: hope, fear and ambiguity,* (Geneva, Lutheran World Federation, 1976).
Loth 1963	H. Loth, *Die christliche Mission in Sudwestafrika, 1842–93,* (Beerlin, 1963).
Louis 1967	W. R. Louis, 'The South West African origins of the sacred trust', *African Affairs,* 66 (262), 1977.
Manpower 1971–5	South Africa, *Manpower surveys for South West Africa,* (Pretoria, 1971, 1973, 1975).
Mbamba 1977	A. M. Mbamba, *Possibilities for the future development of livestock ranching in an independent Namibia,* (MA, Sussex, 1977).
Melber/Hubrich 1976	H. Melber & H-G. Hubrich, *Namibia, Geschichte und Gegenwart: zur Frage der Dekolonisation einer*

Siedlerkolonie, (Bonn, ISSA, 1976).

Melber 1979   H. Melber, *Schule und Kolonialismus: das formale Erziehungswesen Namibias,* (Hamburg, Inst. fur Afrika-Kunde, 1979).

Memorandum 1918   Great Britain, *Memorandum on the administration of the German colonies with special reference to the treatment of the natives,* (Cd. 9146, London, 1918).

Moorsom 1973   R. J. B. Moorsom, *The political economy of Namibia to 1945,* (MA, Sussex, 1973).

Moorsom/ Clarence-Smith 1975   R. J. B. Moorsom & W. G. Clarence-Smith, 'Underdevelopment and class-formation in Ovamboland, 1845–1915', *Journal of African History,* 16(3), 1975.

Moorsom 1977   R. J. B. Moorsom, 'Underdevelopment, contract labour and worker consciousness in Namibia, 1915–72', *Journal of Southern African Studies,* 4(1), 1977.

Moorsom 1979   R. J. B. Moorsom, 'Labour consciousness and the 1971–2 contract workers' strike in Namibia', *Development and Change,* 10, 1979.

Moorsom 1980a   R. J. B. Moorsom, 'The origins of the contract labour system in Namibia, 1900–26', York University, Centre of Southern African Studies, *Collected Seminar Papers, 1978/ 9,* (York, 1980).

Moorsom 1980b   R. J. B. Moorsom, 'Namibia in the frontline: the political economy of decolonisation in South Africa's colony', *Review of African Political Economy,* 17, 1980.

Morris 1974   J. Morris, 'The black workers in Namibia', in R. Murray et al., *The role of foreign firms in Namibia,* (Uppsala, 1974).

Murray 1972   R. Murray, 'An initial survey of the pattern of expropriation of the mineral resources of Namibia by the South African government and overseas companies,' in L. Lazar, *Namibia,* (London, 1972).

Murray 1974   R. Murray, 'The Namibian economy', in R. Murray et al., *The role of foreign firms in Namibia,* (Uppsala, 1974).

Murray 1978   R. Murray, *Namibia: a survey of the mineral industry and its significance,* (Commonwealth Secretariat, London, 1978).

Nachtwei 1976   W. Nachtwei, *Namibia: von der antikolonialen Revolte zum nationalen Befreiungskampf,* (Mannheim, 1976).

N.S.C. 1977   Namibia Support Committee, *The Turnhalle: South Africa's neo-colonial solution for Namibia,* (London, 1977).

N.S.C. 1979   Namibia Support Committee, *South Africa's sham elections in Namibia,* (London, 1979).

N.S.C. 1980   Namibia Support Committee, *Foreign companies in Namibia: a shortlist of Western firms,* (London, 1980).

O'Callaghan 1977   M. O'Callaghan, *Namibia: the effects of apartheid on culture and education,* (Paris, UNESCO, 1977).

Odendaal 1964   South Africa, *Report of the commission of enquiry into South West African affairs, 1962–3 (Odendaal Commission),* (Pretoria, RP 12–64).

Palgrave 1877   Cape Colony, *W.C. Palgrave: mission to Damaraland and Great Namaqualand in 1876,* (Cape Town, 1877).

Pendleton 1974   W. C. Pendleton, *Katutura: a place where we do not stay*, (San Diego University Press, 1974).

Rhoodie 1967   E. M. Rhoodie, *South West: the last frontier in Africa*, (New York, 1967).

Rijneveld 1977   A. J. Rijneveld, *Economic exploitation: the case of Namibia*, (typescript, Rotterdam, 1977).

Roberts 1980   A. Roberts, *The Rossing file*, (London, CANUC, 1980).

Rogers 1978   B. Rogers, 'Notes on labour conditions at the Rossing mine', *S.A. Labour Bulletin*, 4(1−2), 1978.

Rogers 1980   B. Rogers, *White wealth and black poverty*, (Greenwood) Press, 1980).

Serfontein 1976   J. H. P. Serfontein, *Namibia?*, (Randburg, 1976).

S.I.D.A. 1979   Swedish International Development Agency, *Namibia: negotiations and 'elections'*, (Stockholm, 1979).

Simons 1972   R. Simons, 'The Namibian challenge', paper submitted to the *Namibia International Conference*, (Brussels, 1972).

Slonim 1973   S. Slonim, *South West Africa and the U.N.*, (Johns Hopkins University Press, 1973).

S.A.L.B. 1978   South African Labour Bulletin, *Double issue on Namibia*, 4(1−2), 1978. Includes interviews with black workers and documents from the workers' struggle.

SWA Survey, 1967 & 1974   South Africa, Dept. of Foreign Affairs, *South West Africa Survey, 1967, 1974*. (Pretoria, 1967, 1975).

Stals 1969   E. L. P. Stals, 'Die aanraking tussen blankes en Owambos in Suidwes-Afrika, 1850−1915', *Archives Yearbook for SA History*, 31(2), 1969.

Sundermeyer 1973   W. Sundermeyer, *Wir aber suchten Gemeinschaft*, (Witten, 1973).

Swanson 1967   M. W. Swanson, 'South West Africa in trust, 1915−39', in P. Gifford & W.R. Louis (eds), *Britain and Germany in Africa*, (Yale University Press, 1967).

Thomas 1978   W. H. Thomas, *Economic development in Namibia*, Munich/Mainz, 1978).

Totemeyer 1977   G. Totemeyer, *South West Africa/Namibia*, (Randburg, 1977).

Troup 1950   F. Troup, *In face of fear*, (London, 1950).

U.N. 1974   U.N. Office of Public Information, *Namibia: a trust betrayed*, (New York, 1974).

UNIN 1977   U.N. Institute for Namibia (UNIN), *Towards Manpower Development for Namibia* (draft report prepared by R.H. Green), Lusaka, 1977.

UNIN 1978b   UNIN, *Land use and development in Namibia*, (Consultant C. Nixon, Lusaka, 1978).

UNIN 1979a   UNIN, *Toward Agrarian Reform: policy options for Namibia*, (based on the work of S. Mshonga, Lusaka, 1979).

UNIN 1979b   UNIN, *Constitutional options for Namibia: a historical perspective*, based on the work of M. Bomani & C. U C. Ushewokunze, Lusaka, 1979).

Vedder 1934   H. Vedder, *Das alte Sudwestafrika*, (1934).

Vedder 1938   H. Vedder, *South West Africa in early times*, (shortened

	translation, OUP, 1938).
Voipio 1972	R. Voipio, *Kontrak — soos die Owambo dit sien,* (Johannesburg, Christian Institute, 1972).
Wellington 1967	J. H. Wellington, *South West Africa and its human issues,* (Oxford, 1967).
Winter 1977	C. Winter, *Namibia: the story of a bishop in exile,* (London, 1977).
Witbooi 1929	H. Witbooi, *Die dagboek van Hendrik Witbooi,* (Cape Town, Van Riebeeck Society, 1929).
W.C.C. 1971	World Council of Churches, *The Cunene dam scheme,* (Geneva, 1971).

Resource List

SWAPO Missions Abroad

Provisional Headquarters, C.P. 953, Luanda, People's Republic of Angola. Telephone 39234, Telex 3069/SWAPO/AN. The Department of Information and Publicity, the Women's Council and the National Union of Namibian Workers (N.U.N.W.) can also be contacted at this address.

Algeria Office, 20 Rue Dirah, Hydra-Algiers.

Botswana Office, P.O. Box 146, Francistown.

Cuba Office, Calle 21a no. 21432, 4218 y 214, Atabay, Havana.

East Africa Office, P.O. Box 2603, Dar-es-Salaam, Tanzania.

Egypt Office, 5 Ahmed Hishmat Street, Zamalek, Cairo.

Ethiopia Office, P.O. Box 1443, Addis Ababa.

Finland Office, Domusacademica B216, Leppasuoinkatu 7, Helsinki 10.

German Democratic Republic Office, Schonholderweg 20, Berlin.

Libya Office, P.O. Box 4491, Tripoli.

Nigeria Office, Flat 16 Crescent A, Federal Government Housing Estate, Victoria Island, Lagos.

Observer Mission to the U.N., 801 Second Avenue, Room 1401, New York, N.Y. 10017, U.S.A.

Scandanavian Office, Karduansmakargatan 4,3tr, 11152 Stockholm, Sweden.

U.K. and Western European Office, 188 North Gower Street, London NW1 2NB, U.K.

West Africa Office, B.P. 6110, Dakar, Senegal.

Yugoslavia Office, CAVPJ, Boulevard Lenin 6, 11070 Belgrade.

International organisations

Afro-Asian People's Solidarity Organisation (A.A.P.S.O.), 89 Abdel Aziz All Saoud Street, Manial, Cairo, Egypt.

All-African Council of Churches, P.O. Box 20301, Nairobi, Kenya.

Information Centre of the World Peace Council, Lonnrotinkatu 25 A5 krs. 00180 Helsinki 18, Finland.

Lutheran World Federation, 150 Route de Ferney, 1211 Geneva 20, Switzerland.

O.A.U. Liberation Committee, Dar-es-Salaam, Tanzania.

Office of the United Nations Commissioner for Namibia, DC-328, United Nations, New York, N.Y. 10017, U.S.A.

Organisation of African Trade Union Unity (O.A.T.U.U), P.O. Box 701, Accara, Ghana.

Organisation of African Unity (O.A.U.), P.O. Box 3243, Addis Ababa,

Ethiopia.
Pan African Women's Organisation, 23 Boulevard Col. Amirouch, Algiers, Algeria.
United Nations Centre Against Apartheid, United Nations, New York, N.Y. 10017, U.S.A.
United Nations Institute for Namibia, P.O. Box 33811, Lusaka, Zambia.
World Council of Churches, 150 Route de Ferney, 1211 Geneva 20, Switzerland.

Solidarity organisations
Africa Groups in Sweden, Grev Turegatan 15, 11446 Stockholm, Sweden.
American Committee on Africa, 198 Broadway, New York, N.Y., 10038, U.S.A.
Anti-Apartheid Beweging, Postbus 10500, Amsterdam, Holland.
Anti-Apartheid Bewegung, Blucherstrasse 14, 53 Bonn 1, Federal Republic of Germany.
Anti-Apartheid Movement, c/o A. Kusuhara, 1072 Okamura, Isogo-Ku Yokohama, Japan 235.
Anti-Apartheid Movement, Newport Chambers, 50 Courtenay Place, P.O. Box 9154, Wellington, New Zealand.
Anti-Apartheid Movement, 89 Charlotte Street, London W1P 2DQ, U.K.
Comite centre le colonialism et l'apartheid, Avenue beau 14, 1410 Waterloo, Belgium.
Committee of Solidarity with the People of Africa and Asia, Idanostr. 5. 2 Hoot, Sofia, Bulgaria.
Committee on Southern Africa (K.Z.A.), Da Costastraat 88, Amsterdam, Holland.
Episcopal Churchmen for South Africa, Room 1005, 853 Broadway, New York, N.Y. 10010, U.S.A.
Fellesradet for det Serlige Afrika, Goteborggaten 8, Oslo 5, Norway.
Finnish Africa Committee, Bulevardi 13, A9, Helsinki, Finland.
International Defence and Aid Fund, 104/5 Newgate Street, London EC4, U.K.
Irish Anti-Apartheid Movement, 20 Beechpark Road, Foxrock, Co. Dublin, Eire.
Landskomitee Sydafrika Aktion, Hejrevej 38, DK-2400, Copenhagen NV, Denmark.
Moveimente Portugues centre o Apartheid, Rua Artilharia Um, 105,3, Lisbon, Portugal.
M.R.A.P., 120 Rue St Denis, 75002 Paris, France.
Namibia Support Committee, 188 North Gower Street, London NW1, U.K.
Polish Solidarity Committee, Patac Kulturyi Nayki, Strefak, Warsaw, Poland.
Solidarity Committee, Prague, Czechoslovakia.
Solidarity Committee, Thalmannplatz 8–9, 108 Berlin, German Democratic Republic.
Southern Africa Liberation Committee, 4th floor, 322 Castlereagh Street, Sydney 2000, Australia.
Soviet Solidarity Committee, 10 Kropotkinskaya Street, Moscow, U.S.S.R.
Toronto Committee for the Liberation of Southern Africa, 427 Bloor Street West, Toronto, Ontario, Canada.

AFRICA TITLES FROM ZED PRESS

POLITICAL ECONOMY

DAN NABUDERE
Imperialism in East Africa
Vol I: Imperialism and Exploitation
Vol II: Imperialism and Integration
Hb

ELENGA M'BUYINGA
Pan Africanism or Neo-Colonialism?
The Bankruptcy of the OAU
Hb and Pb

BADE ONIMODE
Imperialism and Underdevelopment in Nigeria:
The Dialectics of Mass Poverty
Hb and Pb

MICHAEL WOLFERS AND JANE BERGEROL
Angola in the Frontline
Hb and Pb

MOHAMED BABU
African Socialism or Socialist Africa?
Hb and Pb

ANONYMOUS
Independent Kenya
Hb and Pb

YOLAMU BARONGO (EDITOR)
Political Science in Africa: A Radical Critique
Hb and Pb

OKWUDIBA NNOLI (EDITOR)
Path to Nigerian Development
Pb

EMILE VERCRUIJSSE
Transitional Modes of Production:
A Case Study from West Africa
Hb

NO SIZWE
One Azania, One Nation:
The National Question in South Africa
Hb and Pb

BEN TUROK
Development in Zambia: A Reader
Pb

J.F. RWEYEMAMU (EDITOR)
Industrialization and Income Distribution in Africa
Hb and Pb

CLAUDE AKE
Revolutionary Pressures in Africa
Hb and Pb

ANNE SEIDMAN AND NEVA MAKGETLA
Outposts of Monopoly Capitalism:
Southern Africa in the Changing Global Economy
Hb and Pb

CONTEMPORARY HISTORY/REVOLUTIONARY STRUGGLES

AQUINO DE BRAGANCA AND IMMANUEL WALLERSTEIN (EDITORS)
The African Liberation Reader: Documents of the National Liberation
Movements
Vol I: The Anatomy of Colonialism
Vol II: The National Liberation Movements
Vol III: The Strategy of Liberation
Hb and Pb

EDWIN MADUNAGU
Problems of Socialism:
The Nigerian Challenge
Pb

MAI PALMBERG
The Struggle for Africa
Hb and Pb

CHRIS SEARLE
We're Building the New School!
Diary of a Teacher in Mozambique
Hb at Pb price

MAINA WA KINYATTI
Thunder from the Mountains:
Mau Mau Patriotic Songs
Hb

EDUARDO MONDLANE
The Struggle for Mozambique
Pb

BASIL DAVIDSON
No Fist is Big Enough to Hide the Sky:
The Liberation of Guinea Bissau and Cape Verde: Aspects of the African
Revolution
Hb at Pb price

BARUCH HIRSON
Year of Fire, Year of Ash:
The Soweto Revolt — Roots of a Revolution?
Hb and Pb

SWAPO DEPARTMENT OF INFORMATION AND PUBLICITY
To Be Born a Nation:
The Liberation Struggle for Namibia
Pb

PEDER GOUWENIUS
Power to the People:
South Africa in Struggle: A Political History
Pb

HORST DRECHSLER
Let Us Die Fighting:
The Struggle of the Herero and Nama Against German Imperialism
(1884-1915)
Hb and Pb

GILLIAN WALT AND ANGELA MELAMED (EDITORS)
Mozambique: Towards a People's Health Service
Pb

ANDRE ASTROW
Zimbabwe: A Revolution that Lost its Way?
Hb and Pb

RENE LEFORT
Ethiopia: An Heretical Revolution?
Hb and Pb

TONY AVIRGAN AND MARTHA HONEY
War in Uganda: The Legacy of Idi Amin
Hb and Pb

LABOUR STUDIES

DIANNE BOLTON
Nationalization: A Road to Socialism?
The Case of Tanzania
Pb

A.T. NZULA, I.I. POTEKHIN, A.Z. ZUSMANOVICH
Forced Labour in Colonial Africa
Hb and Pb

LITERATURE

FAARAX M.J. CAWL
Ignorance is the Enemy of Love
Pb

KINFE ABRAHAM
From Race to Class
Links and Parallels in African and Black American Protest Expression
Pb

OTHER TITLES

A. TEMU AND B. SWAI
Historians and Africanist History: A Critique
Hb and Pb

ROBERT ARCHER AND ANTOINE BOUILLON
The South African Game:
Sport and Racism
Hb and Pb

WOMEN

RAQIYA HAJI DUALEH ABDALLA
Sisters in Affliction:
Circumcision and Infibulation of Women in Africa
Hb and Pb

CHRISTINE OBBO
African Women:
Their Struggle for Economic Independence
Pb

MARIA ROSE CUTRUFELLI
Women of Africa:
Roots of Oppression
Hb and Pb

ASMA EL DAREER
Woman, Why do you Weep?
Circumcision and Its Consequences
Hb and Pb

MIRANDA DAVIES (EDITOR)
Third World — Second Sex:
Women's Struggles and National Liberation
Hb and Pb

**You can order Zed titles direct from Zed Press, 57 Caledonian
Road, London, N1 9DN, U.K.**